Teaching for Diversity and Social Justice

Readings for Diversity and Social Justice: An Anthology on Racism, Antisemitism, Heterosexism, Ableism, and Classism

Edited by: Maurianne Adams, Warren J. Blumenfeld, Rosie Castañeda, Heather W. Hackman, Madeline L. Peters, Ximena Zúñiga

Readings for Diversity and Social Justice was inspired by the highly successful *Teaching for Diversity and Social Justice: A Sourcebook* and is the first reader to cover the scope of oppression in America. *Readings for Diversity and Social Justice* contains a mix of personal and theoretical essays and is designed as an introduction to the six "isms": racism, sexism, anti-semitism, heterosexism, classism, and ableism. The anthology also contains articles challenging students to take action to end oppressive behavior and to affirm diversity and social justice. The selections include writings from some of the foremost names in the field—bell hooks, Iris Marion Young, Beverly Daniel Tatum, Cornel West, Michael Omi, Gloria Anzaldúa, Suzanne Pharr, and many other distinguished scholars. *Readings for Diversity and Social Justice* can be used as a companion to *Teaching for Diversity and Social Justice*, or as a stand-alone text.

Readings for Diversity and Social Justice is also published by Routledge. For information on ordering the anthology or to receive an exam copy, please contact our Customer Service Department at 1-800-634-7064. Fax: 1-800-248-4724. Email: *cserve@routledge-ny.com*.

ISBN: 0-4159-2634-3

Teaching for Diversity and Social Justice

A SOURCEBOOK

edited by

Maurianne Adams

Lee Anne Bell

Pat Griffin

Routledge New York & London

Published in 1997 by
Routledge
29 West 35th Street
New York, NY 10001

Published in Great Britain by
Routledge
11 New Fetter Lane
London EC4P 4EE

Printed in the United States of America on acid-free paper.

Library of Congress Cataloging-in-Publication Data

Teaching for diversity and social justice: a sourcebook / editors,
Maurianne Adams, Lee Anne Bell, Pat Griffin.
p. cm.
Includes bibliographical references and index.
ISBN 0-415-91056-0 (hardbound: alk. paper)
ISBN 0-415-91057-9 (pbk: alk. paper)
1. Critical pedagogy—United States. 2. Social justice—Study and
teaching—United States. 3. Multicultural education—United States.
4. Teachers, training of—United States. I. Adams, Maurianne.
II. Bell, Lee Anne, 1949– . III. Griffin, Pat.
LC196.5.U6T43 1997
370.11'5—dc20 96-37658
CIP

To our life partners

John, Ravi, and Kathy

for their unconditional love and support

CONTENTS

Part III: Issues for Teachers and Trainers

TABLE OF FIGURES AND HANDOUTS

TABLE OF APPENDICES

ACKNOWLEDGMENTS

Preparing, writing, and editing a sourcebook for the newly emerging field of social justice education has been a daunting task. The collaborative approach discussed throughout this volume has been lived out during the three years we worked together on this challenging project. We have been inspired and supported by the dedication and unfailing support of our families, colleagues, friends, and students, only a few of whom we are able to acknowledge here.

We owe a tremendous debt to those colleagues and friends who generously took time, under tight deadlines, to review all or part of this manuscript in various stages of completion, and provided valuable feedback, critique, and encouragement along the way. Many thanks to: Julie Andrzejewski, Sue Books, Judi Chamberlin, Mark Chesler, Judy Dorney, Peter Frederick, Jan Goodman, John A. Hunt, Amy Kesselman, Simi Linton, Lily McNair, K. Ravishankar, Spencer Salend, Nancy Schniedewind, Rickie Solinger, Mary Deane Sorcinelli, Jill Tarule, Lorraine Taylor, Cooper Thompson, and Ximena Zúñiga.

Mary McClintock is in a class by herself. We offer a tribute to her particular genius with libraries, computers, and data bases of all sorts, her humor and sound judgment, and her formidable knowledge of the field of social justice education.

We continue to learn from and be inspired by the graduate students in the Social Justice Education Program at the University of Massachusetts/Amherst School of Education who teach the courses described here. Their creativity, resourcefulness, and passion for teaching have contributed greatly to this approach and sustained us in our years of learning and writing about social justice education. We owe special thanks to Peg Brigham Alden, Bob Bureau, Ginni Fleck, Cindy Gallagher, Mary Gannon, Heather Hackman, Yehudit Heller, Stephanie Jo Kent, Madeline Peters, Sue Pliner, Kim Wysmierski, Elise Young, and Dvora Zipkin for sharing instructional materials and information.

We acknowledge our debt to Stephen Botkin, Georgeanne Greene, Elinor Levine, Kathy Phillips, and Valerie Young, whose original early work is reflected in several of the single-issue curriculum designs.

We want to thank the authors who contributed to this volume for their enthusiasm and belief in this project, their patience with our inevitable and seemingly endless revisions, and their dedication to social justice education as a life project.

We are grateful to our editors, Jayne Fargnoli and Alex Mummery, for their early enthusiasm for this project and commitment to seeing it through during a stressful and difficult period.

A very special acknowledgment goes to Bailey Jackson and Jerry Weinstein, whose original thinking, vision, and inspired teaching and mentorship have been the indispensable foundation for everything in this volume.

Finally, despite the scope of this project, the experience of collaborating as an editorial and writing team has been remarkably easy, stimulating, and rewarding. We are grateful for many energizing conversations as the work before us challenged and stretched our understanding of social justice education, and for the laughter and wonderful meals we shared at Maurianne's kitchen table. We discovered in the process that a writing team that includes three very different writing styles can come together to take advantage of the best of each, without strain on our friendships.

PREFACE

This is the book we wish had been available when we began teaching courses on issues of oppression twenty years ago. In this book we address both theoretical and practical issues that confront faculty who introduce diversity and social justice content in their classrooms. The book provides a unified framework for helping students understand and critically analyze several forms of social oppression including racism, sexism, heterosexism, antisemitism, ableism, and classism, as well as the parallels and interconnections among them.

Social justice education includes both an interdisciplinary subject matter that analyzes multiple forms of oppression (such as racism and sexism), and a set of interactive, experiential pedagogical principles that help students understand the meaning of social difference and oppression in their personal lives and the social system. In an increasingly abrasive and polarized American society, social justice education has the potential to prepare citizens who are sophisticated in their understanding of diversity and group interaction, able to critically evaluate social institutions, and committed to working democratically with diverse others.

We have designed this sourcebook for use in higher education (black studies, women's studies, teacher education, sociology, psychology, student affairs and diversity curricula for general education programs), adult formal and non-formal education, and workplace diversity and staff development programs. It can also be adapted for upper-level high school courses.

This book reflects twenty years of collaboration among several generations of faculty and graduate students. Much of our early work on diversity and social justice was intuitive, but, as we grounded our practice in the emerging anti-oppression and social justice literatures, we developed an approach that interweaves theory and practice. Most of the contributors have studied and taught together as graduate students and colleagues at the University of Massachusetts/Amherst School of Education. All have shared in developing a common body of theory and practice.

The book is divided into three sections. The first section consists of four chapters that lay out the theoretical foundations and frameworks upon which our practice is based. Chapter 1 situates our understanding of oppression and social justice in the broader literature, while chapter 2 lays out the specific conceptual foundations for our courses. Chapter 3 reviews themes and principles from various pedagogical frameworks that form the roots of our practice, and chapter 4 describes the principles of design we use to construct social justice education curricula.

Part II consists of curriculum designs that illustrate our approach. In chapter 5 we provide a format and specific activities introducing key concepts that are used in all of the following curriculum designs. Chapter 5 also presents the assumptions and goals that underpin the curriculum designs that follow in chapters 6–11. Given the understandable temptation for instructors to move directly to the specific curriculum designs that may interest them, we strongly encourage readers to read chapter 5 first and use it in conjunction with the following six designs. Chapters 6–11 present curriculum designs on specific single issue topics: Racism, Sexism, Heterosexism, Antisemitism, Ableism, and Classism. Each of these chapters provides structured activities and handouts. Citations are gathered at the back of the volume, followed by a selective list of video resources organized by topic. Chapter 12 presents a curricular overview for a course that includes multiple topics introduced sequentially within a semester format and discusses how such a course fits into a general education curriculum. This chapter also addresses issues of grading, feedback, and building a community of instructors.

The curriculum designs described in chapters 5–12 are based on actual courses that we offer for undergraduate general education and teacher education credit and as graduate courses in the Social Justice Education Program. These single and multiple issue courses are taught by faculty like the authors, or advanced graduate students who have completed coursework in the program that covers content similar to that in chapters 1–4, 13–15.

Part III examines additional issues and challenges for social justice education. Chapter 13 discusses specific facilitation issues that arise in social justice courses and provides practical strategies to address classroom process. Chapter 14 examines what we need to know about ourselves in order to be effective teachers of this content. Chapter 15 explores what we need to know about our students. These three chapters use examples from our own practice to illustrate problems and issues that arise in social justice teaching with suggestions for how to address them, and pull together many of the themes and issues discussed in earlier chapters.

We hope that what we have written will be of use to both novice and experienced social justice educators. The curriculum designs are written in a step-by-step format, which can be easily followed or modified. Instructional activities that are described in one chapter and used in others, are cross-referenced and indexed. The single issue curriculum designs include commentary on the structure of the activities as well as discussion of facilitation and processing issues that may arise during the course. Information for lectures and historical timelines are included in the text or in Appendices. The readings assigned to our students are listed at the end of the volume, along with video resources and citations.

The curriculum designs are structured in the format of an introductory module plus four modules that can be taught over a two and one-half day period. A diagram suggesting how these designs might be revised to fit a more traditional once- or twice-a-week semester format is also provided at the back of the book. Instructors may use the curriculum designs with the diagram to mix and match activities from a variety of chapters. They may also choose to create their own designs, using the foundation and conceptual tools provided in Part I. Instructors who are preparing to teach, or are already teaching about issues of oppression and encountering difficulties, can draw on the practical information in Part III.

We have tried to balance specific descriptions with flexible alternatives. Our intention is to be descriptive rather than prescriptive, to provide sufficient detail so that those readers coming new to social justice subject matter or teaching process can see precisely how they might proceed and tailor curriculum designs to fit their own circumstances.

We have deliberately used clear and accessible language, and provided our own definitions where we use terms with specific meanings. We recognize, however, the complexity and fluidity of the language of social group and social identity naming. Our decision here has been to adopt terms preferred by people from targeted groups themselves: "people of color" rather than "nonwhite"; "gay, lesbian, bisexual" rather than "homosexual"; "people with disabilities" rather than "handicapped." Specific ethnicities are capitalized but not hyphenated (African American, Asian American) and racial designations are capitalized only when used as proper nouns (Black, Latino, White). We have asked the authors of each curriculum design to address other considerations of language usage in their respective chapters.

Our approach to teaching is primarily active and experiential. We have tried in the curriculum designs to provide sufficient instructions so that someone experimenting with this pedagogy for the first time may be successful. We have also provided in the theoretical foundations of Part I and the practical examples of Parts II and III, information to help the reader better understand the roots of this approach and strategies for using it effectively in the classroom. For example, social identity development is *described* in chapter 2, but *applied* in chapters 3, 4, 12, and 15.

There are social justice issues, such as Ageism, that we have not included in this volume because we have not yet fully developed curricula to address them. Readers may find Part I as well as the curriculum designs useful for constructing new designs to address manifestions of oppression not included in this volume, or combinations of social justice issues. We also acknowledge that there are different approaches to social justice education, some of which are noted in chapters 1 and 3.

We have tried to situate our work clearly, so that readers who hold different perspectives from ours can still locate us in a broader body of work on the theory and practice of anti -oppression and social justice education. All of the course curriculum designs we present in this sourcebook express our particular perspectives on the dynamics of social oppression. These include a belief that social groups in the United States exist within constructed and unequal hierarchies in which they experience differential access to power and privilege, resulting in an unjust and oppressive system. Difference in such a system is not neutral, but rather provides the basis for stratification among different groups of people. We acknowledge throughout this volume the ways in which students are challenged as they encounter this perspective, and we suggest ways they can be encouraged to stay engaged with this material, however difficult the process.

Our goal in social justice education is to enable students to become conscious of their operating world view and to be able to examine critically alternative ways of understanding the world and social relations. As such, we find traditional lecture methods insufficient for this type of learning. Rather we call upon a variety of pedagogical practices to encourage students to actively engage with us, with each other, and with the informational materials, as they examine these topics and relate to their social world. Our hope is that students will learn to critique current social relations and to envision more just and inclusive possibilities for social life.

We look forward to an ongoing dialogue with readers about the theory and practice of social justice education. With such a dynamic field, we expect that the theory, the practice, and the language will continue to evolve.

Amherst, MA
May 1996

Maurianne Adams
Lee Anne Bell
Pat Griffin

PART ONE

Theoretical Foundations and Frameworks

1

Theoretical Foundations for Social Justice Education

Lee Anne Bell

This chapter sets in context the approach to oppression and social justice described in this book. It provides a way for readers who approach oppression and social justice from other positions to see where we connect with, and in some cases differ from, other orientations. Our intention is to foster a broad dialogue among the many people who struggle, as we do, to find more effective ways to challenge oppressive systems and promote social justice through education.

The chapter examines the persistent and the everchanging aspects of oppression by tracing ways in which "common sense" knowledge and assumptions make it difficult to see oppression clearly. We discuss the value of history for discerning patterns that are often invisible in daily life but which reflect systemic aspects of oppression as it functions in different periods and contexts. Concepts are presented that enable us to freeze and focus on specific aspects of oppression in our teaching while remaining conscious of the shifting kaleidoscope of a dynamic and complex social process.

What Is Social Justice Education?

We believe that social justice education is both a process and a goal. The goal of social justice education is full and equal participation of all groups in a society that is mutually shaped to meet their needs. Social justice includes a vision of society in which the distribution of resources is equitable and all members are physically and psychologically safe and secure. We envision a society in which individuals are both self-determining (able to develop their full capacities), and interdependent (capable of interacting democratically with others). Social justice involves social actors who have a sense of their own agency as well as a sense of social responsibility toward and with others and the society as a whole.

The process for attaining the goal of social justice we believe should also be democratic and participatory, inclusive and affirming of human agency and human capacities for working collaboratively to create change. We do not believe that domination can be ended through coercive tactics and agree with Kreisberg (1992) in a "power with" vs. "power over" paradigm for enacting social justice goals. This book focuses on developing educational processes for reaching these goals.

We also realize that developing a social justice process in a society steeped in oppression is no simple feat. For this reason we need clear ways to define and analyze oppression so that we can understand how it operates at various individual, cultural, and institutional levels. While this is inevitably an oversimplification of a complex social phenomenon, we believe that the conceptual frameworks presented here can help us make sense of and hopefully act more effectively against oppressive circumstances as these arise in our teaching and activism.

Why Social Justice Education Needs a Theory of Oppression

Practice is always shaped by theory, whether formal or informal, tacit or expressed. How we approach social justice education, the problems we identify as needing remedy, the solutions we entertain as viable, and the methods we choose as appropriate for reaching those solutions are all theoretical as well as practical questions. Theory and practice are intertwining parts of the interactive and historical process which Freire calls praxis (1970).

Articulating the theoretical sources of our approach to social justice education thus serves several important purposes. First, theory enables us to think clearly about our intentions and the means we use to actualize them in the classroom. It provides a framework for making choices about what we do and how, and for distinguishing among different approaches. Second, at its best, theory also provides a framework for questioning and challenging our practices and creating new approaches as we encounter inevitable problems of cooptation, resistance, insufficient knowledge, and changing social conditions. Ideally we keep coming back to and refining our theory as we read and reflect upon the emerging literature on oppression, and as we continually learn through practice the myriad ways oppression can seduce our minds and hearts or inspire us to further learning and activism. Finally, theory has the potential to help us stay conscious of our position as historical subjects, able to learn from the past as we try to meet current conditions in more effective and imaginative ways.

Defining Features of Oppression

Pervasiveness: We use the term "oppression" rather than discrimination, bias, prejudice, or bigotry to emphasize the pervasive nature of social inequality woven throughout social institutions as well as embedded within individual consciousness. Oppression fuses institutional and systemic discrimination, personal bias, bigotry, and social prejudice in a complex web of relationships and structures that saturate most aspects of life in our society.

Restricting: On the most general level, oppression denotes structural and material constraints that significantly shape a person's life chances and sense of possibility. Oppression restricts both self-development and self-determination (Young, 1990). It delimits who one can imagine becoming and the power to act in support of one's rights and aspirations. A girl-child in the United States in 1996, for example, especially if she is poor or of color, is still unlikely to imagine herself as President of the country. Some one hundred and thirty years after the abolition of slavery,

African Americans as a group have yet to achieve full equality in the United States. And despite rhetoric that anyone can get ahead if they work hard enough, a father's economic status is still the best predictor of the status of his offspring.

Hierarchical: Oppression also signifies a hierarchical relationship in which dominant or privileged groups benefit, often in unconscious ways, from the disempowerment of subordinated or targeted groups (Wildman, 1996; McIntosh, 1992; Young, 1990; Frye, 1983; Miller, 1976). Whites, for example, gain privilege as a dominant group because they benefit from access to social power and privilege not equally available to people of color. Thus, as a group, Whites earn more money than other racial groups, hold the majority of positions of power and influence, and command the controlling institutions in society (Hacker, 1992). White-dominated institutions negatively affect the life expectancy, infant mortality, income, housing, employment, and educational opportunities of people of color (Bell, 1992; Gregory & Sanjek, 1994).

Complex, multiple, cross-cutting relationships: Power and privilege are relative, however, since individuals hold multiple and cross-cutting social group memberships (Collins, 1990). An upper-class professional man who is African American (still a very small percentage of African Americans overall) may enjoy economic opportunities not available to most women, yet at the same time face limitations not endured by white co-workers, male or female. Despite his economic and professional status and success, he may be threatened by police, unable to hail a taxi, and endure hateful epithets as he walks down the street (Cose, 1993; Dill & Zinn, 1990; Feagin & Sikes, 1994; West, 1993).

Internalized: Oppression resides not only in external social institutions and norms but also within the human psyche as well (Fanon, 1968; Freire, 1970; Miller, 1976). Oppressive beliefs are internalized by victims as well as benefactors. The idea that poor people somehow deserve and are responsible for poverty, rather than the economic system that structures and requires it, is learned by poor and affluent alike. Homophobia, the deep fear and hatred of homosexuality, is internalized by both straight and gay people. Jews as well as gentiles absorb antisemitic stereotypes.

How do we capture such complex social phenomena in clear and understandable terms that neither oversimplify nor rigidify processes that are lived by diverse human beings in historically specific and individually particular ways? What connects the experiences of a poor woman on welfare with a professional woman facing a glass ceiling at work? What commonalities are shared by African Americans segregated in northern ghettos and gay and lesbian people harrassed on the streets? In what ways do Native Americans on reservations and Jews stereotyped in the media face a similar threat? How is avoidance and isolation of people with disabilities connected to assumptions that people who speak English with an accent are ignorant? In what ways is it possible, or even desirable, that these examples be subsumed under a unified theory of oppression?

"Isms": Shared and Distinctive Characteristics: In grappling with these questions, we have come to believe in the explanatory and political value of identifying both the particular characteristics of specific forms of oppression such as ableism or classism, as well as the patterns that connect and mutually reinforce different oppressions in a system that is inclusive and pervasive. In this book we examine the unique ways in which oppression is manifested through racism, sexism, classism, antisemitism, ableism, and heterosexism, and the dimensions of experience that connect "isms" in an overarching system of domination. We look, for example, at the existence of a dominant or agent group and (a) subordinate or target group(s) in each form of oppression as well as the differentials of power and privilege that are dynamic features of oppression, whatever its particular form. At the same time we try to highlight the distinctive qualities and appreciate the historical and social contexts that distinguish one form of oppression from another. In this model, diversity and the appreciation of differences are inextricably tied to social justice and the ways that power and privilege construct difference unequally in our society (see chapter 5).

From our perspective, no one form of oppression is the base for all others, and no simple definition includes them all, but all are connected within a system that makes them possible. This view differs from others such as that of Young (1990) who describes distinctive types of oppression that may or may not be connected within a unitary system. We believe that eradicating oppression ultimately requires struggle against all its forms, and that building coalitions among diverse people offers the most promising strategies for challenging oppression systematically. Therefore we highlight theory and practice that demonstrate the interconnections among different forms of oppression and suggest common strategies to oppose it.

Learning from History

Knowledge of history helps us trace the patterns that constitute oppression over time and enables us to see the long-standing grievances of different groups in our society. Current debates on issues such as affirmative action, for example, cannot be fully understood without also addressing the historical experiences of slavery, legal and de facto segregation, relocation, and racial violence that have locked African Americans, Native Americans, and Asian Americans out of positions that would allow economic and social advancement as a group. Similarly, stereotypes of Jews can only be fully explored in the context of identifiable historical cycles in a three thousand year history of exploitation, exclusion, and expulsion. Historical context is vital for understanding how stereotypes develop in one context with particular meanings, and continue as unquestioned fact down through the ages.

Historical knowledge also offers hope as well as evidence that oppressive circumstances can change through the efforts of human actors. We can see through history how slavery was abolished, women gained the right to vote, and unions organized and improved working conditions for large numbers of people, to name a few examples (Zinn, 1980). History can suggest strategies for acting in the present to address current problems and learn from past mistakes. For example, the coalitions and ruptures between suffragists and abolitionists of the nineteenth century have been instructive for a twentieth-century women's movement that seeks to be inclusive (Lerner, 1986). Historians have recently begun to look more closely at the 1950s and the roots of various liberation movements in what is popularly known as a quiescent period in United States history (Marcus, 1992). Yet the seeds for mass movement that sprang up in the 1960s and 1970s were sown during that "conservative" period. As we encounter a period in many ways similar to the 1950s perhaps we can recognize the seeds for similarly activist movements in the years ahead.

As we move toward an understanding of the interlocking nature of different forms of oppression we can also trace connections among movements that may not have been as clearly visible then as they are now in hindsight. For example, new historical studies illuminate ways in which the civil rights movement and African American struggles for equality and self-determination inspired Native Americans, Puerto Ricans, and Chicanos as well as the new left and antiwar movements, and the feminist, gay/lesbian/bisexual and disability rights movements (Gitlin, 1987;

Goodman, 1983; Marabel, 1984; Marcus, 1992; Morris, 1991; Oboler, 1995; Shapiro, 1993). We can study these histories to learn how better to build coalitions and avoid internal divisions.

Constructing an Inclusive Theory of Oppression

In this section we examine concepts from the literature on racism, sexism, and classism that contribute to a general theory of oppression and social justice that is inclusive of various "isms." We touch on contributions from activists in the civil rights, new left, and women's liberation movements of the 1960s and 1970s, as well as more recent movements for equality and social change. The history of ideas developed in these movements grounds our theoretical understandings in lived experience and highlights the contradictions and conflicts in different views of oppression and social justice as these are lived out in various periods and contexts. Our discussion here highlights broad themes rather than rendering an inclusive and detailed account of the rich and well-developed academic and social movement traditions to which we are indebted.

Racism: The social science literature on racism and insights about racism that emerged from the civil rights movement of the late 1950s and early 1960s profoundly shaped the way scholars and activists have come to understand oppression and its other manifestations. The civil rights movement fired the imagination of millions of Americans who applied its lessons to an understanding of their own situations and adapted its analyses and tactics to their own struggles for equality. For example, Native American, Chicano, and Puerto Rican youth styled themselves after the African-American youth in SNCC and the Black Panther Party (Oboler, 1995). The predominantly white student antiwar movement drew directly from the experiences of the black freedom struggles to shape their goals and strategies (Gitlin, 1987). Early women's liberation groups were spawned within SNCC itself as black and white women applied the analyses of racial inequality to their own positions as women (Echols, 1989; Evans, 1979; Sayres, 1984), as did Latinas within the Puerto Rican Youth (Oboler, 1995). The gay liberation and disability rights movements also credit the civil rights movement as a model for their organizing and activism (Marcus, 1992; Shapiro, 1993). Poor people's movements and welfare rights likewise drew upon this heritage (Piven & Cloward, 1982).

Of the many valuable legacies of the civil rights movement and the academic traditions focusing on racism, we highlight here two key themes. One is the awareness that racism is a system of oppression that not only stigmatizes and violates the dominated group (Fanon, 1968; Freire, 1970; Memmi, 1965), but also does psychic and ethical violence to the dominator group as well (McIntosh, 1992; Bowser & Hunt, 1981; Terry; 1975). The idea that oppression affects, albeit in different ways, both the dominant and subordinate group, has been used by many other groups to make sense of their experiences of oppressive relationships and social institutions.

The second broad theme is that racism functions not only through overt, conscious prejudice and discrimination but also through the unconscious attitudes and behaviors of a society that presumes an unacknowledged but pervasive white cultural norm (Segrest, 1994; Frankenberg, 1993; Omi & Winant, 1986; Said, 1993). The notion of cultural imperialism challenges the alleged neutrality of cultural assumptions that in fact define and reinforce white supremacy and exposes racial images embedded in language and cultural practices that are promoted as neutral and inclusive. The concept of unmarked and unacknowledged norms that bolster the power position of the dominant group is an important one for examining other forms of oppression as well. Feminists, for example, use the idea to examine practices of male supremacy and patriarchy (MacKinnon, 1989) while gay and lesbian rights activists use it to analyze heterosexual privilege (Frye, 1983; Rich, 1979).

Classism: The new left movements of the late 1960s and early 1970s espoused ideals of political democracy and personal liberty and applied their political energy to make power socially accountable (Bowles & Gintis, 1987). New left critiques of power built on Marxist theory to examine issues of domination and exploitation and to focus on the structural rather than individual factors that maintain oppressive economic and social relations. They also critiqued the tendency to conflate democracy with capitalism to suppress exploration of alternative economic and social arrangements.

In our teaching we draw on new left analyses to examine how power operates through normalizing relations of domination and systematizing ideas and practices that are then taken as given. These analyses remind us to continually ask "in whose interest" prevailing systems operate. This question of power and the interests it serves has been a useful analytic tool for examining oppression in all of its multiple forms. Asking who benefits and who pays for prevailing practices helps to expose the hierarchical relationships as well as the hidden advantages and penalties embedded in a purportedly fair and neutral system.

Sexism: The women's liberation movement developed important theoretical and analytic tools for a general theory of oppression and liberation (Evans, 1979). Through consciousness raising groups women collectively uncovered and deconstructed the ways that the system of patriarchy is reproduced inside women's consciousness as well as in external social institutions, and challenged conventional assumptions about human nature, sexuality, family life, and gender roles and relations (Dinnerstein, 1976; Chodorow, 1978; Firestone, 1970). Consciousness raising groups provided a process for naming how members of subordinate groups can collude in maintaining an unequal system, identified the psychological as well as social factors that contribute to internalizing oppressive beliefs, and explored how to raise consciousness to resist and challenge such systems both inside our own consciousness and externally in the world. Feminist practice also sought to create and enact new ways of being that were liberatory. Insights from feminist theory and practice have been fruitfully used by other groups to raise consciousness, to develop an analysis of their own psychological and social assumptions and practices as these collude in maintaining oppression, and to experiment with alternative practices

Multiple Issues: Women of color, lesbians, Jewish feminists, and poor and working-class women brought forth critiques from within the women's movement that questioned a unitary theory of feminism and highlighted the multiple and diverse perspectives, needs, and goals of different feminists (Collins, 1990; Hull, Scott, & Smith, 1982; Moraga & Anzaldúa, 1981). These challenges have been used to critique unitary theories of class, race, and gender and to proliferate a range of analyses and ideas about oppression(s) that take into account both the multiple identities people hold and the range of experiences of oppression lived within any given group (Spelman, 1988). Women of color who are lesbians and poor, for example, experience oppression in multiple and distinctive ways that demand more complex analyses of the mechanisms of oppression in the lives of diverse groups of people (Lorde, 1984).

More recently, postcolonial studies and postmodern theories, and ongoing discussions within various social movements, have begun to challenge simple binary categories such as black/white, heterosexual/homosexual, male/female, and notions that essentialize, or treat as innately given, the groupings created within an oppressive social order (Mohanty, Russo, & Torres, 1991; Trinh, 1989). The inadequacy of defining the experience of individuals and groups in simplistic binary terms is reflected through challenges within the gay/lesbian movement raised by bisexual, transsexual, and transgender people and within black movements by biracial and multiracial people. The range of experiences of people holding multiple identities and diverse social group memberships poses continuing challenges to theories of oppression to account for their experiences.

Individual and Group Identity

How can we help our students think more broadly about group identity, how group identity is used to oppress, and the positive value of self-ascribed group memberships without reducing the complexities involved? In the United States we are socialized to view life in individual terms. Our Constitution and public ethos proclaim and celebrate the rights of individuals. Yet, in what meaningful sense can we say that a self "stands free from history and social affiliations" (Young, 1990)? As members of human communities our identities are fundamentally constructed in relation to others and to the cultures in which we are embedded (Bakhtin, 1981; Epstein, 1987; Vygotsky, 1978). In a very real sense, it is impossible to separate our individual identities from the various social group memberships we hold.

When these group memberships co-exist within an unequal system, they inevitably generate multiple and conflicting personal meanings. People often affirm their group identity(ies) as a source of nurturance, pride, and meaning at the same time as they are victimized by the dominant group's characterization of their group in ways they experience as oppressive and reject as invalid.

Oppression cannot be understood in individual terms alone, for people are privileged or oppressed on the basis of social group status. One of the privileges of dominant group status is the luxury to simply see oneself as an individual. A white man, for example, is rarely defined by whiteness or maleness. If he does well on his job, he is acknowledged as a highly qualified individual. If he does poorly, the blame is attributed to him alone.

Those in subordinated groups, however, can never fully escape being defined by their social group memberships. A Puerto Rican woman, for example, may wish to be viewed as an individual and acknowledged for her personal talents and abilities. Yet she can never fully escape the dominant society's assumptions about her racial/ethnic group, language, and gender. If she excels in her work, she may be seen as atypical or exceptional. If she does poorly, she may be seen as representative of the limitations of the group. In either case, she rises or falls not on the basis of individual qualities alone, but always also partly as a member of her group(s).

This does not mean that all members of a particular social group will necessarily define themselves in exactly the same way. A person's group identity may be central, as religious identity is to a traditionally observant Jew. Or it may be mainly background, only becoming salient in certain interactional contexts, as Jewish identity may become for an assimilated Jew when confronted with antisemitism (Young, 1990). In both cases they share the burden of the social conditions facing them as targets in an unequal society.

Group identity is also an historical and contextual phenomenon. Latinos in the United States, for example, are an extremely diverse group comprising people from many different countries of origin, speaking various languages, from divergent racial, ethnic, and socio-economic groups, who arrived in the United States under widely different conditions of immigration, colonization or slavery in many time periods (Anzaldúa, 1987; Oboler, 1995). The label Latino may include a Spanish speaking, upper-class white man from Cuba as well as a Mayan speaking, Indian woman from Mexico or Guatemala. The dominant society lumps these individuals together in a group labeled "Hispanic" to which certain stereotypes are applied. On one level they thus could be said to share a common group experience of oppression in a historical United States context, and indeed, this is often the basis for political organizing across different groups of Latinos. On another level, their experiences are so divergent as to have little in common at all except when compared to the experiences of non-Latinos.

A popular view of Americanization is that people from all of these various groups will ultimately merge together to create one unified group that is a blend of all the cultures involved. This view of the United States as a "melting pot" often points to successive waves of European immigration in the eighteenth and nineteenth centuries as evidence of this process. This view, however, ignores Anglo American conformity that required white immigrant groups such as the Germans, Irish, Italians, and Scandinavians to divest themselves of their native ethnic cultures and languages and adopt Anglo European, middle-class cultural norms and values (McLemore, 1993; Steinberg, 1989). It also ignores the continued exclusion of nonwhite groups, particularly Native Americans and Americans of African, Caribbean, and Indian descent.

One of the most invidious mechanisms of oppression is the eradication of subordinate group cultures through the imposition of the dominant group's culture and language. The ideal of assimilation rests on the assumption of a "supposedly unitary majority culture" (Omi & Winant, 1986; Said, 1993), which in fact is the dominant Anglo European culture. In such a context, individuals and groups gain equality by becoming as much like the privileged group as possible. This process automatically marginalizes those who can never "pass" into the dominant culture by virture of race, gender, or other noticeable difference and strips people of cultural aspects they value. At its worst, this process in the United States has led to the near extermination of the native people of this continent (Churchill, 1995; Wright, 1992; Stannard, 1992).

The tension between individual and group identity(ies) is complicated further by the fact that group identity is also for many people self-consciously chosen and affirmed as a fundamental aspect of self-definition. Self-ascription, "belonging to a group with others who similarly identify themselves, who affirm or are committed together to a set of values, practices and meanings" is an important concept to many in our society (Young, 1994, 34). The emergence of black consciousness, gay pride, feminist solidarity, disability rights, red power, la raza, and other affirmations of group identity exemplifies the importance of self-ascribed group status to people who are devalued by the dominant culture.

Finally, neither individual identities nor social groups are homogeneous or stable. Individuals are constituted partly by group relations and affinities that are "multiple, cross-cutting, fluid and shifting" (Young, 1990, 48). Postmodern writers have argued persuasively against the notion of a unitary subject and essentialist notions of group identity that ignore the fluid and changing ways that people experience themselves both as individuals and as members of different social groups over the course of a lifetime (Anzaldúa, 1987; Mohanty, Russo, & Torres, 1991). "Despite our desperate, eternal attempt to separate, contain, and mend, categories always leak" (Trinh, 1989, 94).

Hegemony, Reproduction, and the Operations of Power

We usually think of oppression in stark terms of naked power, the master beating the slave, for example. The political movements for equality over the past few decades have succeeded in challenging some of the most glaring abuses of power. Yet, while advances have been made, the basic relations of domination have been remarkably resistant to change. Young notes how general patterns of inequality continue to be reproduced even in the face of deliberate efforts to change them (1990).

Gramsci put forth the idea of hegemony to explain the way in which power is maintained not only through coercion but also through the voluntary consent of those dominated (Morrow & Torres, 1995). Hegemony describes how a dominant group can project its particular way of seeing social reality so successfully that its view is accepted as common sense, as part of the natural order, even by those who are in fact disempowered by it (Tong, 1989). Hegemony helps us understand power as relational and dynamic, something that circulates within a web of relationships in which we all participate, rather than as something imposed from top down (Foucault, 1980). Power consists not simply in a person or group in power unilaterally imposing its will on another person or group, but rather an ongoing system that is mediated by well-intentioned people acting as agents of oppression, usually unconsciously, by simply going about their daily lives (Young, 1990).

The exclusion of people with disabilities from many jobs, for example, does not require overt discrimination against them. Business as usual is sufficient to prevent change. Physical barriers to access go unnoticed by those who can walk up the stairs, reach elevator buttons and telephones, use furniture and tools that fit their bodies and functional needs, and generally move in a world that is designed to facilitate their passage.

Hegemony is also maintained through "discourse," which includes ideas, texts, theories, and language. These are embedded in networks of social and political control that Foucault called "regimes of truth" (1980). Regimes of truth operate to legitimize what can be said, who has the authority to speak, and what is sanctioned as true (Kreisberg, 1992). For example, until women began speaking about spousal abuse, a husband's authority to physically control his wife often went unchallenged, rendered invisible through the language of family privacy and assumptions about sexual consent in marriage.

Oppression operates through everyday practices that do not question "the assumptions underlying institutional rules and the collective consequences of following those rules" (Young, 1990, 41). One important mechanism for challenging oppression, then, is to make visible and vocal the underlying assumptions that produce and reproduce structures of domination so that we can collectively begin to imagine alternative possibilities for organizing social life (Freire, 1970).

For example, the assumptions of heterosexual privilege are mostly unchallenged and invisible in our society. Social norms, rituals, and language, as well as institutional rules and rewards, presume the existence of exclusively heterosexual feelings and relationships. The language and symbols of love, attraction, family, and sexual and emotional self-development largely ignore the existence of homosexual, bisexual, transgender, and other possibilities of human potential. Well-meaning heterosexual people may bemoan gay-bashing and hate-based assaults on gays and lesbians, but assume that the system is basically fine as it is. They only see extreme examples of prejudice and live their lives unaware of the daily exclusions, insults, and assaults endured by those who are not heterosexual. Heterosexism also conceals how this regime operates not only to oppress gay, lesbian, bisexual, and transgender people but also to constrain and limit heterosexuals to narrowly gender-defined rules of behavior and options for self-expression as well.

Privilege and Penalty: Internalized Domination and Subordination

The normalization of oppression in everyday life is achieved when we internalize attitudes and roles that support and reinforce systems of domination without question or challenge. As Audre Lorde so eloquently states, "the true focus of revolutionary change is to see the piece of the oppressor inside us" (1984, 123). Both agents, those who are privileged in the hierarchy of oppression, and targets, those who are victimized and penalized, play a role in maintaining oppression.

For members of subordinate or targeted groups, internalized subordination consists of accepting and incorporating the negative images of themselves fostered by the dominant society (Bartky, 1979; Lipksy, 1977; Miller, 1976; Fanon, 1968; Freire, 1970; Memmi, 1965; Sennett & Cobb, 1972). It includes such feelings as inferiority and self-hatred and often results in self-concealment, resignation, isolation, powerlessness, and gratitude for being allowed to survive (Pheterson, 1990). Dominated groups collude in maintaining systems of oppression both because they internalize the false belief that the system is correct and as a means of survival. Women may actively accept the belief that men are more capable in politics and business and women more naturally suited to housework and childcare. They may unquestioningly adopt assumptions about female limitations and negative stereotypes of women as weak, overemotional, and irrational. Women may also support male dominance as a means of survival because to challenge it means risking jobs, relationships, and physical security.

Internalized acceptance of the status quo among subordinate groups can also lead them to turn on members of the group who challenge it. This horizontal hostility (see chapter 2) blocks solidarity among group members and prevents organizing for change. For example, gay and lesbian people who stay in the closet and pass as heterosexual in order to survive may resent activists who insist on being open and actively challenging discrimination against their group. This division within the community helps to maintain the system of heterosexism and prevents solidarity and working together for change.

Members of dominant or privileged groups also internalize the system of oppression and through their collusion with the system operate as agents in perpetuating it. Internalized domination is the incorporation and acceptance by individuals within the dominant group of prejudices against others and the assumption that the status quo is normal and correct. It includes feelings of superiority, and often self-consciousness, guilt, fear, projection, and denial (McIntosh, 1992; Frankenberg, 1993; Pharr, 1988).

Dominants learn to look at themselves, others, and society through a distorted lens in which the structural privileges they enjoy and the cultural practices of their group are represented as normal and universal. The privilege of dominant groups is reinforced in both language and material practices. For example, in spite of rhetoric that the United States is a secular nation, Christian symbols, holidays, and rituals are routinely integrated into public affairs and institutions. Other religious and spiritual traditions held by large numbers of Americans, including Jews, Muslims, Hindus, and Native Americans, are invisible or marginalized so much so that when members of these groups protest they are often viewed as challenging the American (Christian) way of life. Similarly, even the most modest proposals to change the economic system to more equitably distribute goods and services is taken as a challenge to the American (capitalist) way of life.

Dominants also engage in horizontal hostility toward members of their own group who challenge the status quo. For example, Whites who challenge racist practices may be labeled by other Whites as troublemakers, extremists, or bleeding hearts. Pressure against rocking the boat or "making trouble" can discourage dominants from challenging inequality and discrimination and block change. Often by simply doing nothing, dominants perpetuate the system as agents of the status quo.

Freire argued that members of both subordinate and dominant groups are dehumanized by oppression (Freire, 1970). Part of the task of change is to engage people from both groups in examining the costs of maintaining systems of domination. The impetus for change more often comes from members of oppressed groups since those who are oppressed by a system usually have the most incentive to change it. They are also more likely to develop a critical perspective about the dominant society and to see more clearly the contradictions between myths and reality (Freire, 1970; Hartsock, 1983; Harding 1991; Collins, 1990). The "subjugated knowledges" of oppressed groups, those truths and insights about the social world that are suppressed, define the world and the possibilities for human existence differently and offer valuable alternative visions of what is possible (Collins, 1990). Thus, it is important to listen to the analyses and experiences of members of target groups to get a clearer understanding of how oppression operates and to imagine alternative ways of organizing social life.

Dominants also have an important role to play in challenging oppression and creating alternatives. Throughout our history there have always been people from dominant groups who use their power to actively fight against systems of oppression (Aptheker, 1993; Wigginton, 1992; Zinn, 1980). White abolitionists, middle- and upper-class anti-poverty crusaders, and men who supported women's rights are examples. Dominants can expose the social, moral, and personal costs of maintaining privilege so as to develop an investment in changing the system by which they benefit, but for which they also pay a price. Some argue this commitment comes through friendship (Spelman, 1988), others that it comes only through mutual struggle for common political ends (Sleeter, 1993; Mohanty, Russo, & Torres, 1991). In either case, dominants too need to identify the role they play in maintaining the system and the price they pay for privileged status in an unequal hierarchy.

For example, when millions of Americans are homeless and hungry, those who are comfortable pay a social and moral price. The cost of enjoying plenty while others starve challenges our ability to see ourselves as good people living in a just society. It also prevents us from examining underlying structural problems in the economic system that ultimately make all working and middle-class Americans vulnerable in a changing international economy. The productive and creative contributions of people who are shut out of the system are lost to all of us. Rising violence and urban decay make it increasingly difficult for anyone to feel safe on city streets. Reduced social supports, limited affordable housing, and scarcities of food and potable water loom as a possible future for all who are not independently wealthy, particularly as we reach old age.

Consciousness, Agency, and Resistance

Given the power of systems of domination to saturate both the external world and our individual psyches, how do we challenge and change them? In a context where we are all implicated, where we cannot escape our social positions, how do we find a standpoint from which to act (Lewis, 1993)? A commitment to social justice requires a moral and ethical attitude toward equality and possibility and a belief in the capacity of people as agents who can act to transform their world (Freire, 1970; Weiler, 1991). Hegemony is never total, it is always open to contestation (Morrow & Torres, 1995). The contradictions between espoused social principles and lived experience offer one place to begin.

Our approach to social justice education begins with people's lived experience and works to foster a critical perspective and action directed toward social change (Bell & Schniedewind, 1987; Kreisberg, 1992; Lewis, 1993). We take the position that people in both dominant and subordinate groups have a critical role to play in dismantling oppression and generating visions for a more socially just future. The specific standpoints of particular social groups are important. Within homogeneous groups, people can analyze policies and practices that support oppression and build group solidarity and support from the particular vantage points of their group(s). Heterogeneous coalitions among different groups can then develop strategies further and build support for change that draws on the energies, and differential insights and access to power of members from various groups.

The civil rights movement illustrates well the potential of a coalition of empowered people with their allies. Each group brought its own perspective and moral commitment to the struggle. Black Americans brought a collective personal integrity and willingness to risk their lives which forced American society as a whole to confront the ugly truth of racism. Jews, who were the largest group of whites to participate, drew on their own experiences of oppression to mobilize support and commitment in white communities. Whites with access to power and privilege not available to most black Americans acted as allies in the struggle for change by passing laws in Congress, using the media to publicize the struggle and joining in actions where white lives were more likely to gain police protection. Together they forged a coalition for change that inspires social movements to this day.

We can also learn from studying the factors that led to the demise of the civil rights movement in order to be more effective allies and work in coalition with others without erasing or suppressing difference in the name of false unity (Albrecht & Brewer, 1990; Bunch, 1987; Kaye/Kantrowitz, 1992; Reagon, 1983). As individuals and groups we can only have partial visions. Coalitions can bring together multiple ways of understanding the world and oppressive structures within it. Specific skills of perspective taking, empathic listening, and self-examination are useful to this process. So are practicing and sharing effective ways to work as allies to actively create alternatives to individual isolation and the suppression of political culture. Through dialogue we can find creative ways to encourage each other to begin to "imagine otherwise" (Lather, 1991). Social justice courses are one arena for practicing skills and developing collective strategies for change.

Conclusion

As historical circumstances change and emerging social movements take up the issue of oppression in the United States, new definitions and understandings will evolve. Through highlighting the historical and contextual nature of this process we hope to avoid the danger of reifying systems of oppression as static or treating individuals as unidimensional and unchanging. History illustrates both how tenacious and variable systems of oppression are and how dynamic and creative we must continue to be to rise to the challenges they pose. The concepts and processes we present in this text are continuously evolving. We hope the work presented here will contribute to an ongoing dialogue about social justice education theory and practice.

This chapter situates the approach taken in this volume within the broader discourses on oppression and social justice in academic and social change realms. In the next chapter, Bailey Jackson and Rita Hardiman describe in more detail the specific conceptual foundations for the curriculum designs to follow. They present the theoretical models developed in their early work that undergird the social justice courses we teach at the University of Massachusetts/Amherst.

2

Conceptual Foundations for Social Justice Courses

Rita Hardiman, Bailey W. Jackson

The preceding chapter places social justice education within a broad framework of historically situated discourses on oppression and liberation. In this chapter we describe how the conceptual models that undergird our practices and the curricula presented in this volume developed out of our early practice at the University of Massachusetts/Amherst School of Education, and how they continue to evolve.

Our conceptual model includes a definition of oppression in which individuals play a variety of roles in a multilayered and dynamic script. The model includes the dominant and subordinate social roles, as oppressor and oppressed (or agent and target of oppression), in interaction with the structural characteristics that hold the overall script in place. We introduce a matrix of the systemic aspects of the oppression script and the role relations and interactions within it. Finally, we present a generic model of social identity development based on our earlier work on black identity development (Jackson, 1976a, b) and white identity development (Hardiman 1979, 1982) in order to understand and anticipate how these roles may interact with each other and change over time in relation to a person's various social group memberships.

During the late 1970s and early 1980s we used the identity development models in courses on racism, cultural bias, and counseling from a racial perspective. Our interactions with colleagues and students engaged in the women's, gay liberation, and disability rights movements, and workshops focusing on antisemitism and classism, led us to see striking parallels and commonalities in the manifestations of different forms of oppression. We also explored the applicability of social identity development for other peoples of color (Kim, 1981), biracial people (Wijeyesinghe, 1992), and women and members of other social identity groups within the contexts of racism, sexism, antisemitism, heterosexism, ableism, and classism. We then extended the racial identity models to a generic model that examines how members of agent and target groups experience internalized domination or internalized subordination and change their sense of relationship to other members of their target or agent group at various stages of consciousness.

Our thinking on these issues was informed by the work of Fanon (1967, 1968), Freire (1970, 1973), Memmi (1965), Goldenberg (1978), and Miller (1976). Rather than asking historical questions, such as "How did this come to be?" or "Which isms are foundational to other isms?" our goal became one of understanding, recognizing, and describing the generic characteristics of oppression. Our starting point is that once systems of oppression are in place, they are self-perpetuating. We want to understand the structures of self-perpetuation, the roles people play in the system of oppression and how these roles interact. Eventually our generic model of social identity development came to be subsumed within the general model of oppression.

According to our model, *social oppression* exists when one social group, whether knowingly or unconsciously, exploits another social group for its own benefit. Social oppression is distinct from a situation of simple brute force in that it is an interlocking system that involves ideological control as well as domination and control of the social institutions and resources of the society, resulting in a condition of privilege for the agent group relative to the disenfranchisement and exploitation of the target group.

Oppression is not simply an ideology or set of beliefs that assert one group's superiority over another, nor is it random violence, harassment, or discrimination toward members of target groups. A condition of social oppression exists when the following key elements are in place:

- The agent group has the power to define and name reality and determine what is "normal," "real," or "correct."
- Harassment, discrimination, exploitation, marginalization, and other forms of differential and unequal treatment are institutionalized and systematic. These acts often do not require the conscious thought or effort of individual members of the agent group but are rather part of business as usual that become embedded in social structures over time.
- Psychological colonization of the target group occurs through socializing the oppressed to internalize their oppressed condition and collude with the oppressor's ideology and social system. This is what Freire refers to as the oppressed playing "host" to the oppressor (1970).
- The target group's culture, language, and history is misrepresented, discounted, or eradicated and the dominant group's culture is imposed.

Social oppression then involves a relationship between an agent group and a target group that keeps the system of domination in place. Recognizing the importance of collusion to the system of oppression does not mean that targets share equal responsibility for their situation with agents, or that they collude willingly. Rather, the collusion of targets is the result of agents taking control over time of the institutions of a society, as well as the minds, ideology, language, culture, and history of the targets.

Part of the method of establishing dominance in the system of oppression is the naming of the target group by the agent group. The ability to name reflects who has power. Agent groups establish their dominance by controlling how targets are named. The eradication or chipping away of a group's identity is not always a visible or conscious process. Rather it happens gradually, and in many respects, unconsciously. Over an extended period of time, a system of domination becomes institutionalized so that conscious intent is no longer necessary to keep power and privilege in the hands of the agent group.

While oppression is reproduced in the institutions and structures of society, individual people also play a role in its operation and maintenance. Some groups and individuals are victims or targets of injustice and oppression and other groups and individuals are agents who reap the benefits of illegitimate privilege by virtue of their social group membership(s).

The Social Oppression Matrix

In our model, social oppression is maintained and operationalized at three levels: the individual, the institutional, and the societal/cultural. The matrix below illustrates the dynamic workings of these three levels along three dimensions that operate to support and reinforce each other: the context, the psychosocial processes, and the application.

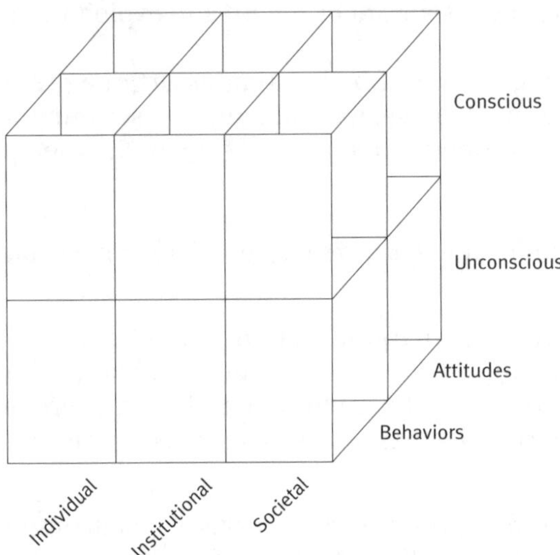

Figure 2.1. Oppression Model

The Context

The context axis interacts with all three levels: individual, institutional, and cultural/societal. The actual boundaries are more fluid than the lines in the diagram would suggest and all three levels are mutually reinforcing.

Individual Level: At the individual level, we focus on the beliefs or behaviors of an individual person rather than on institutional or cultural practices. Here we refer to conscious or unconscious actions or attitudes that maintain oppression. Examples include harassment, rape, racial/ethnic/religious slurs, and behavior that excludes targets.

An individual agent or target is also affected by and has an effect on institutions in that individuals are socialized, punished, rewarded, and guided by institutions that maintain and perpetuate oppressive structures. In turn, the individual has an effect on the institutions and the broader culture to the extent that he/she works, consumes, teaches, votes, and lives the values of the dominant society/culture.

Institutional Level: Institutions such as the family, government, industry, education, and religion are shapers of, as well as shaped by, the other two levels. The application of institutional policies and procedures in an oppressive society run by individuals or groups who advocate or collude with social oppression produces oppressive consequences. Examples are the unequal treatment of African Americans and poor people of all races by the criminal and civil justice system, housing and employment discrimination against gays and lesbians, unequal access to quality education for the poor and working classes, and exclusion from social and cultural institutions such as civic groups and social clubs that have historically excluded women, men of color, and Jews.

Societal/Cultural Level: Society's cultural norms perpetuate implicit and explicit values that bind institutions and individuals. In an oppressive society the cultural perspective of the dominant groups is imposed on institutions by individuals and on individuals by institutions. These cultural guidelines, such as philosophies of life, definitions of the good, normal, health, deviance, and sickness, often serve the primary function of providing individuals and institutions with the justification for social oppression. Examples of these cultural guidelines and norms abound in the perception of homosexuality as sick or evil, the acceptance of the nuclear family as the only model of a "good" family, and assumptions in the media and court systems about what rape victims did to incur the rape.

The Psycho-Social Processes

Psycho-social processes describe the types of involvement relative to one's advocacy, participation, support, or collusion in a system of social oppression. These processes are conscious or unconscious (Katz, 1978), dominative or aversive (Kovel, 1970), involving active or passive acceptance (Jackson, 1976; Hardiman, 1982). *Conscious* processes involve knowingly supporting the maintenance of social oppression through individual, institutional, and social/cultural attributes. *Unconscious* processes represent unknowing or naive collusion with the maintenance of social oppression and occur when the target or agent comes to accept the dominant logic system and justifies oppression as normal or part of the natural order, for example, Asians who have eyelid surgery, Blacks who use skin-lightening products, and ethnic groups who anglicize their names to sound less Jewish, Polish, or Italian.

The Application

The application dimension acknowledges that oppression is manifested at both the attitudinal and behavioral levels of individual and system interaction. The *attitudinal level* describes the individual and systemic values, beliefs, philosophies, and stereotypes that feed the other dimensions, for example, the stereotype that Jews control the economic system, that gays and lesbians are child molesters, or stereotypes that Asians are sneaky and inscrutable. The behavior variable describes the actions of individuals and systems that support and maintain social oppression, such as an individual who threatens a person of color seeking to move into a new apartment or neighborhood, or the institutional practice in banks of "redlining" neighborhoods where people of color live.

Roles in the System of Oppression

The terms we use to describe members of oppressed and oppressor groups are *target* and *agent* of oppression. *Targets* are members of social identity groups that are disenfranchised, exploited, and victimized in a variety of ways by the oppressor and the oppressor's system or institutions. Target groups are those which, in Goldenberg's terms, are subject to containment, having their choices and movement restricted and limited; are seen and treated as expendable and replaceable, without an individual identity apart from the group; and are compartmentalized into narrowly defined roles (1978). Young (1990) says targets are people subjected to exploitation, marginalization, powerlessness, cultural imperialism, and violence. Targeted or stigmatized people are kept in their place by the agents' ideology which supports oppression by denying its existence, and blames the condition of the oppressed on themselves and their own failings. Memmi (1965) argued that oppression, if it lasts long enough, becomes so familiar to oppressed people that they accept it and cannot imagine recovery from it.

Agents are members of dominant social groups privileged by birth or acquisition, who knowingly or unknowingly exploit and reap unfair advantage over members of target groups. Members of agent groups are also trapped by the system of social oppression that benefits them, and are confined to roles and prescribed behavior for their group. Freire (1970) observes that a paradox of social oppression is that oppressors/agents are also dehumanized because they have engaged in a process of stealing the humanity of others.

Freire notes that oppression is perpetuated from generation to generation as new generations become its heirs and are shaped in its climate. Agents, due to their power to define reality, see themselves and are seen by others as normal or proper, whereas targets are likely to be labeled as deviant, evil, abnormal, substandard, or defective. Unlike targets, agents are frequently unaware that they are members of the dominant group due to the privilege of being able to see themselves as persons rather than as stereotypes. In this way, agents are also subject to psychological colonization because, once the oppressive structures are in place, oppression becomes normalized and succeeding generations of agents learn to accept their inheritance of dominance and privilege as the natural order—the way things are, and always will be.

Agents and targets vary among different nations and cultures, but in the United States, we consider the following groups as agents and targets because of the pervasive and systemic hierarchies that hold in place their unequal status relative to each other:

	AGENTS	**TARGETS**
Race and Ethnic	Whites	People of Color
Gender	Men	Women
Sexual Orientation	Heterosexuals	Gay men, Lesbians, and Bisexuals
Religion	Christians	Jews, Muslims, and Other Religious Minorities
Physical/ Psychological/ Developmental Disability	Able persons	Disabled Persons
Class	Owning and Middle Class	Poor and Working Class
Age	Middle/Adult	Young and Elderly

Multiple Identities: Many people are likely to have both agent and target identities. There are gendered, raced, classed people of different religions and sexual orientations, young and old, able-bodied and -minded or disabled. This adds another level of complexity to our attempt to understand the dynamics of oppression, particularly as it is influenced by the behaviors and attitudes in each role. Although we acknowledge the implications of multiple social group identities and the reality that most people play both the target and agent role, here for purposes of clarity, we focus on specific agent or target identities as a still point in a dynamic picture.

Relationships Within and Between the Roles in the System of Oppression

Collusion (Internalized Subordination or Domination): *Internalized subordination* refers to ways in which targets collude with their own oppression. People who have been socialized in an oppressive environment, and who accept the dominant group's ideology about their group, have learned to accept a definition of themselves that is hurtful and limiting. They think, feel, and act in ways that demonstrate the devaluation of their group and of themselves as members of that group. For example, internalized subordination is operating when target group members question the credentials or abilities of members of their own social group without cause, yet unquestioningly accept that members of the agent group are qualified, talented, and deserving of their credentials. Internalized subordination also operates when target group members curry favor with dominant group members and distance themselves from their own group, often unconsciously.

Through internalized subordination, members of target groups learn to collude with their own oppression or victimization. Conscious collaboration occurs when target group members knowingly, but not necessarily voluntarily, go along with their own mistreatment to survive or to maintain some status, livelihood, or other benefit, as when a person of color silently endures racist jokes told by a boss. Such collusion is often seen by the target group member as necessary to "live to fight another day." The more insidious form of collusion is unconscious, not knowing that one is collaborating with one's own dehumanization, as when a woman blames herself for the actions of her rapist or batterer. Likewise, a woman who silently accepts sexual harassment as a condition of work life is colluding with her own oppression, even if not consciously or intentionally doing so.

Internalized domination refers to the behaviors, thoughts, and feelings of agents, who through their socialization as members of the dominant group, learn to think and act in ways that express internalized notions of entitlement and privilege. Examples of internalized domination include men talking over and interrupting women in conversation, while simultaneously labelling women as chatty. There is an absence of feeling that one has to prove oneself, or that one's status, talent, and qualifications would be questioned in any situation on the basis of social identity. Agents learn to expect to be treated well and accommodated, as when English-speaking United States citizens travel outside the United States and expect people in other countries to speak English or accommodate their culture to suit Americans. Extreme examples include the "erasure" of target group members by failing to acknowledge their existence or importance. Historical presentations that Columbus discovered America erase the existence of native peoples who preceded him by several thousand years.

Target and Agent Interaction: Vertical and Horizontal Relationships

Because our work involves anti-oppression education in the classroom, we have focused upon how oppression impacts individual consciousness and identity development. To help students understand how oppression is manifested at the individual level by agents who dominate in interaction with targets who collude, we developed the model of vertical and horizontal relationships presented below. This model draws from Fanon (1968) and Freire (1970) regarding horizontal aggression and violence.

The relationship between agent and target can be viewed as a one-up and one-down pattern, with agents operating out of internalized privilege, in a manner oppressive to targets, who simultaneously collude to some degree out of their own internalized subordination. This representation necessitates isolating for the sake of analysis only one social identity membership at a time. For example, to represent a male–female relationship as one of a dominant male and subordinate female requires ignoring that the male may be gay, or a person of color, or disabled, and the woman may be heterosexual, white, or able-bodied. While we acknowledge that this single identity focus is limiting, and represents neither the complexity of any one person's multiple identities nor the reality of a person's different agent and target identities, we present this scenario to illustrate the hierarchical relationship between agent and target.

Vertical Interaction: Vertical interaction exemplifies conscious and unconscious dehumanization and denial of rights of the target by the agent, as well as the target's collusion with social oppression. We describe this one-up, one-down interaction as a vertical relationship, because the parties occupy different hierarchical positions, with the agent, literally above or over the target. One simple illustration is a male supervisor harassing a female employee (agent behavior: dominance), while the female employee remains silent and does not challenge the behavior (target behavior: collusion)

Horizontal Relationships: The term horizontal is used to reflect relationships and interactions between members of the same social group, who, at least on one dimension of social identity, are "equal" in status. This term comes from the terms horizontal violence, or horizontal hostility, used by Pharr (1988*)* to represent the phenomenon of oppressed people directing rage at being oppressed inward and back on each other, rather than directing it outward toward the more dangerous and powerful victimizer. Horizontal relationships may take two forms:

- ***Target–Target***: The conscious and/or unconscious attitudes and behaviors exhibited in interactions between members of the same target group, that support and stem from internalized subordination (for example, women who ostracize or label other women for not conforming to sex-role defined behavior).
- ***Agent–Agent***: The conscious and/or unconscious punishments that agents bestow on other agents who violate the ideology of the oppressive system (for example, teasing and hazing by men toward men who share equal responsibility for child care and household maintenance). Agent/agent relationships also include conscious or unconscious rewards given to those who actively support or passively accept the oppressive system. For example, a reward may be as invisible as retaining membership in an informal social group at work in which valuable information about career opportunities is shared.

Thus far, we have defined social oppression and shown how as a pervasive system it works at the individual, institutional, and cultural/societal levels, and how assigned social roles interact to keep the system in place. The final section of this chapter addresses how oppression affects the identity development of targets and agents as they are socialized into dominant or subordinate social groups. The model presented below and illustrated in Figure 2.2 provides a developmental profile of targets and agents as participants in oppression and liberation who are capable of change.

Social Identity Development Theory

The generic social identity development theory is an adaptation of black identity development theory (Jackson, 1976) and white identity development theory (Hardiman, 1982). Social identity development theory has also been influenced by other theorists and applications to other social groups (Cross, 1971, 1978, 1991; Helms, 1990; Kim, 1981; Schapiro, 1985). Social identity development theory describes attributes that are common to the identity development process for members of all target and agent groups.

We present the stages, for purposes of conceptual clarity, as if a person were to move neatly from one stage to the next. In reality most people experience several stages simultaneously, holding complex perspectives on a range of issues and living a mixture of social identities. This developmental model can be helpful in understanding student perspectives and selecting instructional strategies, but we caution against using it simplistically to label people.

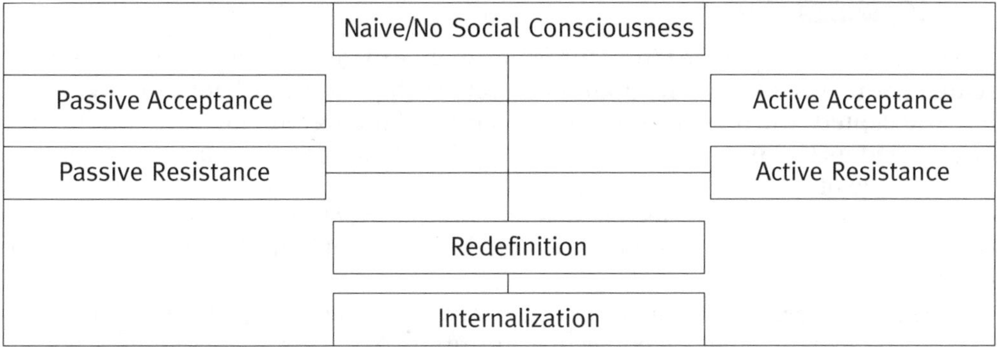

Figure 2.2. Stages of Social Identity Development (Hardiman & Jackson, 1992).

Stage I—Naive/No Social Consciousness

At birth and during early childhood, agents and targets are unaware of the complex codes of appropriate behavior for members of their social group. They naively operate from their own needs, interests, and curiosity about social group differences and break rules and push against the boundaries of social identity group membership. Through these boundary violations they begin to learn lessons about what it means to be a member of their social identity group—agent or a target.

In the transition from Naive to Acceptance consciousness, agents and targets become aware of the differences between themselves and members of other social groups. While they may not feel completely comfortable with people who are different, they generally don't feel fearful, hostile, superior, or inferior. Children at this stage display an interest in understanding the differences between people and often ask questions that embarrass or threaten adults, such as "Why do people have different skin color?" or "Can two women get married?" This stage is brief and covers the period between birth and three to four years of age.

The events that transform children from a naive or unsocialized state to a stage of Acceptance of their social dominance or subordination are numerous. The most significant socializers appear to be parents, who are role models of attitudes and behaviors, and who convey important messages through their words and silences, actions and inactions; the formal education system, including teachers, and the formal and informal curriculum; peers, who set the standards for appropriate and inappropriate behavior; religious organizations; the mass media; and the larger community with its norms, laws, social structures, and cultures that set the limits, formal and informal, for the behavior of citizens. (See cycle of socialization in chapter 5.)

Two related changes take place as the young agent or target moves into the Acceptance stage. One, they begin to learn and adopt an ideology or belief system about their own and other social identity groups. Another is they begin to learn that the world has rules, laws, institutions, and authority figures that permit certain behaviors and prohibit others, even if these rules do not make sense, and violate other principles such as freedom, equality, and axioms such as "do unto others." Both types of learning are immensely powerful, pervasive, and consistent, so much so that the acceptance of this socialization to some degree seems inevitable. This socialization process results in the second stage of identity development, Acceptance.

Stage II—Acceptance

The stage of Acceptance represents some degree of internalization, whether conscious or unconscious, of the dominant culture's logic system. People at this stage have "accepted" the messages about the nature of their group identity, the superiority of agents (Whites, heterosexuals, men, Christians), and the inferiority of targets (people of color, gays, lesbians and bisexuals, women, Jews). The Acceptance stage has two manifestations, passive and active, which refer to the relative consciousness and intentionality with which a person holds to the dominant belief system.

Agent in Acceptance: As agents in the Passive Acceptance stage have learned and to some degree internalized codes of appropriate behavior, conscious effort is no longer required to remind them of what to do and how to think. Dominant beliefs and actions are part of their everyday life, as when a white store clerk carefully watches black customers to see if they are shoplifting, or a Christian manager sets a date for an important meeting on a Jewish holiday. Questions that arose during the naive stage have been submerged and repressed such that individuals are able to live their lives without doubt. When questions occasionally arise, there is a built-in system of rationalization to fall back on and provide answers.

For those raised in the Active Acceptance stage, instruction about the inadequacies, weaknesses, deviance, and basic inferiority of targeted people occurs in a very direct manner. They are told in many ways "that's how those people are"—Mexicans are lazy, Jews control the banks, women are dumb, gays are sinners, and the disabled are objects of pity. People raised in a Passive Acceptance environment learn to blame the victim for the effects of oppression (Ryan, 1971). The key difference between Active and Passive messages is whether they are overt or covert.

Agents of oppression who have adopted an Acceptance consciousness are generally unaware that they have privileges as dominant group members of an oppressive society. They are usually unaware that they think of themselves and other agents as superior. More subtle is the assumption that the agent's experience is normative or "the way things are done." Therefore men should of course be heterosexual and masculine and those who deviate are sick or abnormal. Passive acceptance of the agent's perspective as normative is more subtle than outright belief in superiority, but in practice it has many of the same negative effects as active acceptance.

Agents of oppression who move from the Naive stage into the entry and adoption phase of Active Acceptance tend to express their superiority more directly. In the extreme form, agents at Active Acceptance may join organizations (KKK, Christian Identity) that are designed to promote supremacy. Many agents who are in the Active Acceptance stage devote their lives to maintaining their dominant perspective and privilege.

Most agents are well into their adult years before encountering events or circumstances which begin the transition to the Resistance stage. This transition marks a confusing and often painful period. Information or experiences that contradict the Acceptance world view have been initially ignored or passed off as isolated or exceptional. Gradually as the individual begins to encounter more conflicting information these isolated incidents form a discernible pattern. The contradictions that initiate the transition period can occur in the form of a personal connection or friendship with a target, or through signficant social events or information presented in books, media, and formal education.

Agents begin to experience difficult emotions during this exit phase and entry into Resistance consciousness. Their accepted identity as White, male, Christian, or heterosexual comes under scrutiny and they are often afraid and uncertain what the implications of this self-examination will be. The questioning that begins during this exit phase of Acceptance builds into the stage of Resistance.

Targets in Acceptance: Targets in the Acceptance stage have learned and accepted messages about the inferiority of targets and target culture. Often these negative/oppressive messages are held simultaneously and in contradiction to more positive messages about their social group conveyed by same group adults or social peers. Typically, the person lives with and rationalizes varying degrees of cognitive dissonance on a daily basis.

Some targets operate at a Passive Acceptance consciousness, unaware of the degree to which their thoughts, feelings and behaviors reflect the dominant group ideology. Some women prefer to work for men or to purchase services from male doctors, dentists, and lawyers because of an ingrained belief that women are not smart or capable enough to handle these jobs.

Targets in the Active Acceptance stage more consciously identify with the dominant group and its ideology. For example, some people of color are opposed to civil rights laws and affirmative action because they believe that people of color are less successful due to their own laziness and pathological culture.

Socialization of targets into the dominant world view is essentially an invisible process that is difficult to unlearn. Targets who retain this world view for life successfully rationalize efforts on the part of others to change their consciousness. Even targets who experience an urge to question their current status may find themselves seduced into remaining in place by the rewards offered by agents.

Targets who reach the exit phase of an Acceptance world view begin to acknowledge the collusive and harmful effects of the learned logic system and behavior patterns. Sometimes external events are so blatant that the person is hard pressed not to recognize the existence of oppression. Other times an individual may encounter someone of their own group who is a powerful role model, as when a lesbian in Acceptance encounters an "out" lesbian who spurs her to reject internalized homophobia, and a closeted existence.

Stage III—Resistance

The Resistance stage is one of increased awareness of the existence of oppression and its impact on agents and targets.

Agents in Resistance: As a result of experiences and information that challenge the accepted ideology and self-definition, agents entering Resistance reject earlier social positions and begin formulating a new world view. This is a dramatic paradigm shift from an ideology that blames the victims for their condition to an ideology that names one's own agent group as the source of oppression as agents become aware that oppression exists and causes the disparity between agent and target groups. Furthermore, agents begin investigating their own role in perpetuating oppression. For example, a white person may become aware for the first time of white privilege in employment, recreation, travel, or schooling.

Anger is a prevalent feeling at this stage—anger toward other agents and the nature of the agent's social group identity. Some agents wish they weren't members of their dominant group and distance themselves from other agents who don't share their new consciousness. Some zealously confront other agents for their group's oppressive actions and attitudes. Others are ostracized because their behaviors and attitudes threaten other agents who are in the Acceptance stage.

Agents in Resistance begin to develop a systemic view of how their identity has been shaped by social factors beyond their control as they re-examine the roles agents play in supporting oppression. This occurs particularly for liberal agents who have been involved in helping targets assimilate into the agent's culture and society. When the problem is redefined as an agent problem, the strategies for addressing it change. This new understanding helps some move beyond guilt and feeling overwhelmed by personal responsibility. Having negotiated the conflict between their own values and societal definitions of appropriate behavior for their group, they begin to move towards a new identity. At Resistance agents develop an awareness of their social identity, but one which is not necessarily positive. The task of Redefinition then is to engage in a process of renaming and developing a social identity that is positive and affirming.

Targets in Resistance: Acknowledgment and questioning of the cumulative experiences of oppression and their negative effects lead targets to the Resistance stage. Targets generally begin by questioning previously accepted "truths" about the way things are, for example, that men are superior, or that any person of color who works hard enough can realize their dreams. Gradually target group members become more skilled at identifying the oppressive premises woven into the fabric of all aspects of their social experience. They may also begin to feel intensified hostility toward agents, and other targets who collude with agents.

The overt expression of hostile reactions to oppression marks the transition from the entry to the adoption phase of Resistance. At this point the target group member has fully internalized the antithesis of the earlier Acceptance consciousness, and may experience increased and sometimes overwhelming anger, pain, hurt, and rage. The combination of these powerful emotions and the intellectual understanding of how oppression works may feel all-consuming. At this stage members of the target group often adopt a posture as anti-agent, for example anti-White, anti-male, anti-straight. Identity is defined in opposition to the oppressor.

Some targets may find that the Resistance stage results in losing benefits acquired when they colluded with the Acceptance consciousness and may choose a path of Passive Resistance, in hopes that they will be able to stay in favor with agents, while rejecting oppression. This strategy typically proves too frustrating and contradictory to sustain.

For most targeted people at Resistance the primary task is to end the pattern of collusion and cleanse their internalized oppressive beliefs and attitudes. During the course of the Resistance stage, targets often discover that they have become proactive and do have some power, even if not of the same type and quantity available to members of agent groups. Also, the targets begin to recognize that a considerable amount of energy has been put into "Who I am not." As they move toward the new question "Who am I?" they exit Resistance and enter Redefinition.

Stage IV—Redefinition

The focus of the Redefinition stage is on creating an identity that is independent of an oppressive system based on hierarchical superiority and inferiority.

Agents in Redefinition: At this stage agents begin to redefine the social group identity in a way that is independent of social oppression and stereotyping of targeted group(s). In prior stages agents have not been concerned with their own social identity but focused on targeted people and *their* problems (Acceptance). Or they have *reacted* to the social issue of oppression (Resistance). The experiences in Resistance leave agents feeling negatively about their social group membership, confused about their role in dealing with oppression, and isolated from many other members of their social group. Developing a positive definition of their social identity and identifying aspects of their culture and group that are affirming are necessary parts of this stage. Men who form groups to examine their socialization and critically assess the definition of masculinity that they have internalized illustrate agents at this stage.

In contrast to the negative feelings about their social group identity in Resistance, people in Redefinition develop pride in their group and a sense of personal esteem. There is a recognition that all groups have unique and different values that enrich human life, but that no culture or social group is better than another. The transition from Redefinition to Internalization emanates from the need to integrate and internalize this new social identity within one's total identity. Having established a sense of pride in themselves and their group, they are now ready to act more spontaneously on their values in everyday life.

Targets in Redefinition: In the Redefinition stage targeted people are primarily concerned with defining themselves in terms that are independent of the perceived strengths and/or weaknesses of the agent and the agent's culture. The Redefinition stage is particularly significant for targets because it is at this juncture that they shift their attention and energy away from a concern for their interactions with agents toward a concern for primary contact with members of their own social group who are at the same stage of consciousness. This type of behavior tends to be viewed negatively in an oppressive society and is often seen as counterproductive by liberal agents who view themselves as kind and benevolent. Members of targeted groups who are in Redefinition are generally labeled troublemakers or separatists. Agents who have worked to get subordinates into dominant social institutions will be particularly confused and/or put off by this apparent "self-segregating" and ungrateful behavior by targeted people. Targets in Redefinition, however, do not see interaction with agents as useful in their quest for a positive or nurturing identity.

Renaming is one primary concern in this stage as targets search for paradigms that facilitate this task. This search often begins with the formation of a new reference group consisting of other targeted people with a Redefinition consciousness.

Targeted people who are still embedded in the Acceptance or Resistance stages of consciousness are not likely to share the same concerns and personal needs as those experiencing Redefinition, and they are generally not supportive of the issues that Redefining people are attempting to address. Many targets form support groups and networks of like-minded people to focus on issues of self-definition.

The search for a social identity often involves reclaiming one's group heritage. Through revisiting or exploring one's heritage/culture, targets in Redefinition often find values, traditions, customs, philosophical assumptions, and concepts of time-work-family that are appealing and nurturing. They rediscover many aspects of their heritage that have been handed down through the generations and still affect their way of life today. They become clearer about the uniqueness of their group and come to realize they are considerably more than merely the victims of oppression. As they experience their group identity in a way that engenders pride, they may adopt a new name such as disabled rather than handicapped, or Black or African American rather than Negro. When people in Redefinition begin to contemplate the implications that this new sense of self has for all aspects of life, they exit Redefinition and enter Internalization.

Stage V—Internalization

In the Internalization stage, the main task is to incorporate the identity developed in the Redefinition stage into all aspects of everyday life. Even though targets have internalized consciousness, they are still likely to revisit or encounter situations that trigger earlier world views. For example, a Jew may feel that other Jews are acting "too Jewish" in a corporate setting and suddenly realize how they have bought into antisemitic stereotypes. The process of refining identity can be ongoing as new sources of history or past feelings and thoughts characteristic of earlier stages reemerge. As long as a person lives in an oppressive society, the process of uncovering previously unrecognized areas of Acceptance and Resistance will be ongoing even though their predominant consciousness may be in Redefinition or Internalization.

Agents in Internalization: Agents at this stage, aware of their past and concerned about creating a more equal future, try to apply and integrate their new social identity into other facets of their overall identity, since change in one dimension will undoubtedly affect all others. Implicit in the term Internalization is the assumption that the new aspects become a natural part of behavior so that people act unconsciously, without external controls, and without having to consciously think about what they are doing. The new behavior becomes spontaneous.

Targets in Internalization: At this stage targeted people are engaged in the process of integrating and internalizing their newly developed consciousness and group pride. They realize that the process of redefining identity is a valuable learning and consciousness expanding experience. It is now time to test this new sense of self in a wider context than the supportive reference group focused on in the Redefinition stage and to determine what effects this new social identity will have on the many social roles that people play. Targets at the Internalization stage begin by interacting and often renegotiating with the significant people in their lives for the purpose of establishing the type of social interactions that will serve their new social identity. Even in situations where their perspective is not valued and renegotiation does not succeed they find that their new self-esteem and self-concept can provide the necessary sustenance to prevail.

Another significant aspect of Internalization consciousness is the appreciation of the plight of all targets of any form of oppression. Having moved through the liberation process for their own experience of oppression, it becomes easier for the person with an Internalization consciousness to have empathy for members of other targeted groups in relation to whom they are agents (for example, a heterosexual Latino who can now acknowledge and explore Christian or heterosexual privilege). It is less likely that a target in Resistance or Redefinition consciousness will be able to acknowledge coexistent agent identities. Furthermore, those who find themselves victims of more than one form of oppression (for example, black women or disabled Jews) find that their developmental process in one area of their social identity may be useful in dealing with other of their targeted identities as well. There is essentially no exit phase for this stage; the ongoing task is one of lifelong exploration and nurturance.

Conclusion

In this chapter, we have presented a definition of social oppression, a matrix of the interlocking levels and types, a description of the roles and relationships among agents and targets, and a developmental model of the social identity process. These foundational concepts undergird the curriculum designs in chapters 5–12. The next chapter turns from key concepts that underlie course content to the principles that support our pedagogical approach and teaching process.

3

Pedagogical Frameworks for Social Justice Education

Maurianne Adams

> Many teachers who do not have difficulty . . . embracing new ways of thinking, may still be as resolutely attached to old ways of practicing teaching as their more conservative colleagues. . . . Even those of us who are experimenting with progressive pedagogical practices are afraid to change.
>
> —bell hooks, *Teaching to Transgress*

Topics that arise in social justice education classrooms such as prejudice, discrimination, and inequality, are affectively loaded for both teachers and students and linked to strongly held beliefs, values, and feelings (Weinstein & Bell, 1982; Schoem, 1993). As we turn our attention in this chapter from subject matter to teaching practice, or from *what* we teach to *how* we teach, we face these five pedagogical dilemmas:

(1) balancing the emotional and cognitive components of the learning process;

(2) acknowledging and supporting the personal (the individual student's experience) while illuminating the systemic (the interactions among social groups);

(3) attending to social relations within the classroom;

(4) utilizing reflection and experience as tools for student-centered learning; and

(5) valuing awareness, personal growth, and change as outcomes of the learning process.

These pedagogical dilemmas have been explored over many years in educational communities as disparate as laboratory and intergroup education, community organizing, women's studies, black studies, and adult literacy education. This chapter reviews some of the pedagogical traditions and epistemologies that have evolved into social justice educational practice. Readers may situate themselves within one or more of these broad teaching and learning traditions and find that key practices in areas with which they are more familiar are reinforced or elaborated within others with which they may be less familiar.

Although the social justice practice described here continues to evolve through experimentation and reflection, it is also grounded upon a considerable pedagogical literature reaching back at least to the middle of this century. These foundations are traced in greater detail in my book on social justice pedagogy (Adams, forthcoming). Here, I suggest in broad brush strokes, the major debates about pedagogy that have provided key elements for social justice educational practice.

Laboratory and Intergroup Education

Experiments in group process and intergroup communication took place in the 1940s among interracial community leaders and social psychologists engaged in a precursor of social justice education. Kurt Lewin, a German Jewish refugee from Nazism, was studying intergroup prejudice and devising methods for direct action in community settings in 1944. His experiments with training groups ("T-groups") and "action research" (Lippitt, 1949; Benne, 1964; Marrow, 1969) combined the personal with the systemic and used simulations and role plays in a set of procedures called "laboratory training," which examined interracial conflicts and provided opportunities to "get into the shoes of the other" (Lippitt, 1949).

Laboratory training stresses learning about the self in group-based social situations that focus on the following (adapted from Golembiewski & Blumberg, 1977):

- ***presentation of the self:*** opportunities to disclose attitudes, beliefs, and behaviors for the purposes of feedback and learning;
- ***feedback:*** information from others that enables participants to understand the impact of what they say or do;
- ***climate:*** a learning environment that provides trust and nondefensiveness, so that participants can change and correct language and behavior that is inappropriate;
- ***cognitive organizers or maps:*** models derived from research and theory that help participants to organize and generalize from experiences within the group;
- ***experimentation, practice, and application:*** opportunities to try out and practice new patterns of thought and behavior, in order to transfer them to back-home situations.

Reflective practices such as "processing," "debriefing," and "feedback" are central to social justice teaching. Processing and feedback help participants understand their impact on each other, contextualize interpersonal and intergroup miscommunication, and bring undercurrents of conflict and criticism out into the open where they can be constructively addressed (Lippitt, 1949). Small group simulations and interaction provide specific, socially situated examples of otherwise elusive abstractions about racism, classism, and other oppressions that can then be interpreted and analyzed ("processed") from multiple perspectives. These ideas have been enriched by the problematizing of participant status and positionality (Bell, 1995; Ellsworth, 1989).

The laboratory tradition also provides methods for generating data on attitudes, stereotypes, and misinformation. These data reflect the affective "inside" of interracial misunderstandings as they emerge in the here-and-now of the classroom. Such data can be presented by participant observers through sensitive and respectful feedback to defuse difficult situations and enhance participant learning. The group dynamics literature provides many useful ideas about staging simulations and conducting process observation and feedback which can be adapted to social justice topics (see Bradford, Gibb, & Benne, 1964; Golembiewski & Blumberg, 1977; Pfeiffer & Jones, 1974; Eitington, 1984). Lewin's insistence (1948) upon the necessary interaction among education, research, action, and explicit transfer from the laboratory situation to daily experience is also evident in social justice education.

Human Relations, Intergroup, and Multicultural Education

Experiments in intergroup and intercultural consciousness raising groups and black-white sensitivity training occurred throughout the 1940s and 50s (Williams, 1947; American Council on Education, 1949; Cook, 1954). These approaches assumed that awareness and knowledge would by themselves reduce prejudice and were used frequently in the 1950s school and military desegregation, the 1960s civil rights movement and anti-racism training pioneered by SCLC and SNCC, and continued with 1970s affirmative action and equal opportunity staff development programs (Hayles, 1978; York, 1994). These efforts aimed to increase intergroup respect and communication competence.

Sociological analyses of race relations at the systemic level added the understanding of power differentials (Hayles, 1978). Multicultural education in some instances, for example, combined a systems perspective with focus on personal change (Sleeter & Grant, 1994; Nieto, 1996; Suzuki, 1984; Schniedewind & Davidson, 1983). These were informed by an emerging social science literature of race relations that described specific intervention strategies (Argyris, 1970, 1975), analyzed resistance to change (Coch & French, 1948; Mill, 1974), focused upon the dominance and privileges of the white majority (Terry, 1975; Wellman, 1977; Hardiman, 1982, 1994; Segrest, 1994), and generated research concerning conditions under which intergroup contact might reduce or exacerbate racial tensions and prejudice (Amir, 1969, 1976; Sherif, 1961, 1967). Experience-based personal awareness and social action strategies recur as techniques of choice in anti-racism and anti-sexism workshops and course syllabi (Cross et al., 1982; Wolverton, 1983; Rozema, 1988; Frankenberg, 1990; Freedman, 1994; Katz, 1978; Sargent, 1974, 1977; Sherover-Marcuse, 1981; Schoem et al., 1993).

Multicultural theorists such as Suzuki (1984), Banks (1991), Banks and Banks (1995), Nieto (1996), Grant (1992), and Sleeter and Grant (1994) also focus on transformative pedagogical practices. Suzuki, for example, proposes principles that integrate an experiential, personal focus and collaborative and democratic classroom processes, with attention to social identity, sociocultural and historical context, and community-based experiments for change (Suzuki, 1984).

Nieto stresses decision-making and social action skills and invokes Freire's call for a critical pedagogy that "is based on the experiences and viewpoints of students rather than on an imposed culture" (1996, 321). Sleeter and Grant call for education that is multicultural and social reconstructionist to empower young people to make social changes (1994). These writers make important distinctions between human relations approaches that do not focus on social power and oppression, and those that integrate personal awareness with a social justice orientation.

Cross-cultural and International Training

Cross-cultural training programs, more internationally oriented than domestic "intergroup education" efforts (Noronha, 1992), were begun in the 1950s for student programs abroad (Batchelder & Warner, 1977), the Peace Corps (Chaffee, 1978; York, 1994) and overseas work by United States citizens (Downs, 1978; York, 1994). Because of the importance that international education attached to adapting to and acting within unfamiliar and often ambiguous social situations, cross-cultural training favored experience-based learning, feedback, application, and transfer.

> Education in the classroom teaches one to deal with emotionally loaded questions of value and attitude by analyzing and talking about them in an atmosphere of emotional detachment. Such a scholarly, scientific attitude is appropriate to the task of understanding; but by sidestepping direct, feeling-level involvement with issues and persons, one fails to develop the "emotional muscle" needed to handle effectively a high degree of emotional impact and stress (Harrison & Hopkins, 1967, 440).

Intercultural pedagogy enables students to effectively handle feelings elicited by emotionally laden real-world situations and events (Condon, 1986) and models the value of cultural reciprocity among multiple learning styles (Adams, 1992; Anderson & Adams, 1992; see also chapters 5 and 15).

Experiential Education

A core premise of experiential education is that "all learning is experiential" and that most formal, traditional classrooms focus too much on the product at the expense of the process (Joplin, 1995). The primary impetus behind experiential education can be found in the legacy of John Dewey (Hunt, 1995; Boud et al., 1993; Griffin & Mulligan, 1992; Kolb, 1984), with some debt as well to Lewin and Piaget (Chickering, 1977; Kolb, 1984) and to Habermas and Freire (Criticos, 1993; Saddington, 1992; Brookfield, 1993). Dewey understood "reflective experience" to mean the process by which the personal and social meanings of experience interact and become one (Hunt, 1995).

Except for the work of Kolb (1984), much of the writing on experiential education, and pedagogy generally, has remained "undertheorized" (Lusted, 1986) and devoted primarily to practical and pragmatic concerns. Experiential pedagogies usually start from a structured experience and focus the learner's reflections upon that experience. "Experience alone is insufficient to be called experiential education, and it is the reflection process which turns experience into experiential education (Joplin, 1995, 15). Joplin's "action-reflection" cycle grounds experiential education in reflective analysis of a "challenging action," which is preceded by a "focus" and followed by a "debrief" (Joplin, 1995).

The core principles and practices (see Proudman, 1995) of experiential education, however, have been problematized by practitioners who question "the embodied location of experience and the social organization of the process" (Bell, 1995, 9).

> We talk about concrete experience, but I do not know what this means. To me experience "exists" through interpretation. It is produced through the meanings given it. Interpretations of lived experiences are always contextual and specific. Experiences are contingent; interpretations can change. . . . Perhaps remembering an experience recomposes it so that its meaning changes (Bell,1995, 10, 15).

Social identity, voice, and positionality are important considerations for social justice pedagogy discussed later in this chapter.

Black Studies and Ethnic Studies

Black and ethnic studies emerged from the civil rights and black consciousness movements (Cole, 1991; Suzuki, 1984) that fused racial pride with social action and insisted that education be made relevant to real-world problems of injustice. These programs incorporate a powerful critique of university educational practices and curricula, questioning "*what* is taught in the liberal arts curricula of America's colleges and universities; *to whom* and *by whom* it is taught; *how* it is taught; and *why* it is taught" (Cole, 1991, 134).

The pedagogies of black studies were informed by Freire's vision of student agency and empowerment within a transformed teaching and learning process (McWhorter, 1969). This emphasis emerges in black feminist pedagogy as well (Butler, 1985). Other pedagogical concerns in black studies are the relationship of the classroom to everyday experience in community and the rootedness of theory in action (Bunch and Powell, 1983; see also James and Farmer, 1993). Black feminist pedagogies have elaborated these concerns for a "methodology that places daily life at the center of history" (Russell, 1983, 272) and in which "the classroom is the first step in (students') own transformation" (Coleman-Burns, 1993, 141). Barbara Omolade (1987), for example, writes about connecting the personal with the political or historical.

> This method works well to empower students, drawing them out, helping them to make sense of what they already know and have experienced. The creation of an intellectual partnership . . . lessens the power imbalance and class differences . . . yet reinforces the knowledge that can be received from the instructor, the readings, and the discussion (Omolade, 1987, 35).

The themes of personal experience in the classroom, socially relevant learning, and taking a critical or oppositional stance to received knowledge, can be seen in Gloria Ladson-Billings' characteristics of "culturally relevant teaching" (1995; see also Foster, 1988), which affirm everyone's *membership in a larger community*, envision teaching as a way to give back to one's community, and utilize a Freirean "mining" rather than "banking" teaching mode (Ladson-Billings, 1995, 478–79). Culturally relevant teachers *maintain equitable and reciprocal teacher-student relations* within which student expertise is highlighted, teachers encourage their entire classes rather than singling out single learners, and students are partly responsible for each others' academic success. Culturally relevant teachers *see knowledge as doing*, discuss their pedagogical choices and strategies with their students, and teach actively against a "*right-answer* approach" (author's italics, 1995, 482).

Feminist Pedagogies

The centrality of pedagogy to the women's movement can be seen in accounts of its originating moments by women activists in SNCC and SDS (Evans, 1979; Howe, 1984b).These consciousness-raising pedagogies, however, were not all that new. Florence Howe traces her own understanding that "all education is political" and her experiments with teaching that "turns upside down" the traditional roles of teacher and learner to her experiences teaching in Mississippi's Freedom Schools (Howe, 1984a). Howe describes the use, in the Mississippi Freedom Schools, of a pedagogy designed to raise the consciousness among black students, a pedagogy that

> begins on the level of the students' everyday lives and those things in their environment that they have either already experienced or can readily perceive, and builds up to a more realistic perception of American society, themselves, the conditions of their oppression, and alternatives offered by the Freedom Movement (Howe, 1984a, 10).

This is the pedagogy that, in the women's movement, came to be known as consciousness-raising.

Consciousness Raising

"The educational endeavor, to feminists, is a consciousness-raising process, explicitly directed to social transformation" (Bricker-Jenkins & Hooyman, 1986). This process starts from the telling of women's individual stories, but moves to discussion of commonalities of experience in areas such as childhood, jobs, motherhood, or sexual relationships. Consciousness raising involves a "process of transformative learning" that awakens personal awareness, leads to critical self-reflection and analysis, discovers group commonality among a "class" of situations, and provides "an ongoing and continuing source of theory and ideas for action" (Sarachild, 1975, 147).

Twenty years later, consciousness raising remains a key feminist strategy (Klein, 1987; Hart, 1991), with its postmodern emphasis on "personal stories (which) gain new readings both by the teller and by the other group members" (Damarin, 1994, 35). For example, Estelle Freedman describes her use of peer-facilitated "small groups" to create safe spaces in which her students discuss their personal reactions to classroom learning and integrate the personal with the academic (1994; see also Ferguson, 1982). A similar site, although differently named, can be recognized in the leaderless and often overlapping "affinity groups" described by Elizabeth Ellsworth as "safer home bases" for support, clarification, common language, and the basis for dialogue among differently situated social groups.

> Once we acknowledged the existence, necessity, and value of these affinity groups, we began to see our task not as one of building democratic dialogue between free and equal individuals, but of building a coalition among the multiple, shifting, intersecting, and sometimes contradictory groups carrying unequal weights of legitimacy within the culture and the classroom (Ellsworth,1989, 1994, 317).

Like Ellsworth's affinity groups, we use homogeneous caucus groups to generate themes and issues for discussion, to provoke self-reflection and generate action strategies that can then be discussed by the class as a whole. Homogeneous caucus groups may be leaderless, although structured by guiding questions or a project, or joined by a facilitator who shares the social identity of the group.

Interactive Learning and Teaching

Some of the rationale for the cooperative, interactive, and dialogic teaching modes of social justice education derives from research examining women's silence in traditional classrooms (Sandler & Hall, 1982; Sadker & Sadker, 1992) or from theories of women's development based on relational and emotional dimensions of women's socialization and experience (Maher, 1985; Clinchy, 1993; Belenky, Clinchy, Goldenberger, & Tarule, 1986; Gilligan, 1982). Here feminist affirmation of student-based, active learning in collaborative small groups, converges with pedagogical traditions of Freirean and experiential practice.

Teachers who practice interactive and collaborative pedagogies engage their students as active co-investigators who learn to take multiple perspectives on their own prior knowledge and beliefs, on each others' viewpoints, and on the course content (see Maher, 1985). In this sense "voice" relates to reciprocity and interaction: "Who speaks? Who listens? And why?" (hooks, 1994, 40). Because "it is one thing for students to know about cooperation, and another for them to experience it," feminist educators structure experiences that hold students accountable for cooperation, help students practice the requisite communication and shared leadership skills, and reward interdependence (Schneidewind, 1985, 1993).

Being "Other" in the Classroom

Analyses of who is "other" in the women's studies classroom direct our attention to differentials in power and status for both students and teachers (hooks, 1984; Washington, 1985; Butler, 1985; De Danaan, 1990). As the dynamics of power, positionality, and authority play out, silences among and between students of the European American, heterosexual, middle-class majority and students marginalized by racial or ethnic, gay, lesbian or bisexual experiences dampen what Spelman calls "the heart of the educational exchange . . . the lively exchange among students" (1985, 241). Interactive feminist classroom pedagogies sometimes result in the not surprising reproduction, within hypothetically democratic classrooms, of dominance and marginalization (Crumpacker & Vander Haegen, 1987).

bell hooks notes that in diverse ethnic communities as distinct from classrooms, women have not been silent: "for black women, our struggle has not been to emerge from silence to speech but to . . . make a speech that compels listeners, one that is heard" (1989, 6). Ellsworth argues that student silence may not be the result of "voicelessness" but of "not talking in their authentic voices." "What they/we say, to whom, in what context . . . is the result of conscious and unconscious assessments of the power relations and safety of the situation" (1989, 1994, 313). Students from both dominant and marginalized groups maintain silence in the classroom out of fear of being patronized or polarizing the class; anger, anxiety, or hostility; ignorance of each others' life experiences; resistance to being forced to speak; lack of skills or practice in intergroup communication or background for understanding their different cultural styles (Spelman, 1985; Da Danaan, 1990; hooks, 1984; Kochman, 1981). Feminist strategies to encourage students to value their own and each others' voice include working toward community based upon "a shared commitment and a common good that binds us" (hooks, 1994, 40) and using the institutionally derived classroom authority of the professor to endorse a process of community building.

The implications of positionality provide an impetus for the social justice educator to acknowledge the partiality and situatedness of different perspectives and truth-claims in the classroom. Maher and Tetreault's ethnography suggest that students and teachers can and do struggle to remain aware that their viewpoints are partial and oppositional, but while they may "challenge and undermine the social structures they inhabit . . . they cannot completely step outside them" (Maher & Tetreault, 1994, 203). "What is perceived as marginal at any given time depends on the position one occupies" (Laurie Fink, quoted in Maher & Tetreault, 1994, 164).

Power, Authority, Voice

Feminists have pointed to two sources of asymmetry in the classroom based on the instructor's institutional power, status and authority, and her race, gender, class, age, or other social status relative to her students.

> Do we know what powers we do have and want to have? Do we know what powers our students have, and what powers we hope they might come to have? Are we *clear* about the powers, *wanted and unwanted,* that we as teachers have? (Spelman, 1985, 244, author's italics)

Feminists asking how best to use our power and authority present a range of options. Some say that "the teacher's power should be abandoned, but not her skills and knowledge" (Hoffman, 1985, 148), suggesting a distinction between the traditional teacher-student hierarchy and a place where women's expertise can be recognized:

> I, at least, wanted the feminist classroom to be a place . . . in which teachers and students alike participated in a learning process, rather than a place in which we presented ourselves as experts who would tell our students facts . . . which they would dutifully record in their notebooks (Mumford, 1985, 89; see Fisher, 1981).

Margo Culley uses her authority as a bridge, explaining that as students accept the instructor's authority ("I mean the authority of her intellect, imagination, passion") they can also begin to "accept the authority of their own like capacities" (Culley, 1985, 215).

Barbara Omolade argues that this "authority with, not authority over" is complicated by the multiple ways in which teacher and students are both alike and not alike. She says "I *am* just like my students" in relation to white male privilege, white female and black male status. "But as an employed intellectual who uses my mind and my skills to instruct others, I have greater status than my sister students in the classroom and in the society" (1987, 34, author's italics). Lisa Delpit adds a further alternative, to teach "the culture of power" (1988) as a way of bringing students from nondominant social groups into an understanding of the classroom codes that reflect the culture of those who have power.

Social justice educators, like these feminist teachers, acknowledge that a nonauthoritarian classroom depends on students' learning how to initiate and maintain democratic structures, and accept greater responsibility for decision-making (Schniedewind, 1987). Social justice education also draws from feminist pedagogy the principle that "power over" must be clarified and made explicit as it bears on classroom norms, behaviors, grading, and evaluation. An instructor's "power with" can model for students who are similarly situated how they, too, might gain similar power—if not institutional power, at least the power of intelligence and knowledge that the institution credentializes (Culley, 1985). This, of course, is not a simple process when we remember that institutional processes of evaluation have "been used in racist and sexist and elitist ways, which serve to diminish students' integrity and humanity" (Omolade, 1987, 36).

Safety and Emotions in the Classroom

Classroom safety is integrally tied to respect and the expression of emotion, especially emotions perceived as negative, such as fear, discomfort, threat, pain, anxiety, hostility, and anger.

> Students must feel secure that their comments will be treated with respect whether or not the faculty member or the class agrees with them. Students must have confidence that faculty members are in control of the discussion and will intervene, if necessary, to prevent personal expressions from provoking personal attacks by some who may find them offensive. At the same time, the faculty members must balance the need for creating a safe space with their obligation to see to it that blatantly false beliefs are subjected to mature and thoughtful criticism. Striking the correct balance is no easy task (Rothenberg, 1985, 124–25).

Feminist teachers recommend establishing explicit classroom norms to ensure respect and confidentiality, to guide the handling of conflict and "triggers" (see chapter 5), and to focus discussion not on the person but on ideas (see also Rothenberg, 1985; Cannon, 1990; Thompson & Disch, 1992; Tatum,1992).

The feminist themes of process, voice, positionality, safety, power, and authority are related in feminist pedagogy to validating womens' feelings and emotions. The "connected" way of knowing described by Belenky, Clinchy, Goldenberger, and Tarule (1986) combines feeling with thought, and emotion with ideas. Believing that "the central role for the emotions in feminist education is their function in helping us explore feminist beliefs and values," Fisher uses student experiences as a basis for improvisation, simulation, dialogue, and questioning, in order to integrate emotion with thought (1987). This valuing of emotion and feelings has led social justice educators to appreciate a process orientation as well.

> [We] know that it isn't information alone that educates people. If it were, we would already have a very different world than we do. . . . Our experience is that, when we focus on process in the teaching of oppression, learning occurs at an unusually deep level. Students are engaged at both cognitive and affective levels. . . . The information students gain through the experiences of connection, empathy, and identification is not readily forgotten (Romney, Tatum, & Jones, 1992, 98, 107).

Social Action

How to live out their new awareness of contradictions, reshaped beliefs and values, and shifts in direction or identity are momentous considerations for students. "Action is the natural antidote to both denial and despair" (Romney, Tatum, & Jones, 1992, 107; see Tatum, 1994). Beverly Tatum has said pointedly that raising awareness without also raising awareness of the possibilities for change "is a prescription for despair. I consider it unethical to do one without the other" (1992, 20–21).

Social justice educators make these connections between awareness and action by helping students recognize various spheres of influence in their daily lives; analyze the relative risk factors in challenging discrimination or oppression in intimate relations, friendship networks, and institutional settings; and identify personal or small group actions for change. (Examples are in chapter 12 and the fourth modules of chapters 6–11).

Critical Pedagogies and Liberatory Education: Paulo Freire

The purpose of Freire's pedagogy is to enable the oppressed to understand that oppressive forces are not part of the natural order of things, but rather the result of historical and socially constructed forces that can be changed. The goal of liberatory education is praxis (connecting theory and practice) on the part of the oppressed who thus become actors in their own history. Freire also examines internalized oppression (see chapter 2), by which he means "the duality which has established itself" inside the consciousness of the oppressed:

> They are at one and the same time themselves and the oppressor whose consciousness they have internalized. . . . Only as they discover themselves to be "hosts" of the oppressor can they contribute to the midwifery of their liberating pedagogy (Freire, 1970, 32–3).

Liberatory pedagogy not only envisions the recovery of the voices, experiences, and perspectives of marginalized students from their "internalized oppression," but also empowers the teacher to use her classroom authority on behalf of the "truth claims" of these marginalized experiences. One key element in Freire's pedagogy, of tremendous value to social justice educators, is his contrast between banking education and problem-posing or dialogic education (1970).

> A Freirean critical teacher is a problem-poser who asks thought-provoking questions and who encourages students to ask their own questions. Through problem-posing, students learn to question answers rather than merely to answer questions. In this pedagogy, students experience education as something they do, not as something done to them (Shor, 1993, 26).

Because dialogue requires critical thinking, it can also generate critical thinking. In this sense, dialogue is not a "technique, a mere technique, which we can use to get some results" (Shor & Freire, 1987, 13); rather, as a communicative process that reflects social experience in order to understand the social and historical forces at work, it enables participants to develop "critical consciousness" (see Smith et al., 1975). This process enables students to name and discuss "coded situations" to uncover "generative themes": "Problem-posing is a group process that draws on personal experience to create social connectedness and mutual responsibility" (Wallerstein, 1987, 34; see Shor, 1992, 1987; Freire 1970, 1973; and Smith et al., 1976 for accounts of these processes).

The teacher's role in Freirian pedagogy is to provide structure and ask questions until students begin asking questions of themselves and of each other. It is also "to provide necessary information that promotes critical thinking" (Wallerstein, 1987, 41). Chairs arranged in circles rather than in rows facing a teacher's desk, reinforce the imagery of co-learners and co-teachers. Small groups provide spaces for group listening or action brainstorming. The democratic classroom becomes, in effect, a laboratory of democratic social practice.

Social and Cognitive Developmental Models

The shift of focus from a teacher's own lectures or content-coverage to what students are actually learning raises questions for the social justice educator. Who is the learner? What are her/his processes of understanding and meaning-making? What are the effects of classroom contexts or of group and interpersonal dynamics?

Educational theorists and psychologists have long turned to psychosocial and cognitive developmental theory for guidance in understanding issues that engage students across the lifespan and shifts or transitions in meaning-making or consciousness (Pascarella & Terenzini, 1991; Oser et al., 1992). But this body of theory has not paid sufficient attention to social status, positionality, or different life experiences (Bidell & Fischer, 1992; Rogoff, 1984; Rogoff et al., 1984). Two major traditions that address these questions are social identity and cognitive development theory.

Social Identity Development Theories

Erikson acknowledged the formative and socializing role played by the social groups significant to a growing person (1964, 1968), but failed to relativize or problematize the basis of the identity construct within normative Western concepts of self. Thus, Erikson's concept of "negative identity" has been used to deny or devalue the different pathways experienced by members of nondominant identity groups such as women, people of color, poor people, and gays, lesbians, and bisexuals. At the same time, paradoxically, "negative identity" has also paved the way for analyses of internalized subordination (see discussion in chapter 2).

Social identity *development* models, whether focussing upon race, sexual orientation, or gender, derive from but also diverge from their Eriksonian prototype in several important ways. They highlight dimensions of dominant (agent) and subordinate (target) identity development that are adversely affected by the stratifying processes of societal privilege and domination (for Whites, heterosexuals, Christians, or males) on the one hand, and of societal oppression and subordination (for people of color, gays, lesbians or bisexuals, females, or Jews) on the other. They describe developmental processes by which a person's internalized stereotypic and negative beliefs about self can be brought to the surface, analyzed, and transformed into an identity that is not dependent either upon subordination or domination. These models have been created in the historical context of social liberation movements: black identity development models in the civil rights movement (Jackson, 1976; Cross, 1971), "coming out" models in the gay liberation movement (Cass, 1979, 1984) and "feminist identity" models in the women's movement (Block, 1973; Downing & Roush, 1985).

When looked at generically, the social identity development models share several key assumptions: (1) both dominant and targeted group members' identity development is influenced by the pervasiveness of racism or other specific forms of oppression; (2) identity development evolves through sequential shifts or stages of consciousness toward greater complexity, inclusiveness, and differentiation; (3) identity development has as its goal liberation from internalized oppression or internalized domination; (4) individual interactions within groups as well as between groups are affected by differences in levels of consciousness; and (5) stage is a convenient metaphor for describing evolving states of consciousness or world views.

If the limits and distortions of unitary social identity models are acknowledged, these models can serve as guidelines for understanding how others see the world (Icard, 1986; Gonsiorek, 1995). We can appreciate that students evolve ways of thinking about oppression through years of unexamined experiences within family, peers, and community. They develop a "tried and fully tested identity" which "helps the person feel centered, meaningful, and in control, by making life predictable" (Cross, 1995, 60). Not surprisingly this identity may be vigorously defended against discordant information or experiences presented in the social justice classroom.

Our goal as educators is to provide information and experiences that students can incorporate into their own developmental journey, in ways that make sense to them. Even as we feel a responsibility to challenge and contradict all stereotypic beliefs or attitudes, the decision to shed these beliefs or attitudes belongs to the student, not us (Hardiman & Jackson, 1992). Recalling our own ongoing shifts of world view and challenges to the inevitable residue of our own internalized domination or oppression can help us be empathic in this process (see chapters 2 and 14).

Finally, it is important to understand that human beings are never "in" a stage. Stage is a metaphor for growth or change; *lens, world view, perspectives, consciousness level* are equally appropriate metaphors. What "develops" is a person's increasingly informed, differentiated, and inclusive understanding of within group and between group commonalities and differences, and a personalized awareness of how these understandings bear on one's everyday behaviors. Beverly Tatum uses the metaphor of a spiral staircase:

> As a person ascends a spiral staircase, she may stop and look down at a spot below. When she reaches the next level, she may look down and see the same spot, but the vantage point has changed (Tatum, 1992, 12).

Cognitive Development Theory

The values, beliefs, and biases that both students and instructors bring to classes on social justice, the tenacity of stereotypes and entrenched modes of thinking, the unexpectedly emotional attachments to beliefs and thought processes rooted in trusted home, school, and religious communities, are forces that suggest a powerful and multidimensional cognitive developmental agenda (Harro, 1986; Gallos, 1989; Schoem, 1993; Dunn, 1993; Bidell et al., 1994; Adams & Zhou-McGovern, 1994).

Theories of cognitive development among college students and adults (Perry, 1970, 1981; Kitchener, 1982; Belenky et al., 1986; Baxter Magolda, 1992; King & Kitchener, 1994) illuminate the evolution of momentous shifts in thinking from concrete to abstract, simple to complex, external authority to internal agency, and clear-cut certitudes to comfort with doubt, uncertainty, and independent inquiry (King & Kitchener, 1994; Baxter Magolda, 1992; Pascerella & Terenzini, 1991; Mentkowski et al., 1983). These cognitive patterns act as filters through which a person can organize and "make" meaning from experiences, interactions, and ideas.

Studies have shown that students in college gradually develop skills in complex thinking, self-reflection, tolerance for uncertainty and ambiguity, and ability to take on multiple and divergent perspectives (Mentkowski et al., 1983; Baxter Magolda, 1992; King & Kitchener, 1994). These cognitive skills constitute intellectual characteristics which may be considered necessary if not sufficient thresholds for social justice and social diversity education. College curricula that deal with social justice and diversity call for many of the qualities described in the developmental literature on critical thinking (Kurfiss, 1988; Knefelkamp, 1974), such as openness to conflicting perspectives from readings or classroom discussions, and the ability to reflect upon one's experiences, prior beliefs, and feelings, from one's own as well as another's perspective.

The process of cognitive development outlined by Perry (1970, 1981) and Belenky, Clinchy, Goldenberger and Tarule (1986) maps movement through qualitatively different views of knowledge from certainty, through uncertainty, toward relativistic or contextual thought. For the social justice educator, students who utilize *dualistic* or *received knowing* are especially challenging in their insistence upon clear answers, unambiguous data, certainty, and external authority firmly located in the teacher. Such students may find it especially difficult to relinquish societally-endorsed beliefs and stereotypes on complex issues of race, gender, class, or sexual orientation when the end point is unclear and the intellectual and emotional journey fraught with uncertainty.

> My students express some disappointment, particularly early in the semester, that I do not provide them with "answers" to the questions of intergroup relations. Students frequently come to my course with a dualistic worldview, looking for just two sides to every issue—a right side and a wrong. They come ready to argue and defend what they view as right and attack and ridicule what is wrong, or they feel guilty if they might be perceived as being in the wrong. . . . It takes a considerable amount of time as well as personal and intellectual work for students to accept the absence of answers and to bring an intellectual perspective that incorporates many competing and complementary views of individual issues (Schoem, 1993, 17).

Dualistic thinking and *received knowing* are indicators of conceptual limits upon students' readiness to listen, respond to, and learn from each other's divergent experiences and viewpoints.

The transitional stages of *multiplicity* and *subjective knowing* represent a crucial turning point after which students can more comfortably think complexly and draw upon intuition, feelings, or "common sense" as new sources of internal authority (Kurfiss, 1988). These newly acquired world views bring with them new confidence and skills in handling multiple perspectives, acknowledging and critically examining differences and commonalities between one's own and others' world views, and coordinating the concrete and personal dimensions of experience with abstract and societal constructs or perspectives.

The presence of some dualistic and many early multiplistic thinkers in social justice classes calls for several pedagogical strategies: (1) draw upon the concrete, personal, and experiential as the grounding for abstract knowledge; (2) take ample time to help students process sources of contradiction or conceptual confusion, both at the personal level and at the level of theory; (3) provide explicit course structure and support for the inevitable student-generated dissonance and contradiction; (4) make explicit use of our own authority as teachers to endorse and explain more complex thinking modes. For example, instructors can have students devise open-ended questions for which there are no "correct" answers and use their authority to model respect and appreciation for peer perspectives as a valid source of knowledge about social diversity.

The journey from a dichotomous to a contextual way of thinking also takes a student toward a broader and more inclusive ethical perspective (see Kohlberg and Higgins, 1989), and from an external to an internal locus of authority and responsiblity. It helps account for students' initial resistance to multiple perspectives, explains some of a student's anxiety in the absence of certainties in social justice problem-solving, and sheds light on the cognitive skills needed for abstract thought in an emotionally charged, personalized domain such as social justice education. It provides empirical support for an educational process that affirms the internal locus of judgments and decisions as well as the broadening of authority and knowledge away from the teacher to include self and peers (Knefelkamp, 1974; Adams & Zhou-McGovern, 1994).

Major Elements of Social Justice Education Practice

As social justice educators, we try to plan approaches that are safe and respectful for all participants as we engage them with information and discussions that are likely to elicit emotional as well as intellectual reactions. We try to be aware of the range of their agent and target social identities and their likely responses from various cognitive developmental levels. We believe that we ignore the beliefs and knowledge students bring to our classes at our peril. It is our aim to help them develop credible sources, honest personal reflection, and critical thinking as the basis for a larger and more adequate view of their complex social roles and responsibilities as social agents.

The pedagogies examined in this chapter are rooted in academic traditions that have been nourished from a variety of sources and perspectives. Out of these distinctive traditions has evolved a body of social justice education practice, which includes the following principles:

(1) *Balance the emotional and cognitive components of the learning process*: Teaching that pays attention to personal safety, classroom norms, and guidelines for group behavior.

(2) *Acknowledge and support the personal (the individual student's experience) while illuminating the systemic (the interactions among social groups)*: Teaching that calls attention to the here-and-now of the classroom setting and grounds the systemic or abstract in an accumulation of concrete, real-life examples.

(3) *Attend to social relations within the classroom*: Teaching that helps students name behaviors that emerge in group dynamics, understand group process, and improve interpersonal communications, without blaming or judging each other.

(4) *Utilize reflection and experience as tools for student-centered learning*: Teaching that begins from the student's world view and experience as the starting point for dialogue or problem-posing.

(5) *Value awareness, personal growth, and change as outcomes of the learning process*: Teaching that balances different learning styles and is explicitly organized around goals of social awareness, knowledge, and social action, although proportions of these three goals change in relation to student interest and readiness.

These social justice principles create new roles, challenges, and opportunities for students to take responsibility for their own learning and participation in learning groups, respect each other, avoid blame or snap judgment, and give themselves and each other room to make mistakes while learning. Students learn to look critically at messages about "the other" coming from the media and other sources of cultural information, practice new behaviors and communication skills, and develop social change scenarios.

The ideas presented here may seem overwhelming to someone socialized and skilled within the traditional lecture-and-discussion mode of higher education. It is encouraging to know that these principles of social justice teaching are virtually the same as principles of effective college teaching for *all* students (Chickering & Gamson, 1987). These teaching principles appear in handbooks for enhancing social diversity in college classrooms and campuses (such as Green, 1989) and also in the new research on college teaching and learning for everyone (Hatfield, 1995; Bruffee, 1993; Meyers & Jones, 1993; Oser et al., 1992). Writing as a teacher who was herself "socialized" in the academic tradition (Adams, 1992), I recommend a gradual, incremental approach to experimenting with these new pedagogies. A first step might be to use the activities illustrated in the curriculum designs of chapters 5–11 for developing student-generated guidelines that create a fair, safe, respectful atmosphere, where students can take risks and both students and teacher are allowed to learn from their mistakes.

> We know that . . . changing *what* we teach, means changing *how* we teach (Culley & Portuges, 1985, 2, authors' italics).

4

Designing Social Justice Education Courses

Lee Anne Bell, Pat Griffin

If we are to be intentional about social justice education we need a clear and well-thought out blueprint for enacting our goals. We need to focus our courses in ways that will join our students where they enter and build upon the questions and concerns they bring. We also need to understand the challenges to self that emerge when confronting socialization to change oppressive assumptions, beliefs, and behaviors (Arnold, Burke, James, Martin, & Thomas, 1991). Finally, we need to set goals for learning that make sense educationally and are reachable within the time constraints of our courses. To address these and other issues we discuss the following elements that scaffold our approach to designing social justice education courses:

- ***Preassessment:*** Identifying relevant characteristics of students and developing goals appropriate to the learning needs of the group.
- ***Matching the environment to student learning process:*** Attending to the experiential phases learners often go through in a social justice education class and structuring an environment that supports them appropriately at different points in the course.
- ***Structuring Content:*** The selection of specific class activities to address key concepts in social justice education and match these to student learning needs.
- ***Sequencing:*** Developing an appropriate progression of activities to attend to both content and process as these evolve during the class.
- ***Accommodating a variety of learning styles:*** A description of different student learning styles and building in a variety of ways to accommodate them.

- ***Making adjustments as the class unfolds:*** A discussion of the importance of flexibility in making design changes while a class is in progress.

The design considerations we present here may seem complicated and perhaps overwhelming on first reading. These ideas were developed over many years of teaching social justice education courses and integrate a variety of models and sequences. We encourage our readers to focus on one or two design issues at a time to develop facility in applying them and to find out how they work in your courses. Then gradually add others as you go. Also, a few of the models, such as Figure 4.1 below, may not be relevant to your educational setting if you are unlikely to have the option of homogeneous classes.

Preassessment

Three interrelated questions are relevant as we anticipate and prepare to teach a new course: What is the course focus? What are the characteristics of the students who are taking the course? Given the answers to the first two questions, what should be the goals of the course? The answers to these questions can help us match both overall goals and specific class activities to the particular needs of a group.

Single Issue vs. Multiple Issue Focus: Courses can have a single issue focus (racism *or* classism, for example) or a multiple issue focus (sexism, heterosexism, *and* ableism). Single issue courses, while examining one form of oppression in depth, can also explore how different issues of oppression intersect and help students understand the many parallels and connections among different forms of oppression. For example, a course on sexism will also examine how women from different social classes, racial groups, religions, abilities, or sexual orientations experience sexism.

Another approach to social justice education might be to analyze current events or controversial topics using either a single issue or an integrated focus. For example, a course could focus on such topics as affirmative action or a campus visit by an anti-gay speaker and construct class activities around this event. With an integrated focus, current events or controversial topics can be examined from several different perspectives. Students in a course using an integrated focus could, for example, analyze an event or issue through the lenses of race, gender, sexual orientation, and socio-economic class perspectives.

Heterogeneous or Homogeneous Group: In most of the single issue courses discussed in this volume, students are assumed to be a heterogeneous group of agent and target group members in relation to the topic of the course. Thus, in a racism course it helps to anticipate, if possible, the mix of students of color, white students, and biracial students. In a sexism course, for example, we might vary the design based on the number of men and women enrolled. If we don't have approximately equal numbers of agents and targets enrolled, we would avoid planning activities that place the smaller number (either agent or target) in a vulnerable position in a class environment in which they might already feel on the spot. As a general guideline, we try to ensure that at least one third of a mixed class is either agent or target group members. Figure 4.1 illustrates the combinations of issues and group demographics that could be planned for in a social justice education course.

	Homogeneous Group	Heterogeneous Group
Single Issue	■ Addresses one ism ■ Participants are all agents or all targets with regard to this ism ■ All women sexism ■ All white racism	■ Addresses one ism ■ Participants include agent and target group members ■ Mixed sexism ■ Mixed racism
Multiple Issues	■ Addresses multiple isms ■ Participants all share one agent or target group identity ■ Class on racism and sexism with lesbian, gay, bisexual participants	■ Addresses multiple isms ■ Participants are a variety of agent and target groups across a range of isms ■ Class on several isms with a mixed group of participants

Figure 4.1. Social Justice Education Instructional Models (Rita Hardiman, 1995).

Multiple Identities and Interests: Students who have multiple target identities bring a different world view to the course and different needs than students with a single or no targeted identity. In a sexism course with gay men and lesbians or people of color, for example, we can anticipate and provide ways to explore how students encounter sexism differently through their experience of heterosexism and racism. International students, students for whom English is not a first language, or students with disabilities may require modifications to make sure that readings and other class activities are accessible to everyone.

Students' professional interests are also relevant for planning. If the course includes a variety of majors and career orientations, a more generic approach to the course topic or the use of professional caucuses to apply the material might be called for. If students are preparing to be teachers, we can emphasize the role of educators and schools in perpetuating or addressing oppression. Finally, it is useful to know whether students are graduate or undergraduate, traditional or nontraditional, or a mixture. Each group brings to the course a different combination of work and life experiences that we consider in planning classes to meet their needs and interests.

Students' Prior Experiences in and Motivations for Taking Social Justice Education Classes: For students with no prior experience in a social justice education course, we anticipate less familiarity with an experiential approach that includes personal exploration and the expression of feelings. We therefore might need to spend more time with introductory activities, reviewing participation guidelines, providing a rationale for our interactive experiential approach, and establishing a safe and supportive environment. Students with no prior experience in social justice education might be less open to challenges to their understanding of social justice than students who have already had some experience with these issues.

It is also worthwhile to know what motivates students to take the course. Some students select social justice education courses because they are genuinely interested in the content and are excited about learning. Other students take the course because they are required to (as a degree requirement for their major field, for example) or because it is expedient (simply because they need another credit or find the idea of a weekend course appealing). With a group of "volunteers" who have chosen the course because of interest in the topic, we can assume a higher level of commitment to exploring issues and engaging classmates in discussion. With a group of "hostages" whose presence in the course is not a choice, but simply to meet program requirement, there is more potential for hostility and resentment at being asked to actively participate in discussions that challenge their understanding of issues they might not even perceive to be connected to their personal or professional lives. With these students, we might need to spend more time exploring the nature of the topic and its relevance to their lives.

One way to obtain relevant information is to ask students to fill out a personal profile sheet in which they identify their social group memberships and prior experiences in social justice education courses (see chapter 15). Other options for preassessment include interviewing students informally beforehand or talking with other teachers who are familiar with the students who will be taking the course.

Stages of Social Identity Development Likely to be Represented in the Class: The social identity development model described in chapter 2 can be helpful in anticipating how different students may respond to learning about oppression and interacting with others in the course. In our single issue courses, we find that most undergraduate students in the agent group reflect acceptance or resistance stages while students from target groups often demonstrate a broader range of stages. Identity development models can help us plan activities and promote discussions to engage students and pose appropriate challenges that will make sense to their frame of reference and help them build upon current knowledge and awareness (see Tatum, 1992; Hardiman & Jackson, 1992; Hardiman, 1994).

Though students will most often reflect a variety of social identities and developmental stages, as well as a range of prior experiences with social justice education, what we learn about our students beforehand can help us plan more effectively to meet students where they are and engage them in activities that reflect their felt concerns and questions. At the same time, we need always to treat this information tentatively, as a place from which to begin rather than a definitive assessment.

Determining Class Goals: Three broad goals for social justice education courses are: to increase personal awareness, expand knowledge, and encourage action. The relative emphasis we place on each of these goals will vary with the prior knowledge and experience of the group.

Increase personal awareness: Increasing personal awareness includes helping students learn more about their own socialization and social identities, and the conscious and unconscious prejudices and assumptions they hold. Through examining personal awareness students can develop greater clarity about the differential treatment they receive as a result of their own social group memberships. They learn to identify and challenge what are often unexamined beliefs about themselves and others and understand how these beliefs have been established through an unequal system based on hierarchies of privilege and power. Course content also helps students recognize how specific forms of oppression are manifested in their everyday lives through interpersonal interactions, institutional practices, and cultural norms which guide their behavior as individuals.

Expand knowledge: To expand knowledge, we ask students to examine historical, economic, and social information that defines and reflects oppression. We provide data in the form of statistics about access to social resources such as health care, housing, employment, education, and government and examine incidents of violence and harassment and institutional discrimination experienced by target groups in the United States. We also discuss the history of disenfranchised groups so that students have an understanding of forces beyond themselves that shape individual and group behavior and learn about the ways people from various social groups have struggled against oppression in every historical period. Through readings, videos, lectures, and discussion we engage students in learning about the structural and institutional features of oppression and use this knowledge to analyze current examples of oppression in our society.

Encourage action: We hope that students will create meaningful ways to apply their new awareness and knowledge rather than feel overwhelmed by it. We provide support for identifying possible actions they can take, practicing self-chosen interventions, and planning ways they can continue to act and get support for their actions beyond the course. Our goal is to enable students to see themselves as agents of change, capable of acting on their convictions and in concert with others against the injustices they see.

We try to touch upon all of these goals in every course, but the relative emphasis depends on a number of factors such as: who the students are, what the course topic is, and how long the course will last. For example, with students who have never thought much about racism and are taking a course to fulfill a requirement, we place more emphasis on increasing awareness and knowledge. With students who have a basic understanding of racism and are already committed to addressing it, we would spend more time on providing knowledge and planning action.

Matching Environment to Student Learning Process

One very important consideration in our design for social justice education is attending to the disequilibrium people experience as they are confronted with the reality and pervasiveness of social oppression. Confrontation with the effects of oppression invariably calls into question deeply held assumptions about the social world and can literally throw students off balance. This instability can be frightening as students experience contradictions and begin to realize that previous ways of making sense of the world no longer seem adequate. However, in a supportive learning environment disequilibrium can also be exhilarating as students grapple with contradictions and seek more satisfactory ways to make sense of social reality.

Kegan (1982) provides a sequence for understanding this process of disequilibrium that we find useful as we plan our courses. He identifies three positions that learners take in a progressive sequence as they confront, engage, and eventually incorporate new learning. He calls these positions: defending, surrendering, and reintegration (described below). This sequence provides a framework for making sense of the various psychological reactions or positions students may experience at different stages in their learning and helps us to be empathic with their internal struggles for meaning at each stage.

For each position, Kegan identifies a corresponding facilitating or classroom environment. He calls these facilitating environments: confirmation, contradiction, and continuity (Kegan, 1982, 118–20). The progression of facilitating environments offers a framework for creating appropriately supportive conditions in which students can first open up to and engage with new ideas (as they are defending), then grapple with contradictions and challenges to previous knowing (surrendering), and finally incorporate new information and ways of making sense of the social world (reintegration). The following description is an adaptation of Kegan's sequence to the social justice classroom (adapted in Bell & Weinstein, 1982).

Initial Phase

Psychological Position of Defending (Embeddedness). From a social-psychological perspective, whether consciously or unconsciously, people develop and internalize a set of beliefs about social justice issues through living in this society. Each of us could be said to be *embedded* in a particular way of making sense of the world. Unchallenged, this embeddedness leads us to take for granted our world view as given, natural, and true, as simply "the way things are." In the social justice education classroom these beliefs will be exposed to examination and questioning, unsettling the taken for granted world view. This challenge inevitably disturbs a person's equilibrium, can be experienced as threatening and will often raise a person's defenses.

Corresponding Facilitating Environment: Confirmation (Holding On). The way students experience the environment of the classroom has a powerful effect on whether or not they are willing to entertain conflicting information and internal disequilibrium. If the environment is perceived as threatening, a person's defenses may be fairly rigid. They will tend to ignore challenges to their world view and any conflicting information will be rationalized to fit the present belief system. If the environment is perceived as supportive, a person's defenses may be more permeable. In this case, despite the experience of internal conflict, there can be an attraction to new information and interest in grappling with contradictions and discrepancies that are perceived.

For these reasons, the initial phase of a social justice education course is very important. Our goals in this phase are to create an environment in which students feel *confirmed* and validated *as persons* even as they experience challenges to their belief system. We want to construct an environment that is supportive and trustworthy, one in which uncomfortable and challenging issues may be raised and explored, where students can express discomfort, confusion, anger, and fear and know they will be treated with dignity and respect.

An example from a heterosexism workshop may be illustrative. Many students, especially heterosexual students, enter the course with little or no awareness of heterosexism and homophobia. Because of the unconscious homophobia endemic in our society, they may feel uncomfortable with the topic, apprehensive about what they might learn about their own feelings, and insecure with having a lesbian or gay instructor. Homosexual and bisexual students on the other hand may be quite aware of heterosexism and homophobia but fearful that they will be exposed or unfairly treated in the course. To create a *confirming* environment we want to help people break the ice and identify some commonalities they share. We also want to establish and model ground rules of listening respectfully and speaking truthfully from our own experience. We identify stereotypes and assumptions that the culture fosters about homosexuality and bisexuality and acknowledge the misinformation we all receive in order to make it possible to openly examine taboo topics. Once students experience support and realize it is safe to not have all the answers, to be confused or uninformed, and to make mistakes despite their best intentions, they may be able to relax their defenses enough to engage with classroom activities and information that question their assumptions about social reality.

Phase Two

Psychological Position of Surrendering (Differentiation). If we have succeeded in creating a supportive environment, students may now feel secure enough to open up to contradictions to their old belief system and begin a process of exploration. They become willing to examine and differentiate ideas and feelings and try on different ways of making sense of the world. This process can be confusing, disorienting, and, at times, frightening. Students might feel out of control, without known boundaries or familiar ground, and may experience a sense of loss or *surrender* as they literally "excavate the ground they stand on" (Barker, 1993, 48). As they learn new information they may also experience strong emotions such as anger, resentment, and a sense of betrayal by those who were supposed to tell them the truth about the social world. At the same time, they may feel a sense of freedom as they consider, discard, and eventually construct new ways of making sense of the world.

Corresponding Facilitating Environment : Contradiction (Letting Go). The supportive environment for this second position is one that allows students to immerse themselves fully in whatever contradictions and conflicts arise as a consequence of engaging previously unknown ideas and exploring their own and other's feelings and experiences. The course content and process deliberately pose and explore contradictions and encourage students to seek new ways to make sense of the material they encounter. This process is akin to Freire's notion of education for critical consciousness (1970, 1973).

At this point the environment shifts. It does not overprotect or enable students to avoid feelings of discomfort, confusion, fear, and anger. Such feelings are an inevitable and ultimately helpful part of the learning process. Through engaging with challenging information and participating in experiential activities, students are encouraged to let go of the comfortable and familiar and explore new territory.

To continue with the example from the heterosexism course, the environment now shifts to encourage exploration of feeling and identification of *contradictions* and discontinuities between what we are taught and what is hidden from us. A representative activity for this phase is one in which students engage in guided imagery focusing on close same-sex friendships from childhood. One male student remembered his best boyhood friend and focused on a time when the two little boys were playing in the bathtub, splashing each other and began exuberantly flipping each other's penises. He recalled the spontaneity and sheer abandon of free play until his mother came into the bathroom and froze in horror. Not a word was said but the game abruptly ended. As he recalled this long forgotten episode, the student realized that an unspoken barrier had arisen between him and his friend that affected their closeness, as well as his ability to be physically close to other men. He could then bring in other associations and learnings that reinforced the lessons of homophobia and begin to examine the high price he pays as a heterosexual in limiting his ability to express intimacy and caring toward male friends.

Phase Three

Psychological Position of Reintegration (Transforming). Once students have left familiar ground and explored new territory, both affectively and intellectually, they are in a position to integrate what they have learned and establish a new foundation. This balance is gradually achieved as a new set of beliefs becomes "home base" for interpreting experience and creating meaning. The past is not wholly rejected, but reinterpreted and reconstructed into a new frame of reference as students come into a new "self-possession" (Harris, 1988).

Facilitating Environment: Continuity (Staying Put). The environment once again shifts to encourage the development of stability and *continuity* based on new insights and knowledge. Activities are designed to help students articulate and confirm what they have learned and think about what this might mean for their actions beyond the course. Opportunities are provided to imagine taking new actions, the likely consequences of such actions, and types of support that could be called upon to sustain these changes. As they consider the future we encourage them to develop ongoing systems of support for sustaining themselves beyond the course so they can continue a process of learning about social justice issues and acting on their convictions.

To conclude the heterosexism workshop example, students were asked to imagine typical interactions with friends, family, and co-workers and reflect upon new insights about homophobia as these informed how they wished to behave in the future. The man in the previous example decided he wanted to develop more closeness and intimacy with his male friends and openly discuss with them the homophobic feelings that blocked such intimacy. He also wanted to look more closely at the messages he might be communicating to his own sons and make sure he was allowing them a full expression of feelings. It is important to recognize and affirm that each student chooses and develops his or her own action plan suited to their particular learning and comfort level.

In our experience, the process described above approximates fairly closely the psychological processes most students seem to move through in social justice education courses. However useful a guide, though, the map is not the territory. We can't always know whether students are engaged in these ways, nor whether the exploration they take up in class will continue beyond the course. Occasionally some students choose not to engage in the ways we hope they will. They may hold on to their frame of reference and refuse to explore contradictory information. We hope this process allows respect for those students as well.

The following figure summarizes the three psychological phases described above. Below we provide examples of the specific kinds of activities that structure content in each phase of the course to provide the appropriate facilitating environments as the course unfolds.

Experiential Sequence	Facilitating Environment
Defending (Embeddedness)	Confirmation (Holding On)
Surrendering (Differentiation)	Contradiction (Letting Go)
Reintegrating (Transforming)	Continuity (Staying Put)

Figure 4.2. Experiential Sequence and Facilitating Environment (adapted from Kegan, 1982, in Bell and Weinstein, 1982).

Confirmation Phase

Post an agenda and class objectives. This step provides an explicit structure that students can rely upon, and if desired, adjust to meet their own needs. It helps students anticipate what the focus of the course will be and have some sense of what will occur in the course. This process also enables students to share responsibility for following the agenda or identify ways the agenda does not meet their needs and adjusting it accordingly.

Begin with introductions and expectations. This step recognizes the unique identity of each participant and lets people know they will not be treated as anonymous members of a class, but are indeed central to the course. They begin to understand that they will be asked to learn about and listen to each other. This step also helps students begin to identify and develop their own goals for learning.

Facilitators can then clarify ways the course will and will not meet the expressed expectations and adjust the design accordingly. This step also supports the notion of an explicit agenda that can be adapted to meet student needs and expectations where possible.

Acknowledge feelings. During a social justice education course many different feelings arise as students grapple with perspectives and information that challenge their previous understanding. It is essential to acknowledge that these feelings are a natural and appropriate part of the learning process. Providing students with some guidance for how to recognize, listen to, and learn from feelings encourages their expression in ways that help rather than hinder learning. The introduction of concepts such as "learning edge," "comfort zone," and "triggers," for example, provides students with a language and a process to use in examining and making sense of feelings (see chapter 5).

Use low risk self-disclosure and interaction in the early stages of the course. Introducing activities early in the course where students can comfortably interact with each other and discuss their own thoughts and feelings at a low-risk level establishes a norm of interaction and self-disclosure at the outset. This initial interaction should be low risk so that students can comfortably practice what for many might be a novel experience of sharing feelings and personal experiences in the context of a classroom.

Establish group norms for respectful interactions. Creating a list of guidelines for interactions and asking the class to agree to abide by these guidelines provides clear boundaries for appropriate interactions. Mutually agreed upon guidelines create a climate of safety in which students can feel responsible for themselves and each other and trust that they will be supported during the course.

Contradiction Phase

Once the confirmation phase of the course is established, we move into the contradiction phase in which activities encourage students to explore their own perspectives and face the challenges posed by new information and different perspectives. Learning activities in the contradiction phase can focus on any of the several key concepts identified in chapter 5 and exemplified in the course designs in this volume: a) personal socialization and experience; b) historical context; c) manifestations at the individual, institutional, and societal/cultural levels; d) power and privilege; e) collusion and internalization; f) horizontal oppression; g) agents as allies, targets as empowered.

Validate personal risk-taking. Support and encourage students to take risks in exploring perspectives, feelings, and awarenesses that contradict their prior understanding. Validate students who express confusion or ask questions that reflect their personal struggle with issues discussed in the course.

Encourage full discussion. Encourage everyone to participate in class discussions and elicit a variety of perspectives so that differences can be openly aired and explored. Inviting divergent perspectives enables students to work with contradictions and have their own thinking challenged.

Allow contradictions and tensions to emerge. Resist the tendency to smooth over tensions, resolve contradictions, or relieve uncomfortable moments in class. These experiences are an essential part of the learning process in a social justice education course. As long as students use participation guidelines, the experience of discomfort with new perspectives and tension among different perspectives can help students work through their own learning.

Continuity Phase

During the continuity phase of the course students turn their attention to thinking about how to integrate new awareness and knowledge into their lives and bring their course experience to a close. We focus on helping students identify actions they want to take as they further their learning and concretize their new perspectives in actions. Our intention is to help students feel optimistic about social change rather than feel overwhelmed by the enormity of social oppression. Students also need to think about how to nurture their developing understanding of and commitment to acting against social injustice. The following guidelines help in planning this phase of the course.

Identify a wide variety of action possibilities. Encourage students to identify actions that match their personal level of comfort. This means acknowledging and valuing actions at all levels of risk, from reading about racism, to objecting to racist jokes or comments in their classes or at the family dinner table, to joining a Third World Caucus or white ally group on campus.

Identify ways that students can get support for their actions against social injustice. Developing support for new awareness of and commitment to address social justice issues that extend beyond the course boundaries is an essential part of helping students bridge the gap between class and their school, work, and personal lives. Helping students develop support groups from class or learn about existing community or campus groups to join provides a way for students to nurture relationships with others who share their developing commitments.

Bring the class experience to a close. Help students achieve a sense of closure by providing a way for them to summarize learnings, appreciate classmates, and identify next steps in continuing their learning.

The following table includes the phases in the facilitating environment and examples of the methods or structure in each phase. Each method or structure is intended to address the psychological concerns students have as they move through the different learning phases of the course.

Facilitating Environment	**Structure/Method**
Confirmation (Establishing the Climate)	Post Agenda and Objectives Begin with Introductions and Expectations Acknowledge Feelings Use Low Risk Self-Disclosure Establish Norms for Group Communication
Contradiction (Initiating the Encounter)	Validate Personal Risk Taking Encourage Full Discussion Allow Contradictions to Emerge
Continuity (Closure/Transition Out of Course)	Summarize Plan Action/Applications Develop On-goingSupport Evaluate the Course Close the Course

Figure 4.3. Methods to Match Facilitating Environments.

Structuring Learning Activities

With the model in Figure 4.3 as a broad framework, we then plan each class learning activity. In general, the internal structure of individual learning activities follows a basic progression:

(1) Advance Organizers

(2) Encounter/Activity

(3) Processing/Discussion

(4) Transition to Next Activity

Advance organizers introduce new information or conceptual frames for students to use in examining key issues and their own experiences. Examples of advance organizers include definitions of key terms, and introduction to concepts such as stereotyping, the cycle of socialization, and the multiple levels of oppression. In an ableism class, for example, students might be introduced to the concept of stereotyping through defining the term and noting several characteristics of stereotypes. This prepares students for the next phase of the learning process, the encounter.

The encounter or activity is a structured interaction or confrontation with one or more key concepts. Examples of activities include role plays, case studies, a brainstorming session, an interactive lecture, a video, a discussion, or a worksheet. This activity is designed to engage students with the issues experientially so they can interact with the material and each other. In the ableism class, students might be asked to brainstorm a list of words and images they have learned about people with disabilities. As they see the list of negative words and images applied to people with disabilities, they learn how pervasive these images are in the culture.

Processing enables each student to reflect on the previous encounter to identify personal meaning, questions, and contradictions and to draw new learnings from the activity. During processing, facilitators pose questions that ask students to discuss what happened in the encounter, how they felt about it, what they learned from the interaction, and to listen to the similar and different ways others in the class experienced the activity. During this discussion students can express confusion, ask questions, make observations, and challenge their own and others' thinking. In our hypothetical ableism class, after completing the brainstorm activity, students might reflect upon and discuss the following questions: "What feelings do you have as you look at the list we have created?," "What surprises you about the list?," "What questions do you have about any of the terms on the list?," "What themes do you notice when you look at this list of images?"

The transition to the next activity does not necessarily wait until resolution occurs. Students can be left with questions and contradictions that are carried into the next activity. If learning activities are sequenced in a way that flows naturally from one theme to the next, summarizing the main points while processing one activity and introducing the next one will make sense. Encourage students to stay with contradictions and questions as they move into the next activity. After discussing the questions posed during the processing phase of the activity, facilitators can help students make a bridge to the next activity by saying, "Now that we have identified some of the stereotypes we have learned about people with disabilities, let's look more closely at where these messages come from." The class could then move into an experiential activity or short lecture focused on socialization.

Sequencing Learning Activities

The overall progression of learning activities within any one curriculum design is another important consideration in designing social justice education courses. We consider several factors in selecting and sequencing activities so that the overall flow of the course makes sense to students. This careful sequencing also enables us to introduce concepts and activities in an incremental way that builds upon student awareness and learning at different phases of the course (Weinstein, 1988).

Low to Higher Risk Sequencing. Learners need to feel safe in order to be willing to express and examine deeply held feelings, confusions, and assumptions about the issue. Low risk activities in the beginning of a social justice education course are designed to help students get acquainted, understand interaction guidelines, and engage in superficial discussions before moving to activities that require more risky disclosure of feelings and perspectives. Moving from individual reflection to discussions in pairs or small groups before engaging in whole group discussions is also a way to progressively increase the level of risk as discussions proceed.

Concrete to Abstract Sequencing. This sequencing principle reflects our belief that students learn best when their understanding of oppression is firmly rooted in concrete experiences and examples that provide a foundation for analysis of abstract concepts and the multiple levels on which oppression operates.

Personal to Institutional Sequencing. In most of our courses we begin with personal content, then introduce an institutional and cultural focus. We start with a personal focus because this level is easier for students to explore initially. After examining their own experience and socialization, and gathering information from many sources including readings, lectures, and discussions, students are usually better prepared to explore how oppression operates on institutional and cultural levels.

Difference to Dominance (or Diversity to Justice) Sequencing. This sequence first focuses on helping students describe and understand their own experiences as members of different social groups and listen to others in the course talk about their experiences and perspectives. The focus is on respecting, understanding, and acknowledging difference. After this, the concepts of dominance, social power, and privilege are introduced to help students understand that difference is not neutral, that different social groups have greater or lesser access to social and personal resources and power.

Psychological and Logical Sequencing. The structure of the course should make both psychological and logical sense to both facilitators and participants. Logical sequence requires beginning with what people already know and presenting information that can be gradually integrated into expanding levels of analysis. Psychological sequence refers to how participants negotiate the course at the psychological and emotional levels. The low risk to higher risk sequence supports effective psychological sequencing.

What? So What? Now What? Sequencing. This sequence is a guide for organizing process as well as content by increasing awareness (What), thinking and analysis (So what) and experimenting with new behavior (Now what) (Borton, 1970, 93). It begins by asking "What" students currently know and feel in order to identify the information and supportive climate needed for initiating an activity or the course as a whole. The question, "So What?" refers to how students process an activity or activities to draw meaning that expands their awareness and knowledge. The question "Now What?" addresses the implications of what students have learned and the next steps to be taken given new knowledge and awareness.

The table below summarizes the three previous sections to combine facilitating environments, methods/structures, and sequencing. This chart can be helpful as a planning guide when designing a course.

Facilitating Environment	Methods/Structure	Sequences
Confirmation	Agenda/Objectives Introductions Warm Up Fears/Expectations	What? So What? Now What? Psychological and Logical Difference (Diversity) to Dominance (Justice) Personal to Institutional Concrete to Abstract Low to Higher Risk
Contradiction	Advance Organizers Definitions Activity (simulation, discussion, video, lecture, panel presentation, etc.) Transition	
Continuity	Action Planning Support Closure	

Figure 4.4. Environment, Methods, and Sequences.

Learning Style Preferences

As instructors, we all have certain learning style preferences and often teach in ways that favor our own preferred learning style. To avoid this tendency and to consciously accommodate a variety of student learning styles in our instructional designs, we find a useful guide in the experiential learning model developed by Kolb (Kolb, 1984; Smith & Kolb, 1986; Anderson & Adams, 1992; further discussed in chapter 15) . This model provides guidance for selecting as well as sequencing learning activities to meet a range of learning style preferences as shown in Figures 4.5 and 4.6.

The Kolb model identifies four learning modes: concrete experience, reflective observation, abstract conceptualization, and active experimentation. For each learning mode, the model lists instructional activities that are appropriate to that style. In planning a course, the model can be used as a checklist to insure that we have planned a range of activities so that all four learning modes are likely to be engaged during a course. For example, using the model as a guide to evaluate whether the course designs in this volume include a variety of learning preferences, we note that simulations such as Star Power in the classism course, role playing in the sexism course, and speakouts in the antisemitism course engage students in a direct and concrete manner (concrete experience). The processing questions that follow each activity, film, or lecture illustrate reflective observation. We note that the conceptual model of individual, institutional, and cultural levels of oppression is explained and used to analyze the dynamics of the ism explored in each course

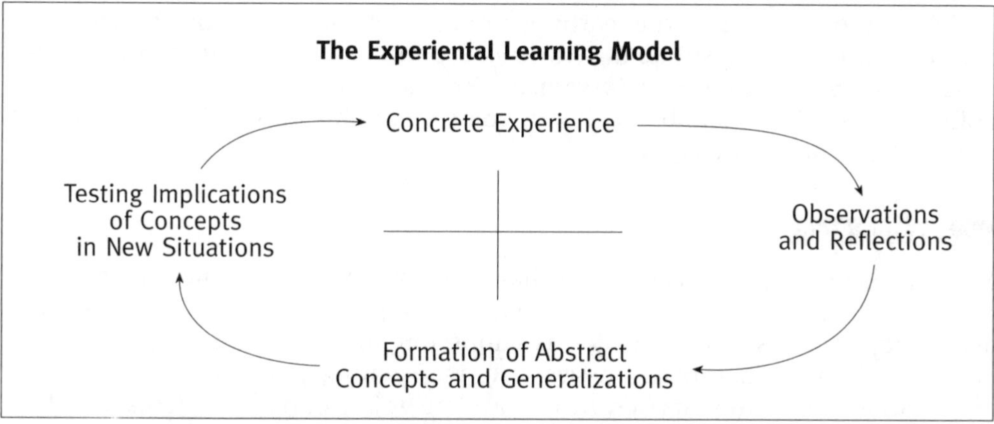

Figure 4.5. The Experiential Learning Model.

Source: Smith & Kolb, 1986, 12. Copyright: © 1986 by David A. Kolb and Donna M. Smith. Reproduced with permission from McBer & Company, Inc., 116 Huntington Ave., Boston, MA, 02116.

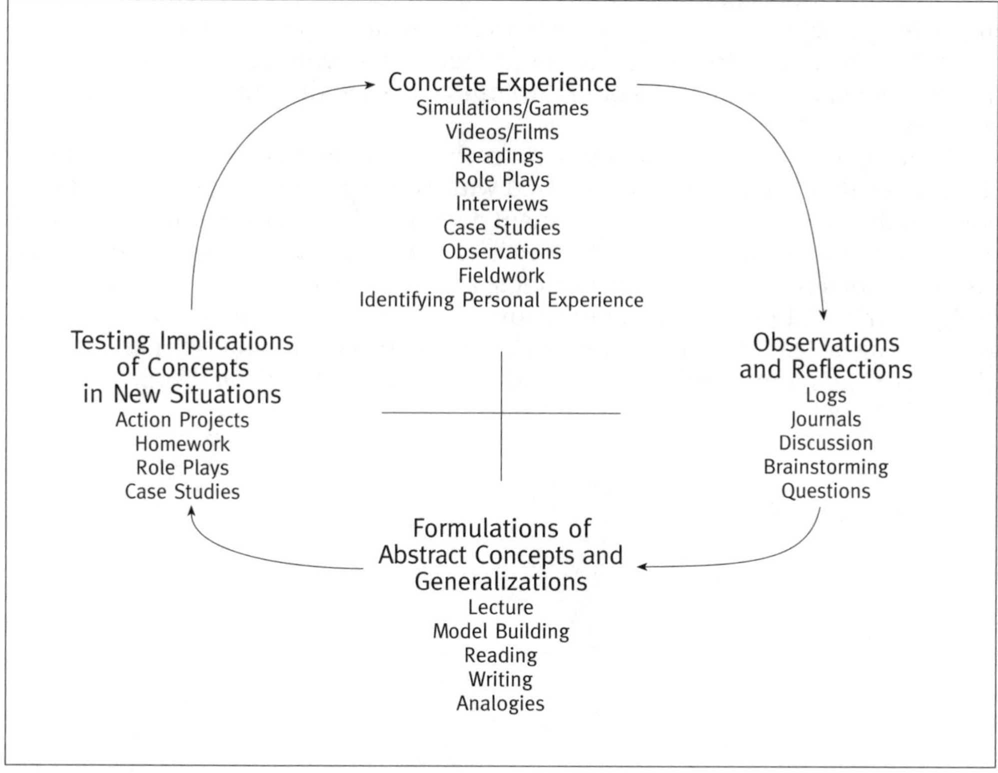

Figure 4.6. Instructional Activities that Support Different Aspects of the Learning Cycle.

Source: Svinicki & Dixon, 1987, 142. Reprinted with permission of The Helen Dwight Reid Educational Foundation. Published by Heldref Publications, 1319 Eighteenth St. N.W., Washington, D.C. 20036–1802. Copyright: c 1987.

(abstract conceptualization). Finally, we see that students develop action projects to apply learnings about racism, sexism, ableism, and other forms of oppression to at home situations (active experimentation). This sequence is evident in the general flow of the modules in each design in this volume as well as within the flow of specific activities.

Kolb's model illustrates the learning strengths of each style and the preferred learning situations of students with those particular strengths. Most courses include students who represent several different learning style preferences and the Kolb model enables us to be deliberate in our planning and include a variety of learning activities in each class.

Design Adjustments

Many times the design that facilitators have prepared prior to the start of the course requires adjustment once the course begins. Having the flexibility to make needed design adjustments based on what is happening in the moment is an essential design skill. Many factors can necessitate redesigning a course. Preassessment information about students may be incomplete or inaccurate. Incidents in a class may require a change in design to capitalize on a spontaneous learning opportunity that presents itself unexpectedly during the class. Student expectations for the course may not match the design. Activities may take longer than the time allotted for them in the original design and facilitators need to change plans as a result. Informal student evaluations in the midst of the course may signal the need to make design adjustments (see chapter 15 for further discussion). In all of these cases, it is necessary to reevaluate the design and decide how to make adjustments that will maintain the flow of the course while addressing the essential key concepts.

The design tools presented in this chapter are offered to help facilitators have confidence that what they have planned will enable students to explore difficult issues in the most supportive environment possible. These activities are sequenced to help students understand the dynamics of oppression in their own lives and in the larger society. We hope these principles will also be useful in developing new designs for social justice education courses to meet the particular needs of the groups you teach. With practice, these principles can become a routine part of planning and a basis from which to create and explore new activities and approaches to social justice education.

PART TWO

Curriculum Designs for Addressing Diversity and Social Justice

5

Introductory Module for the Single Issue Courses

Pat Griffin

This chapter describes the introductory module for each of the single issue courses described in chapters 6–11. The activities in this session are designed to introduce students to the basic dynamics of oppression described in chapter 2. This session introduces basic vocabulary, key concepts, and the overall theoretical perspectives upon which each single issue design is based. Students learn and practice using participation guidelines followed in all of the single issue courses. Students also learn that, though there are multiple levels on which oppression operates, in these courses they will be focusing on developing individual awareness, knowledge, and action plans. Because this session describes oppression as an overarching phenomenon, students also begin to understand the interconnections and interactions among the different forms of oppression.

Introductory Module: Chapter 5

Chapter 6	Chapter 7	Chapter 8	Chapter 9	Chapter 10	Chapter 11
Racism	Sexism	Heterosexism	Antisemitism	Ableism	Classism

This introductory module takes three to four hours to complete. Depending on the class format and flexibility we have presented selected parts of this introductory module in one-and-one-half hour evening sessions and a more in-depth version in an eight hour all day session. Course facilitators can choose selected parts of this introduction if time constraints do not allow for completion of the entire segment. We believe, however, that all introductory modules should include the following fundamental parts *prior* to the four modules presented in each of the single issue designs:

- Individual introductions of participants and their goals.
- Identification of discussion guidelines.
- Review of class outline, evaluation criteria, and other administrative information.
- Introduction to the oppression model.
- Identification of participant identities related to the specific course topic.
- Definition of basic vocabulary: oppression, agent/target, privilege, ally, prejudice, social power.

Single Issue Focus

In the course designs described in chapters 6–11 of this book, we examine one form of oppression at a time in classes of 25–30 students. We focus on racism, sexism, classism, heterosexism, ableism, and antisemitism. In each design we discuss parallels and interconnections among the different forms of oppression and class readings are chosen to help students understand these connections. We teach these single issue courses from a "multi-centered" perspective that recognizes the interactions of other social group memberships with the one under study in the single issue design. For example, in a racism course we encourage students to talk and think about how their gender, sexual orientation, religion, class, and ability interact with their racial identity in affecting their life experiences.

There are advantages and disadvantages to this single issue approach. Focusing on one issue at a time can simplify a complex and difficult process. Students can think about one social identity and concentrate their attention on understanding the dynamics of one form of oppression at a time. For students who have never given much thought to oppression, this focus can facilitate learning. Focusing on one form of oppression at a time also enables that form of oppression to be explored in greater depth than would be possible in a multiple issue approach. One of the disadvantages of the single issue approach is the danger of disregarding the impact of other social group memberships on the dynamics of the topic under study. For this reason it is important to address the impact of other social group memberships in class discussions and readings as well as to invite students to examine the impact of other social group identities on their experiences and perspectives.

Alternative Formats for Presenting Introductory Content

In the instructional format we use, students enrolled in all single issue courses meet together for one evening session early in the semester; then each single issue course meets separately from 9 A.M. to 5 P.M. on a Saturday and Sunday during the semester. That is, racism, sexism, heterosexism, classism, ableism, and antisemitism all meet on different weekends. Each weekend course is one credit. Typically, 25–30 undergraduate or graduate students are enrolled in each weekend course. Students may enroll in one or more weekends during the semester, but they take the introductory session only once.

During the introductory session in which all students participate, we present the information described here. With this format, all students in single issue courses during the semester have been introduced to the same basic foundational information about the dynamics of oppression.

There are numerous options for organizing the activities in the introductory module and the single issue designs that follow. For example, this material can be presented over an extended time with shorter class periods similar to traditional courses that meet two or three times a week for the entire semester (see alternative formats provided at the end of this volume). Though we have chosen to present introductory information to all students enrolled in any single issue course during a separate class session, this material could also be integrated into each single issue design. We encourage social justice education teachers to choose how to present introductory information based on the specific characteristics of your teaching situation.

We have divided each single issue course into four modules that follow this introductory module. Typically, the four modules take place in a Saturday and Sunday morning and afternoon teaching format several weeks after the introductory module. We find that spending two days together focusing on social justice issues enables participants to reach a depth of self-exploration and examination that is more difficult to achieve in a more traditional class format where students meet together for one or two hours, two or three times a week.

Typically, this introductory module introduces theoretical concepts and vocabulary that are used in each of the single issue courses. Within the single issue designs, Module 1 includes activities designed to help participants build community. It also reviews concepts presented in the introductory module, reviews discussion guidelines, previews the specific course agenda, and begins introductory work on the topic for that course. The second and third modules usually focus on developing a more in-depth understanding of how the particular form of oppression works and give participants an opportunity to engage in more discussion and exploration. The fourth module helps participants begin to think about how what they have learned can be integrated into their lives outside the course. Participants identify action plans and develop support networks among classmates or make plans for continuing their learning about social justice issues.

In addition to the in-class activities described in chapters 5–11, we require students to complete selected readings for each course and integrate these readings into written reactions to the course after its completion. These readings are available in single issue packets or grouped together in a multiple issue volume (ed. Adams, Brigham, Dalpes, & Marchesani, 1996) that includes homework questions and follow-up activities for each "ism." The readings are listed at the end of this volume.

Introductory Module	
Saturday Morning Module 1	Sunday Morning Module 3
Saturday Afternoon Module 2	Sunday Afternoon Module 4

Figure 5.1. Single Issue Course Design.

This format can be modified, however, to accommodate different educational contexts. For a more traditional semester course format in which classes meet once a week during a fourteen week semester, the following division might be more appropriate:

Weeks 1–3 = Introductory Module

Weeks 4–6 = Module 1

Weeks 7–9 = Module 2

Weeks 10–12 = Module 3

Weeks 13–14 = Module 4

Several key concepts guide and structure course activities. These concepts provide the focus for the content for all of the single and multiple issue curriculum designs described in chapters 6–12.

- Social Diversity and Social Justice
- Social Oppression and Liberation
- Social Group Memberships: Agents and Targets
- Personal Experience/Socialization
- Prejudice
- Stereotypes
- Social Power
- Privilege and Rights
- Collusion
- Internalized Domination and Subordination
- Historical Context
- Individual, Institutional, and Cultural Levels
- Agent Role: Ally
- Target Role: Empowerment
- Horizontal Oppression
- Parallels, Interconnectedness, Uniqueness
- Multi-centeredness
- Individual and Collective Action
- Social and Individual Change

Figure 5.2. Key Concepts.

These key concepts provide guidance for choosing learning activities. Each learning activity is designed to help students understand one or more of these concepts. Most of these activities in the single issue designs that follow are interchangeable in that, with modification, any learning activity can be used in teaching about several different forms of oppression.

The courses described in chapters 6–11 address social justice issues in the United States. While acknowledging that international events affect the experiences of social groups in the United States and that addressing oppression in other parts of the world is important, it has been our experience that most students in our courses can best begin to explore social justice issues through their own experiences in the United States. Racism in Great Britain or South Africa, while similar to racism in the United States, involves different social groups in different socio-historical contexts. In addition, an explicit United States focus enables students to explore their own participation in perpetuating social injustice. Though our courses focus on the United States, we find that international students enrich class discussions by sharing their experiences both in their home cultures and in the United States.

Moreover, it has been our experience that a rich mix of different social identities, experiences, perspectives, and awarenesses creates the most productive learning environment for all students. The role of the facilitators is to help create a class environment in which students can share their own experiences, express their own beliefs, ask their own questions and hear the experiences, beliefs, and questions of others.

Over the past few years the mainstream media and conservative educators and politicians have raised concerns about "political correctness" on college campuses. These critics charge that this presumed lack of tolerance for the expression of any views that contradict a progressive party line stifles debate and violates basic principles of free speech. Social justice education courses are sometimes targeted as examples of this intolerance whereby students are indoctrinated in a class atmosphere that discourages dissent and the free expression of beliefs.

While it is accurate to say that our courses present a definite perspective on social justice, it is also important to recognize that, within the framework of these courses, students are encouraged, not discouraged, to express their beliefs and to talk about their experiences. Students are encouraged to be critical of and reexamine their experiences and beliefs in light of other perspectives presented in class, but are not evaluated on the congruence of their beliefs with the perspectives presented by other students or the facilitators. (See chapter 12 for evaluation.)

Underlying Assumptions

Several underlying assumptions create a philosophical foundation for our social justice education practice. Facilitators who plan to use this sourcebook should be aware of what these assumptions are. We also share these assumptions with our students.

It is not useful to argue about a hierarchy of oppressions. We believe that little is gained in debating which forms of oppression are more damaging or which one is the root out of which all others grow. Though we acknowledge that some students believe that there is an urgent need to address one form of oppression over others, we present the perspective that each form of oppression is destructive to the human spirit. We do, however, identify ways in which specific forms of oppression are similar or different, but do not rank the differences identified. Our courses are based on the belief that even if we could eliminate one form of oppression, the continued existence of the others would still affect us all.

All forms of oppression are interconnected. Each participant in our courses is a collage of many social identities. Even though a course is focused on sexism, for example, each student's race, class, religion, sexual orientation, ability, and gender affect how that student experiences sexism. We encourage students to explore the intersections of their different social group memberships and also to understand the similarities in the dynamics of different forms of oppression.

Confronting oppression will benefit everyone. Most people can understand how confronting sexism will benefit women or how addressing ableism will benefit people with disabilities. We also believe that men and non-disabled people will benefit from the elimination of sexism and ableism. Unfortunately, some participants react to social justice education as if engaged in a conflict in which one group wins and another loses. However, when people are subjected to the effects of oppression based on their social group membership, their talents and potential achievements are lost to all of us. Even if we are not members of a particular disadvantaged social group, we all have friends, co-workers, or family members who are targeted by some form of oppression. In addition, we might become members of disadvantaged social groups in the future if we become disabled or have a change in economic circumstances. Another way we are hurt by oppression is that many people who are members of groups that benefit from oppression live with a burden of guilt, shame, and helplessness and are never sure if their individual accomplishments are earned or the result of advantages received due to their social group membership. Confronting oppression can free members of all social groups to take action toward social justice. The goal in eliminating oppression is an equitable redistribution of social power and resources among all social groups at all levels (individual, institutional, and societal/cultural). The goal is not to reverse the current power inequity by simply alternating the groups in power positions.

Fixing blame helps no one, taking responsibility helps everyone. We present the perspective that there is little to be gained from fixing blame for our heritage of social injustice. We are each born into a social system and are taught to accept it as it is. Nothing is gained by feeling shame about what our ancestors did or what our contemporaries do to different groups of people out of fear, ignorance, or malice. Taking responsibility, in contrast, means acting to address oppression. Rather than becoming lost in a sense of helplessness, our goal is to enable students to understand how they can choose to take responsibility in their everyday lives for confronting social injustice.

Confronting social injustice is painful AND joyful. Most students do not want to believe that they can harbor unfair prejudices about groups of people. Confronting these prejudices in themselves and others is difficult. Students need to open themselves to the discomfort and uncertainty of questioning what is familiar, comfortable, and unquestioned. Facing the contradictions between what students have been taught to believe about social justice and the realities of the experiences of different social groups is complex. Students learn that some of what they were taught is inaccurate. Some information they need was not taught at all. Students need to be assisted through this process with hope and care. At the same time, we believe that understanding social oppression and taking action against it can be a joyful and liberating experience. Some students' lives are changed in exciting and life affirming ways as a result of their experiences in social justice education courses. They find ways to act on their beliefs and make changes in their personal lives that profoundly affect their personal and professional relationships.

OVERVIEW OF INTRODUCTORY MODULE

Agenda

1. Introductions—30 mins.
2. Course Description—15 mins.
3. Interaction Guidelines—20 mins.

4. Comfort Zones, Learning Edges, Triggers—30 mins.
5. Identifying Social Group Memberships—20 mins.
6. Identifying Social Group Status—20 mins.
7. Describing An Oppression Model—60–90 mins.
8. Closing and Preparing for Module 1—15–30 mins.

Supplemental Activities

1. Agent and Target Role in Eliminating/Maintaining Oppression (30 mins.)
2. Levels and Types of Oppression (30 mins.)

Figure 5.3. Overview of Introductory Module.

Introduction to Single Issue Curriculum Designs

3–4 hours
Goals:

- Develop a common vocabulary.
- Develop a common understanding of oppression dynamics.
- Identify and practice group participation guidelines.
- Explore social identities and experiences.

Activities

1. Introductions (30 minutes).

Ask participants to find a partner and then ask each person to take two minutes to share a) their name, b) what they are studying in school or what their work is, c) what led them to take this class, d) an expectation they have about the class, and e) what other social justice-related classes or workshops they have attended previously. Return to the whole group and ask each person to briefly introduce themselves to the group by giving their name and what they hope to learn from the class. Introduce yourself and other co-facilitators. Describe your interest in and commitment to social justice education. Sometimes telling a personal story about the first time you attended a social justice education class or workshop helps to ease student anxiety and also models the kind of personal sharing that is expected in the class.

2. Class Description (15 minutes).

Describe the class outline, work requirements, grading information, and attend to other administrative matters.

3. Class Participation Guidelines (20 minutes).

Because the course content is challenging and the class process is experiential and interactive, participants need some basic discussion guidelines in order to develop trust and safety. Ask the participants to identify guidelines that would help them participate fully in class activities. This can be accomplished in groups of three to five and then shared with the whole group or brainstormed as a whole group activity. Some of the guidelines we find helpful include the following:

- Set own boundaries for sharing.
- Speak from experience and avoids generalizing about groups of people.

- Respect confidentiality.
- Keep personal information shared in the group.
- Share air time.
- Listen respectfully to different perspectives.
- No blaming or scapegoating.
- Focus on own learning.

Figure 5.4. Sample Guidelines.

4. Comfort Zones, Learning Edges, and Triggers (30 minutes).
(This activity can be integrated into the single issue designs if time constraints require shortening the introductory module.)

The concepts of comfort zones, learning edges, and triggers can serve as guides to help students understand and explore their reactions to class activities and other students' perspectives. Present the following information to participants.

Comfort Zone: We all have zones of comfort about different topics or activities. Topics or activities we are familiar with or have lots of information about are solidly inside our comfort zone. When we are inside our comfort zone we are not challenged and we are not learning anything new. When we are participating in a discussion or activity focused on new information or awareness, or the information and awareness we have is being challenged, we are often out of our comfort zone or on its edge. If we are too far outside our comfort zone, we tend to withdraw or resist new information. The goal in this class is to learn to recognize when we are on the edge of our comfort zone.

Learning Edge: When we are on the edge of our comfort zone, we are in the best place to expand our understanding, take in a new perspective, and stretch our awareness. We can learn to recognize when we are on a learning edge in this class by paying attention to our internal reactions to class activities and other people in the class. Being on a learning edge can be signaled by feelings of annoyance, anger, anxiety, surprise, confusion, or defensiveness. These reactions are signs that our way of seeing things is being challenged. If we retreat to our comfort zone, by dismissing whatever we encounter that does not agree with our way of seeing the world, we lose an opportunity to expand our understanding. The challenge is to recognize when we are on a learning edge and then to stay there with the discomfort we are experiencing to see what we can learn.

Ask participants to take two minutes each to share with a partner a time they can remember being on a learning edge with new information or a new skill. Provide some examples of your own to model self-disclosure and to help participants to understand what you are asking them to identify. For example, talk about learning a new sport skill or dance, taking a difficult academic class, or being in another country where you were not familiar with the culture or language. Ask participants to respond to this question: What internal cues will alert you that you are on a learning edge in this class? Encourage students to recognize pounding hearts, sweaty palms, butterflies in the stomach, excited focused attention, confusion, fear, or anger as all cues to recognize that they are on a learning edge.

Triggers: Triggers are words or phrases that stimulate an emotional response because they tap into anger or pain about oppression issues. Typically, triggers often convey, consciously or unconsciously, a stereotypical perception or an acceptance of the status quo. (See Responding to Triggers in Appendix 5A.) Examples of triggers include:

- "I don't see differences, people are people to me."
- "What do you people really want anyway?"
- "I think men are just biologically more adapted to leadership roles than women."
- "I feel so sorry for people with disabilities. It's such a tragedy."
- "If everyone just worked hard, they could achieve."
- "Homeless people prefer their life."
- "I think people of color are blowing things way out of proportion."
- "If women wear tight clothes, they are asking for it."

Invite students to identify a process for naming triggers in ways that encourage open and respectful dialogue. Put a sheet of newsprint on the wall and have students write down triggers that are used during class. Later, with some distance from the event, these triggers can be discussed. Ask students who are triggered to explain why. Invite students who triggered someone else to listen and try to understand what was upsetting about their comment. Help them to clarify what they meant or to acknowledge new information. Encourage participants to view these discussions as "food for thought" rather than attempts to change individual participants on the spot. No one can focus effective attention on personal learning when they feel defensive or chastised.

Commentary

Many students come into social justice education courses with some fear that they will "make a mistake" by triggering someone else. Encourage students to look at triggers as learning opportunities for everyone. Though agents are usually more likely to say something that triggers target group members in a class, anyone can say something that can trigger anyone else regardless of social group membership. Sometimes agents are triggered by what other agents say and target group members can be triggered by someone from their own group as well.

5. Identifying Social Group Memberships (20 minutes).

List different categories of social identity on newsprint or on an overhead:

Gender
Class
Sexual Orientation
Physical/Developmental/Psychological Ability
Race
Religion
Age

Figure 5.5. Identifying Social Group Memberships.

Define social group: A group of people who share a range of physical, cultural, or social characteristics within one of the categories of social identity. Write the following examples of social group memberships on newsprint or an overhead:

Gender:	Female, Male, Transgender people
Race:	Black, White, Latino, Asian/Pacific Islander, Native American, Biracial
Ethnicity:	African American, Cuban, English, Chinese, Sioux
Sexual Orientation:	Bisexual, Lesbian, Gay, Heterosexual
Religion:	Christian, Jew, Muslim, Hindu
Class:	Poor, Working Class, Middle Class, Owning Class
Age:	Young People, Young Adults, Middle-Aged Adults, Old People

Figure 5.6. Social Groups.

Using the Social Group Membership Profile in Appendix 5-B, ask participants individually to indicate their social group memberships for each social identity category. Tell them they will be describing their profile with one other person whom they choose. Stress to students that the social group memberships listed are examples and not meant to be exhaustive. Invite students to add other social group memberships that best describe themselves. For now, ask students only to fill in the membership column; the status column is filled in later in this introductory session.

Social Group Membership Profile		
Social Identities	**Membership**	**Status**
Race		
Gender		
Class		
Age		
Sexual Orientation		
Religion		
Ability/Disability		

Figure 5.7. Social Group Membership Profile.

Commentary

Providing students with this framework often raises questions about the names used to represent different social groups. This framework is tentative and fluid. Its purpose is to provide students with a common understanding, not to impose particular language. We stress that the issue of self-definition is extremely sensitive, open to interpretation and contradiction and constantly in flux. We invite students to describe different names they prefer for their social groups and to ask questions about how other groups name themselves. Students might also have questions about which groups are included among the social groups within each identity category. For example, Jewish students sometimes identify as an ethnic or racial group.

Again we stress that this framework is an imperfect model that cannot fairly represent the full range of perspectives or complexity embedded in a consideration of social group memberships. For now, invite students to use the model in whatever way feels comfortable for their own self-definitions and experience. These issues can be taken up in more detail in the single issue classes that follow.

Completing this profile also raises questions about how to identify social group memberships that are not as clearly differentiated as gender, race, or religion usually are. Biracial and multiracial students might also have difficulty categorizing themselves. We encourage these students to name themselves by indicating the racial heritages of both their parents. Participants typically ask questions about how to define different age cohorts and how to identify social class membership. Provide students with some initial (and flexible) guidelines for making these decisions and emphasize that these categories are arbitrary, to be revisited and stretched in the single issue courses. For age, we recommend that students think of ages 1–17 as young people, 18–29 as young adults, 30–60 as middle–aged adults, and 60 on as old people. These age categories reflect employment discrimination. We encourage participants to think of their parents' or caregivers' occupations when identifying social class. These guidelines help students identify their social group memberships without having to get too deeply into any one topic at this point. Make sure students know that they can leave blank any social group memberships they choose not to disclose, and may control what they wish to disclose in paired sharing and whom they wish to share with.

After participants have completed their individual profile, ask them to choose a partner and discuss the following questions which you will write on the chalkboard or newsprint:

- Which of your social group memberships were easiest to identify?
- Which of your social group memberships were most difficult to identify?
- What questions are raised for you in trying to identify your social group memberships?

After about 15 minutes, ask everyone to bring their attention back to the large group and ask for volunteers to give their answers to the questions discussed in pairs.

Processing

Ask students how this process enabled them to think about themselves in new ways. Ask them what they think accounts for our being more aware of some social group memberships and less aware of others. Describe some of your own social group memberships and your own awareness of them. Point out that everyone belongs to multiple social groups, though most of us are more aware of some than others.

6. Identifying Status Associated with Social Group Membership (20 minutes).

Put the following chart on newsprint or on an overhead transparency and ask participants what they notice about how different social groups are arranged in the two columns on the right side of the chart. Ask them what the social groups in each column have in common.

RACE	Whites	Blacks, Latinos, Asians, Native Americans, Biracial People
GENDER	Men	Women
CLASS	Owning Class, Upper Middle Class	Lower Middle Class, Working Class, Poor
SEXUAL ORIENTATION	Heterosexuals	Lesbians, Gay Men, Bisexual People
RELIGION	Gentiles, Christians	Jews, Muslims, Hindus
ABILITY	Non-Disabled People	Disabled People
AGE	Young and Middle-Aged Adults	Young People, Old People

Figure 5.8. Social Groups and Status.

Participants are typically able to identify the groups who are in the middle column as people in society that, as a group, are viewed as "superior," "normal," "the best group to be in." The social groups in the right column are identified as "disadvantaged," "inferior," "discriminated against," or "needing help." Point out that what they are identifying are differences in status between the groups listed in the two columns.

7. Describing the Oppression Model (60–90 minutes).

This is the model that forms the foundation for this course. It is not the only way to understand oppression, but it is the model we will be using in these courses. It is important to stress the tentative nature of this model and that it is an attempt to take a snapshot of dynamic and complex phenomena for the purposes of understanding and identifying a common vocabulary. In this spirit, invite students to raise questions about it and identify its limitations as well as its usefulness in helping us to understand social oppression. Describe to participants how oppression is an overarching phenomenon with individual manifestations based on different social identity categories (see explanations in chapters 1 and 2):

Social Identity Category	**Form of Oppression**
Race	Racism
Gender	Sexism
Sexual Orientation	Heterosexism
Religion	Antisemitism
Physical, Developmental, Mental Ability	Ableism
Class	Classism
Age	Ageism

Figure 5.9. Social Identity Categories and Forms of Oppression.

Point out that under religion, we have listed only one form of religious oppression, antisemitism. Acknowledge that there are many other religious groups that are targeted in the United States, Muslims and Hindus, for example. We focus on antisemitism here because it is the form of religious oppression we address in the courses to follow. NOTE: The antisemitism curriculum design can be used as a template to study other forms of religious oppression in the United States.

Describe how all individual forms of oppression share several characteristics:

a) Each form of oppression is perpetuated by a socialization process. Use the Cycle of Socialization Model (Appendix 5C) to illustrate how we all learn to accept dominant thinking about social differences. Talk about how we come by our prejudices honestly. We were each born without prejudice into a world that has systematically taught us to accept an oppressive system. We learned this from people who love and care for us: parents, teachers, friends. What we learn is reinforced in schools and by the media as well as other institutions with which we interact. To change how this system operates it is necessary to take individual and collective action for social change. (See chapter 6 for a more elaborate description of how the cycle of socialization works.)

b) Each form of oppression has agent and target social groups. Within each form of oppression there is a group of people with greater access to social power and privilege based upon their membership in their social group. We call this group the agent group. We call groups whose access to social power is limited or denied the target group. Other descriptors for these two groups include the following: Agent: Dominant, Oppressor, Advantaged. Target: Subordinate, Oppressed, Disadvantaged.

Social Power: Access to resources that enhance one's chances of getting what one needs or influencing others in order to lead a safe, productive, fulfilling life.

Privilege: Unearned access to resources (social power) only readily available to some people as a result of their social group membership.

Use the following table to identify agent and target groups for each form of oppression.

Form of Oppression	Agent Groups	Target Groups
Racism	Whites	Blacks, Latinos, Asians, Native Americans, Biracial People
Sexism	Men	Women
Classism	Owning Class, Upper Middle Class	Lower Middle Class, Working Class, Poor
Heterosexism	Heterosexuals	Lesbians, Gay Men, Bisexual People
Antisemitism	Gentiles, Christians	Jews
Ableism	Non-Disabled People	Disabled People
Ageism	Young and Middle-Aged Adults	Young People, Old People

Figure 5.10. Forms of Oppression and Agent/Target Groups.

Point out that members of both agent and target groups are capable of prejudice, abuse, violence, and hatred, although only the agent groups have the institutional and cultural power to back up their prejudices against the target groups. For example, individual people of color might have prejudices against white people and individual women might have prejudices against men, but as a group, neither people of color nor women hold many positions of power in major institutions in the United States to turn their prejudices into widely held institutional and social policy.

Ask participants to turn their attention to their individual social group membership profiles. Have them identify their status (agent or target) for each of their social group memberships. Invite participants to use the table as a guide for completing this activity. After they have completed this task, ask participants to answer the following questions with a partner:

- For which social group memberships was it easiest to identify your status?
- For which social group memberships was it more difficult to identify your status?
- When you look at your overall profile, what surprises you?
- Which social group memberships are you most aware of on a daily basis?
- Which ones are you least aware of?
- Which ones would you like to learn more about?

After participants have discussed their responses to these questions, call their attention back to the large group and invite volunteers to talk about their answers to the questions.

Facilitation Issues
This activity invites participants to see themselves as members of several social groups, some of which receive privileges and some of which do not. Ask participants to be aware of how their collage of social group memberships interact as they focus on one issue of oppression at a time. For example, a disabled working-class man will experience his agent identity as a man in ways that are different from a non-disabled, upper-middle-class man. If there are men in the class who do not have any targeted identities, ask them to think about their experience as young children and recall their feelings about the absence of power and privilege available to young people.

c) Oppression is based on negative stereotypes of targeted groups that are often well known to agents and targets. Describe how within each form of oppression, members of both agent and target groups usually can readily identify negative stereotypes of the targeted groups whether they subscribe to these stereotypes or not. (See chapter 9 for a definition and discussion of stereotype.) Their knowledge of stereotypes is frequently not related to actual experience with target groups. Ask participants to quickly call out a few stereotypes of men and women to illustrate how easily we can generate lists of stereotypes for different social groups. Make it clear that calling out stereotypes does not indicate one's agreement with them.

d) Each manifestation of oppression operates on multiple levels. Many people perceive racism, sexism, or other forms of oppression to be individual acts of meanness or hatred only. To fully understand oppression it is essential that participants recognize that it operates on multiple levels:

- ***Individual:*** Attitudes and actions that reflect prejudice against a social group.
- ***Institutional:*** Policies, laws, rules, norms, and customs enacted by organizations and social institutions that disadvantage some social groups and advantage other social groups. These institutions include religion, government, education, law, the media, and health care system.
- ***Societal/Cultural:*** Social norms, roles, rituals, language, music, and art that reflect and reinforce the belief that one social group is superior to another.

Ask participants to work in groups of three to brainstorm examples of oppression at each level. Encourage them to identify examples from several of the forms of oppression discussed. Allow five minutes, then ask participants to call out several examples of individual, institutional, and societal/cultural oppression. Write these examples on three separate sheets of newsprint or on the chalkboard. Ask participants if they have any questions about the examples. Clarify any examples that are unclear.

8. Preparing for the single issue classes and ending the Introductory Module (15–30 minutes).

Remind students that the next part of the class will focus on one specific form of oppression. Make sure all students know when and where the next class will meet. Tell them what reading assignments they have to do in preparation for the class. If there is time, end the introductory session by asking each participant to identify a) something they learned that will stay with them from the introductory module and b) one thing they are looking forward to in their single issue course.

Supplementary Activities

If more time is available for the Introductory Module, the following activities and information can be added.

Supplemental Activity 1

Agent and target group members play a role in either perpetuating oppression or eliminating it. NOTE: This is a fifth characteristic of oppression that can be inserted in Activity 7 (30 minutes).

Oppression can be both vertical and horizontal.

Vertical oppression: when agents enforce subordinate status upon targets.

- White male legislators pass laws affecting women and people of color
- Heterosexual people harass or make fun of lesbians and gay men

Agent to Agent Horizontal Oppression: When agents enforce dominant status with other members of the agent group

- Gentile parents discourage a daughter's romantic interest in a Jewish man
- Boys who don't conform to traditional "masculine" interests and behaviors are harassed by other boys

Target to Target Horizontal Oppression: When target group members enforce subordinate status among their own group or, if there is more than one target group, when one target group enforces subordinate status with another target group.

- Lesbians and gay people oppose the participation of other gay people in Pride Marches who think, act, and look too stereotypical
- African American people vandalize shops run by Koreans

Internalized Subordination: When members of the target social group have adopted the agent group's ideology and accept their subordinate status as deserved, natural, and inevitable.

- A woman believes she is less qualified for a job than a man
- A disabled person believes he cannot live independently without supervision from social workers

Internalized Domination: When members of the agent group accept their group's socially superior status as normal and deserved.

- A heterosexual who believes only heterosexuals are good parents
- A man who only considers men qualified for the job

Collusion: When people act to perpetuate oppression or prevent others from working to eliminate oppression.

- Able-bodied people who object to strategies for making buildings accessible because of the expense
- Jews avoid associating with other Jews who act too "Jewish"

Empowerment: When target group members refuse to accept the dominant ideology and their subordinate status and take actions to redistribute social power more equitably.

- Working-class and poor mothers organize to fight cuts to welfare benefits and demand better child care programs
- Students with disabilities sue a school to gain access to all buildings and programs

Ally: A member of the agent group who rejects the dominant ideology and takes action against oppression out of a belief that eliminating oppression will benefit agents and targets.

- A man objects to sexist jokes told in the men's locker room
- White people join an organization working on addressing racism in the workplace

Figure 5.11. Definitions of Key Terms: Overview.

Supplemental Activity 2

The following information can be included in Activity 7 as part of the discussion of oppression as a multi-leveled phenomenon (30 minutes).

In addition to working on multiple levels, oppression can be both conscious and unconscious and can be perpetuated by omission and commission. Provide participants with an example of each at all three levels. If time permits, ask them to think of a few more examples of each.

Individual Unconscious:

- A high school teacher assumes all of her students are interested in dating classmates of the other sex
- A teacher who prides himself on being fair to all of his students calls on boys to answer questions three times more often than he calls on girls

Individual Conscious:

- Someone uses racial slurs to refer to Blacks and Puerto Ricans
- A parent asks to have his child moved out of a gay teacher's classroom

Institutional Unconscious:

- Students celebrate Christmas in school, but not other winter religious holidays
- A town hall building does not have an entrance that is accessible to people using wheelchairs

Institutional Conscious:

- A state adopts a law prohibiting the legal recognition of lesbian and gay relationships
- An employment agency steers Blacks toward low paying, domestic or custodial positions

Societal/Cultural Unconscious:

- Standards of beauty for women are based on white norms: blond, fine hair, blue eyes, and fair skin
- A belief in individual merit and hard work being rewarded by economic success leads to a belief that poor people are lazy and undeserving

Societal/Cultural Conscious:

- English is designated as the "official" language in the United States
- European culture is assumed to be superior to other cultures

Appendix 5A

RESPONDING TO TRIGGERS

A trigger is something that an individual says or does or an organizational policy or practice that makes us, as members of social groups, feel diminished, offended, threatened, stereotyped, discounted, or attacked. Triggers do not necessarily threaten our physical safety. We often feel psychologically threatened. We can also be triggered on behalf of another social group. Though we do not feel personally threatened, our sense of social justice feels violated.

Triggers cause an emotional response. These emotions include hurt, confusion, anger, fear, surprise, or embarrassment. We respond to triggers in a variety of ways, some helpful and others not. Our guide in developing a full repertoire of responses to triggers is to take care of ourselves and then decide how to respond most effectively. Some of these responses are effective and some are not. What responses we choose depend on our own inner resources and the dynamics of the situation. This list is not intended to be all-inclusive and is in no order of preference.

Leave: We physically remove ourselves from the triggering situation.

Avoidance: We avoid future encounters with and withdraw emotionally from people or situations that trigger us.

Silence: We do not respond to the triggering situation though we feel upset by it. We endure without saying or doing anything.

Release: We notice the trigger, but do not take it in. We choose to let it go. We do not feel the need to respond.

Attack: We respond with an intention to hurt whoever has triggered us.

Internalization: We take in the content of the trigger. We believe it to be true.

Rationalization: We convince ourselves that we misinterpreted the trigger, that the intention was not to hurt us, or that we are overreacting so that we can avoid saying anything about the trigger.

Confusion: We feel upset but are not clear about why we feel that way. We know we feel angry, hurt, or offended. We just don't know what to say or do about it.

Shock: We are caught off guard, unprepared to be triggered by this person or situation and have a difficult time responding.

Name: We identify what is upsetting us to the triggering person or organization.

Discuss: We name the trigger and invite discussion about it with the triggering person or organization.

Confront: We name the trigger and demand that the offending behavior or policy be changed.

Surprise: We respond to the trigger in an unexpected way. For example, we react with constructive humor that names the trigger and makes people laugh.

Strategize: We work with others to develop a programmatic or political intervention to address the trigger in a larger context.

Misinterpretation: We are feeling on guard and expect to be triggered, so that we misinterpret something someone says and are triggered by our misinterpretation, rather than by what was actually said.

Discretion: Because of dynamics in the situation (power differences, risk of physical violence or retribution, for example), we decide that it is not in our best interests to respond to the trigger at that time, but choose to address the trigger in some other way at another time.

Discussion Questions

- Which responses are most typical for you when you are triggered? As a target group member? As an agent group member?
- Are there differences in how you respond to triggers depending on your different social identities?
- Which responses would you like to add to your repertoire?
- Which responses do you use now and would like to stop using or use more selectively?
- What blocks you from responding to triggers in ways that feel more effective?
- What can you do to expand your response repertoire?

Appendix 5B

SOCIAL GROUP MEMBERSHIP PROFILE

Social Identities	Examples of Social Group Memberships
Race:	Black, White, Asian, Latino/a, Native American, Biracial, Pacific Islander
Gender:	Woman, Man, Transgender
Class:	Poor, Working Class, Middle Class, Owning Class
Physical/Mental/ Developmental Ability:	Able, Disabled
Sexual Orientation:	Lesbian, Gay, Bisexual, Heterosexual, Asexual
Religion:	Catholic, Jew, Protestant, Buddhist, Hindu, Muslim
Age:	Young People, Old People, Middle-Aged Adults, Young Adults

Personal Social Group Membership Profile		
Social Identities	**Membership**	**Status**
Race		
Gender		
Class		
Age		
Sexual Orientation		
Religion		
Ability/Disability		

Appendix 5C

CYCLE OF SOCIALIZATION DIAGRAM
Created by B. Harro (1982).

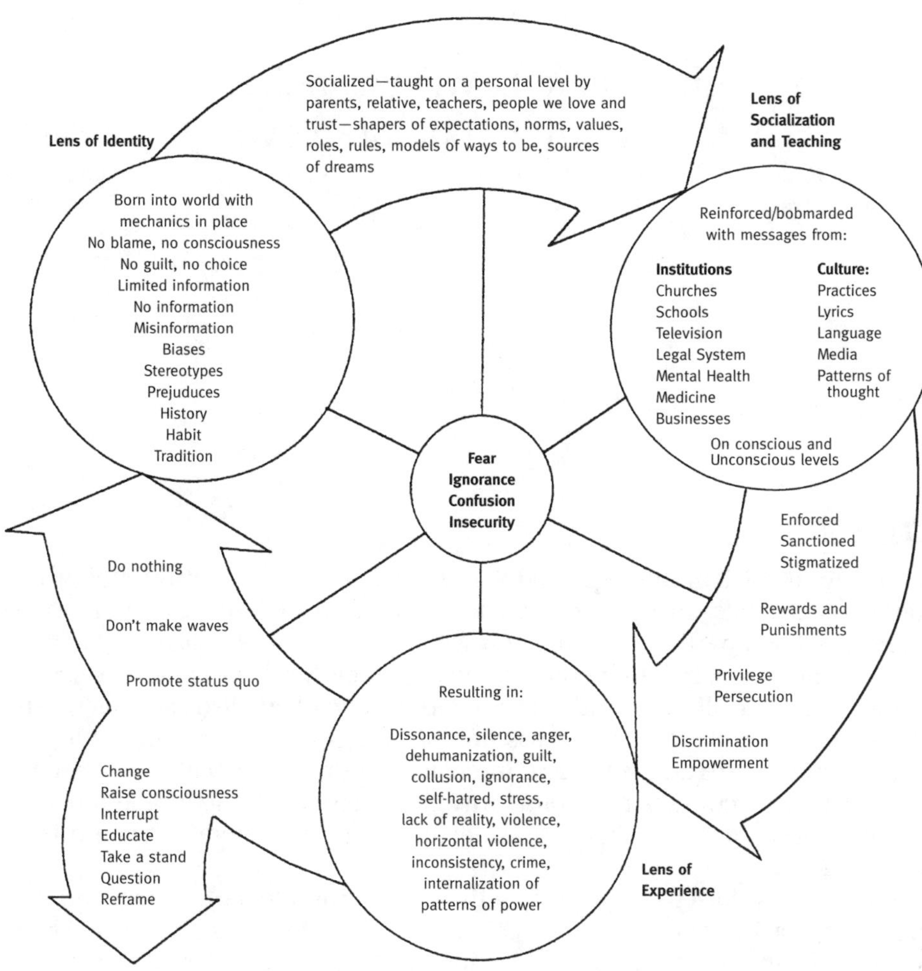

6

Racism Curriculum Design

Charmaine L. Wijeyesinghe,
Pat Griffin, Barbara Love

Introduction

Teaching about racism in the United States is a complex and emotional process. Participants typically bring to class a wide range of feelings, experiences, and awarenesses. Most participants sincerely want to learn about racism and how they can play a role in making their communities, schools, and workplaces welcoming places for people of all racial and cultural heritages. Yet fear, distrust, anger, denial, guilt, ignorance, naivete, and the wish for simple solutions can fill the learning process with surprises and emotional intensity. In our experience, however, participation in racism courses can transform awareness and encourage anti-racist action to reflect a more sophisticated understanding of and increased commitment to ending racism.

Our approach is based on the perspective that race is a social construction rather than a biological or genetic essence (Omi & Winant,1986). This perspective is supported by work in physical anthropology showing that there is at least as much variation among people within racial groups as there is between different racial groups (Jacoby & Glauberman, 1995). We believe that racial categories do, however, have potent social meaning. An understanding of the history of how racial categories in the United States have been constructed and legislated by North Americans of European descent to justify privilege, colonialism, murder, and theft of whole cultures forms the basis for our work (Takaki, 1993). This history is evident when various racial categories have been created or changed to meet the emerging economic and social needs of white United States culture (Steinberg, 1989). Racial categories artificially emphasize the relatively small external physical differences among people and leave room for the creation of false notions of mental, emotional, and intellectual differences as well.

In our racism classes we identify people of European descent as the agent group and people of African, Asian, Native American, and Latin descent as the target groups. The complexities inherent in addressing racism become immediately apparent as we encounter this key question: What are the indicators or determinants of racial identity if we believe race is socially constructed? Is it physical appearance? Is it family of origin? Is it cultural or political affiliation? Is it language? What about white-skinned Latinos? Why are Jews not identified as a targeted racial group? How about biracial people? What about the history of discrimination directed at Irish Americans in the United States? Where do Arabs or others of Middle Eastern heritage fit in this model? What about a white person with a distant Native American ancestor?

We address these questions in a variety of ways. First, we acknowledge that the models we use for understanding racism are not the only way to address these issues and that we are providing a starting point for discussion. We believe that any attempt to categorize people is inherently problematic and we invite different perspectives. Second, we make it clear that we are focusing on racism in the contemporary United States. Third, we invite participants to focus on not only how they identify themselves, but also how others identify and respond to them based on their skin color, language, and culture as they negotiate their lives in the United States. For example, we encourage a person of primarily European heritage who has a distant Native American ancestor to consider the extent to which he or she is targeted by society because of this heritage, and how and if this ancestry affects their ability to gain access to the benefits offered in society. Our goal is to enter a dialogue that will challenge students to understand racism and to become clearer about how their own racial identities affect their experience of relative privilege or disadvantage.

It is important when planning a racism course to take into account issues in the campus environment and in the broader social context that affect how students are thinking and feeling. A number of these issues shape the beliefs students bring into the class and are discussed in the section that follows.

Belief in Meritocracy and Individualism

Many students bring a firm belief that, in the United States, if individuals work hard, they will earn economic and social rewards that are just and fair. White students often express resentment about legislated interventions such as affirmative action or school busing because these strategies violate their belief in the fundamental fairness of American society by giving racial minorities or women what they see as an unfair advantage. When students bring these concerns to classes they provide excellent opportunities to explore the history of racism in the United States, differences between prejudice and power, white skin privilege and rights for all, patterns of discrimination, and the dehumanizing effects of racism on white people even though they are not targeted by it.

Theories of Racial Inferiority or Superiority

The publication of Herrnstein and Murray's *The Bell Curve* (1994) and the ensuing discussion of innate genetically coded abilities provide some white students with an easy explanation for the persistence of underachievement, poverty, and crime among African Americans and a misinformed justification for inequality and racial stratification (Fraser, 1995). This explanation also allows them to avoid understanding their own privilege and the need to take action against racism. Teachers in racism courses must be prepared to address the issues raised by these genetic or biological explanations for racial inequity and to help students understand them in the larger context of racism as a social and cultural phenomenon. Discussion of these issues provides opportunities to talk about how science can be misused to perpetuate racism.

Conflict and Antagonism Among Targeted Racial Groups

Sometimes conflicts arise within and among groups of Black, Asian, Latino, and Native American students. For example, there are rival antagonisms among young Black and Puerto Rican people that erupt in violence and loss of life, and inner city Blacks who resent Korean or Chinese shopkeepers in their neighborhoods. When this conflict is focused on claims about who is more oppressed, we believe it is important to acknowledge the differences in heritage and history of oppression for different groups in the United States as well as the differences in how targeted racial groups are treated. However, we focus on understanding the underlying dynamics of racism that affect all of these groups. Therefore, we stress the benefits of building coalitions and identifying costs of horizontal oppression and our belief that inter- and intra-group hostility is a by-product of racism in which targeted groups are forced into competing with each other for scarce resources.

Tendency to Focus on One Targeted Racial Group

It is important not to frame racism exclusively as a Black-White issue or as an issue based solely on skin color. This tendency might be more or less likely depending on the demographics of the geographic area in which the course is taught. Participants need to understand the particular dynamics of racism among racial groups in their geographic area as well as to become aware of racism in other parts of the United States. It is important to address the complexities of racism by including all targeted racial groups in class readings, discussions, and examples and by acknowledging the effects of color as well as culture and language on the treatment of targeted racial groups.

The Place of Ethnicity in a Racism Class

The relationship between race and ethnicity is not a simple one. We define ethnicity as a sub-category of race. In this chapter, we use the broad racial categories of White, Black, Asian, Latino/a, and Native American. Within each of these racial categories are many ethnic identities which often become blurred or lost within the broader racial designation. For example, the Asian racial category includes ethnic groups such as Chinese, Japanese, Thai, Cambodian, Vietnamese, and Pacific Islanders. White students often do not think of themselves as members of ethnic groups and may not know much about their German, Italian, Irish, French, English, or Scottish heritages. One of the trade offs for white ethnics who migrated to the United States was to give up their ethnic heritage in return for unnamed racial privilege. The same process, of course, did not occur for People of Color whose ethnicity gets subsumed under race. Understanding and identifying white ethnicity, especially European ethnicity, sometimes helps students understand how derivatives of Anglo European culture have come to embody the essence of what we mean by "American" culture. Identifying their ethnicity can also help white students affirm aspects of their white identities. We believe white students are better prepared to address racism with a sense of affirmation rather than shame or guilt about being white.

Some participants are confused about whether to identify Jewishness as a racial, ethnic or religious identity. Because Jews have a distinct religion, a rich tradition, language, culture, and history, they have been historically identified as both a racial and an ethnic group. We believe that there are unique historical aspects of Jewish oppression that distinguish it from contemporary United States racism targeting Blacks, Asians, Latinos, and Native Americans. We address the historical oppression of Jews as a separate issue in our courses and do not address it in our discussions of contemporary racism in this chapter. (See chapter 9 for a discussion of anti-semitism.)

Students with Biracial or Multiracial Identities

Discussing racial identities and racism with the implicit assumption that all students can clearly place themselves in one racial category or another denies the experience of many people. In reality, most of us are a mix of various racial and ethnic identities. The already complex nature of racism is complicated further for people who identify themselves as biracial and whose families include both agents and targets. As in other forms of oppression where some people do not fit neatly into binary categories (bisexuals, transgendered people), it is important to acknowledge the full diversity of experience with regard to racism.

Black Nationalism and Other Social Movements Encouraging Racial Pride Among Targeted Groups

As targeted racial groups become impatient, frustrated, and angry about the intransigence of racism in the United States, they identify strategies and philosophies that promote racial pride and empowerment for themselves and other members of their targeted racial groups. Many white students (and faculty) regard some of the spokespersons or leaders of these groups as divisive and controversial. Teachers need to be prepared to help all students understand these issues in the context of racism and to challenge students to consider the histories of oppression endured by targeted racial groups that leads to their advocacy of racial pride and empowerment.

Allegations of Separatism

On some campuses, Black, Latino/a, Asian, or Native American students prefer to live together in designated sections of residence halls, join separate fraternaties and sororities or other campus-based organizations, or participate in separate events like dances, Pow-Wows, and black homecomings. Many campuses also sponsor cultural centers for students of African, Asian, Latino/a, or Native American descent. In addition, many colleges include academic programs in African American, Asian, Native American, and Latino/a Studies. White students sometimes struggle to understand why these "special" programs are needed and express concern that their existence encourages segregation and, therefore, makes racism worse. These issues, when raised in a racism class, become opportunities to help students understand the pervasiveness of white culture on most campuses and the tendency to notice and name actions of target group members differently from the naming of actions of their own group. (White students' living and socializing together is not thought of as separatism.) Students can also learn the differences between chosen separation and forced segregation and the need for the former in a racist society.

Issues of Naming

Deciding what language to use to refer to different racial groups is a challenging process. Self-chosen names preferred by different racial groups change over time and there is no unanimity in preference for one name over another among members of the same racial group. The rigidity of insisting that only one name is acceptable antagonizes participants and violates the need to name oneself rather than be named.

In this book we have chosen to refer to the agent group in racism as Whites. We refer to the several racial groups targeted by racism as People of Color. Some groups prefer ALANA, which includes African, Latino, Asian, and Native American. When referring to specific targeted racial groups we use the terms Asian, Black, Latino, and Native American. We recognize that other names are preferable to some people and encourage facilitators to choose racial group names that are consistent with geographical norms and the needs of targeted groups to name themselves, rather than be named by agents.

Overall Goals

The overall goals of the design are to:

- Identify and discuss participants' racial and ethnic heritages.
- Understand our socialization into a racist culture.
- Learn definitions and guiding assumptions about race and racism.
- Increase awareness and understanding of individual, institutional and societal/cultural manifestations of racism.
- Understand conscious and unconscious racism.
- Explore the concepts of white privilege, collusion, internalized racism, and empowerment.
- Understand the experiences of people from different racial heritages.
- Explore the costs and benefits of working to end racism.
- Identify ways of taking action against racism in the personal, institutional, and community lives of participants.

OVERVIEW OF RACISM MODULES
Introductory Module (See chapter 5)

Module 1 (3 hours) Activities	**Module 2 (3 1/2–4 hours)** Activities
1. Welcoming, Warmup Activity, and Introductions (30 mins.) 2. Review of Goals, Guidelines, Agenda, Assumptions (20 mins.) 3. Definitions of Key Terms (25 mins.) 4. Ethnic Identity and Pride Activity (40 mins.) 5. Personal Timeline/Cycle of Socialization (60 mins.) 6. Closing (15 mins.)	1. Warmup Activity (10 mins.) 2. Definitions of Cultural & Institutional Racism (15 mins.) 3. Racism at the Cultural Level & Gallery Walk (60 mins) 4. Institutional Racism (90 mins.) Option 1: Video Option 2: Design a non-racist institution Option 3: Racism Timeline 5. Building a Web of Racism (30 mins.) 6. Closing (15 mins.)

Module 3 (3 1/2 hours) Activities	**Module 4 (3 1/2–4 hours)** Activities
1. Check-In, Agenda Review (15 mins.) 2. Review of Definitions of Key Terms (10 mins.) 3. Caucus Groups (105–120 mins.) 4. Dialogue Between Caucus Groups (60–75 mins.) 5. Closing (15 mins.)	1. Warmup Activity & Check-In (30 mins.) 2. Characteristics of an Ally (20 mins.) 3. Costs & Benefits of Interrupting Racism (15 mins.) 4. Action Continuum (15 mins.) 5. Spheres of Influence (20 mins.) 6. Action Planning (20 mins.) 7. Taking It with You (45–60 mins.) 8. Closing (30 mins.) 9. Evaluation (15 mins.)

Handout 6.1. Overview of Racism Modules.

Racism Curriculum Design

Module 1

Time Needed: 3 hours
Goals:

- Review definitions and assumptions related to racism.
- Identify and reflect on our own racial heritage(s) and identity (ies) and how our personal histories have affected our sense of heritage and identity.
- Understand our own socialization into a racist culture.
- Learn how racism is manifested in our own lives at the individual and interpersonal levels.

Key Concepts: oppression, prejudice, discrimination, social power, stereotype, race, ethnicity, racism, racial identity.

Activities:

1. Welcome, Warmup Activity, Introductions (30 minutes).

As participants enter the room, give them a copy of the reading packet for the session, a name tag, and a blank index card. Once all of the participants have arrived, welcome the group. Introduce yourself and give a brief summary of your background. To assess the hopes and concerns of participants, ask them to write an expectation that they have for the course on one side of the index card. On the other side of the card, they will indicate a fear or concern that they have about the course. Participants should not put their names on their cards. Collect the cards, reshuffle, and pass them out again so that each person receives someone else's card. Participants then introduce themselves, by name, describing something about themselves, and reading the hope and fear card that they received. Tell the group that the guidelines described in the next section encourage a safe space where these concerns are addressed.

2. Review Of Goals, Guidelines, Agenda, Housekeeping Details, Assumptions (20 minutes).

The general goals of the class and the guidelines noted in the introductory module described in chapter 5 should be posted and reviewed. Review the outline of the agenda. Remind participants of the starting and ending times of the class, where food and beverages are available during the breaks, the location of rest rooms, and any other details related to general personal comfort. In addition, invite participants to tell you of any particular comfort, access, or learning needs they may have.

3. Definitions of Key Concepts (25 minutes).

Using newsprint or overheads, present each term defined below and give examples of each. The more general concepts of *social group, oppression, prejudice, social power, stereotype, agent,* and *target* should be reviewed first (see chapter 5). Use examples of racism for each of these terms. For example, a discussion of stereotypes could include the misinformation that all Blacks are good basketball players, Native Americans are alcoholics, Latinos are promiscuous, Asians are good in math and science (see chapter 9 for a definition of stereotypes). Examples of the social power of agents (Whites) include the power to set, interpret, and enforce rules of conduct (the overwhelming majority of legislators, police, judges, and lawyers are white), the power to create societal images of what is valued in culture (by controlling the images presented in language or media), and the power to control access to certain opportunities (education, recreational facilities, social, or service organizations).

Additional terms that relate more specifically to racism can follow the presentation of the more general concepts.

Discrimination: The differential allocation of goods, resources, and services, and the limitation of access to full participation in society based on individual membership in a particular social group.

Race: A social construct that artificially divides people into distinct groups based on characteristics such as physical appearance (particularly color), ancestral heritage, cultural affiliation, cultural history, ethnic classification, and the social, economic, and political needs of a society at a given period of time. Racial categories subsume ethnic groups.

Ethnicity: A social construct which divides people into smaller social groups based on characteristics such as shared sense of group membership, values, behavioral patterns, language, political and economic interests, history and ancestral geographical base. Examples of different ethnic groups are Cape Verdean, Haitian, African American (Black); Chinese, Korean, Vietnamese (Asian); Cherokee, Mohawk, Navajo (Native American); Cuban, Mexican, Puerto Rican (Latino); Polish, Irish, and French (White).

Racial and Ethnic Identity: An individual's awareness and experience of being a member of a racial and ethnic group; the racial and ethnic categories that an individual chooses to describe him or herself based on such factors as biological heritage, physical appearance, cultural affiliation, early socialization, and personal experience.

Racism: The systematic subordination of members of targeted racial groups who have relatively little social power in the United States (Blacks, Latino/as, Native Americans, and Asians), by the members of the agent racial group who have relatively more social power (Whites). This subordination is supported by the actions of individuals, cultural norms and values, and the institutional structures and practices of society.

Individual Racism: The beliefs, attitudes, and actions of individuals that support or perpetuate racism. Individual racism can occur at both an unconscious and conscious level, and can be both active and passive. Examples include telling a racist joke, using a racial epithet, or believing in the inherent superiority of Whites.

Active Racism: Actions which have as their stated or explicit goal the maintenance of the system of racism and the oppression of those in the targeted racial groups. People who participate in active racism advocate the continued subjugation of members of the targeted groups and protection of "the rights" of members of the agent group. These goals are often supported by a belief in the inferiority of People of Color and the superiority of white people, culture, and values.

Passive Racism: Beliefs, attitudes, and actions that contribute to the maintenance of racism, without openly advocating violence or oppression. The conscious and unconscious maintenance of attitudes, beliefs, and behaviors that support the system of racism, racial prejudice, and racial dominance.

Handout 6.2. Definitions of General Concepts I: Racism (adapted from Hardiman and Jackson, 1980).

4. Ethnic Identity and Pride Activity (40 minutes).

This activity provides an opportunity to look at the varied parts of our ethnic and cultural heritage. Racially and ethnically, we are a patchwork of cultures and ethnicities put together in a person, family, tribe, clan, or community. We use the patchwork quilt as metaphor for the racial, cultural, and ethnic mixtures we represent, individually, and collectively as a group and as a society. Give the following directions to participants:

A. Take a piece of paper and divide it any way you want to by folding or dividing it into four sections.

B. In the different sections of the paper, describe the following aspects of your identity:

- Section 1: Where you are from. Draw a pictorial or symbolic representation of where your ancestors are from.
- Section 2: How you identify yourself racially/ethnically.
- Section 3: Describe an aspect of your racial/ethnic heritage that you are proud of.
- Section 4: Describe what you know about the heritage of your first or last name.

C. After participants have completed all four sections, ask each one to describe the patches on their quilt to the entire class. At the end of participant descriptions, ask each person to tape the patches on their quilt together on the wall to form a group quilt.

Processing

Ask participants to talk about how hard or easy it was to complete this activity. Participants can also talk about what they learned about their sense of racial and ethnic identity from doing the activity. While this activity may take a considerable amount of time, this sharing in the large group allows participants to learn about each other's background including similarities and differences in their experiences and sets a tone for self-disclosure. If time is limited, participants can talk about their quilt in small groups, and then discuss insights in the larger group.

Commentary

In our experience, Whites and People of Color vary in their responses to this activity. Whites often find it difficult to identify aspects of their experiences which they would attribute to their racial background, or may feel embarrassed by talking about being "proud of being white" since this feeling has often been associated with attitudes of white supremacy.

People of Color often identify with both their racial and ethnic heritage. White participants may be surprised to hear about the differences in experiences, since People of Color are often identified by race and assumed to have the same experience as others in their racial group, regardless of differences in their ethnicity. The scope of the questions for this activity can be broadened to include questions based on their class, gender, sexual orientation, religion, or physical ability, as well as their race. This allows participants to talk about how other agent and target identities affect how they see themselves racially.

Break (15 minutes)

5. Personal Timeline/Cycle of Socialization (60 minutes).

The goal of this activity is to draw out participants' early memories of being consciously or unconsciously taught messages about race and racial groups in order to build an awareness of how racism has affected their lives. Ask participants to reflect on the following series of questions, and talk with a partner about their answers. Ask participants to change partners for each new question. Keep time and tell participants when they should finish their discussion and move to a new partner. Some potential questions are listed here. The actual number and nature of questions chosen will depend on the time allotted to this activity, and the makeup of the group.

Questions:

- When were you first aware of yourself as a member of a particular racial group?
- When were you first aware of people from other races? Which races?
- When did you first witness or experience someone being treated differently because of his/her racial group?
- When was a time that you were proud of your racial identity?
- When was a time you realized that you would be treated differently because of your race?
- What are some times when you had (have) friends from different racial groups?
- Any other significant event in your life related to race or racism.

After participants have completed these questions, ask them to return to the large group.

Processing

Ask for some examples of what people learned from answering the questions and listening to the answers of others. Draw connections between the different experiences where appropriate, and begin to call attention to examples of early learning about race and racism and where they came from. After about 10–15 minutes of discussion, move the discussion to the cycle of socialization shown in Appendix 5C as a way of illustrating how we are systematically socialized by individuals, culture, and the institutions of society to accept a system of racial dominance and racism. Highlight the messages that people received about race and racial groups from family members that were both subtle and blatant, such as, locking car doors when driving through certain neighborhoods, making jokes about members of various targeted racial groups, not allowing them to play or eat at certain people's houses, disapproving of interracial couples, or avoiding in-depth socializing with people from diverse racial groups. Use the following text as a guide for describing the cycle of socialization:

> We are born without racist attitudes, values, or beliefs. Though we are born into social identity groups, we have no information about ourselves or about others. It is through the socialization process that we acquire the sets of attitudes, values, and beliefs that support racism.

Our early experiences reflect the influence of the culture and its institutions in socializing us to accept racist norms, values, and beliefs. Family, peers, and community are among our early socializing influences.

A variety of cultural influences support the socialization of racism. Powerful white role models such as the President of the United States, judges, Congress people, police officers, teachers, doctors, news commentators, television personalities, and historical figures are presented to us as contributing to the development of the country. The use of Whiteness as the standard of normality is an often unconscious part of this socialization. The designation "flesh" as a color for crayons, or "nude" as a color for women's hosiery, helps to internalize a notion of the pigmentation of White as normal. Linguistic socialization includes the assignment of positive virtues to Whiteness and negative values to Blackness. For example, heroes wear white hats and villians wear black hats; a pure heart is white, but an evil heart is black.

These early messages about race and racism are reinforced by our contact with other institutions including the media, schools, religious institutions, the judicial system, and the political system among others. In the educational system, this is reflected through differential access to education, including access to adequate preparation, being taught and counseled in a way that promotes growth and development, or the ability of some students to gain acceptance to colleges and universities because of a "legacy" of family attendance at a particular institution.

The media exert a major socializing influence on us. One example is the differential portrayal of People of Color and Whites. The majority of actors, commentators, writers, and producers are White. People of Color are often relegated to stereotypical or minor roles or roles depicting them engaged in criminal activity or violent behavior. This association is combined with limited portrayals of People of Color engaged in positive roles. In addition, People of Color are often associated with public assistance or with appeals for charity.

Religious institutions contribute to racist socialization in a variety of ways. Positive Christian religious figures are light skinned, while "villains" such as Judas and Cain are portrayed as dark skinned. The story of Noah is construed to provide a religious justification for slavery, as when Ham is told that he and his children would be servants.

The combination of messages that we receive from our families, our communities, the surrounding culture, and the institutions of society combine to create a social system based on the "Rightness of Whiteness," the systematic oppression of People of Color, and the collusion by individuals in the cycle of racism.

6. Closing (15 minutes).

As a way of drawing this section to a close, ask participants to briefly say how they are feeling, using one word or one sentence.

Facilitation Issues:
This section of the course is important since it sets the foundation and the tone for the modules that follow. Issues of trust and safety are usually paramount in the minds of participants. Working together to develop and *practice* the guidelines is important. You can be an active role model from the start by describing your own thoughts and feelings. Participants may feel embarrassed by examples of their own racism or internalized racism. They may exercise caution: Whites because they are afraid of offending People of Color; People of Color because they may not feel safe with white facilitators or participants.

Whites may sit back and wait for People of Color to teach them about racism, since some white participants will assume that they themselves know little about racism and will need to hear about it from the "people who have it done to them." Some of the People of Color may assume that they know everything there is to know about racism from their own experiences, and may be skeptical that they will hear or learn anything new. In groups where there are few People of Color, be particularly attentive to safety issues, and be sure that these participants are not asked to be educators for the entire group or spokespeople for their entire racial group. Assigned readings can provide information for all students to draw upon and elaborate.

Activities that examine participants' early experiences often carry an emotional component which facilitators should be aware of and ready to address. For some People of Color, recounting early experiences with racism can involve re-living situations where they or members of their family were targets of prejudice, discrimination, or violence, and may cause them to re-experience the emotions felt at that earlier time. For some Whites, realizing that parents and people who were close to them consciously or unconsciously taught them stereotypes about other racial groups may cause discomfort, anger, or sadness. It is critical in the processing of activities which stimulate strong emotional responses to affirm that one of the costs of racism is the emotional pain that it causes all people. We try to create safety for people to express some of those painful emotions while maintaining a clear focus that our goal is to create a productive learning environment.

It may be helpful to have one facilitator presenting or processing an activity while the other monitors the group for signs that individuals are in distress or need attention privately during a break.

Module 2

Time Needed: 3 1/2 to 4 hours
Goals:

- Understand conscious and unconscious racism.
- Identify and discuss institutional and cultural manifestations of racism.
- Examine the cultural and institutional privileges attached to Whiteness in society.

Key Concepts: culture, cultural racism, institutions, institutional racism.

Activities:

1. Warmup Activity (10 minutes).

Lead a general warmup of your choosing, one that can bring the group together, insure people know each other's names, and begin to get people interacting comfortably together (see Pfeiffer & Jones, 1972–81, 1982–present; Silberman, 1990; Eitington, 1984 for examples).

2. Definitions of Cultural and Institutional Racism (15 minutes).

On newsprint or overheads, discuss the following definitions:

Culture: Aspects of a social environment that are used to communicate values such as what is considered good and desirable, right and wrong, normal, different, appropriate, or attractive. The means through which society creates a context from which individuals derive meaning and prescriptions for successful living within that culture (language and speech patterns, orientation toward time, standards of beauty, holidays that are celebrated, images of a "normal" family).

Cultural Racism (Racism at the Cultural Level): Those aspects of society that overtly and covertly attribute value and normality to white people and Whiteness, and devalue, stereotype, and label People of Color as "other," different, less than, or render them invisible. Examples of these norms include defining white skin tones as nude or flesh colored, having a future time orientation, emphasizing individualism as opposed to a more collective ideology, defining one form of English as standard, and identifying only Whites as the great writers or composers.

Institutions: Established societal networks that covertly or overtly control the allocation of resources to individuals and social groups and that set and influence cultural norms and values. Examples of social institutions include the legal and criminal justice system, various forms of media, banks, schools, and organizations that control access to, or the quality of employment and education. In addition, since religious groups, family units, governmental bodies, and civic organizations influence social norms, policies, and practices, these agencies can also be defined as social institutions.

Institutional Racism (Racism at the Institutional Level): The network of institutional structures, policies, and practices that create advantages and benefits for Whites, and discrimination, oppression, and disadvantage for people from targeted racial groups. The advantages created for Whites are often invisible to them, or are considered "rights" available to everyone as opposed to "privileges" awarded to only some individuals and groups.

Handout 6.3. Definitions of Cultural and Institutional Racism.

3. Racism at the Cultural Level/Brainstorm and "Gallery Walk" (60 minutes).

In this activity, give participants examples of culture in the United States: language, music, literature, orientation to time, dress, family configurations. List some examples of these on newsprint. Discuss these examples with the group and ask participants to generate additional examples which you add to the newsprint.

Divide the participants into small groups of three to four. Assign each group one of the manifestations of culture from the list and ask them to think of specific examples of how it supports or maintains racism. Give each group a piece of newsprint and ask them to write their examples on it. After groups have had enough time to think of and record examples, ask them to post their newsprint around the room.

Ask participants to walk around the room and read the examples developed by each group. Attach an extra sheet of newsprint to the bottom of each list so that participants may add additional examples. Ask participants to note the similarities and connections among the various manifestations of cultural racism. A blank piece of newsprint can be posted at the front of the room and participants invited to jot down a thought or feeling after they have viewed all of the newsprint from the small groups.

Some examples of cultural racism:

Holidays and celebrations: Thanksgiving and Christmas are acknowledged officially on calendars. "Traditional" holiday meals, usually comprised of foods representing the dominant culture, have become the norm for everyone. The commemoration of the birth of certain Whites is accepted while the commemoration of persons of other racial groups, such as Martin Luther King Jr., are questioned or resisted in some states. Holidays associated with non-European cultures are given little attention in United States culture, for example, Three Kings Day, Kwanzaa, Chinese New Year, Cambodian New Year.

Personal traits: Characteristics such as independence, assertiveness, modesty, are valued differently in various cultures.

Language: "Standard English" usage is expected in most institutions in the United States. Other languages are sometimes expressly prohibited or tacitly disapproved of.

Standards of dress: If a student or faculty member dresses in clothing or hairstyles unique to their culture, they are described as "being ethnic," whereas the clothing or hairstyles of Europeans are viewed as "normal."

Standards of beauty: Eye color, hair color, hair texture, body size, and shape ideals exclude most People of Color. For instance, black women who have won the Miss America beauty pageant have closely approximated white European looks. One black musician who won great "crossover" appeal used surgery and cosmetics to eliminate features that were distinctly "Black" or "African."

Cultural icons: Jesus, Mary, Santa Claus, for example, are portrayed as white. The devil and Judas Iscariot, however, are often portrayed as black.

Use of language: The adjective "white" usually refers to good and pure, while "black" usually refers to evil, bad, impure.

Relationship to Time: In the European value system, time is money, and efficiency is of maximum significance. In other cultures, emphasis is placed on relationships and community. Europeans view time as specific, compartmentalized, incremental, and quantifiable segments. Other cultures view time as a continuum flowing infinitely.

Processing

As participants complete the gallery walk, re-convene the large group and ask people for any new thoughts, ideas, or additions to the lists. In bringing this activity to a close, re-emphasize that racism is more than individual actions and beliefs; it is part of the cultural fabric of our society.

Break (15 minutes)

4. Institutional and Cultural Racism (1 1/2 hours).

Option 1: Video.

To provide some variety in the mode of presentation, and to accommodate differences in preferred learning styles, we recommend showing a video, which illustrates different manifestations and effects of racism. *Skin Deep, A Class Divided,* or *The Color of Fear* are excellent videos for this activity (see the video reference list at the end of this volume).

Preview videos ahead of time to become familiar with the content and to develop processing questions to spark discussion after participants view the video. The video should be thirty minutes to an hour, with about half an hour set aside for processing participant's responses. Help focus analysis of the video by asking participants to note examples of individual, cultural, and institutional racism, and the connections among these as they watch the program.

Other activities that can highlight the three levels of racism include having participants 1) design a non-racist institution or 2) discuss a short presentation of the history of racism in the United States, using as a base a Timeline of Racism, such as the one at the end of this chapter. Each of these alternative activities is described below.

Option 2: Designing a Non-Racist Institution.

The goal of designing a non-racist institution is to have participants increase their awareness of racism by identifying attitudes, behaviors, policies, and practices which would have to be changed if an institution were to become non-racist. After brainstorming a list of societal institutions in the large group, divide participants into small working groups. Ask them to create a non-racist institution, on large sheets of newsprint, using words and symbols. Participants should explore questions such as:

(1) What is the underlying philosophy of this institution towards race?

(2) How does this institution acknowledge race, if it does at all?

(3) What racial groups are represented in this institution, and what positions and roles do they fill?

(4) What are some of the norms and values of this institution?

Add other questions that tap into how the hypothetical society or organization might address racism on the individual, cultural, and institutional levels.

Option 3: Racism Timeline.

Discuss a short presentation of the history of racism or the experiences of different racial groups in the United States (Bennett, 1961, 1988; Kivel, 1996; Takaki, 1993) using a Timeline of Racism such as the one in Appendix 6A and drawing upon assigned readings. The Racism Timeline should be written on newsprint or presented as overheads so that it is visible to all participants. Review the information included on the timeline. Choose one of the formats described below.

(1) Present a brief lecture based on materials noted above.

(2) Put historical events on cards or sheets of paper and the dates on another sheet of paper. Give different participants the sheets with dates printed on them and

other participants the sheets on which the events are printed. Participants should find their matching dates and events. Participants holding the sheets with dates should have several people clustered around them at the end of the activity.

(3) Post dates in sequence around the room. Give participants 3 x 5 inch cards on which events are described. Ask them to tape their cards on the posters (stand in the space) with the appropriate date.

(4) In advance, construct a racism history quiz. Participants complete the quiz, then discuss the answers to the quiz. Participants can score their quiz, give themselves a grade and discuss how much or little they knew about the history of racism and why.

(5) Construct in advance a racism history "Jeopardy" game, using the format of the Jeopardy television show.

Processing

(1) What feelings did you have as you completed this activity?

(2) What is one thing that you learned in this activity?

(3) What surprised you about this activity?

(4) What do you want to find out more about as a result of this activity?

(5) For the history activity: What events described in this activity did you learn about in school?

5. Building a Web of Institutional Racism (30 minutes).

The objective of this activity is to build an actual web in the classroom to illustrate how various institutions work together to systematically limit the full participation of People of Color in society. The actual web symbolizes the "web" of institutionalized racism.

Begin this activity by briefly reviewing the definitions of institutions and institutional racism (see chapter 7 for complete directions to this activity).

The following is an example of how various institutions are connected to perpetuate racism: financial institutions are connected to housing in that a bank manager may see People of Color as a greater financial risk than Whites and thus be less likely to offer them mortgages. Without a mortgage, people cannot afford to buy a home.

As an alternative to using cards and yarn in this activity, the web can be created on paper by writing the various institutions in a circle when they are first generated by the larger group, and then drawing lines to symbolize the connections the group makes among these institutions

Processing: See Sexism Curriculum Design (chapter 7) for directions for processing this activity.

6. Closing (15 minutes).

As a way to bring closure to this module, ask participants to identify a thought, a feeling, a question, or something that they want to share with the class. Go around the circle and give participants the option to pass if they wish.

Facilitation Issues

We have encountered participants, especially Whites, who discount examples of cultural or institutional racism as atypical or exemplifying the over-sensitivity of People of Color. Some participants may charge that there is reverse racism in education and employment as a result of affirmative action or non-discrimination policies. Still others may feel that the slight increase in the number of People of Color in positions in government, the media, or other professions are indications of the end of racism.

In responding to these statements, encourage participants to say more about what *they* understand the issue to be, so that they are pushed to go beyond a surface analysis to think of the issues underlying their position. It is our experience that participants often base their positions on traditional societal norms and beliefs which they take for granted without deeper reflection. Feeling comfortable with these challenges to "common sense" understandings of social inequity is difficult for participants who have never considered these issues before.

Module 3

Time Needed: 3 1/2 hours
Goals:

- Encourage Whites to explore the concept of White privilege and the costs and benefits of colluding with the system of racism.
- Encourage People of Color to explore the concepts of internalized subordination and empowerment.
- Listen to the experiences of people from different racial groups and create the opportunity for dialogue.

Key Concepts: White privilege, collusion, ally, internalized racism, horizontal racism, empowerment.

Activities:

1. Check-In and Review of the Agenda for the Day (15 minutes).

Ask participants what differences in their own perceptions they have noticed in light of the previous discussions. For example, have any of them noticed examples of racism in television shows? End this activity by reviewing the goals and activities of this module, and reminding participants of the guidelines that were identified in Module 1.

2. Definitions (10 minutes).

Introduce the following key concepts:

White Privilege: The concrete benefits of access to resources and social rewards and the power to shape the norms and values of society which Whites receive, unconsciously or consciously, by virtue of their skin color in a racist society. Examples include the ability to be unaware of race, the ability to live and work among people of the same racial group as their own, the security of not being pulled over by the police for being a suspicious person, the expectation that they speak for themselves and not for their entire race, the ability to have a job hire or promotion attributed to their skills and background and not affirmative action (McIntosh, 1992).

Collusion: Thinking and acting in ways which support the system of racism. White people can actively collude by joining groups which advocate white supremacy. All people can collude by telling racist jokes, discriminating against a Person of Color, or remaining silent when observing a racist incident or remark. We believe that both Whites and People of Color can collude with racism through their attitudes, beliefs, and actions.

Horizontal Racism: The result of people of targeted racial groups believing, acting on, or enforcing the dominant (White) system of racial discrimination and oppression. Horizontal racism can occur between members of the same racial group (an Asian person telling another Asian wearing a sari to "dress like an American"; a Latino telling another Latino to stop speaking Spanish), or between members of different, targeted racial groups (Latinos believing stereotypes about Native Americans; Blacks not wanting Asians to move into a predominantly Black neighborhood).

Internalized Racism: The result of people of targeted racial groups believing, acting on, or enforcing the dominant system of beliefs about themselves and members of their own racial group. Examples include Blacks using creams to lighten their skin, Latinos believing that the most competent administrators or leaders are white, Native Americans feeling that they cannot be as intelligent as Whites, Asians believing that racism is the result of People of Color not being able to raise themselves "by their own bootstraps."

Ally: A white person who actively works to eliminate racism. This person may be motivated by self-interest in ending racism, a sense of moral obligation, or a commitment to foster social justice, as opposed to a patronizing agenda of "wanting to help those poor People of Color." A white ally may engage in anti-racism work with other Whites and/or People of Color.

Empowered Person of Color: An empowered Person of Color has an understanding of racism and its impact on one's life without responding to the events and circumstances as a victim. Rather, being empowered means the capacity to engage individuals and institutions with an expectation of being treated well.

Handout 6.4. Definitions of General Concepts II: Racism.

3. Caucus Groups (1 3/4–2 hours).

This activity is only appropriate if the facilitation team includes a white person and a Person of Color. Invite participants to join one of two groups: People of Color or White. Encourage mixed race participants to choose either the white or people of color group depending on which group they identify with more strongly. Tell participants that they will spend the next hour or so in these groups, and that they will have the opportunity to share insights and thoughts about their small group discussion with the larger group afterward. The white facilitator then gathers the white participants, and takes them to the room that has been designated for their caucus group. The facilitator of color gathers the People of Color and takes them to their designated room. This dividing up, moving, and re-settling will take about 5–10 minutes and can constitute the break for this section. Once in the caucus groups, each facilitator begins the discussion by reviewing the questions that form the focus for that particular group.

Questions for People of Color Caucus Group:

(1) What thoughts do I have about meeting in caucus groups?

(2) How have I been affected by internalized racism and horizontal racism? How do I collude with the system of racism?

(3) How can I empower myself and others in the group to deal with racism in our lives, and to take action to end racism.

(4) What are the costs and benefits of actively confronting racism, and doing anti-racism work?

Questions for White Caucus Group:

(1) What thoughts or feelings do I have about meeting in caucus groups?

(2) How have I benefited from white privilege?

(3) How can I move from feelings of guilt and shame about racism to taking responsibility for my role as an agent of racism?

(4) What are the costs and benefits of becoming an ally to People of Color, and doing anti-racist work?

The closing discussion should include attention to issues that participants have about leaving their caucus group to rejoin the large group. Strategies to address these concerns include talking about how participants feel about their time together and about re-joining the larger group, discussing how to maintain safety and trust in the larger group, and the fairness of holding particular expectations of the other group(s).

4. Dialogue Between Caucus Groups (60–75 minutes).

When the caucus group time is over, bring the groups back together. Reiterate that the purpose of the caucus groups was to allow members of the agent and target groups to have separate time to discuss some of the specific ways that racism influences their lives. By referring back to the guidelines and asking the groups to acknowledge, though not necessarily agree with, each other's concerns, the exchange of information between the groups can begin.

Structure the dialogue so that each group has the same amount of uninterrupted time. Some suggested topics for white students to focus on include: a) What I want People of Color to know about me, b) Something I learned about racism, c) Something that makes me proud to be a member of my racial group, d) A question I have, e) Something I am planning to change in my attitudes or actions. Suggested topics for Students of Color to address include: a) Something about race or racism I never want to hear again, b) Something I want white students to know, c) Something that makes me proud to be a member of my racial group, d) Something I am planning to do to address racism, e) A question I have. After one group has presented, members of the other group(s) may ask questions for clarification, but should not question the legitimacy of the experience. If there are more than two groups, adapt the time spent in this section to accommodate additional report outs.

In closing the dialogue, make connections between this activity and those in the other modules and highlight how racism affects all of us. Whites are affected by denial of racism, since it requires them to develop an inaccurate sense of the impact of race on society. They are also affected by their emotions once they recognize racism. Racism can form barriers against authentic, open friendships between Whites and People of Color. People of Color are limited in their access to goods and services, and in their ability to establish a full and positive sense of self. All people have received misinformation and partial information about race and racism. Initiating change requires a conscious effort to break the system of racism, and an assessment of the costs and benefits of both keeping the system going or interrupting it.

Commentary

We have found that caucus groups are an effective way to encourage a level of sharing, challenge, and reflection that participants are less likely to experience in the mixed group. Caucus groups work well when participants have some level of awareness of racism provided by the activities in Modules 1 and 3. The facilitators in each caucus group should share the same racial identity as the participants in that group (White or Person of Color). If there are more than two facilitators, each can go into the appropriate caucus group, or can facilitate additional caucus groups of Whites or People of Color, depending on the racial background of the facilitator and the number of participants in either the target or agent racial groups.

Issues Associated with Splitting the Group: The splitting of the larger group into target and agent groups often has a profound effect on participants. White participants can experience some anxiety and doubt that they can have a meaningful conversation about racism without People of Color in the room. Many participants of color express a sense of relief that they will have a space to talk about their experiences without having to monitor what they say in the presence of Whites. They may also feel safer talking in a group just for People of Color because discussing how they collude with racism in the mixed group can be seen as airing dirty laundry in front of Whites. The distinct experiences of inter-group conflicts among Asian, Latino, Native American, and African heritage students can also add complexity to caucus group discussions.

As much as possible, encourage people to choose the racial group to which they feel personally connected and to which the culture assigns them. White people in interracial relationships may feel as if they are treated like a Person of Color when they are with their partners. They still receive privilege as a white person, even though they may have been subjected to racial prejudice because of their relationships with a Person of Color. Use the questions for each group as a way to help participants decide where they belong. For example, the group for People of Color will be discussing internalized racism, a concept not applicable to Whites. Unless a person experiences white skin privilege, the discussion in the white group will not be relevant to his or her experience.

Issues in the White Group: In the white group, some participants may deny that they as individuals receive privilege from racism, or that they collude, even passively, with the racist system. One way of highlighting the power and privilege of participants' white identities is to encourage them to explore the similarities in their experiences as Whites, and the differences related to other social identities. For example, a white lesbian, a white Jew, and a white man in a wheelchair will probably still have the same experience of seeing mostly white people in the media, being taught in school by mostly white people, living in districts represented by mostly white Congress people, and not being targeted *exclusively* because they are white. Help participants distinguish between denying privilege or being overwhelmed by guilt on the one hand, and being a responsible ally on the other.

Issues in the People of Color Group: Participants in this group may start a discussion about which targeted racial group has been hurt the most by racism, or attempt to create "a hierarchy of hurt." When this type of discussion occurs in the caucus group, it can be used as an opportunity to address horizontal oppression, the result of which creates tensions between targeted groups that deflect attention away from the racism of the dominant culture. While differences in experience and history need to be acknowledged, a comparison of who is hurt most by racism is generally non-productive, and tends to reinforce racist stereotypes and inaccurate information about different racial groups. The concept of empowerment, that is also part of the discussion for this group, calls us to move beyond this competitive system and to create new coalitions where the experiences of different targeted racial groups can be heard and valued.

Issues in Creating the Dialogue Between Groups: The dialogue between caucus groups can be a powerful experience for participants. For some Whites, it may be the first time that they hear directly the perceptions of People of Color or the emotional intensity that accompanies these experiences. For some People of Color, it may be the first time that they hear Whites taking responsibility for white privilege or talking about how they also are hurt by racism. When the report out from either group involves intense emotions, participants will need support to fully attend to and process the experience. Whites who are struggling with guilt feelings will need to be reminded of the difference between guilt and responsibility or encouraged not to retreat into denial because their emotions cause them discomfort. People of Color who are centered in their own experience of racism may discount the experiences of Whites, or may want to respond by challenging the legitimacy of Whites' feelings.

5. Closing (15 minutes).

Ask students in turn to use one word to describe how they are feeling about the topic of racism right now.

Module 4

Time Needed: 3 1/2 to 4 hours
Goals :

- Identify ways to take action against racism in personal, work, and community settings.
- Provide a framework for developing a personal agenda for action (next steps).
- Explore ways of empowering ourselves to eliminate racism in various areas of everyday life.
- Explore challenges faced in implementing action strategies.

Key Concepts: ally, spheres of influence, continuum of action strategies, re-entry

Activities:

1. Warmup Activity, Check-In, Goals and Agenda Review (30 minutes).

Choose a warmup activity to get participants energized for this portion of the design. After this activity, take time to allow participants to talk about reactions and thoughts since the last part of the class. At the end of this time, review the goals, concepts, and agenda for this module.

2. Characteristics of an Ally (20 minutes).

Begin this activity by reviewing the definition of an ally (see Characteristics of an Ally in Appendix 6B). To build on this definition and make it more concrete, ask participants to form pairs, and discuss a time when each of them experienced someone acting as an ally. This example may or may not be related to issues of race. Their discussion should focus on what that person did that made him or her a good ally, how others responded to the actions of the ally, and what participants can learn from this person's actions that they can apply to being an ally against racism.

After the pairs have been together for about ten minutes, ask participants to report out on some of the characteristics of good allies. Record these characteristics on newsprint as they are called out and post them on the wall for reference during the following activities. In this series of activities, encourage Whites to think of themselves as allies both to People of Color and to other Whites who are interrupting racism. People of Color can think of how they can support members of their own racial group, members of other targeted racial groups, and Whites who are interrupting racism.

3. Costs and Benefits of Interrupting Racism (15 minutes).

Ask participants to brainstorm some of the costs and benefits of interrupting racism. Examples include risking the loss of friends who choose to collude with racism, or giving up access to goods or services if certain companies are found to have racist practices. Sample benefits can include knowing others more fully without the fear, prejudice, or mistrust that racism engenders and having more accurate information about the contributions to society that are made by all racial groups. Record examples of costs and benefits identified by the group on newsprint and post this list next to the characteristics of good allies.

4. Action Continuum (15 minutes).

To prepare participants for developing their own personal action plan, present the *Action Continuum* (see Appendix 6C). Give examples of strategies for taking action against racism, such as reading a book on race or racism, attending a cultural or political event focused on different racial groups, confronting someone making a racist remark, or boycotting a company with racist business practices.

Break (10 minutes).

5. Spheres of Influence (20 minutes).

Present the Spheres of Influence (see Appendix 7E) and ask participants to brainstorm strategies for combating racism in each sphere. Participants can refer to the Action Continuum (6C) for ideas. For example, in the sphere of the self, a person could read a book, explore the concept of white privilege or internalized domination, or attend a cultural or educational event that will push his or her learning edge a little further. In the sphere of work, a person could examine the environment and culture of his/her workplace to see how inclusive it is of the values, contributions, and experiences of People of Color. During this activity, discuss how each action carries a certain level of risk which may vary in light of each person's circumstances. Interrupting a racist joke may seem easier with friends, but more risky with parents or a boss. Record the ideas generated by the group on newsprint and post them on the walls so that they can be used as references during the next activity.

6. Action Planning (20 minutes).

Give each participant an Action Planning Worksheet (see Appendix 7F). Ask each participant to identify at least three areas in which he or she can interrupt racism in the future, using any of the strategies in any of the spheres of influence. The action should be realistic in terms of that person's willingness and ability to carry out that particular action strategy. For example, a college age participant who is planning to confront her parents about racism, should be encouraged to identify the costs and benefits of different ways of dealing with her parents, and to identify realistic goals for this intervention, given her economic situation. Similar issues relate to a participant who is going to confront a boss or institutional policy that perpetuates racism in his/her workplace.

Give participants about ten minutes to create a change contract for themselves and to discuss it with a partner. Instruct the partner to ask questions about the timeline for completing the action strategy, possible outcomes of the strategy, the support needed in order to carry out the strategy, and sources of encouragement and support that can be used during the implementation of the strategy.

Remind participants to develop realistic action plans, while also stretching a bit beyond their comfort zone. A person's place on the action continuum will be a function of each person's awareness of racism, readiness, and willingness to take action, and where he/she is in terms of personal comfort zone (see chapter 5). For some participants at the beginning stages of awareness of racism, reading a book may be most appropriate. This action will give them more information and does not require them to confront someone else. Other participants who have more awareness of racism but who have not confronted racism in interpersonal interactions may be interested in strategies for interrupting racist or stereotypical comments or jokes. Participants who have worked to interrupt racism at the individual level can be encouraged to do anti-racist work at a community or organizational level, such as joining a local or national organization working for change, or participating in letter writing campaigns or boycotts against companies that discriminate based on race.

The more fully participants can develop their action plan (timelines for taking action, things that might block progress, things that might facilitate progress, potential support systems), the more they can use others in the class for feedback and support. Encourage participants to commit at least one strategy to paper.

7. Taking It with You (45–60 minutes).

Action plans encourage participants to carry their new awareness into their life outside of the class. To help participants make the transition from their experience in class to doing anti-racist work outside the class, divide participants into groups of four for a short discussion of implementation issues. Encourage participants to consider the level of risk for each of the activities in their contract, how they can minimize this risk, and what tools, such as listening skills or more information, they will need to effectively carry out their strategies. Some participants may want to to get more feedback on their action plans. Others may want to role play how they might interrupt someone making a racist remark or have a conversation with a relative about a previous incident of racism. Facilitators can serve as consultants to help individuals or groups use this time as effectively as possible.

8. Closing (30 minutes).

We believe that it is important to end the course by having facilitators and participants exchange appreciation for the level of attention, risk taking, care, and commitment that group members demonstrated throughout the course. As a closing activity, invite participants to talk about a new learning that they have had while in the class, a feeling that they have about the class, something that they are taking away from the class, or someone in the group whom they would like to appreciate.

9. Evaluation (15 minutes).

Participant feedback on the course provides invaluable information to the facilitators. Provide a method and time for both verbal and written feedback about the class activities and facilitators.

Appendix 6A

TIMELINE OF SELECTED KEY EVENTS IN THE STRUGGLE FOR RACIAL EQUALITY IN THE UNITED STATES 1819–1988

1819 Congress passes "civilization act" to assimilate Native Americans.

1827 *Freedom's Journal*, first African-American newspaper appears.

1830 Congress passes Indian removal act.

1831 Cherokees turn to courts to defend treaty rights in *Cherokee Nation v. Georgia.*

1831–1838 Indian tribes resettled in West in Trail of Tears.

1835–1842 Seminoles resist removal in Second Seminole War.

1848 Treaty of Guadalupe Hidalgo cedes Mexican territory in Southwest to the U.S.

1857 *Dred Scott v. Sanford* endorses southern views on race and territories.

1859 John Brown raids Harper's Ferry.

1863 Emancipation Proclamation; African-American soldiers join Union army.

1865 President Johnson begins Reconstruction; Confederate leaders regain power; white southern governments pass restrictive black codes.

1866 Congress passes Civil Rights Act and renewal of Freedman's Bureau over Johnson's veto.

1876 Battle of Little Big Horn; Sioux annihilate white troops led by General Custer.

1880–81 Helen Hunt Jackson's *A Century of Dishonor* influences public conscience about poor government treatment of Indians.

1882 Congress prohibits Chinese immigration for ten years, bowing to pressure from nativists in the West.

1883 Supreme Court in civil rights cases strikes down 1875 Civil Rights Act and reinforces claim that the federal government cannot regulate behavior of private individuals in matters of race relations.

1887 Dawes Act dissolves tribal lands and grants land allotments to individual families.

1890 Wounded Knee massacre; final suppression of Plains tribes by U.S. army.

1895 Booker T. Washington gives Atlanta Compromise speech.

1896 *Plessy v. Ferguson* upholds doctrine of "separate but equal" among Blacks and Whites in public facilities.

1899 *Cummins v. County Board of Education* applies "separate but equal" doctrine to public schools.

1898 Race riot erupts in Wilmington, North Carolina.

1902 Chinese immigration excluded indefinitely by Congress.

1905 Niagara Falls Convention promotes more militant pursuit of African-American rights.

1906 Race riot erupts in Atlanta, Georgia.

1909	NAACP founded.
1914	During Mexican Revolution U.S. troops invade Mexico.
1915	D. W. Griffith directs *Birth of a Nation.*
1917	Whites attack African Americans in race riots in East St. Louis, Illinois.
1919	Chicago race riot one of many in the "Red Summer."
1923	Ku Klux Klan activity peaks.
1931	Nine African-American men arrested in Scottsboro affair.
1934	Wheeler Howard Act restores lands to tribal ownership.
1939	Marion Anderson performs at the Lincoln Memorial.
1941	African Americans threaten to march on Washington to protest unequal access to defense jobs; Fair Employment Practices Committee (FEPC) prohibits discrimination in war industries and government.
1942	120,000 Japanese Americans sent to relocation camps.
1943	Ban on Chinese immigration lifted.
1948	Truman appoints Presidential Committee on Equality of Treatment and Opportunity in the Armed Services.
1954	*Brown v. Board of Education* rules "separate but equal" illegal.
1955	Rosa Parks arrested; Montgomery bus boycott begins.
1957	Little Rock desegregation crisis; Congress passes Civil Rights Act; Martin Luther King, Jr. founds SCLC.
1960	Sit-in Greensboro, North Carolina; SNCC formed; Kennedy elected president.
1961	Freedom Rides protest segregation in transportation; National Indian Youth Council formed.
1962	James Meredith enters University of Mississippi.
1963	Civil Rights march on Washington and King "I Have a Dream Speech"; bombing of Baptist Church in Birmingham, Alabama; JFK assassinated.
1964	Economic Opportunity Act allocates funds to fight poverty; Civil Rights Act outlaws discrimination in jobs and public accommodations; murder of Schwerner, Chaney, and Goodman; riots break out in first of the "long hot summers"; Democratic National Convention fails to seat the delegation of the Mississippi Freedom Democratic Party.
1965	Malcolm X assassinated; Voting Rights Act allows federal supervision of voter registration; Watts explosion; young African-American men in Mississippi refuse to enlist in demonstration against the war in Vietnam; Cesar Chavez organizes United Farm Workers strike.
1966	King begins Chicago campaign to organize vs. landlords; founding of Black Panther Party in Oakland, California; Mohammed Ali refuses to fight in "white man's war" and his boxing title is taken away; SNCC calls for withdrawal from Vietnam.
1967	Race riots erupt in Newark, Detroit, and other cities; King begins Poor People's Campaign; George Wiley starts Welfare Rights Organization.
1968	King assassinated; African-Americans riot in 168 cities and towns; Civil Rights Act bans discrimination in housing.

1970	Soledad Prison prisoners organize and prisoner support groups are formed on the outside; National Guard called to Jackson State and Kent State (students are shot at both schools).
1971	Inmates revolt at Attica Prison.
1978	*Bakke v. University of California* outlaws quotas but upholds affirmative action.
1980	Race riots break out in Chattanooga and Miami.
1982	Voting Rights Act of 1965 renewed.
1988	Congress apologizes and awards $20,000 to each of the surviving 60,000 Japanese-American internees.

Source: Compiled by L. A. Bell from Norton, M.B. et al. (1994). *A People and a Nation: A History of the United States* (fourth edition). New York: Houghton-Mifflin.

Note: This timeline focuses primarily on African-American and Native American events since 1800. Many options exist for constructing timelines for particular periods and focusing on the histories of particular or multiple groups. The point is to demonstrate both the recurring struggles and the occasional victories as a result of organizing and protest over time.

Appendix 6B

BECOMING AN ALLY

What Is an Ally?

An ally is a member of the agent social group who takes a stand against social injustice directed at target groups (Whites who speak out against racism, men who are anti-sexist). An ally works to be an agent of social change rather than an agent of oppression. When a form of oppression has multiple target groups, as do racism, ableism, and heterosexism, target group members can be allies to other targeted social groups they are not part of (lesbians can be allies to bisexual people, African American people can be allies to Native Americans, blind people can be allies to people who use wheelchairs).

Characteristics of an Ally

- Feels good about own social group membership; is comfortable and proud of own identity
- Takes responsibility for learning about own and target group heritage, culture, and experience, and how oppression works in everyday life
- Listens to and respects the perspectives and experiences of target group members
- Acknowledges unearned privileges received as a result of agent status and works to eliminate or change privileges into rights that target group members also enjoy
- Recognizes that unlearning oppressive beliefs and actions is a lifelong process, not a single event, and welcomes each learning opportunity
- Is willing to take risks, try new behaviors, act in spite of own fear and resistance from other agents
- Takes care of self to avoid burn-out
- Acts against social injustice out of a belief that it is in her/his own self-interest to do so
- Is willing to make mistakes, learn from them, and try again
- Is willing to be confronted about own behavior and attitudes and consider change
- Is committed to taking action against social injustice in own sphere of influence
- Understands own growth and response patterns and when she/he is on a learning edge
- Understands the connections among all forms of social injustice
- Believes she/he can make a difference by acting and speaking out against social injustice
- Knows how to cultivate support from other allies

Appendix 6C

ACTION CONTINUUM

Actively Participating	Denying, Ignoring	Recognizing, No action	Recognizing, Action	Educating Self	Educating Others	Supporting, Encouraging	Initiating, Preventing

Supporting Oppression ◄——► Confronting Oppression

Actively Participating: Telling oppressive jokes, putting down people from target groups, intentionally avoiding target group members, discriminating against target group members, verbally or physically harassing target group members.

Denying: Enabling oppression by denying that target group members are oppressed. Does not actively oppress, but by denying that oppression exists, colludes with oppression.

Recognizing, No Action: Is aware of oppressive actions by self or others and their harmful effects, but takes no action to stop this behavior. This inaction is the result of fear, lack of information, confusion about what to do. Experiences discomfort at the contradiction between awareness and action.

Recognizing, Action: Is aware of oppression, recognizes oppressive actions of self and others and takes action to stop it.

Educating Self: Taking actions to learn more about oppression and the experiences and heritage of target group members by reading, attending workshops, seminars, cultural events, participating in discussions, joining organizations or groups that oppose oppression, attending social action and change events.

Educating Others: Moving beyond only educating self to question and dialogue with others too. Rather than only stopping oppressive comments or behaviors, also engaging people in discussion to share why you object to a comment or action.

Supporting, Encouraging: Supporting others who speak out against oppression or who are working to be more inclusive of target group members by backing up others who speak out, forming an allies group, joining a coalition group.

Initiating, Preventing: Working to change individual and institutional actions and policies that discriminate against target group members, planning educational programs or other events, working for passage of legislation that protects target group members from discrimination, being explicit about making sure target group members are full participants in organizations or groups.

Created by P. Griffin and B. Harro, 1982.

7

Sexism Curriculum Design

Diane Goodman, Steven Schapiro

Introduction

Almost thirty years have passed since the reawakening of the women's movement in the United States and other Western societies. During that time, the struggle against sexism, and for women's rights and gender equity, has profoundly impacted society in the United States. This struggle has led to a reexamination of gender roles and patriarchal institutions, and a growing awareness of the relationship between sexism and other forms of oppression, such as racism, classism, heterosexism, and ableism. Yet despite, and in some ways because of the progress that has been made, there is also an anti-feminist backlash, with a reemphasis in the culture on hyper-masculinity and hyper-femininity as gender norms (evidenced in films, music lyrics, and MTV videos), an effort to redefine women as sex objects and to glorify the traditional nuclear family structure. Violence against women appears to be on the rise (from date rape to sexual harassment in schools), and women and children comprise an increasing percentage of those living in poverty. Women still earn only seventy-five cents compared to every dollar earned by men, and men still control nearly all of our institutions (Costello & Stone, 1994).

Nonetheless, we often hear today that we are in a post-feminist era: that the struggle for gender equality is over as more and more women enter the professional and business world and take on positions of leadership, and many men try to overcome the limits of traditional gender roles and take on a greater share of homemaking and parenting responsibilities. Many younger women and men see the issue as a matter of individual choice and ask what all the fuss is about. On many campuses, continuing efforts to critique the sexist bias in the disciplines and curriculum, and call attention to the sexist use of language and patterns of violence against women, are frequently met with charges of "feminist-fascism," "p.c. police," and "white-male bashing."

A profound confusion and ambivalence exists in American society today about sexism and feminism, so it is important that those interested in facilitating courses on these issues be aware of this complex context and prepare to facilitate discussion about the "hot topics" on campuses today.

Sexual Harassment, Date Rape, and Sexual Codes of Conduct

What is unwanted sexual attention? When does no mean no? What is consent? How are these terms defined and what are colleges and workplaces doing about them? Media attention on the Thomas-Hill hearings, the William Kennedy Smith date rape trial, highly publicized charges of sexual assault on many campuses, and the strict sexual codes of conduct that some colleges have enacted, bring these issues to the forefront. Recent studies suggest a disturbing pattern of sexual harassment in our middle schools and high schools (Stein et al., 1993; AAUW, 1993).

Both women and men need to know their rights and responsibilities. Women need to know that they do not have to tolerate unwanted or non-consensual sexual attention or contact and that recourse is available. Men who are concerned with acting in ways that are supportive and respectful of women need more information and dialogue in order to break old patterns of behavior and learn new ones. Those who hold actively sexist views need at the very least to understand the legal implications of sexist behavior.

The Myth of Equality

While women have increased representation in most professions, significant patterns of job segregation and wage gaps persist. Women are still largely absent from fields requiring backgrounds in math and science, and more and more women can find no work at all that provides a living wage. With this "feminization of poverty," women and children in women-headed households represent an increasing proportion of those living below the poverty line (Polokow, 1993). While studies show that men have been taking on some of the burden of household and child-care responsibilities, women still do far more than their share (Hochschild, 1989; Schor, 1992). Among working-class women, who have always had to work, the situation has changed little over the years. The intersection of racism and classism means that poor and working class women of color have benefited least from the increased economic opportunities available to women (Amott & Matthei, 1991).

The Interaction of Gender with other Social Group Memberships

Recognizing the ways in which race, class, and other social group memberships interact in defining one's identity and experiences of sexism is important. Facilitators need to be aware of the various ways in which sexism is experienced and also to understand how the various "isms" interact to reinforce one another. While sexism may be a primary concern among white heterosexual women and men, the same may not be true for lesbians, gay men and people of color, who may see racism or heterosexism as primary in their lives. Students bring all aspects of themselves into the classroom, and they need to understand how their multiple social identities shape their perspectives and experience of sexism, and that of others. We should therefore be careful not to assume a youthful, white, heterosexual middle-class standard of "normality."

The "Men's Movement" and Men's Rights Issues

In recent years, a men's movement has arisen with multiple forms. One form is reflected in the work of Robert Bly (1990), Sam Keen (1991), and others who emphasize male bonding and a rediscovery of what they call the "roots of deep masculinity." While some aspects of this "mytho-poetic" movement support the reexamination of masculinity, other aspects appear to promote a view of men as victims of women. Another "men's movement" among fundamentalist Christian groups, called The Promise Keepers, draws tens of thousands of men to large rallies in football stadiums across the country. This movement reinforces traditional concepts of masculinity and femininity and reassures men of their "rightful" place as heads of the family, breadwinners, and protectors of women. There are also men's rights groups organized in opposition to the women's rights movement that focus on specific issues such as child custody, child support and alimony, and opposition to affirmative action.

The more long-standing men's movements, including the pro-feminist, anti-sexist men's movement reflected in the National Conference on Men and Masculinity, men's groups working against violence against women, and those allied with the gay liberation movement, are more aligned with the goals of feminism. These profeminist men's groups acknowledge that while men may be limited by traditional gender roles and thus have a stake in the continuing redefinition of masculinity, their role as oppressors of women (both actively and passively) must be confronted. Their goal is for men to take responsibility for male behavior and to act in support of women's rights (Kimmel & Messner, 1993; Stoltenberg, 1993).

Participant Issues

As we attempt to educate people about sexism we often face not only ignorance and lack of awareness, but also a backlash of defensive attitudes that deny and discount the issue. Many suggest that women now "have it all" and that men need to protect their rights. Reactions may differ due to age and generation. For people who feel that they have adjusted well to traditional gender roles, talking about change can threaten their sense of identity and well-being. Women who attend the sexism class may not want to see themselves as oppressed and/or may fear losing the approval of men in their lives and thus shun the label "feminist" and discount the problems that they experience. Women in the group commonly come to the defense of individual men in the group, or of men in general. Men may not want to acknowledge male privilege and their role as oppressors, reacting defensively to threats to the status quo. They frequently become angry at what they may see as "male-bashing" or blaming men for the problem. The goal of the workshop is to provide a safe place for participants to explore assumptions and gain new information and perspectives that open the possibility for change.

OVERVIEW OF SEXISM MODULES
Introductory Module (see chapter 5)

Module 1 (3 hours) Activities	**Module 2 (3–3 1/2 hours)** Activities
1. Welcome, Warmup Activity, and Introductions, (30 mins.) 2. Goals, Guidelines, and Agenda (20 mins.)	1. Warmup Activity (10 mins.) 2. Cycle of Socialization: Sexism (30 mins.) 3. Definitions: Sexism and other

3. Attitudes toward Gender (40 mins.) 4. Act Like a Man/Act like a Woman (45–60 minutes) 5. Definitions: Sex and Gender (10 mins.) 6. Closing (15 mins.)	related terms (15 mins.) 4. Media Images of Women and Men (120–150 mins.) 5. Homework and Closing (15 mins.)
Module 3 (3 1/2–4 hours) Activities	**Module 4 (3 1/2 hours)** Activities
1. Current Images of Women and Men in Advertising (30–40 mins.) 2. Status of Women Quiz (30 mins.) 3. Institutional Sexism (60–90 mins.) Option A1: Video Option A2: Create a Sexist Institution (60–90 mins.) Option B: Violence against Women Option C: Web of Sexism . 4. Closing (10 mins.)	1. Feminisms: Definition and Theoretical and Historical Overview (45 mins.) 2. Men as Allies (20 mins.) 3. Strategies for Change (30 mins.) 4. Spheres of Influence (30 mins.) 5. Action Planning (30–45 mins.) 6. Closing (15–30 mins.) 7. Evaluation (10 mins.)

Handout 7.1. Overview of Sexism Modules.

Module 1

Time Needed: 3 hours
Goals:

- Create a positive learning environment.
- Develop an understanding of the ways gender role messages are communicated and reinforced, and the personal effects of these messages.

Key Concepts: gender roles, gender role socialization, gender identity, biological sex.

Activities:

1. Welcome, Warmup Activity and Introductions (30 minutes).

See Racism, chapter 6, for general instructions for this section.

2. Review Goals, Guidelines, and Agenda (20 minutes).

Ask participants to write on one side of a 3 x 5 inch card a hope they have for this course and on the other side a fear about the course. Collect, shuffle, and redistribute the cards. Ask each participant to read the hope and fear on the card they received and use these to discuss goals for the course and guidelines for participation.

3. Attitudes toward Gender (40 minutes).

Ask participants to pair up with a person they do not know. Tell them each person will have two minutes to answer the following question: What do you like about being female or male? After two minutes, ask people to let the other person have a turn. After approximately four minutes call time and ask them to find a new partner for a new question. Ask the second pair to discuss: What do you dislike about being female or male? Repeat the process for a third time and ask them to discuss: When was the first time you became aware that boys and girls were treated differently because of their sex? After participants have discussed all three questions, bring the whole group together again.

Processing:
For each question, ask volunteers to describe their responses to the whole group. Draw connections between what participants report and what the course will be addressing. For example, you can point out that the group will be discussing both the advantages and limitations placed on people because of their sex, and exploring differential treatment of boys and girls, men and women.

4. Act Like a Man/Act Like a Woman (45–60 minutes) (Adapted from Paul Kivel, 1992).

Divide the group into same-sex groups of about four each. Give each group a sheet of newsprint. Ask each group to list collectively what they learned growing up about how to act like a man (for male groups) or a woman (for female groups). They should consider the overt and covert messages from family, peers, neighborhood, media (TV, movies, books), schools, and churches/synagogues/temples.

Draw a large box on two sheets of newsprint or the chalkboard. Put the heading "Act Like a Man" on one and "Act Like a Woman" on the other. Begin with either the women's or men's group and ask each group to report the items on their list. If there is more than one group for men or for women, ask all the groups of one sex to report first before moving to the second group. Ask the groups not to repeat what another group has already listed. List the responses in the boxes labeled "Act like a Man" or "Act Like a Woman" respectively so that there is one list for each sex.

Processing:
After the lists are recorded, discuss the following questions with the group:

- What do you notice about the lists?
- Which messages have been useful? Not useful?
- What are some advantages of following these messages? What are disadvantages? (List advantages and disadvantages as the discussion proceeds.)
- How do these messages keep people in "boxes"?
- What are some of the consequences of stepping out of the box?

This discussion focuses on what is gained and lost by going along with gender messages and what we risk by stepping outside of these roles. It helps participants identify the costs and benefits of obeying these expectations. This can demonstrate both what male as well as female participants have to gain by challenging sexism (less pressure to succeed and be the breadwinner, greater emotional expressiveness), as well as how men are socialized to receive privileges in the society (given and assumed to be qualified for positions of leadership and authority).

This is also an opportunity to address how homophobia helps reinforce traditional gender roles. You can discuss (drawing upon the participants' responses) how the fear of being labeled "gay" or "lesbian" keeps people in traditional gender roles. This limits opportunities for both sexes to express all aspects of themselves, explore a full range of interests, and develop close and intimate relationships with members of their own sex.

Commentary:
Based on how people typically respond, these issues can be highlighted:

- Generally the female and male messages are opposite and complementary: Boys/men should be assertive and in charge; girls/women should defer to men and let them take the initiative.
- Often we get conflicting messages: Girls may be told that they can be anything they want to be, but don't be too threatening to boys, get married, and have children; boys may be told to be sensitive, but also be tough and don't show your feelings.
- Messages and expectations may differ due to age and social/cultural identities (race, ethnicity, class, religion). For example, younger women may have had more gender-role flexibility than older women. Some religious traditions prescribe more strict adherence to traditional gender roles than others. In the same way, ethnic and cultural groups vary in their adherence to gender role prescriptions.
- Sex roles can be limiting to both females and males. Both sexes can be discouraged or prevented from behaving in ways or exploring interests that do not conform to accepted gender roles

5. Definitions (10 minutes):

Post and review the following definitions with participants.

Biological Sex refers to the physiological and anatomical characteristics of maleness and femaleness with which a person is born.
Gender Identity refers to one's psychological sense of oneself as a male or female.
Gender Role refers to the socially constructed and culturally specific behavior and expectations for women (femininity) and men (masculinity).

Handout 7.2. Definitions of General Concepts I: Sexism.

Clarify the difference between biological sex and gender roles. Discuss how the previous activity illustrates how we learn the gender roles that are considered appropriate for our biological sex, and how our gender identity may differ from the gender roles that are expected of us. In some groups, issues about transgender persons may be raised. Definitions and information that may be useful in this discussion can be found in the chapter on Heterosexism and in Appendix 8A.

6. Closing (15 minutes).

Go around the circle and ask participants for a one sentence reaction to activities and information addressed so far.

Commentary:
Facilitators can create a supportive environment by enforcing the guidelines developed in order to allay fears that people are going to be personally attacked, or that

the class will sanction male-bashing. Encourage all members to participate in the activities, monitoring pairs and small groups as well as whole group discussions for equitable participation. Help all students develop an investment in the class in order to explore how sexism is an issue that affects everyone.

Some participants may resist the notion that gender expectations and stereotypes affect them, maintaining that each person is an individual. Beginning with their own experience and listening to similarities and/or differences in comparison with others in the group can help them discover commonalities and learn how gender role expectations affect others.

These initial activities also help you assess the knowledge level of group members, their openness to discussing this topic, and their skills in working collaboratively. This information can be useful to anticipate issues and challenges that might arise later in the course. If needed, you can spend some time addressing potential problem areas early on to prevent them from escalating later in the class. For example, it might be useful to review effective communication skills and to note typical patterns of unequal participation in mixed-sex groups to help ensure more equitable and productive discussions throughout the rest of the course.

Module 2

Time Needed: 3–3 1/2 hours
Goals:

- Understand the process of gender role socialization and the influence of social institutions upon our gender identity and behavior.
- Learn a common language and theoretical framework from which to understand and discuss sexism.
- Explore how advertising promotes and reinforces gender roles, objectifies women and men, and encourages violence against women.

Key Concepts: personal, institutional, and cultural sexism; prejudice, privilege, oppression, social power.

Activities:

1. Warmup Activity (10 minutes).

Select any activity that will help the group members get to know each other's names and feel comfortable interacting during the course (see Pfeiffer & Jones, 1972–81, 1982–present; Silberman, 1990; Eitington, 1984 for descriptions of warmup activities).

2. Cycle of Socialization: Sexism (30 minutes).

Using a diagram of the cycle of socialization as your guide (Appendix 5C), illustrate each part of the cycle with reference to gender socialization and sexism. Use experiences from your own life and solicit examples from the group.

- ***Individual Socialization:*** The early messages we receive directly and indirectly about what it means to be a girl or a boy. Use examples generated from the "Act Like a Man/Woman" activity.

- ***Institutional and Cultural Practices:*** The way the culture and our institutions reinforce sexist messages and shape our behavior.

Schools often do not include adequate information about women in history or their contributions to society, literature by women, females in central, competent roles in books, or support or encouragement for girls or boys to pursue non-traditional careers.

In the media, women are often depicted as sex symbols, and held to unrealistic and limited standards of beauty. Issues relating to women and girls in the news are also underreported or marginalized.

In the workplace, women and men are often channeled into traditional jobs; women's competence is often questioned and tested when they are in non-traditional positions. There are also pay and promotional inequities as well as sexual harassment.

- ***Reinforcement and Collusion:*** Both men and women are socialized to accept stereotyped expectations, norms, and practices, for example, sexist jokes and comments. In the workplace, male administrators do not include women in meetings, decision-making and the sharing of informal information. Women may prefer to work with men, defer to male opinions and male bosses, and fail to support other women. Co-workers do not see men and women who question or challenge sexist practices and gender inequities as "team players." These "troublemakers" may be punished with the loss of employment, promotions, or other opportunities. Women who challenge the status quo may be labeled "bitches," "women's libbers," and men can be called "wimps" and ostracized by other men.

Commentary:

Since the point here is not to blame people who have socialized us, make clear to participants that people often perpetuate sexism unknowingly, simply by going along with the status quo. This is especially true for parents, caretakers, and teachers who generally have our best interests at heart and do not consciously intend to miseducate us. People are limited by their own knowledge and awareness.

Discuss how our other social identities and experiences with other forms of oppression affect how we are socialized and how we experience sexism. In part, this comes from our own families and cultures. For example, some women may receive more encouragement and opportunity for educational and professional advancement than others based on variables such as race, class, disability, and degree of support from family members. Remind people to be respectful of the range of others' experiences.

3. Definitions (10 minutes).

Review the definitions of prejudice, privilege, right, and social power. If they were already presented in the introductory module (see chapter 5), you can review them more quickly. If this is the first time participants are encountering these terms, you may need to spend more time explaining them.

Sexism: The cultural, institutional, and individual set of beliefs and practices that privilege men, subordinate women, and denigrate values and practices associated with women.

Social Power: Access to resources that enhance one's chances of getting what one needs in order to lead a comfortable, productive, and safe life.

Right: A resource or state of being that everyone has equal access to, regardless of their social group membership.
Privilege: A resource or state of being that is only readily available to some people because of their social group membership.
Prejudice: A set of negative personal beliefs about a social group that leads individuals to prejudge people from that group or the group in general, regardless of individual differences among members of that group.
Oppression: A systemic social phenomenon based on the perceived and real differences among social groups that involve ideological domination, institutional control, and the promulgation of the oppressor's ideology, logic system, and culture to the oppressed group. The result is the exploitation of one social group by another for the benefit of the oppressor group.

Handout 7.3. Definitions of General Concepts II: Sexism.

This activity can be used to generate discussion about these terms or simply to present a perspective and language that will be used in this class. You should have a good understanding of any definitions you present and be prepared to provide examples.

It is not uncommon for males to challenge the notion that men are not oppressed or that women are not sexist. Acknowledge that, in fact, individual women can mistreat men and have prejudices against them. In certain contexts, women may have power to discriminate against individual men (women bosses, teachers, police officers), but lack social power in society at large. Reinforce the fact that women, as a group, do not hold social power in society as heads of major corporations, institutions, or media concerns, or as high elected officials or military commanders, and therefore are not able to oppress men as a group. There are not institutionalized policies and practices that systematically negatively affect men as a group. Participants should be able to make the distinction between individual prejudice and systemic oppression. If someone disagrees with this perspective, do not push the point. After participating in other class activities on institutional and societal/cultural sexism, it may be easier for participants to understand these concepts.

If women come to the defense of individual men in the group, or of men in general, point out how women are socialized to take care of men and urge participants to focus on their own experience and learning. If men in the group are angry at what they see as "male-bashing," let them express their point of view while once again communicating that there is no personal blame intended, but that we all need to understand sexism as a structural and systemic issue, while taking responsibility for our own behavior.

4. Media Images of Men and Women(120–150 minutes).

Introduce the videos by discussing how the media is an example of one institution that powerfully influences gender roles. Acknowledge that these videos may seem dated and ask participants to consider how much of what they present is still true of more recent advertisements.

First show the video *Stale Roles and Tight Buns*. Afterwards, give participants a few minutes to write their reactions to the video. Then form small mixed-sex groups of approximately four people to discuss:

- Their reactions to the video
- Which images they found most powerful and why

Next show the video *Still Killing Us Softly.* Afterwards, ask participants to discuss their reactions in pairs. Each person should have approximately three minutes to speak. Keep track of time so both people get a full three minutes. Then have participants come together as a large group. Discuss the videos using these questions, which may be posted on newsprint:

- What are your overall reactions (thoughts and feelings)?
- How do you think these messages about men and women affect you and others? For example, how do they affect self-esteem, body image, eating disorders, relationships among women and among men?
- What do these advertisements imply about race, class, disability, ethnicity, sexual orientation, and age?
- What connections do you draw between these ads and violence against women?
- How do these ads harm women and men?
- What images do current advertisements promote?

Some students, most often men, believe that the videos, particularly *Still Killing Us Softly,* take the issue too far and overinterpret the advertisements. Some students may focus on one specific example in the video and challenge the interpretation of it. Instead of debating each advertisement, focus the discussion on the overall and cumulative message of how ads shape perceptions of ourselves and others. Since most people find the videos compelling, allowing participants to share their feelings and the ways they have been affected by these images can help demonstrate the impact of the media on people's lives.

The videos and the discussion may bring up painful feelings for some participants. Be aware of emotional reactions and ensure that the issues are discussed in a thoughtful manner, using the guidelines established at the beginning of class. Be prepared to provide necessary support and to suggest resource material.

Alternative Ways to Discuss the Videos

There are many ways the videos can be discussed. Other alternatives include: 1) discussions in same-sex groups before a whole group discussion; 2) after reactions in pairs or in small mixed groups, a fishbowl format of same-sex groups in which one sex discusses their reactions while the other listens; or 3) after discussions in small mixed groups, a fishbowl of representatives from each small group to share what was discussed in their groups.

You can decide which format would be most effective for a particular group based on the degree of trust, comfort with sharing personal information in groups, the relationship between the males and females in the group, and time available.

5. Homework and Closing (15 minutes).

As a homework assignment, ask participants to review the portrayal of women and men in advertisements in various magazines. It is most effective if they consider ads from different types of magazines such as *Good Housekeeping, Sports Illustrated, New Woman, Ebony, Newsweek, Esquire, Vogue.* Have them pay attention to issues of race, ethnicity, class, disability, age, and sexual orientation. Ask participants to bring to the next session at least three examples of advertisements that reflect contemporary images of women and men.

Ask each participant to complete the following sentence: "One thing I am feeling or thinking about today's session is ________." Go around the circle allowing each person to *briefly* share their response. People may pass if they wish.

Module 3

Time Needed: Approx. 3 1/2–4 hours
Goals:

- Analyze the current images of women and men in advertisements.
- Examine the institutional and cultural manifestations of sexism.

Key concepts: institutional and cultural sexism.

Activities:

1. Current Images of Women and Men in Advertising (30–45 minutes).

Have participants form small groups of four or five people. Give each group a sheet of newsprint or poster board and some glue. Ask participants to briefly present the three ads they brought in for homework, identifying the magazines and what they think are the underlying messages. The ads should be glued onto the newsprint to form a collage. Have each group identify the main messages or themes in the collage.

Processing:
Have each group post their collage and discuss the main themes (not describe each ad). Ask participants to compare their themes with those raised in the videos and discuss any new insights this activity adds to their understanding of sexism.

2. Status of Women Quiz (30 minutes).

Have participants form pairs. Hand out a copy of the quiz to each pair. (See Appendix 7A and Commentary below for how to develop a quiz.) Ask each pair to discuss and answer each question. When the pairs have completed the quiz, review the quiz with the whole class, soliciting their answers and providing the correct information.

Processing:
After reviewing the quiz, go over the answers in Appendix 7B and ask participants to identify information that surprised or raised questions for them. Emphasize that sexism results not only from individual and interpersonal behaviors, but also from a larger social system in which women are denied equal rights. Help students make the connections between individual circumstances and the unjust social, political, and economic realities that women face. Be sure you can reference the facts cited and encourage them to do their own exploration if they question your statistics. Have participants do the quiz in pairs or small groups. This makes the activity more fun, and peer discussion encourages participants to think more carefully and thoroughly about the information.

We have provided a sample quiz. There are many ways to keep the quiz updated or to expand it. Check newspapers, magazines, and journal articles, recently published books, the organizations listed under resources, government reports (Census Bureau, Bureau of Labor Statistics, Office of Education), and regularly updated books of statistical data, such as *The American Woman* (Costello & Stone, 1994), and *WAC Stats* (Women's Action Coalition, 1993), which are listed among the citations. In constructing the quiz, be sure to include information that illustrates where progress has been made. The questions on the fact sheet can also be expanded to include a more global perspective that considers the status of women internationally.

3. Institutional Sexism (60–90 minutes).

Options for Module 3

There are several ways to address institutional sexism in Module 3. We suggest Option A described below. Two other alternatives, Option B and Option C are also presented following Option A. The choice depends on your skills and the interests and readings covered by the group. All three options in Module 3 begin with the "Current Images of Women and Men in Advertising" and the "Status of Women Quiz" activities, and end with some form of closing activity or wrap-up.

OPTION A focuses on exploring one example of institutional sexism that would be relevant to participants. OPTION B focuses on violence against women. We recommend that instructors choose this option only if they have strong facilitation skills, are comfortable dealing with this topic, are able to handle some of the emotions that may arise for participants, and have sufficient information to address misconceptions. OPTION C is geared for groups and teachers that are fairly knowledgeable about sexism and can think about it in more complex ways. Participants are expected to think about the interlocking institutional manifestations of sexism and envision non-sexist institutions.

OPTION A

1. Video: Institutional Sexism (75–105 minutes):

Choose a video on institutional sexism issues that is relevant to the group, such as employment, economics, health, or education. (See video resources at the end of the book for suggestions.) Choose one that is a half hour to one hour in length. Allow at least 30–45 minutes to discuss the video. Develop questions in advance to guide the discussion.

Discussing the Video:

The discussion of the video can utilize any of the formats already covered, such as pairs or small groups, then whole group discussion. Some useful general questions are:

- What are your overall reactions to the video?
- How is what was presented similar to or different from your own experience or previous knowledge?
- What questions or issues did it raise for you?

2. Create a Sexist Institution (60–90 minutes):

With the whole group, brainstorm a broad and inclusive list of social institutions. These could include schools and colleges, restaurants, businesses, government or social service agencies, military, political or religious organizations. Ask participants to form small groups of four to five people and to choose one institution to work on. Give each group newsprint and magic markers. Ask them to design a sexist version of the institution they chose. They should list as many of the behaviors, practices, procedures, policies, and structures that would shape and ensure institutional sexism. Circulate among the groups and assist with any problems that may arise. After about thirty minutes, ask the groups to reunite into a large group and describe their designs.

Processing:
After each group has discussed its design, lead a discussion using the following questions:

- What do you notice about the different institutions that were designed? How are they similar?
- How did you come up with the ideas for your institutions? Were they based on experience or information you already had about institutional sexism?
- What values and attitudes are reflected in these institutions?
- How are these designs similar to what actually exists in real institutions?
- In what ways could these institutions be changed to be less sexist and more equitable?

OPTION B: Violence against Women

Additional Goals:

- To explore gender differences in how fears of personal violence affect our lives.
- To better understand violence against women.

1. Concerns about Personal Safety (30–40 minutes).

Ask the men to brainstorm all the things that they do on a daily basis to feel safe or protect themselves from physical harm from others. Record their answers on newsprint. When the men have finished, ask the same question of the women and record their answers. After both lists are completed, ask participants for their observations on the two lists.

Have them discuss:

- What differences do you notice in the two lists?
- How do you account for the differences?
- How do these concerns affect the lives of men and women?

Processing:
Generally, the men's list is quite short, with items such as locking one's door, while the women's list is quite long, with a wide variety of measures, such as not walking alone, carrying mace, not walking in certain places and at certain times of the day, and checking their car before getting in. Since the men's list is shorter than the women's, asking the men to go first has greater impact in demonstrating the differences between men's and women's experiences.

In summary, note how women are much more concerned about their safety on a daily basis. While men may give some thought to physical safety, they generally have little worry about sexual assault, which is of paramount concern for most women. As a result of sexism, women and men experience different feelings of safety and ability to move about freely in the world.

2. Video: Violence Against Women (Rape/Acquaintance Rape, Domestic Violence, Sexual Harassment) (90–105 minutes).

Choose a video (see video resources at end of book for suggestions) that addresses an issue related to violence against women that is relevant to the group. Choose one that is a half hour to an hour in length. Allow at least 30–45 minutes for discussion. Before showing the video, prepare participants for the content and acknowledge that some people may find it difficult to watch. Give participants the option of choosing to leave the room during all or part of the video. If someone leaves the room, follow-up with them and invite them back when the video is over.

Processing:
Due to the sensitive nature of these issues, we suggest that participants have an opportunity to first react to the video in small same-sex groups or dyads. Appropriate discussion questions will depend on the video selected. Many come with discussion guides. In all cases, encourage students to share their reactions to the video, and their own experiences related to the content, and to make connections with other information and theory discussed in the class so far. Be prepared with accurate information about the topic to dispel myths and stereotypes and to clarify misunderstandings of the issue. Also, be aware of students' emotions and affect during the discussion following the video. Check in with or follow-up with participants as you feel necessary.

OPTION C : For Groups More Knowledgeable about Sexism

1. Web of Sexism (30–45 minutes).

With the group, brainstorm a broad and inclusive list of societal institutions such as large corporations, day care, churches, educational institutions, media organizations, the welfare system, the military, the advertising industry, the legal system, and governmental bodies. Try to think of as many institutions as there are members in the group. Ask each participant to choose one institution they would like to represent and to write the institutions on a badge or index card and tape it to a visible place on their body. (Make sure that each institution is represented by a different person.)

Have the group stand in a circle and call out the name of their institution. Hold onto the end of a ball of string or yarn. Throw the ball to someone in the circle and instruct them to throw the ball to another institution in the circle (wrapping the yarn around her/his wrist before throwing the ball). The participant should then identify how her/his institution and the other institution are aligned or affiliated in supporting sexism, whether overtly or covertly.

For instance, someone representing day care centers could throw the string to someone representing welfare. They could then explain how day care is not widely available to women, making it difficult for women with young children to work outside the home, and that jobs in day care, which are seen as women's work, often do not pay a living wage, again forcing such women to rely on public assistance for support. The person representing welfare might then throw the string to someone representing the media and explain how the media perpetuates the image of women on welfare as lazy and shiftless, having babies in order to get on the dole. The string might then go from the media to the advertising industry, with an explanation of how images of men and women in the media and advertising reinforce each other in an effort to sell products that perpetuate idealized and unrealistic images of men and women in the media.

Each person should continue to toss the string to another, explaining the connection between her/his institution and the next institution, until all in the circle have become part of the giant web. Then, have all in the circle step back until the web is visible as a taut, entwined object, representing those institutionalized practices that keep sexism alive. You can point out that as we cut or weaken some aspects of the web, it becomes less strong and taut, and if we all do our part to undo sexism within the institutions with which we interact, we can begin to unravel the entire web.

If participants have trouble on their own thinking of examples of institutionalized sexism and how various institutions are connected, then ask the group to provide some examples. With a less advanced group, this activity can be framed from the start as more of a group activity, broadening the sources of data, taking the pressure off of individuals, and incorporating information covered in readings or other information sources.

2. Additional Activity: Unraveling the Web (30 minutes).

The group can reverse the process of building the web in order to gradually unravel it, brainstorming ways to attack or work against some of the examples of and connections between the manifestations of institutionalized sexism that have been identified, and throwing the string back to where it came from. For instance, throwing the yarn back from the advertising industry to the media, one could point out possible anti-sexist actions, such as organizing boycotts or letter writing campaigns against companies that use sexist advertising or educating children to become critically aware of the sexist images embedded in many advertisements. (This "unraveling exercise" would double the amount of time needed for the activity.)

Processing:
At the end of the activity, summarize some of the connections made. Emphasize the importance of understanding sexism as consisting of interrelated, institutionalized practices and the need for social change efforts to address these various aspects.

3. Create a Non-Sexist Institution (60-90 minutes).

Conduct the activity in the same way as "Create a Sexist Institution," described above in Option A, except participants will be designing a *non*-sexist one. In designing a non-sexist institution, a group with more knowledge of sexism is challenged to create something new, using their understanding of the dynamics of sexism. This activity encourages them to envision that institutions can change and how they might do so.

Facilitation Issues:
There may be students who are unwilling to question the status quo or consider different perspectives. Some people may feel that you are only focusing on the negative and ignoring all the ways women have achieved equality. Acknowledge that it is important to recognize positive changes and accomplishments as well as areas that continue to need reform. In addition, some participants may continue to challenge the notion that there is any intent behind the institutional patterns of sex discrimination or violence and insist that they are not affected by them. Help students explore the difference between intended and unintended consequences. Explain

how we need to consider the *consequences* of particular behaviors and practices, whether or not they are *intended* to be discriminatory or hurtful.

4. Closing (for all three options) (10 minutes).

Ask participants to complete one of the following statements as a way of summarizing their learnings for this segment of the course: I think. . . . I hope. . . . I feel. . . .

Module 4

Time needed: 3 1/2 hours
Goals:

- Gain a general understanding of feminism(s).
- Identify a range of actions that can be taken to interrupt sexism on the personal, interpersonal, institutional, and cultural levels.
- Plan and commit to taking an action to interrupt sexism.
- Identify and develop strategies for overcoming difficulties in implementing action plans.

Key concepts: feminism(s), feminist movement, ally, spheres of influence, action strategies.

Activities:

1. Feminism(s): Definition and Theoretical and Historical Overview (45 minutes).

Have each participant anonymously write her/his definition of feminism on an index card. Collect cards and redistribute them. Have each person read aloud the new card. Discuss what issues participants included or left out and some assumptions implicit in their definitions. Then present the following definition:

> *Feminism* is the valuing of women, and the belief in and advocacy for social, political, and economic equality and liberation for both women and men. Feminism questions and challenges patriarchal social values and structures that serve to enforce and maintain men's dominance and women's subordination (adapted from Cyrus, 1993, 218–19).

Present a brief theoretical and historical overview of feminism and review the timeline of key events in the struggles for women's rights in the United States. A sample presentation and timeline are provided in Appendix C and D, and can build upon and review information in the reading assignments. We suggest that you post the timeline on the wall for people to view as you read and discuss it. We encourage you to develop your own presentation style for addressing key issues and approaches to feminism.

Commentary:
This activity will help clarify many of the myths and distortions about feminism and the women's movement and illustrate some of the various perspectives within feminism. As the focus of the course shifts from identifying sexism towards working to eliminate it, it is useful for participants to be aware that there are many ways to analyze the causes of sexism and to strategize toward creating greater equality.

Highlight the concept that feminism is not a monolithic movement in which everyone thinks the same way. Show that it has involved many different efforts by a variety of people, and that it has addressed sexism on multiple levels, individual, cultural, and institutional. Understanding that feminism and feminists are not "women who hate men" may open the way for participants to be more supportive and active in feminist causes.

To extend this activity, you can discuss with participants how the definitions presented are similar or different from what they wrote, or heard from the group, and explore the assumptions underlying the various definitions. Participants could discuss why they or others identify with or reject the label "feminist" and men's role in feminism.

2. Men As Allies (20 minutes).

Since this session attempts to help people move from awareness about sexism, to planning actions to interrupt sexism, it is important to help participants think about how they, as women and men, can support each other in their efforts to initiate change at personal and societal levels. The following definition of an ally offers a useful framework for beginning to think about action.

> *Ally:* A member of the agent group who rejects the dominant ideology and takes action against oppression out of a belief that eliminating oppression will benefit both agents and targets. See Appendix 6B for characteristics of allies.

This activity can be a particularly useful way for men to learn about how they can be supportive of women in working against sexism and identify what kinds of actions may be appropriate. It can also lead to a discussion about the responsibility of men to reflect on how they can work on their own behavior, and that of other men, as they attempt to interrupt the norms of behavior that support the status quo. It can also help women to identify ways in which they can support one another in becoming more empowered to take action against sexism.

3. Strategies for Change (30 minutes).

To introduce this activity, remind participants that since sexism has many different manifestations, there are many ways we can work against it in our lives. Refer back to the levels of sexism and the fact sheet to demonstrate this point. Also use the historical perspective to illustrate the various ways people have worked for women's rights and change.

Post one sheet of newsprint titled "individual/interpersonal" and another titled "institutional/cultural." Ask participants to brainstorm as many strategies as they can think of that would address sexism on these two levels. You may want to provide some examples to start the process. Record each idea on the appropriate list. Since this is a brainstorm, focus on generating as many ideas as possible, not on evaluating them. Participants do not need to like or agree with all of the strategies listed. The point is to create as long and inclusive a list as possible. Try to ensure that both lists have several items.

Some possible strategies for *individual/interpersonal* include:

- Interrupt sexist jokes or comments (or do not tell them).
- Change use of sexist or biased language and use gender neutral language.

- Take down sexist posters.
- Change sex-stereotyped behavior, e.g., women: speak up more, be less passive and accommodating, do tasks traditionally assigned to males; men: listen more, do not dominate conversations, do tasks traditionally assigned to females.

Some possible strategies for *institutional/cultural* include:

- Join an activist organization (list some local groups).
- Organize a boycott of a product/movie you find sexist and offensive.
- Write letters to the editor.
- Write letters or organize a letter writing campaign to manufacturers of products/ TV shows that you find offensive.
- Organize educational events.
- Organize a march or demonstration.
- Organize a petition drive.
- Create or change a policy in your school/organization (e.g., regarding sexual harassment, family leaves).
- Investigate and publicize inequitable practices in your school/organization (e.g., hiring and promotion practices, pay scales, funding of sports/activities).

After participants have finished brainstorming, add any additional strategies you can offer. Then ask participants to share "success stories" with the whole group, about times when they actually did act to interrupt sexism. You may want to have the group applaud after each person tells their success story. Reinforce the fact that even small efforts are a step in the right direction.

Processing:
After students have told their "success stories," identify some of the main points or themes that may be helpful for others trying to work for change. Some themes from stories of participants that can be highlighted as points to consider when working for change are:

- Be persistent—change takes time and often occurs incrementally.
- There is power in numbers—working collectively can be more effective than working alone.
- Be well-informed; know your facts.
- Provide workable alternatives to what you are criticizing.
- Be nonjudgmental and constructive when trying to interrupt or change someone's attitudes or behavior.
- Get personal support.

4. Spheres of Influence (30 minutes).

Explain that this activity is designed to help participants look at different spheres of their lives in which they have influence and to identify actions they might take in each sphere to interrupt sexism. In doing so, they can refer to the lists generated in the preceding activity on identifying strategies for change.

Present the spheres of influence (see Appendix 7E), which includes concentric circles starting with self, and then includes friends, family, work, school, and community in ever broader circles. Participants can be given a copy of the spheres of influence to use as a work sheet. Ask participants to brainstorm strategies for combating sexism in each sphere of influence. For example, in the sphere of the self, a person could read a book about feminism or women's history, explore the concept of male privilege or internalized oppression, or attend a cultural or educational event to learn more about some issue in relation to sexism. In the sphere of close friends or family, a person could examine and change their ways of relating to others to act in more empowered or less oppressive ways. For women, that might mean speaking up more for themselves and being less deferential to men. For men, that might mean putting others' needs first and not interrupting or putting down women in conversation. In the sphere of school, a person could examine the percentage of women among tenured faculty or senior administrators, point out the results to others, and, if there are few women in decision-making roles, organize a protest. In the sphere of the community, a person could volunteer to work at a battered women's shelter or organize a group of men to work to oppose violence against women.

Ask participants to draw their own spheres of influence in concentric circles and in each sphere identify and write down one or two actions they might take to interrupt sexism. In groups of three or four, participants should share their ideas for possible actions, thinking together about the possible risks of each action, its chances for success, and its potential impact.

Processing:
In the large group, ask participants to share insights or helpful hints that may have come up in their small groups in regard to choosing and planning actions. Focus the follow-up discussion on the need to select plans that are realistic, have some chance for success, and for which the risks do not outweigh the possible benefits. At this point, suggest that participants who are thinking about actions that can best be taken collectively share their ideas with the large group and see whether there are others who might like to work collaboratively in planning and carrying out an action plan.

5. Action Planning (30–45 minutes).

Ask each participant to decide on one of the possible actions they listed and fill out an Action Planning Worksheet (Appendix 7F), which asks them to consider in depth the possible outcomes of the strategy, the risks and obstacles involved, the timeline for implementation, the supports needed, and where they might find them.

In the same groups of three or four that were used for the spheres of influence, have students share their plans with one another, asking for help in completing the form if necessary. They should also be encouraged to make plans to check in with one another after a set period of time (perhaps two weeks or a month) to let each other know how their actions worked out. Participants can also be asked to write a letter to themselves about their action plan, which you can mail to them in about a month as a reminder.

Processing:
In the large group, ask each participant to briefly describe their plan, in the process making a public commitment to carry it out.

6. Closing (15–30 minutes).

Invite participants to form a circle and say a few words about a significant new learning, a strong feeling, some new understanding that they are taking from the course, or someone whom they would like to appreciate. The facilitators should also join in this activity, sharing their own learnings and feelings, and expressing any appreciations they might have for the group as a whole. It is often a good idea for one of the facilitators to go first and model the level of sharing that might be expected.

7. Evaluation (10 minutes).

Participants should have the opportunity to provide some written, anonymous evaluation of the course.

Appendix 7A

STATUS OF WOMEN QUIZ

1. The total number of men who have served in Congress from its inception through 1992 is 11,096. The total number of women is _____.

2. After the 1992 election, the number of women in the House of Representatives rose from 28 to _____.

3. After the 1992 election, the number of women in the Senate rose from 2 to _____.

4. The references to women on the front page of 10 major and 10 smaller market newspapers around the country averaged _____% during the month of February, 1991.

5. Of the 49,088 roles cast in Screen Actors Guild (SAG) film and TV projects in 1989, the largest number, 41.1%, were male supporting roles. The smallest number ____ were female leading roles.

6. In 1992, women constituted ___ % of all CEO's of regionally accredited colleges and universities.

7. The maternal mortality rate for Whites is 5.9 deaths per thousand; for African Americans, it is ____ per thousand.

8. Families headed by women (no spouse present) increased from 10.9% in 1970 to ____% in 1991. Families headed by men (no spouse present) increased from 2.4% in 1970 to ____% in 1991.

9. In 1992, nearly _____% of employed women who had children under the age of three worked full-time.

10. In 1992, of the nation's 6 million employers, _____ provided some form of child care assistance.

11. In the United States, fathers currently owe mothers _____ dollars in unpaid child support.

12. Nearly ____% of full-time working women, and 37% of full-time working men, earn less than $20,000.

13. In 1984, women overall earned 67.8 cents for every dollar a man earned. In 1992, women earned ____ for every dollar men earned.

14. In 1991, Latinas who worked full time, year round, earned about ____% more than their counterparts in 1976 (earnings are adjusted for inflation).

15. In 1992, the unemployment rate was: for white women ____%; black women ____%; and Latinas ____%.

16. In 1992, the percentage of employed women who were working in administrative support jobs was ______.

17. While there have been significant increases of women in professional jobs, women are only about ____% of skilled blue-collar workers.

18. The average salary of an African American female college graduate in a full-time position is _____ that of a white male high-school dropout.

19. In 1991, the average income for men age 65 and over was ___ % more than the average woman age 65 and over.

20. In 1989, the percentage of U.S. born women who had 4 years or more of college was______ for white women, _____ for black women ______ for Asian women, and _____ for Latinas.

21. The percentage of bachelor degrees awarded to women from 1969/1970 to 1989/90 increased:
    in the Biological Sciences from _____ to _____.
    in Business from _____ to ______.
    in Engineering from _____ to _____.

22. Women are ___ times more likely than men to quit jobs because of sexual harassment and ____ times more likely to transfer.

23. Every ____ seconds a woman is battered in the U.S.

24. ____ % of women have been seriously abused before age 14, ____% by someone in their family.

25. It is estimated that _______ % of rapes are never reported to the police and that less than _______ of the rapists go to jail.

Appendix 7B

STATUS OF WOMEN QUIZ ANSWERS AND REFERENCES

1. Women-134. Source: The Women's Political Action Group, *The Women's Voting Guide,* Berkeley, CA: Earthworks Press, 1992.

2. 28 to 47. Source: "The Democrats Promise Quick Action on Clinton Plan," *The New York Times,* Nov. 5, 1992.

3. 2 to 6. Source: "The Democrats Promise Quick Action on Clinton Plan," *The New York Times,* Nov. 5, 1992.

4. 13%. The lowest average percentage of references to women on the front pages (8%) was found in *The New York Times* and *The Los Angeles Times.* Source: *New York Magazine,* June 1991.

5. 13.9 %. Source: Screen Actors Guild, 1990.

6. 12% (In 1992, 164 public colleges and universities had women CEO's, up from 16 in 1975.) Source: American Council on Education, Office of Women in Higher Education, 1992.

7. 19.5 per thousand. Source: Statistical Abstracts of the United States, 1991.

8. 17.4% for women. 4.5% for men. White women—13.5%, up from 9.1% in 1970; black women—46.4 %, up from 28.2%; and Latinas— 24.4.%, up from 21.8%. White men—4.1%, up from 2.2% ; black men—6.5%, up from 3.7%; and for Latinos—7.4%, up from 5.1%. Source: Bureau of the Census, 1971, 1992.

9. 70%. Up from 64% in 1982. Source: Bureau of Labor Statistics, 1989, 1992.

10. 5,600. Source: The Women's Political Action Group, *Women's Voting Guide,* Berkeley: Earthworks Press, 1992.

11. 24 billion dollars. Source: Report of the Federal Office of Child Support Enforcement, 1990.

12. 75%. Source: Susan Faludi, *Backlash.* New York: Crown Publishers, 1991.

13. 75.4 cents for every dollar. Source: Bureau of Labor Statistics, 1989, 1993.

14. 1% more. Source: Bureau of the Census, 1991,1992.

15. White women—6.9%; Black women—13%; Latina women—11.3%. Source: Bureau of Labor Statistics, January 1993.

16. 27.5 %. Source: Bureau of Labor Statistics, January 1993.

17. 6%. Source: Wider Opportunities for Women.

18. less than

19. 80% more. Source: Bureau of the Census, 1992.

20. White—24.6%; Black 13.3 %; Asian 37.7%; Latina 9.5%. Source: Bureau of Labor Statistics, December 1992.

21. Biological Sciences from 27.8% to 50.7%; Business from 8.7% to 46.7%; Engineering from .8% to 13.8%. Source: National Center for Education Statistics, *Digest of Education Statistics.*

22. 9 times more likely to quit jobs, and 3 times more likely to transfer. Source: *Sexual Harassment: Research and Resources: A Report-in-Progress,* National Council for Research on Women, November 1991.

23. 15 seconds. Source: Coalition of Battered Women's Advocates.

24. 28%; 12%. Source: Naomi Wolf, *The Beauty Myth.* New York: William Morrow, 1991.

25. 85% of rapes are never reported. Less than 5% of the rapist go to jail. Source: National Victim Center and Crime Victims Research and Treatment Center, 1992.

All statistics and sources cited above were compiled by D. Goodman from Women's Action Coalition (1993), *WAC Stats: The Facts About Women,* New York: The New Press, and C. Costello and A. J. Stone (Eds.) (1994), *The American Woman: 1994–95,* New York: W.W. Norton. Both books compile statistics about women from numerous sources and are updated regularly. Sources cited after each correct answer are the original source as listed in *WAC Stats* or Costello & Stone.

Appendix 7C

FEMINISM(S): HISTORICAL AND THEORETICAL OVERVIEW

Different Feminist Perspectives

While there are some shared beliefs, feminists have many different ways of explaining the causes of women's oppression, and they advocate different strategies for liberation. Even though contemporary feminists are moving away from using rigid labels to define different theoretical orientations (e.g., liberal, radical, socialist, psychoanalytic, postmodern), there are various ways feminists conceptualize the problems and the solutions for women's oppression. These are not always mutually exclusive or discrete categories.

One major area of difference focuses upon whether the existing social structures need to be changed or just made more open to women. Some feminists maintain that the goal should be to remove the barriers to women's equal opportunity and full participation within the existing social and political structures and institutions. Other feminists feel that the social structures and values which reinforce dominant/subordinate relations need to be substantially altered, and that all forms of dominance need to be challenged.

Feminists also emphasize different factors as the root of women's oppression. Some stress biology and sexuality, others the class structure, racism, or socialization. Many feminists recognize the interweaving of many of these elements. Various branches of feminism have evolved based on the experiences and perspectives of different groups of women, such as lesbian feminism, black feminism/womanism, Native American and Latina feminisms, ecofeminsm, etc.

More recently, there has been the concern that as feminists have tried to bring to the public's attention the oppression of women, they have made women seem like helpless victims. Some feminists instead encourage the shift of focus to women's strengths and women's empowerment. There are also feminists who are highlighting the importance of the qualities traditionally ascribed to women such as caring, empathy, nurturing, and intuition.

As a result of their analyses, different feminists have emphasized different avenues to seek women's liberation, from education to legislation to social action. Some feminists have worked towards equal opportunity without seeking fundamental institutional change. Some feminists have tried to alter existing institutions and policies, working from within. Other women have decided to create new, alternative organizations and systems, based on feminist principles (cooperation, non-hierarchical structures). An historical perspective illustrates the evolving nature of feminism and feminist struggles.

Brief Overview of the History of Feminism in the United States

The first wave of feminism in the United States grew out of the anti-slavery and other reform movements of the nineteenth century. In 1848, the Seneca Falls Convention called for the end of the subordination of women in all spheres of life. Women's suffrage, the right to vote, eventually became the primary focus leading to the women's suffrage Constitutional amendment in 1920. In the late nineteenth century and early twentieth century the term feminism was introduced to identify various efforts by women to improve their lives and the lives of others: Margaret Sanger, Emma Goldman, and others led a movement to make birth control legal and available to all women, black and white women worked to improve educational opportunities for women, and labor activists struggled to improve the wages and working conditions of women who worked in factories, stores, and offices.

The 1960s began the second wave of feminism. It grew out of the frustrations of white college-educated suburban housewives, and young women of color and white women involved in the peace and civil rights movements. They were concerned with the devaluation of women in everyday life, sexual objectification, violence against women, and the socialization of women to meet the needs of men. They initiated local consciousness-raising groups in which women shared their experiences and reexamined them through feminist lenses.

Feminists worked in a variety of ways to change laws, attitudes, practices and institu-

> tions. NOW and other equal rights groups challenged sex-segregated want ads, sued hundreds of major corporations for sex discrimination, and lobbied in state legislatures to change laws about rape, domestic violence, divorce, and employment. Women working outside the system established battered women's shelters, rape crisis centers, and feminist health clinics. Feminists inside universities created women's studies programs and engaged in research about women in various disciplines (Kesselman, 1995, 396).

Women organized to repeal abortion laws and fight for reproductive freedom. Abortion was legalized in 1973 by the case *Roe v. Wade*, but the struggle to keep it legal continues. "Throughout the 1970s and 1980s, countless women made changes in their individual lives: going back to school or a job, leaving oppressive marriages, developing emotional and sexual relationships with other women, working to develop relationships of mutuality and respect with men" (Kesselman, 1995, 396).

While women and men of different backgrounds have been involved with feminism and women's rights, many of the leaders of the contemporary women's movement who have gained recognition and visibility have been white, middle-class women. Because white women were generally unaware of how their own racial identity impacted their world view and experiences, it made it difficult to confront racism in the women's movement and to form coalitions with women of color. This has led to a closer examination of the ways white privilege and class privilege have ignored or impeded the leadership of poor women and women of color. As feminism has evolved, so has the sensitivity to the differences among women, and the efforts to create a movement which is inclusive of the diversity of women's experiences and concerns.

Throughout the history of women's movements, sympathetic men, concerned about women's oppression, who recognize what they have to gain as well as lose through greater equality between the sexes, have found ways to support the movement's goals. That support has taken form in the organized anti-sexist, pro-feminist men's movement. Centering on the annual National Conference on Men and Masculinity, first held in 1975, the men's movement has included men's consciousness raising groups which has helped men move beyond the limits of the traditional male role and to recognize how their behaviors might be oppressive to women; organized opposition to men's violence against women and a national campaign against homophobia in recognition of the connections between sexism and heterosexism.

Source: This history of feminism and the women's movement is adapted by D. Goodman from A. Kesselman (1995), "A History of Feminist Movements in the U.S.," in A. Kesselman, L. McNair, and N. Schniedewind (Eds.), *Women: Images and Realities, A Multicultural Reader*, Mountain View, CA: Mayfield Publishing Co.

Appendix 7D

TIMELINE OF KEY EVENTS IN THE STRUGGLE FOR WOMEN'S EQUALITY IN THE UNITED STATES FROM 1848

1848	The first Women's Rights Convention was held in Seneca Falls, NY, led by Lucretia Mott and Elizabeth Cady Stanton. Their Declaration of Sentiments stated that "all men and women are created equal."
1849	Elizabeth Blackwell became the first woman doctor in the United States.
1851	Sojourner Truth, ex-slave gave her "Ain't I A Woman" speech drawing a parallel between the struggle for women's rights and the struggle to abolish slavery.
1865	Vassar College opened, one of the first women's colleges.
1869	After the passage of the 14th and 15th amendments granting suffrage to all males, both Black and White, two women's organizations were formed to work for women's suffrage. The National Woman Suffrage Association was led by Elizabeth Cady Stanton and Susan B. Anthony, while the more conservative American Women Suffrage Association was directed by Lucy Stone and Julia Ward Howe.
1896	The National Association for Colored Women, the first national organization of black women, was established, with Mary Church Terrell as first president.
1898	Charlotte Perkins Gilman published *Women and Economics,* in which she decried the wasted efforts and the low economic status of the housewife. She advocated the industrialization of housework and the socialization of child care.
1909	The first significant strike of working women, "The Uprising of the 20,000," was conducted by shirt-waist makers in New York to protest low wages and long working hours.
1915	Margaret Sanger returned from abroad to campaign against the legal barriers to the dissemination of contraceptive information. She and other women, including Emma Goldman, were jailed for their efforts.
1917	Janet Rankin, a Republican from Montana, was the first women elected to serve in Congress.
1920	The 19th amendment was ratified and women finally gained the right to vote.
1923	The Equal Rights Amendment, advocated by Alice Paul and the National Women's Party, was introduced in Congress for the first time.
1925–1945	Medical schools placed a quota of five percent on female admissions. Columbia and Harvard law schools refused to consider women applicants.
1933	Frances Perkins, the first woman to hold a Cabinet post, was appointed to head the Department of Labor by President Roosevelt and served in his cabinet for 12 years.
1940–1960	The number of working women and the proportion of working wives doubled. During World War II, large numbers of women entered the workforce, with "Rosie the Riveter" becoming a national symbol.
1953	Simone de Beauvior's *The Second Sex,* a scholarly and historical analysis of the inferior status of women, was published in the United States.

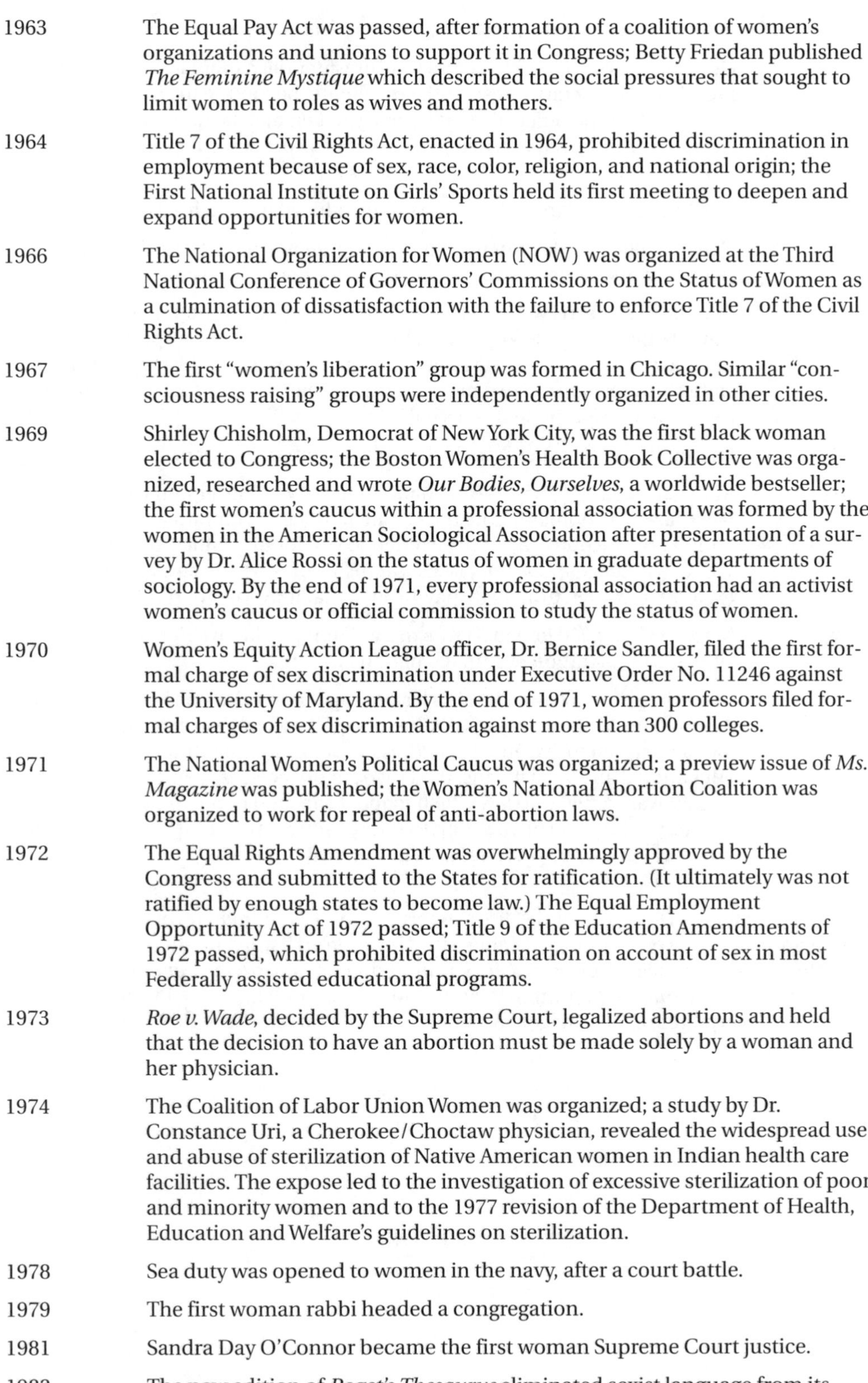

1963	The Equal Pay Act was passed, after formation of a coalition of women's organizations and unions to support it in Congress; Betty Friedan published *The Feminine Mystique* which described the social pressures that sought to limit women to roles as wives and mothers.
1964	Title 7 of the Civil Rights Act, enacted in 1964, prohibited discrimination in employment because of sex, race, color, religion, and national origin; the First National Institute on Girls' Sports held its first meeting to deepen and expand opportunities for women.
1966	The National Organization for Women (NOW) was organized at the Third National Conference of Governors' Commissions on the Status of Women as a culmination of dissatisfaction with the failure to enforce Title 7 of the Civil Rights Act.
1967	The first "women's liberation" group was formed in Chicago. Similar "consciousness raising" groups were independently organized in other cities.
1969	Shirley Chisholm, Democrat of New York City, was the first black woman elected to Congress; the Boston Women's Health Book Collective was organized, researched and wrote *Our Bodies, Ourselves*, a worldwide bestseller; the first women's caucus within a professional association was formed by the women in the American Sociological Association after presentation of a survey by Dr. Alice Rossi on the status of women in graduate departments of sociology. By the end of 1971, every professional association had an activist women's caucus or official commission to study the status of women.
1970	Women's Equity Action League officer, Dr. Bernice Sandler, filed the first formal charge of sex discrimination under Executive Order No. 11246 against the University of Maryland. By the end of 1971, women professors filed formal charges of sex discrimination against more than 300 colleges.
1971	The National Women's Political Caucus was organized; a preview issue of *Ms. Magazine* was published; the Women's National Abortion Coalition was organized to work for repeal of anti-abortion laws.
1972	The Equal Rights Amendment was overwhelmingly approved by the Congress and submitted to the States for ratification. (It ultimately was not ratified by enough states to become law.) The Equal Employment Opportunity Act of 1972 passed; Title 9 of the Education Amendments of 1972 passed, which prohibited discrimination on account of sex in most Federally assisted educational programs.
1973	*Roe v. Wade*, decided by the Supreme Court, legalized abortions and held that the decision to have an abortion must be made solely by a woman and her physician.
1974	The Coalition of Labor Union Women was organized; a study by Dr. Constance Uri, a Cherokee/Choctaw physician, revealed the widespread use and abuse of sterilization of Native American women in Indian health care facilities. The expose led to the investigation of excessive sterilization of poor and minority women and to the 1977 revision of the Department of Health, Education and Welfare's guidelines on sterilization.
1978	Sea duty was opened to women in the navy, after a court battle.
1979	The first woman rabbi headed a congregation.
1981	Sandra Day O'Connor became the first woman Supreme Court justice.
1982	The new edition of *Roget's Thesaurus* eliminated sexist language from its publication.

1983 Sally Ride became the first U.S. woman to travel in space.

1984 Geraldine Ferraro was chosen as vice-presidential candidate with Walter Mondale, Democratic Presidential candidate, becoming the first woman to be named for the office on a major party ticket; marital rape was outlawed in New York, ruling that married men could be prosecuted for raping their wives.

1985 The Equal Rights Amendment was reintroduced in both houses of Congress.

1987 Over 500,000 people marched on Washington in support of lesbian and gay rights, but major news sources opted not to report the event.

1989 Rev. Barbara Harris was consecrated the first female bishop in the Anglican Church; over 500,000 people marched on Washington in support of reproductive freedom, one of the largest such marches in U.S. history; Washington state court recognized two mothers as legal parents when it allowed one of the women to adopt her lover's baby.

1990 Sharon Pratt Dixon became the first black woman mayor of a major U.S. city.

1991 Anita Hill testified about sexual harassment involving Supreme Court nominee Clarence Thomas before the Senate Judiciary Committee, educating the nation and encouraging many women to run for high office; in *United Auto Workers v. Johnson Controls*, the Supreme Court forbade employers from excluding women from high-paying jobs that may involve risk to fetuses.

1992 More than 750,000 joined NOW's march for reproductive rights, the largest single demonstration ever in the nation's capital.

1994 The first national Latina lesbian leadership conference was held in Tucson, Arizona; the Violence Against Women Act (VAWA) of 1994 was signed into law, a comprehensive effort to address violence against women through educational and legal means; the Freedom of Access to Clinic Entrances Act (FACE) was signed into law which made it a federal crime to use force, threat of force, or physical obstruction to injure, intimidate, or interfere with someone obtaining or providing reproductive health services.

Source: Events from 1848 through 1989 are excerpted by D. Goodman from "Rediscovering American Women: A Chronology Highlighting Women's History in the United States" and "Update—The Process Continues" in S. Ruth (Ed.) (1990), *Issues in Feminism: An Introduction to Women's Studies*, Mountain View, CA: Mayfield Publishing Co. Events from 1989 to 1994 are excerpted from *Ms.* magazine, July/Aug. 1992 and Jan./ Feb. 1995.

Appendix 7E

SPHERES OF INFLUENCE

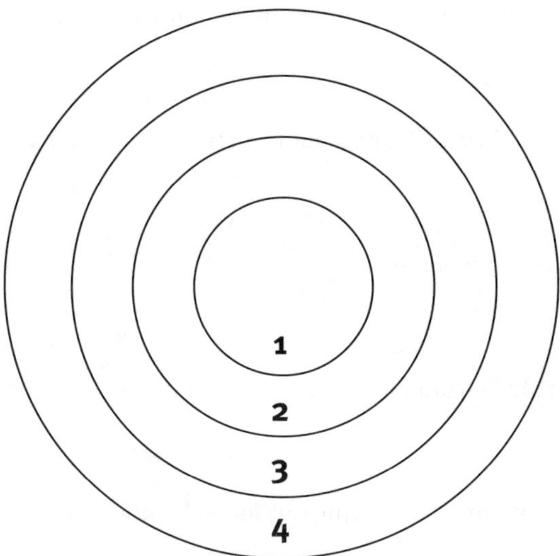

1. Self: Educating yourself, understanding your values and feelings, examining how you want to change
2. Close family and friends: Influencing the people closest to you
3. Social, school and work relationships: Friends and acquaintances, co-workers, neighbors, classmates, people with whom you interact on a regular basis
4. Community: People with whom you interact infrequently or in community settings

Appendix 7F

ACTION PLANNING WORKSHEET

1. What action do you want to take to interrupt or combat sexism?

2. What resources or materials, if any, would you need to achieve your goal?

3. How can you get those resources?

4. What behaviors or steps would taking this action entail?

5. What is a realistic timeline for carrying out the steps involved in this action plan?

6. What hazards or risks are involved?

7. Is this action worth taking that risk? (If not, go back to number one, or think through what could be done to minimize that risk.)

8. What obstacles might you encounter?

9. What could you do to overcome these obstacles?

10. What supports do you have?

11. Where could you find more support?

12. How can you measure/evaluate your success? (How can slow change be differentiated from failure?)

8

Heterosexism Curriculum Design

Pat Griffin, Bobbie Harro

Introduction

The Stonewall Riots in 1969 were a pivotal event in the history of struggle for lesbian, gay, and bisexual rights. Since 1969, societal perspectives on sexuality, gender, and sexual orientation have entered a period of immense change and upheaval in which the social consensus that lesbian, gay, and bisexual people are sick, sinful, and criminal has begun to shift. The medical and religious models that, until 1969 dominated thinking about lesbian, gay, and bisexual people, now compete with a social justice model which defines lesbian, gay, and bisexual people as an oppressed minority (McNeil, 1988). In this changing social context more lesbian, gay, and bisexual people are living openly and demanding recognition as a minority group unjustly subjected to prejudice and discrimination.

In opposition, many conservative religious and political groups view the acceptance of lesbian, gay, and bisexual people as evidence of the moral breakdown of Western civilization and work against any attempt to provide lesbian, gay, and bisexual people with civil rights protection, to portray positive media images, or to include educational programs about them in schools. Between these two extremes, most people approach openly lesbian, gay, and bisexual people or discussions about topics associated with them, with discomfort and uncertainty that reflect socialization into a society where lesbian, gay, and bisexual people have been stigmatized and made invisible.

Visibility and Backlash

The increasing visibility of lesbian, gay, and bisexual people and the issues of concern to them have dramatically affected the social context in which we live and teach. Lesbian, gay, and bisexual characters are included in television shows and movies and some advertisers are beginning to court the lesbian, gay, and bisexual market more aggressively. Media coverage of events such as the congressional hearings about gays in the military, the rally for the 1993 March on Washington for Lesbian, Gay, and Bisexual Rights rally, child custody fights involving lesbian and gay parents, domestic partner benefits coverage by private businesses and municipalities, the passage of anti-discrimination laws in several states, and the passage of referenda in some states denying lesbian, gay, and bisexual people legal protection from discrimination or specifically prohibiting gay marriage, all have brought these issues into the homes, schools, and workplaces of Americans in an unprecedented way.

Despite the increased visibility of lesbian, gay, and bisexual people, most Americans continue to have ambivalent reactions to them. On one hand most people surveyed do not believe that lesbian, gay, and bisexual people should be discriminated against. On the other hand the same respondents do not consider homosexuality an acceptable "lifestyle" (Turque, 1992). This ambivalence is reflected in the fear of AIDS and the continuing association of AIDS with gay men as well as in the reluctance to accept lesbian, gay, and bisexual parents' rights or to acknowledge lesbian, gay, and bisexual families. State-wide referenda on civil rights protection for lesbians and gays and legislation designed to block the legalization of same-sex marriages highlight anti-gay strategies that portray gay rights as "special rights" and the demands of lesbians and gays for inclusion in mainstream United States culture as "promotion" of a "deviant lifestyle."

Educators have been particularly reluctant to acknowledge or address heterosexism and homophobia in the schools (Woog, 1995; Unks, 1995; Sears, 1990). Despite a U.S. Department of Health and Human Services Report (1989) on teen suicide indicating that lesbian, gay, and bisexual young people are two to three times more likely to kill themselves than are other youth, most schools are ill-prepared to address the needs of lesbian, gay, and bisexual students, or lesbian, gay, and bisexual parents with school-aged children. Fears about inappropriately influencing the sexual orientation of young people, addressing sexuality issues in general, and being perceived as advocating or promoting homosexuality, make school officials reluctant to address issues of concern to young lesbian, gay, and bisexual people. Well-organized right-wing religious groups are active in monitoring and opposing any efforts by schools to address issues related to homosexuality. The potential for parental objections to the inclusion of lesbian, gay, and bisexual-related issues in schools causes many school administrators to err on the side of caution rather than risk controversy and conflict.

Hate Crimes and Anti-gay Rhetoric

Violence directed at people thought to be lesbian, gay, and bisexual is a more extreme expression of lack of acceptance. Statistics indicate that lesbian, gay, and bisexual people are among the most frequent targets of hate crimes (Finn & McNeil, 1987). Studies describe the profile of typical perpetrators of hate crimes against lesbian, gay, and bisexual people as groups of school-aged adolescent males who go looking for their victims (Comstock, 1991).

Diversity and Conflict Within the Lesbian, Gay, Bisexual, Transgender Communities

In addition to the responses of the larger society to the increasing visibility of lesbian, gay, and bisexual people and issues that affect them, the diversity among lesbian, gay, and bisexual people and the increasing complexity of issues of concern result in inevitable conflicts within their communities. Acknowledging that there is no monolithic lesbian, gay, and bisexual community surfaces the tensions and prejudices among the diverse groups who all demand inclusion in the sexual minorities community. Over the last few years bisexual women and men; transgender people; lesbians and gay men of color; working class and poor lesbians, gays, and bisexuals; lesbian, gay, and bisexual people with disabilities; and others have stretched the boundaries of issues and identities that need to be addressed and included when we discuss homophobia and heterosexism (Leong, 1996; Ramos, 1994; Ratti, 1993; Silvera, 1992; Weise, 1992; Hutchins & Kaahumanu, 1991; Geller, 1990; Balka & Rose, 1989; Beck, 1989; Roscoe, 1988; Beam, 1986; Smith, 1983). Even the profusion of self-chosen labels reflects the increasing acknowledgment of the diversity under the broad umbrella of queer identities: lesbian, gay woman, gay man, homosexual, queer, butch, fem, lesbian-feminist, lesbian-identified bi woman, faggot, fairy, drag queen, transgenderist, male to female transsexual, dyke, Chicana lesbian, and womanist bisexual are examples of this proliferation of different identities (Sears, 1994; Warner, 1993).

In particular over the last few years transgender people have been explicitly included among the groups under the umbrella of identity groups that defy traditional gender or sexuality expectations. Because of the complicated interplay among gender identity, gender roles, and sexual identity, transgender people pose a challenge to how we think about these issues. Our courses identify lesbian, gay, and bisexual people as the groups targeted by heterosexism because of the common thread of non-heterosexual identity they share. We discuss transgender people in both the sexism and the heterosexism chapters because we believe it is important to identify the interconnections among sexism, heterosexism, homophobia, and transgender issues. Transgender people identify as heterosexual, lesbian, gay, or bisexual (Bornstein, 1994; Feinberg, 1996). It is their transgression of gender boundaries and assumptions about their sexual identity that cause transgender people to be targeted (see definition in Appendix 8A).

Facilitation Issues

Teaching about heterosexism in this complex and dynamic social context presents facilitators with many challenges. We believe it is essential for facilitators to help students understand the connections between sexism and heterosexism. Gender roles are maintained, in part, through homophobia, the fear of being called lesbian or gay (Blumenfeld, 1993, 1992). Maintenance of separate and permanent gender roles and gender identities ensures a hierarchical relationship between genders in which men have more access to social power than do women. For lesbian and gay labels to retain their salience in maintaining male dominance, homosexuality must be strictly stigmatized and silenced. This synergistic relationship between sexism and heterosexism is a basic part of teaching students about the cultural functions of homophobia and heterosexism (Pharr, 1988).

One of the most important challenges to facilitators is the task of constructing an educational experience that acknowledges the complexity of the issues involved without overwhelming students who bring a variety of experiences to the course. Some students will be talking about these issues for the first time. Others might be questioning their sexual orientation during the course and be in transition in their thinking about their sexual identity. Some of these students might claim their lesbian, gay, and bisexual identity during the course. For other students, addressing heterosexism and homophobia requires them to challenge basic and deeply held religious beliefs or personal fears about lesbian, gay, and bisexual people. Lesbian, gay, and bisexual students may also have to confront their internalized homophobia and biphobia (fear or intolerance of homosexual and bisexual people). Heterosexual students learn how issues of gender and sexuality, and homophobia affect their lives. With this challenging mix of participants it is essential to construct a learning environment in which students have control over how much of their personal experiences and sexual identities they choose to disclose as part of the course activities. Establishing an environment that both welcomes self-disclosure and respects the choice not to self-disclose is an important part of helping participants gain the most from the experience.

Overall Goals

- Explore personal feelings, thoughts, and beliefs about homosexuality, bisexuality, and sexual orientation.
- Raise awareness and understanding of the destructive consequences of heterosexism and homophobia.
- Understand heterosexual privilege.
- Understand heterosexism on the individual, institutional, and societal levels.
- Make connections between heterosexism, sexism, and other forms of oppression.
- Learn information that contradicts stereotypes about lesbian, gay, and bisexual people.
- Understand the historical context of present day homophobia and heterosexism.
- Envision a society in which heterosexism and homophobia do not exist.
- Identify personal actions to address heterosexism and homophobia.

Overview of Heterosexism Modules
Introductory Module (see chapter 5)

Module 1 (3 hours) Agenda	Module 2 (4 hours) Agenda
1. Introductions (15 mins.) 2. Agenda, Guidelines, Goals (10 mins.) 3. Definitions (10 mins.) 4. Early Learnings (45 mins.) 5. Understanding the Complexity of Gender and Sexuality (45 mins.) 6. Closing (15 mins.)	1. Opening (25 mins.) 2. Personal Stories (90–105 mins.) 3. Institutional Heterosexism and Heterosexual Privilege (75 mins.) 4. Homework (10 mins.) 5. Closing (15 mins.)

Module 3 (3 hours) Agenda	**Module 4 (4 hours)** Agenda
1. Button Activity(45 mins.) 2. Lesbian, Gay, Bisexual History (90 mins.) 3. Setting Up Caucus Groups (10 mins.) 4. Closing (20 mins.)	1. Caucus Groups (90 mins.) 2. Vision of Non-Heterosexist World (60 mins.) 3. Action Strategies (30 mins.) 4. Closing (45 mins.)

Handout 8.1. Overview of Heterosexism Modules.

Heterosexism Curriculum Design

Module 1

Time Needed: 3 hours
Goals:

- Identify and use effective communication guidelines while discussing heterosexism and homophobia.
- Understand terms commonly used in the study of heterosexism and homophobia.
- Describe the process by which we have learned heterosexism and homophobia, and some of the learned messages.
- Understand the complexity of gender and sexual orientation.
- Understand the connections between homophobia, gender, and sexuality.

Key concepts: socialization, stereotypes, sexual orientation, gender identity, gender roles.

1. Introductions of Facilitators and Participants: (15 minutes).

Introduce yourself to the class and give some background information about yourself, including what motivates you to teach this class. Identify how your other social group memberships (class, race, ethnicity, religion, ability status) affect your experience of heterosexism.

Ask participants to give their names and mention one issue related to heterosexism that they want to see addressed in the class. Record these issues on newsprint and identify anything that is outside the boundaries of the agenda.

Facilitation Issues:
We believe it is important for facilitators to disclose their sexual orientation at some point early on in the course. When both facilitators have identified their sexual identities to participants, they can more effectively use their own personal experiences, including challenges and triumphs, to help participants better understand their experiences.

All participants, especially lesbian, gay, and bisexual participants, need to have control over how much of their own identities and experience they choose to disclose in the course. Disclosing sexual orientation has different meanings and risk levels depending on whether participants are heterosexual, lesbian, gay, or bisexual, and how well they know other participants outside of class. Pressuring lesbian, gay, or bisexual students to identify themselves potentially can put them at risk of being targeted for harassment, violence, or other discrimination out of class. In addition, some participants do not know what their sexual orientation is or resist labeling themselves. Establish an environment that invites self-disclosure, but does not require it and respects participants' decisions not to self-disclose.

2. Agenda, Goals, and Guidelines: (10 minutes).

Post the agenda, goals, and participation guidelines on newsprint or on a chalkboard. Keep them visible for the duration of the course so that you or participants can refer to them. Review all three giving special attention to the guidelines for discussions since an atmosphere of trust and safety are most important. Ask for questions, additions, revisions, and ask for agreement on the guidelines from the whole group with a show of hands.

3. Definitions of Terms:(10 minutes).

Have key definitions posted on newsprint and/or available on a handout. Definitions we usually cover in the beginning of the class are listed here. A more complete list of definitions is included in Appendix 8A. Go over the key definitions and invite participants to ask questions.

Sexism: The individual, institutional, and societal/cultural beliefs and practices that privilege men and subordinate women.

Heterosexism: The individual, institutional, and societal/cultural beliefs and practices based on the belief that heterosexuality is the only normal and acceptable sexual orientation.

Homophobia: The fear, hatred, or intolerance of lesbians and gay men or any behavior that falls outside of traditional gender roles. Homophobic acts can range from name-calling to violence targeting lesbian or gay people.

Biphobia: The fear, hatred or intolerance of bisexual people.

Heterosexual Ally: Heterosexual people who take action against homophobia and heterosexism because they believe it is beneficial to lesbian, gay, and bisexual people and because they believe it is in their own self-interest as well.

Handout 8.2. Definitions of General Concepts: Heterosexism.

4. Early Learnings:(45 minutes).

Ask participants to pair up with someone they don't know. Tell them that you are going to ask a question which each person will answer in turn: one person speaking and the other listening. Each person will have one minute. After one minute, ask them to switch speakers. After both people in the pair have answered the first question, ask them to find another partner. Ask the second question. Change to a third partner, and pose the third question. The questions are as follows:

- What is the first time you remember knowing that there was a sexual orientation other than heterosexual?
- What do you remember learning about gay/lesbian or bisexual people, and from what source did you learn this information?

- How did you learn that you were expected to be heterosexual?

Invite participants to return to the whole group. Ask participants to call out some of the things they learned about lesbian, gay, and bisexual people while you or a co-facilitator write them on newsprint or on a chalkboard. Next make a list of the sources of learned messages. Next ask participants how they learned that they were expected to be heterosexual. Make a list of these items on newsprint.

Early learnings about lesbian, gay, and bisexual people—some typical responses include:

- Child molesters
- Obsessed with sex
- Want to be the other sex
- Hate the other sex
- Had a bad heterosexual experience
- Recruit young people
- Act like the other sex
- Sinners
- Sick

Sources of these learnings:

- Parents, family
- Peers
- Movies, books
- Religious teachings
- Schools

Ways we are taught we should be heterosexual:

- Parents' relationship
- Teased about cross-sex friendships
- Proms, dances, dating
- Look forward to getting married
- Weddings, anniversaries, engagements
- Stigma attached to lesbian, gay, and bisexual people
- Silence about lesbian, gay, and bisexual people
- "Queers Day" at school, playground games like "Smear the Queer"
- Anti-gay namecalling as a put down

Processing:
Ask participants to reflect individually on the group lists. Then ask the following questions:

- What are your reactions to seeing the list of stereotypes of lesbian, gay, and bisexual people?
- Which stereotypes are most familiar to you?
- What do you notice about how and from where we learned about lesbian, gay, and bisexual people?
- Which of these stereotypes do you have questions about now?
- Who actually had lesbian, gay, and bisexual people in your life as you grew up? What do you remember about these people?
- What do you notice about how we learned to be heterosexual?

Acknowledge that we have all learned messages about lesbian, gay, and bisexual people. Check to see if there are differences in messages depending on cultural backgrounds. If so, discuss what might account for those differences. Be sure that people express their reactions in ways that respect the class guidelines.

Help participants make a transition from the early learning and stereotype activities by noting how we all have been socialized into our beliefs about gender and sexuality and what we think is appropriate or acceptable. Refer to the cycle of socialization in Appendix 5C.

Break (15 minutes).

5. Understanding the Complexity of Sexuality and Gender (45 minutes).

The objective of this activity is to help participants think about the complexity of gender and sexuality, and to understand the role of homophobia in maintaining what we accept as "normal." Acknowledge that some participants might disagree with some of the perspectives presented in this lecture. Encourage them to do so and to continue to challenge this and other models presented in class.

Divide students into groups of five. Give each group one or two of the following terms and, based on their understanding of these terms, ask them to develop definitions of each one. Ask them to be ready to write their definitions on newsprint to share with the whole group in about 15 minutes.

Terms to be Defined: biological sex, gender identity, gender role, sexual identity, transsexual, transgender, cross-dresser, lesbian, gay, bisexual, heterosexual.

Ask each small group to post their newsprint on the walls. Invite everyone to do a "Gallery Walk" (browse and read all the definitions). Ask all participants to note definitions that contradict their understandings or definitions that are new to them. After all participants have had a chance to look at all newsprints, ask everyone to return to their seats. Ask what definitions were new. Ask if anyone had different understandings of some of the definitions given.

Talk about how gender and sexuality are far more complex than the either/or categories we have learned. Present the following lecture to clarify the definitions and the relationship of these terms to each other as we will be using them in this course (refer to the list of definitions in Appendix 8A).

Lecture:
We are each born into a physical body and, depending on the physical attributes and genetic make-up of our bodies, we are assigned a biological sex category, either male or female. We are expected to develop a gender identity (our sense of ourselves as male or female) that is consistent with the physical body we are born into. We are then socialized into specific gender roles (socially constructed behavioral expectations of masculinity and femininity) that are consistent with our physical bodies and gender identities. Boys are expected to be aggressive, rough, and physical. Girls are expected to be quiet, diffident, and pleasant. Both girls and boys are expected to develop heterosexual attractions and relationships (sexual and emotional feelings for the other sex). In our society, these routes to gender and sexuality identity are the only acceptable options for men and women. There is, however, far more variability in the relationships among our biological sex (or the bodies we are born into) our gender identity, gender roles, and sexual orientation. Some people do not have a gender identity that matches their biological sex (transsexuals/transgender people). Many people whose gender identity is consistent with their biological sex do not adopt traditional gender roles. They may adopt behaviors and interests that are more associated with the other sex or are gender neutral. Some people enjoy dressing in clothes associated with the other gender role (cross-dressers). Finally, there is a wide range of ways that people can express their sexuality. Heterosexuality is only one option. Lesbian, gay, bisexual identities are also ways in which people express their sexual desires.

How we identify and express ourselves sexually is far more complex and fluid than we are taught to believe. We are socialized to believe that the possibilities for how we identify ourselves are narrow and fixed. In actuality, there are many possibilities for the relationship among our biological sex, gender identity, gender roles, and sexual orientation.

Homophobia plays an important role in maintaining the boundaries around what our society considers "normal." When people violate these gender and sexuality norms, homophobia is one of the primary tools that is used to let people know they are "out-of-bounds." The narrow construction of gender and sexuality we have learned to accept as normal and natural depends in part for its maintenance on stigmatizing lesbians, gay men, bisexual people, and transgender people. Homophobia, biphobia, and transphobia (fear of transgender people) are the glue that holds traditional gender roles and power imbalances between women and men in place. (See "Act Like a Man/Woman" activity in chapter 7.)

After giving this short lecture, invite participants to ask questions. If participants do not agree with the information presented, welcome their perspective and encourage them to remain open to new perspectives as the class continues. Some questions to ask participants include:

- Can you think of times when you or someone you know felt pressure to conform to gender and sexuality norms out of fear of being called lesbian or gay?
- How does this information confirm or contradict your thoughts about gender identity and gender roles?

Next introduce the Klein Grid as a way to help participants acknowledge the complexity of sexual orientation (see Klein Grid in Appendix 8B). This grid helps participants to understand the multi-faceted nature of sexual orientation. Sexual orientation, rather than being a bipolar (heterosexual or homosexual) concept, is in actuality quite complex with several dimensions. The Klein Grid helps participants begin to understand the complexity and fluidity of sexual orientation.

Introduce the Klein Grid by describing the eight dimensions of sexual orientation and the three time periods (past, present, and ideal). Introduce the seven point scale and explain that we can identify our experience on each of the eight dimensions for each of the three time periods. The Klein Grid makes it clear that how we identify ourselves is not simple. Invite participants to complete the Klein Grid on their own outside of class if they wish. The purpose in introducing it here is to illustrate the complexity of sexual orientation. Ask the group for questions and discuss their responses, making the following points:

- The most obvious value of this model is the clear presentation of the complexity of sexual orientation.
- Sexual orientation is not an either/or issue. It is a highly complex predisposition, some aspects of which may change over time.
- Stereotypes about the origin of sexual orientation are not founded in fact. Examples are: women become lesbians because of a "bad experience with a man" or men become gay when they have a weak or absent father or a strong or dominant mother. These erroneous theories had their origin in biased, poorly constructed research of the past or no research at all.
- The best use of this scale is to understand oneself better, or to understand someone else better. It should not be used as a tool for "diagnosis" or labeling.

Ask participants to reflect on the information contained in the Klein Scale and spend five minutes discussing their thoughts with a partner. Use the following questions to guide this discussion:

- How does the Klein Grid confirm or contradict your understanding of sexual orientation?
- How might the Klein Grid affect how we understand our sexual orientation?

Call the class back together and respond to any questions raised during the partner discussions.

Prepare participants for the activities in the next module by telling them that now that we have explored the definitions of sexual orientation and gender, and have identified some of the ways we are socialized into our beliefs about gender and sexuality, we will examine how lesbian, gay, and bisexual people are treated in this culture.

Commentary:
Facilitators need to be familiar with the Klein model to be prepared for this discussion. For more information about the Klein Scale, see Klein, Sepekoff, and Wolf. (1985). "Sexual Orientation: A Multi-Variable Dynamic Process," *Journal of Homosexuality*, 11(1/2), 35–49.

Facilitation Issues:
These conceptual organizers will challenge how some participants understand gender and sexuality. This perspective encourages participants to challenge their beliefs that gender and sexuality are fixed and that there is a consistent relationship among biological sex, gender identity, gender roles, and sexual identity. We believe

it is important to encourage participants to express their reservations and questions about the definitions.

6. Closing (15 minutes).

Ask participants to say one word that sums up something they are thinking or feeling at the end of this module.

Module 2

Time Needed: 4 hours
Goals:

- Understand the impact of homophobia on the lives of lesbians, gay men, and bisexual people.
- Identify the impact of institutional and cultural heterosexist forces on the lives of lesbian, gay, and bisexual people.
- Identify the impact of heterosexual privilege on heterosexual people and lesbian, gay, and bisexual people.

Key concepts: institutional heterosexism, heterosexual privilege, internalized homophobia.

1. Opening (25 minutes).

Invite participants to turn to the person sitting next to them and to express any thoughts, questions, or concerns that have remained with them since the last session. Announce that we will not be able to discuss each one in detail now, but by acknowledging them publicly, we can include as many as possible in the session's discussions.

After about two minutes per person in pairs, go around the group inviting each person to name a question or thought in the form of a "topic title." For example "gay parents," "blatant behavior," "the church and lesbian, gay, and bisexual people," "role playing." It may be useful to write the topics on a public list so that they can be integrated into upcoming discussions (Marcus, 1993).

2. Personal Stories—Panel or Video (90–105 minutes).

Preparation:
Arrange in advance for a panel of speakers from a local lesbian, gay, and bisexual speakers bureau, or invite willing speakers from the course participants or another source, or bring a video or film that describes the personal experiences of lesbian, gay, and bisexual people. *Pink Triangles, A Little Respect: Gay Men, Lesbians, and Bisexuals On Campus,* or *Gay Youth* are good choices (see the video resource list at the end of this volume).

Give panelists information about your participant group (how many people, what they have studied so far on the subject, their approximate age and sex). Be clear with them that they do not need to be experts; they only need to tell some part of their own experience related to being lesbian, gay, and bisexual, and to answer some questions (Blumenfeld, 1993, provides detailed information for setting up a panel). Let panelists know that they do not need to disclose more than they want to, and that they always have the right to refuse to answer any question. Try to identify a panel that includes a range of lesbian, gay, and bisexual identities and also includes women and men of different racial and spiritual heritages. A panel of three to four people provides each speaker with ample time to talk in a sixty to seventy-five minute period.

The Panel:
Introduce this section to participants by saying that the best way to understand the experience of a lesbian, gay, and bisexual person is to hear actual experiences first-hand. For that reason, we have invited a panel of volunteer speakers who are willing to tell their stories to us (or secured a video of people telling their personal stories). Remind participants that everyone speaks from personal experience, and no one person can represent a whole group. Suggest a format that involves everyone on the panel speaking first, and then an open question and answer period.

You can distribute note cards to participants at the beginning of the panel, and if participants seem hesitant to ask questions, invite them to write their questions on the note cards. Collect all the note cards even if nothing is written on them, mix them up, and deliver them to the panelists. This method provides anonymity for participants while still surfacing all of the questions. We recommend, however, that students be encouraged as much as possible to ask their questions aloud. This format is much livelier and the person to person interactions among participants and panelists creates a much more meaningful exchange. Remind participants that panelists always have the option to pass on a question that they don't want to answer. After the panel has finished, thank the panelists for coming to the class, and take a break.

Break (15 minutes).

Processing:
Save thirty to forty-five minutes after the panel has left to process the experience with the following questions. This can be accomplished in small groups or with the whole group. If you use small groups, be sure to return to the whole group to answer questions and hear comments from the small groups.

- What was it like to hear personal stories?
- What new information did you receive?
- What thoughts or questions were stimulated for you?
- What did panelists say that made you uncomfortable?
- How did the panelists challenge some of the stereotypes we identified in Module 1?
- How were the experiences of the panel members similar? Different?

3. Institutional Heterosexism and Heterosexual Privilege (75 minutes).

Prior to beginning this activity, post five newsprints around the room. Write one of the following situations on the top of each newsprint:

- You and your same sex partner are planning a celebration of commitment.
- You and your partner are planning to have a baby.
- Your life partner is sick in the hospital and might die.

- You have been the victim of hate violence because of your sexual orientation.
- You are a teacher or coach in a high school.

Introduce this section by explaining that we will be exploring how institutional forces impact our lives differently, depending on our sexual orientation. Divide the class into groups of four or five. Assign one group to each of the situations on the newsprint. Ask the groups to go stand by their newsprint. Give each group a marker. Read all of the situations aloud and ask participants to imagine that they are lesbian, gay, or bisexual people facing these situations. Each group will have five minutes to work on their situation. Then have all groups rotate clockwise to the next situation. Give them five minutes to work on the new situation. Keep rotating until all groups have worked on all situations posted around the room.

Ask the groups to identify for each situation:

- The institutional policies and practices that would constitute barriers for lesbian, gay, and bisexual people.
- The cultural norms and practices that would constitute barriers for lesbian, gay, and bisexual people.
- The advantages heterosexuals have that are denied to lesbian, gay, and bisexual people.

Each group should work together and write answers on the newsprint. As groups rotate, they should first read what previous groups have written and then add only new thoughts that they have. After all groups have worked on all situations, invite participants to take a gallery walk around the room reading what the groups have added to each situation. After the gallery walk, ask the participants to return to the circle.

Here are some of the issues to address for each of the situations:

You and your same sex partner have decided to have a celebration of commitment. Whom will you invite—parents, siblings, other family, co-workers, friends? Who will pay for the ceremony? How traditional will it be—religious, formal, using vows, symbols, rings, or rituals? What will you wear? Who will preside? Will you take a honeymoon? Will you get time off from work? Will you say what it's for? Will you announce it in the newspaper? Will you apply for domestic partner's benefits at your place of employment? What will you do about gifts, showers, dinners, anniversaries? Will you get joint bank accounts? Will you bring your partner to work gatherings, parties, business trips? What contracts will you enact? How will you choose a lawyer to assist you in creating powers of attorney, wills, health care proxies? What about public displays of affection? Will you apply for family memberships at the Y or the swimming pool, or couple's night at the ski resort? Are there any cultural issues that need to be considered? Are the two of you from different cultural (religion, class, ethnicity, ability status) backgrounds?

Your same sex partner has been in a serious automobile accident, and is in the intensive care unit of the hospital. The hospital has a policy that only immediate family may visit. When you arrive to see him/her, you are asked who you are. What do you say? Do you lie or tell the truth? What if they don't let you in? Do you have insurance coverage that recognizes your relationship? What if your partner's family is hostile towards you or your relationship? What if they don't know about your relationship? Who has decision-making power if your partner can't make medical decisions for her/himself? How do you define your relationship on hospital forms? How will you deal with coming out to doctors and nurses in this stressful situation? Will you get time off from work to visit, care for your partner? What about your partner's hospital roommate? Do you change how you interact in the roommate's presence? Do you hold hands, touch, kiss hello, and good-bye? What if your partner dies? Who will control the funeral arrangements? If children are involved, who will get custody? Will family members contest your partner's wishes? What about property and home ownership? Do you have wills that specify your partner's desires? What if her/his family challenges his/her will? How will the obituary name you—partner, long-time companion, roommate, friend, spouse?

You and your same sex partner have decided to become parents. How will you do it—alternative insemination, intercourse, adoption ? How will you tell your families? Which partner will give birth (if you are women)? How will you decide? If you choose adoption, how will you deal with the agencies' failure to recognize gay/lesbian couples? Which of you will claim to be a single parent? How will you work out custody arrangements in the event of separation, death, challenge by one partner's family? What will the child call her/his parents? Whose medical benefits will be covering the child? Who will have decision-making power in cases of illness or hospitalization of the child? When will you talk to the child about having lesbian, gay, and bisexual parents? How will you help the child to relate to other children and their parents, the school, the medical system? How will you talk to the child about her/his own sexual orientation? If you adopt, would you consider a child from a different cultural background (ethnicity, race, class, religion)? Would you consider a child with a disability? What if you and your partner disagree on the answers to the previous questions? How will you respond when people say, "It just isn't fair to the child."

You have been victimized by anti-gay violence. Is there a hate crime law that includes sexual orientation where this occurred? Are police in these area sensitized to anti-gay violence? Are the police anti-gay themselves and will they take this incident seriously? If you go to the hospital, how will you explain what happened if you are not out? Will you decide not to notify the police or seek medical attention if you are not out or afraid of the reactions of police and medical providers? How will your freedom to move around and go places change? Will your name be in the newspaper? Will your partner be able to take time off from work to care for you?

You are a teacher or coach in a high school. Is there protection against employment discrimination for lesbian, gay, and bisexual people? Is your partner covered by the employment benefit package offered to married heterosexual employees? Will the teacher's union represent you and back you if you are fired because you are gay? Will the principal and school board back you if parents complain about a gay teacher in school? Will you be protected if you are harassed by other teachers or students in the school? Will you be protected from discrimination if you decide to come out to students?

Processing (30 minutes).
Ask if anyone needs clarification on anything they read on any of the newsprints. Ask the group who wrote the item to explain what they meant. Focusing on one situation at a time, ask participants to identify some of the advantages that heterosexuals have in relation to the situations. Have each group call out one of the advantages they listed for each situation. Introduce the concept of *heterosexual privilege* and define it (see definitions at the end of this chapter). Make the point that these "exclusive rights" are another way that the culture and institutions advantage heterosexuals and discriminate against lesbian, gay, and bisexual people. It is not nec-

essary for heterosexuals to give up rights to dismantle privilege, only to give up the exclusivity of those rights. Give some examples of dismantling privilege by giving up the exclusivity, such as:

- Instituting domestic partnership benefits for same gender couples.
- Legalizing adoptions by gay families.
- Passing national, state, or local legislation protecting lesbian, gay, and bisexual people from employment discrimination based on sexual orientation.

Facilitation Issues:
Be aware that there may be lesbian, gay, and bisexual participants in the class, and some of them may have experienced situations similar to the scenarios. This activity could motivate them to come out or it could trigger emotional responses. If anyone chooses to share a personal story or a story of a friend or relative who was discriminated against, this adds an important element of credibility to these hypothetical situations. Any such sharing should be strictly voluntary. It is important to be sure that everyone remembers the guidelines.

4. Homework.(10 minutes).

Bring a wide range of buttons that have slogans or phrases about lesbian, gay, and bisexual rights, issues, and people. For example: "I Support Gay Rights," "Straight But Not Narrow," "Queer," "Bisexual Pride," "Dyke," "Value All Families," "Lesbian Power," or "Gay is Beautiful." Make sure you have enough buttons for everyone and that the buttons represent a wide range of risk; some that would be too threatening for a few people to wear and some that would be fairly easy to wear. Invite participants to browse through the buttons (which you have displayed). Ask them to choose a button to wear wherever they will be going for a day or until the next class meeting. Tell them to be aware of their thoughts and feelings as they look at the buttons and to be aware of what criteria they use for their selection. Encourage them to write down their reactions so we can discuss them during the next section of the class. Explain that we will begin the next class by discussing their "button experiences." Tell them they can also choose NOT to take a button, but they should be aware of what influences their choice. Note that some participants will choose to take the button on and off depending on where they are. Ask them to be conscious of where they feel like they need to do this and where it feels comfortable to wear the button.

Commentary:
If, in your judgment, the button assignment might put students at risk of being targeted by anti-gay harassment or violence, use an alternative homework assignment. Needless to say, student safety should be your first priority. Use your knowledge of the local community in which you are teaching this course to make this decision.

5. Closing (15 minutes).

Instruct participants to meet with a partner and spend five minutes reflecting on this session. Use the following questions as guides. What touched you? What surprised you? What is something useful from this session? What is something you need to think more about? Invite participants to return to the large group and have each person briefly tell one of their insights to the group.

Module 3

Time Needed: 3 hours
Goals:

- Understand major events and patterns in the history of societal perspectives on same-sex relationships.
- Understand heterosexual privilege, internalized homophobia, and collusion.

Key concepts: collusion, internalized homophobia, heterosexual privilege, historical roots of heterosexism.

1. Button Activity (45 minutes).

Ask participants to meet in groups of four or five and discuss the following questions:

- Why did you choose the button you have? or choose not to wear a button?
- Where did you wear your button? or not wear the button?
- What was your own internal reaction to wearing the button? or not wearing a button?
- How did other people react to your wearing the button?

Ask participants to make a circle and invite volunteers to describe their button experience with the whole group. Points to make in this discussion include:

- How homophobia (fear of being perceived as lesbian, gay, and bisexual) affects our decisions.
- How we can all experience homophobia regardless of our sexual orientation.
- Fear is justified in some situations that might be unsafe (might be fired, harassed, ostracized, target of violence).
- Heterosexuals who choose to be allies are sometimes called gay or lesbian to keep them from speaking out.
- Though lesbian, gay, and bisexual people may choose not to disclose their identity, the price of hiding and secrecy is high.
- Contrast wearing the button as a scary or threatening experience with how heterosexuals routinely display their identity in everyday activities (rings, talk of loved ones, pictures of loved ones, public displays of affection, public celebrations).

Break (15 minutes).

2. Lesbian, Gay, and Bisexual History (90 minutes).

Note: This activity takes some preparation by facilitators. We have provided a summary of some significant events in European and United States history that have shaped societal views on homosexuality in the West to use as a guide (see timeline in Appendix 8C) and have included some references that we recommend facilitators read (Katz, 1995; Marcus, 1992; Faderman, 1991; Katz, 1976). There are also some videos available that present historical events (*Before Stonewall* is one example).

Whatever presentation option you choose, we recommend that you create visual aids to use in this activity, such as slides, overheads, or a timeline that can be posted around the room noting significant events and when they occurred, and assign readings that prepare students with historical information.

Option 1:
If facilitators are prepared, much of this information can be presented in a lecture format that is punctuated with contributions from participants who are also knowledgeable about history, and questions to participants about what is being presented, or discussions based on assigned readings.

Option 2:
Another presentation option is to take the summary of significant events provided in the appendix and place these on index cards grouped by different historical eras. Then give these historical groupings of events to small groups of participants who present their era to the rest of the group in chronological order.

Option 3:
Show a video, for example, *Before Stonewall* or excerpts from the PBS series *A Question of Equality,* and then discuss it with participants.

Processing:
After presenting the history, ask participants to take a few minutes of personal time to write down some of their reactions to the history. Also ask them to identify any questions they have or connections they make with the histories of other forms of oppression. After a few minutes call participants back to the large group and use the following questions to stimulate discussion:

- What were your reactions to the history presentation (feelings and thoughts)?
- What did you learn that was new information for you?
- What information contradicted what you had previously thought?
- What themes or recurring patterns did you notice?
- What historical information helped you to better understand the present day reality of heterosexism?
- What events in the most recent part of the timeline do you remember from your own experience?

3. Setting the Context for the Caucus Groups (10 minutes).

Invite participants to think about how they choose to self-identify. In a heterosexism class, there may be participants who are genuinely uncertain which group to join. Some participants who are actively questioning their identity do not know how they identify. Others do not like labeling themselves. Some lesbian, gay, and bisexual participants might be reluctant to identify themselves to others. For these reasons we separate into an all lesbian, gay, and bisexual group for people who identify as lesbian, gay, or bisexual, and a mixed caucus, for people who choose not to identify, who are undecided or unclear about their sexual orientation, or who are heterosexual.

Another option is to have three groups if there are enough facilitators available to provide leadership for all groups. In this case, the caucus choices would be 1) all lesbian, gay, and bisexual, 2) all heterosexual, 3) questioning or resistant to labels. Remind participants about the confidentiality guideline, and invite them to think about which group they want to choose for the next activity. Take a break or begin the caucus groups at the beginning of the next module, so that participants have some time to think about their caucus choice and can go directly to separate caucus rooms after the break.

Facilitation Issues:
See the racism design (chapter 6) for a description of issues associated with dividing a class into agent and target caucus groups. Many of the issues discussed there are similar to issues involved in a heterosexism class. In addition, only facilitators who belong to the caucus group should sit in on that group's meeting. For example, an openly gay facilitator should only go to the lesbian, gay, and bisexual caucus group, and a heterosexual facilitator should only go to the mixed caucus group.

Participants may resist going into caucus groups, offering the argument that this structure "divides us" and causes us to focus on difference rather than similarity. This is an excellent opportunity to talk about the value of meeting with others who share a common social group perspective and also to call attention to the different agendas for each group. In our experience the mixed or all heterosexual group has more difficulty understanding the rationale for caucus groups. The all lesbian, gay, and bisexual group usually appreciates the opportunity to meet separately.

Note: Using caucus groups requires that one or two rooms be available close by. We do not recommend having caucus groups meeting in the same room.

4. Closing (20 minutes).

Go around the circle and ask each participant to say one thing they learned or one question that was raised for them about the lesbian, gay, and bisexual history.

Module 4

Time Needed: 4 hours
Goals:

- Identify concrete examples of collusion, heterosexual privilege, internalized homophobia, and strategies to eliminate them (review definitions in chapter 5).
- Describe an environment that is free of heterosexism and homophobia.
- List concrete action steps participants can choose to take in their lives to work against heterosexism and homophobia.

Key concepts: collusion, internalized homophobia, heterosexual privilege, non-heterosexist environment, strategies for intervention and change.

1. Caucus Groups (90 minutes).

When each group has assembled in the assigned room, give each group its own set of questions for discussion. Tell them that they have one hour in these groups, after which everyone will take a fifteen-minute break and return to the main room to rejoin the other group(s). The discussion agenda for each caucus group is as follows:

All Lesbian, Gay, and Bisexual Group

- What was it like to choose this group?
- What is something that you want to say, but would not say in a mixed group?
- How does internalized homophobia affect your daily life?
- What do you love about being lesbian, gay, and bisexual?
- What can you do to become more empowered?

All Heterosexual, Mixed, and Questioning Groups

- What was it like to choose this group?
- Is there anything you wanted to say, but were uncomfortable saying in front of lesbian, gay, and bisexual people?
- How does heterosexual privilege affect your daily life?
- What makes it difficult to be allies to lesbian, gay, and bisexual people?
- What can you do to become a better ally?

After about sixty minutes, take a break and bring the caucus groups back together. A quick energizing activity is useful at this point to help participants bridge the awkward feelings that sometimes accompany rejoining the whole group after caucusing. After this short energizer activity, post the following sentence stems on newsprint and invite participants to complete any of them by calling out their thoughts. The point of this activity is to listen to what others are saying and focus on understanding and accepting what they are saying.

- Something I want (other groups) to know about me is . . .
- Something I want from (other groups) is . . .
- Something that makes me feel good about being (lesbian, gay, and bisexual) is . . .
- A way I can be a better heterosexual ally is . . .
- A way I can act as a more empowered lesbian, gay, and bisexual person is . . .
- Something I never want said about lesbian, gay, and bisexual people again . . .
- Something I appreciate about one of the other groups is . . .

Alternative activities after the caucus groups include:

- *Speak outs*—Invite one or two people from each group to volunteer to talk about his/her answers to the caucus group questions in front of the whole group.
- *Fishbowl*—Invite members of one caucus group to form a circle in the center of the room and summarize their discussion while the rest of the group observes, and then have caucus groups switch roles.

After everyone has had a chance to complete the sentence stems aloud or completed the alternative activities, introduce the next activity as a way to help move toward a society in which people of all sexual orientations feel good about who they are and have access to the resources and rights they need to live safe, productive, and fulfilling lives.

2. Vision of a Non-heterosexist World (60 minutes).

In order to create a world that is free of heterosexism, we must know what that might be like. This exercise is designed to help us shape that vision. Tell the participants that they will be focusing on one of several situations, and working creatively to imagine it free of heterosexism and homophobia. Present the following scenarios (on newsprint or chalkboard):

- A large family gathering (reunion, wedding, funeral, holiday) where extended family, partners, parents, siblings, and close family friends are gathered.
- A school situation (describe the school in which the participants are enrolled).
- A workplace situation.

Ask the participants to form small groups of no more than five people, and complete the following tasks (groups will have twenty minutes):

1. Choose one of the scenarios.
2. Imagine that through a transformational miracle, that situation has been rendered free of homophobia and heterosexism, and is as equally accepting of lesbian, gay, and bisexual people as it is of heterosexual people. Describe in detail what happens in this new world free of heterosexism and homophobia. Use the following questions as guides, but feel free to go beyond them. Record your ideas on newsprint for presentation to the whole group.

If your group chooses *a family gathering*: what are the relationships like, how do people interact with one another, what roles do people have in the family, with children, and with partners? How is difference dealt with, what are the subtle power dynamics, who dances with whom, what cultural norms or practices are in place? Go into detail in creating a vivid picture of this non-homophobic family gathering. Have fun with it. Feel free to give people names and describe their fictional relationships. You will be invited to present your creation to the other groups.

If your group chooses *a school*: what about the curriculum, the sports program, the social events, the cultural offerings, the possible majors, the organizations, the newspaper, the mascot, the radio station, the student center, the governance system? Also talk about the climate for living and learning, safety on campus, security, the atmosphere of the school. Create what you think would be the most accepting school environment. You will be invited to present your creation to the other groups.

If your group chooses *a workplace*: discuss the organizational structure, the atmosphere, the policies and rules, the dress code, the management system, the technology, the group dynamics, the personnel, the hiring practices, the nonformal gatherings, the lunch groups and discussions, the "company teams," the work groups, the supervision, the grievance process, the benefits packages. Create an open and affirming workplace for all sexual orientations. You will be invited to present your creation to the others groups.

After fifteen minutes of work time, announce that there are five minutes remaining. At twenty minutes, call time, and invite each group to present in turn. Encourage the listeners to express their appreciation for creative thinking as the reports are given. Decide how long reports should be depending on the time available.

After all groups have reported, invite participants to reflect on these visions, and call out some ideas they heard that are actually workable in the present (inclusive language in all official printed material; domestic partnership benefits; a regular lesbian, gay, and bisexual section to the school paper; openly gay or bisexual faculty). Take about fifteen minutes on this last part.

3. Action Strategies (30 minutes).

This section addresses the question of what action we can take to create the change we want (Fahy, 1995). Remind participants that we are all in different stages of readiness to take action. We each need to decide what our personal next step might be. The action continuum may be useful in helping to assess what actions to choose.

Present the action continuum on a handout and on newsprint or poster (see Appendix 6C). Ask participants to identify their typical responses when confronted with an instance of homophobia. There may be more than one typical response. Give a personal example to illustrate this personal assessment (such as, when someone uses exclusive language or makes a heterosexual assumption, I usually just ignore it and go along). After each person has had a chance to think about the question, ask them to form groups of three and briefly describe where they are today on the action continuum as it relates to heterosexism (ten minutes).

Invite each group of three to address the following three questions, coaching each other when there is difficulty (twenty minutes).

- What is a situation in which you would be willing to nudge yourself one notch further on the continuum? Think of an instance where you could take a slightly larger risk than usual. Discuss those situations with each other.
- What are your personal obstacles to change?
- How can you get support?

Invite participants to imagine themselves in specific situations, taking action, encountering barriers, overcoming them, and feeling successful and proud of the stance they took.

4. Closing (45 minutes).

Invite participants to sit (stand) in a large circle together. Go around the circle and ask each person to describe in one sentence their personal action plan. Encourage non-verbal appreciations, but no critiques from others.

Ask participants to reflect on the entire course. Ask them to think back to all the activities, and identify a learning that they will remember. It could be something they learned, something that touched them, something that shocked them, something that surprised them, or something that was confirmed for them.

Conduct a second go around in the circle in which participants are asked to describe their reflections.

Conduct a written evaluation of the course.

Appendix 8A

DEFINITIONS

Sexism: The societal/cultural, institutional, and individual beliefs and practices that privilege men, subordinate women, and denigrate women-identified values.

Heterosexism: The societal/cultural, institutional, and individual beliefs and practices that assume that heterosexuality is the only natural, normal, acceptable sexual orientation.

Sexual Orientation: The desire for intimate emotional and sexual relationships with people of the same gender (lesbian, gay), the other gender (heterosexual), or either gender (bisexual).

Homophobia: The fear, hatred, or intolerance of lesbians, gay men, or any behavior that is outside the boundaries of traditional gender roles. Homophobia can be manifested as fear of association with lesbian or gay people or being perceived as lesbian or gay. Homophobic behavior can range from telling jokes about lesbian and gay people to physical violence against people thought to be lesbian or gay.

Biphobia: The fear, hatred, or intolerance of bisexual women or men.

Heterosexual Privilege: The benefits and advantages heterosexuals receive in a heterosexist culture. Also, the benefits lesbians, gay men, and bisexual people receive as a result of claiming heterosexual identity or denying homosexual or bisexual identity.

Heterosexual Ally: Heterosexual people who confront heterosexism, homophobia, and heterosexual privilege in themselves and others out of self-interest, a concern for the well-being of lesbian, gay, and bisexual people and a belief that heterosexism is a social justice issue.

Gender Identity: One's psychological sense of oneself as a male or a female.

Gender Roles: The socially constructed and culturally specific behavior and appearance expectations imposed on women (femininity) and men (masculinity).

Biological Sex: The physiological and anatomical characteristics of maleness or femaleness with which a person is born.

Transsexual: A person whose biological sex does not match their gender identity and who, through gender reassignment surgery and hormone treatments, seeks to change their physical body to match their gender identity. Transsexuals' sexual orientation can be heterosexual, homosexual, or bisexual.

Transgender Person: A person whose self-identification challenges traditional notions of gender and sexuality. Transgender people include transsexuals and others who do not conform to traditional understandings of labels like male and female or heterosexual and homosexual.

Cross-dresser: A person who enjoys dressing in clothes typically associated with the other gender. Also called a transvestite. Many cross-dressers are heterosexual married men.

Queer: Originally a derogatory label used to refer to lesbian and gay people or to intimidate and offend heterosexuals. More recently this term has been reclaimed by some lesbians, gay men, bisexual people, and transgender people as an inclusive and positive way to identify all people targeted by heterosexism and homophobia. Some lesbians and gay men have similarly reclaimed previously negative words such as "dyke" and "faggot" for positive self-reference.

Pedophile: An adult who is sexually attracted to children. Pedophiles can be male or female and heterosexual or homosexual. Most pedophiles are heterosexual men attracted to female children. Some pedophiles are attracted to children of either gender. It is a myth that most gay men are pedophiles. Police statistics show that well over 90 percent of all reported cases of child molestation involve heterosexual adult males and female children.

Drag Queen: A gay man who dresses in clothes, typically flamboyant and glamorous styles, associated with female movie stars or singers, all with theatrical intent and sometimes with the intention of poking fun at gender roles.

Appendix 8B

KLEIN SEXUAL ORIENTATION GRID

Variable	Past	Present	Ideal
Sexual Attraction			
Sexual Behavior			
Sexual Fantasies			
Emotional Preference			
Social Preference			
Self-Identification			
Hetero/Gay Lifestyle			

1=Other gender or heterosexual only
2=Other gender mostly or heterosexual mostly
3=Other gender somewhat more or heterosexual somewhat more
4=Both genders equally or hetero/lgb (lesbian, gay, bisexual) equally
5=Same gender somewhat more or lgb somewhat more
6=Same gender mostly or lgb mostly
7=Same gender only or lgb only

- Sexual Attraction: To whom are you sexually attracted? For the present, use the past year as a time frame.
- Sexual Behavior: With whom do you have sex?
- Sexual Fantasies: When you daydream, masturbate, or fantasize about sexual experiences, with whom do you imagine having sex?
- Emotional Preference: With whom do you feel intimate loving and emotional connections?
- Social Preference: With whom do you prefer to spend your social time?
- Self-Identification: How do you describe your sexual orientation?
- Heterosexual/Lesbian, Gay, Bisexual Lifestyle: With which "community" do you identify and spend time?

Choose the number that best describes your life for each of these variables in the past, present, and your ideal.

Appendix 8C

LESBIAN, GAY, BISEXUAL OPPRESSION HISTORY TIMELINE
Compiled by Pat Griffin

Before 2500 B.C.E.	Goddess Worship. No conception of sexual orientation, no stigma attached to same-sex sexuality.
1400 B.C.E.–1 C.E.	Greek and Roman Era. No conception of sexual orientation as an identity. Sexual relationships between men accepted as part of culture within strict norms of who takes what role in sex acts.
615–565 B.C.E.	Sappho, living in the isle of Lesbos, celebrates love between women in poems and songs.
1 C.E.–700 C.E.	Rise of Christianity in Western Europe. Extremely repressive period in which all sexuality or nudity except for procreation in marriage is condemned.
390	Theodosius declares Christianity official religion of Roman Empire.
533	Justinian imposes death penalty for adultery and same sex-acts.
900–1100	Veneration of Greek and Roman culture. Increased tolerance for many differences: religious, cultural, sexual. Knights, clerics, popes engaged in same sex acts.
1260–1600	Rise of intolerance. Inquisition, witch hunts. Heresy equated with same-sex acts. Women punished for violating gender order.
1260	Legal code of Orleans prescribes death penalty for same-sex acts.
1431	Joan of Arc burned at the stake for refusal to recant heresy, including her refusal to stop wearing men's clothes.
1481	Pope Innocent gives full sanction to the witch hunts.
1533	First English civil law to call for death penalty for same-sex acts between men (Buggery Law).
1600–1800	China and Japan: Sex between men tolerated into mid 1700s. Emperors, Buddhists, samurai have younger male lovers.
1740	First law punishing male same-sex acts in China.
1600–1800	Colonial America: colonists bring prejudices about sexuality with them from Europe to America. They are scandalized by Native American beliefs about sexuality and nudity. Cross-dressing women and men in some Native American cultures are revered as healers and shamans. Sex between men or between women referred to as "buggery," "the unspeakable sin against God," "sodomy," and "wickedness not to be named among Christians."
1800–1860	United States and Western Europe: Liberalizing of attitudes about sodomy in France, United States, Germany, and England. It is still a crime but not punished by death. Thomas Jefferson recommended that in Virginia sex between men be punished by castration and sex between females be punished by having a hole 1 1/2 inches in diameter bored into the nose cartilage of the offending women.
1810	Napoleonic Code removes all penalties for any sexual activity between consenting adults in France.

1861	England removes death penalty for sodomy.
1869	Hungarian doctor, Karoly Benkert, coins "homosexuality" to describe same-sex acts.
1870–1910	Western Europe and United States: rise of the medical profession's influence. Sodomy becomes homosexuality, a suitable topic for scientific study. Doctors develop a typology for a "Homosexual Personality," also called "inverts," and "the third sex," and "men trapped in women's bodies." Many medical "experts" call for decriminalization of homosexuality because "the poor creatures" are sick, not criminals.
1890s	"Heterosexual" is first used in medical texts to refer to people inclined toward sex with both men and women. By mid 1890s, heterosexual is used exclusively to refer to people who are inclined toward sex with the other sex.
1871	Paragraph 175 of the German Penal Code reiterates that homosexual acts between men is a crime (lays foundation for Nazi persecution of homosexuals).
1895	In England, Oscar Wilde, at the height of his popularity, is arrested, tried, and imprisoned for homosexuality.
1897	Dr. Magnus Hirschfield, a German homosexual, founds the Scientific Humanitarian Committee, the first homosexual rights organization.
1900–1930	Germany and United States: homosexual rights movement flourishes in Germany. Rich urban subculture for homosexual men and women develops in Germany and United States. African American lesbians, gay men, and bisexuals prominent part of the Harlem Renaissance. "Gay" becomes a code word in the homosexual subculture in U.S. Freud "discovers" female sexuality. The "New Woman" (feminists and suffragists) of the 1920s are stigmatized as "lesbians." Doctors "treat" the "symptoms" of homosexuality with a variety of "cures": castration, electric shock, cliterodectomy, hormone injections, lobotomy, untested drugs, commitment to insane asylums, and vigorous exercise and diet programs.
1919	The Institute for Sexual Science is founded in Germany by Magnus Hirschfield.
1923	Emma Goldman becomes one of the earliest public supporters of homosexual rights in U.S.
1924	The Chicago Society for Human Rights is founded by Henry Gerber, the first homosexual rights organization in the United States.
1928	Radclyffe Hall's lesbian novel, *The Well of Loneliness*, is banned in the United States.
1930–1946	Pro-Nazi Forces in Germany target homosexual men as "unGerman." State sanctioned harassment and violence against homosexuals begins.
1933	Hitler becomes Chancellor of Germany and all homosexual organizations are banned. Attacks against homosexuals escalate.
1933–44	Homosexual rights movement in Germany is wiped out. Thousands of homosexual men are sent to concentration camps, few survive. Homosexuals in the camps wore a pink triangle to signify their identity. In the

	United States, despite massive efforts to screen out homosexual men and women from military service, many find each other in the gay urban subcultures of port cities (San Francisco and New York).
Late 1940s	First lesbian newsletter *Vice Versa* started by Lisa Ben (a pseudonym).
1946–1960	Post-war period marks return to traditional family values, domestic tranquility. Cold War begins.
1948	First Kinsey study reveals that homosexual behavior among men is far more widespread than previously thought. Bisexuality highlighted because of Kinsey's research.
1950	The United States Senate authorizes a formal investigation of "homosexuals and other moral perverts" in government. Ushers in a decade of active police and government harassment of homosexual men and women.
1951	Mattachine Society is founded by Henry Hay (homosexual men's organization).
1952	Kinsey does a study of homosexual behavior among females. Eisenhower signs Executive Order barring homosexuals from government service.
1955	Daughters of Bilitis founded by Del Martin and Phyllis Lyon (homosexual women's organization).
1960–1968	Time of social change and breakdown of social consensus on many issues. Minority voices speak out: black civil rights, anti-war, counterculture, women.
1961	U.S. Motion Picture Code rules that homosexuality, previously banned from the screen, can be depicted "with discretion, care, and restraint."
1962	*Life* magazine does feature on emerging gay subculture in America.
1967	The first student homophile organization forms at Columbia University in New York City.
1967	The ACLU changes its position on the constitutionality of legal sanctions against gay people and states publicly that it supports gay rights laws.
1968	The North American Conference of Homophile Organizations adopts "Gay Is Good" as a slogan for the movement.
1969–1976	Period of enormous growth and visibility of the gay rights movement.
June 27, 1969	Stonewall Riots, New York City. During a routine police raid of a gay bar in Greenwich Village, gay men and lesbians fight back for first time, touching off three days of riots and gaining national media attention. This is marked as the birth of the modern gay/lesbian rights movement.
1972	George Weinberg coins "homophobia" to describe an irrational fear of homosexuality. First time anti-homosexual feelings are labeled as pathological.
1973	American Psychiatric Association removes homosexuality from its list of mental disorders.
1975	American Psychological Association removes homosexuality from its list of mental disorders.

1972–1976	36 cities and towns adopt gay rights laws. 25 states repeal sodomy laws. Several mainstream religious groups endorse gay rights laws.
1977–1980	Emerging political conservative and fundamentalist Christian coalition voices resistance to gay rights.
1977	Dade County, Florida recalls gay rights law. Singer Anita Bryant becomes spokeswoman for anti-gay groups. Harvey Milk, first openly gay city supervisor, elected in San Francisco.
1978	Gay rights laws recalled in Eugene, Oregon; Wichita, Kansas; St. Paul, Minnesota. Briggs Initiative introduced and defeated in California (prohibiting gay teachers in schools or any positive discussion of homosexuality in schools). Briggs Initiative look-alike passed in Oklahoma. Harvey Milk and Mayor George Moscone assassinated in San Francisco, November 27.
1979	First national March on Washington for lesbian and gay rights has 100,000 participants.
1980–1991	Increasing swing toward conservatism as Ronald Reagan is elected President.
1981	First cases of AIDS begin to appear.
1982	Wisconsin passes the first state-wide gay rights law in the nation.
1982	The first Gay (Olympic) Games with 1,500 participants. USOC sues organizers and prohibits the use of the word "Olympic" in association with the Gay Games.
1986	Supreme Court rules that a Georgia sodomy law was correctly used to arrest and convict a gay man for having sex with a man in his own bedroom when a police officer came to the home to serve a traffic summons and discovered the two men.
1987	The second national March on Washington for lesbian and gay rights has 700,000 participants. It is the biggest civil rights march in the history of the country. *Time* and *Newsweek* fail to report it. Bisexuals becoming increasingly visible and vocal about being explicitly included in lesbian and gay events and organizations.
1988	Department of Justice releases a report on hate crimes in the United States. Lesbians and gay men cited as most frequent targets.
1988	Act Up (AIDS Coalition to Unleash Power) becomes a prominent direct action group calling national attention to the failure of the government to address AIDS and price gouging by drug companies. This ushers in a new era of militant activism by lesbians, gay men, bisexual people, and heterosexual allies.
1989	American Bar Association endorses gay rights legislation. Massachusetts becomes the second state to pass a gay rights law. Denmark becomes the first country in the world to legalize gay marriages. United States Department of Health and Human Services issues a report on teen suicide: lesbian and gay youth reported to be 2–3 times more likely to kill themselves. Much of the report is suppressed by conservative Republicans.
1990	Beginning of Queer Nation, a direct action protest group of mostly young lesbian, gay, and bisexual people in cities and towns around the country. "Outing" becomes a controversial tactic within LGB commu-

	nity where well-known, but closeted lesbian and gay politicians, movie stars, athletes, etc. are yanked out of the closet by other gays.
1990	Gay Games III in Vancouver, British Columbia, attracts over 7,000 athletes from 26 countries and is the largest athletic event in the world in the last two years. No media coverage. Connecticut and Hawaii become the 3rd and 4th states to enact gay rights laws.
1991	AIDS moves into the 10th year of the epidemic.
1992–1996	Diversification of lesbian, gay, bisexual movement. Religious right leads backlash against gay civil rights.
1992	Coalitions of right-wing Christian fundamentalists and Republicans target lesbians and gay men as responsible for the the breakdown of "traditional family values." Anti-gay rhetoric is prominent part of Republican National Convention. Oregon and Colorado place initiatives on the November ballot that would outlaw gay rights legislation. Colorado initiative wins and becomes model for anti-gay initiatives in other states. Massachusetts becomes first state with Governor's Commission on Lesbian and Gay Youth recommending that all schools address the needs of LGB youth.
1993	President Clinton proposes lifting the military ban on homosexuals resulting in "Don't Ask, Don't Tell, Don't Pursue" policy. Third National March on Washington for Lesbian, Gay, and Bisexual Rights. First time "bisexual" is included in march title. Approximately one million people attend.
1994	Gay Games IV in New York City has 11,000 athletes. 25th anniversary of Stonewall March in NYC. Transgender people protest their exclusion from Stonewall march title. Colorado law ruled unconstitutional by Colorado Supreme Court, goes to Supreme Court. Anti-gay initiatives on ballot in Idaho and Oregon. Hawaii Supreme Court considers legalizing marriage between same-sex couples, resulting in backlash in several other states passing laws barring marriage between same-sex couples.
1996	Supreme Court rules Colorado anti-gay civil rights law unconstitutional.

Source: Information in this timeline was compiled by P. Griffin from the following sources: S. Cavin (1985), *Lesbian Origins*, San Francisco: Ism Press; J. D'Emilio (1983), *Sexual Politics, Sexual Communities: The Making of a Homosexual Minority in the United States, 1940–1970*, Chicago: University of Chicago Press; J. D'Emilio & E. Freedman (1988), *Intimate Matters: A History of Sexuality in America*, New York: Harper & Row; M. Duberman, M. Vicinus & G. Chauncey (Eds.) (1989), *Hidden from History: Reclaiming the Gay and Lesbian Past*, New York: New American Library; R. Eisler (1987), *The Chalice and the Blade: Our Past, Our Future*, San Francisco: Harper & Row; A. Evans (1978), *Witchcraft and the Gay Counterculture*, Boston: Fag Rag Books; L. Faderman (1991), *Odd Girls and Twilight Lovers: A History of Lesbian Life in the Twentieth Century*, New York: Columbia University Press; L. Feinberg (1996), *Transgender Warriors: Making History from Joan of Arc to RuPaul*, Boston: Beacon; J. Grahn (1984), *Another Mother Tongue*, Boston: Beacon; J. Katz (1983), *Gay/Lesbian Almanac*, New York: Harper & Row; J. Katz (1995), *The Invention of Heterosexuality*, New York: Dutton Books; E. Marcus (1992), *Making History: The Struggle for Gay and Lesbian Rights, 1945–1990*, New York: HarperPerennial; R. Plant (1986), *The Pink Triangle: The Nazi War against Homosexuals*, New York: Henry Holt & Co.; U. Vaid (1995), *Virtual Equality: The Mainstreaming of Gay and Lesbian Liberation*, New York: Doubleday; A. Weiss & G. Schiller (1988), "Before Stonewall" in *The Making of a Gay and Lesbian Community*, Tallahassee, FL: Naiad Press.

9

Antisemitism Curriculum Design

Gerald Weinstein, Donna Mellen

Introduction

As we began to write this chapter, we heard on the local news that a synagogue in a nearby community had been spray painted with the words: "Kill The Jews, Heil Hitler" (with customary swastika), and "White Power." Soon after, a large menorah erected on a family's lawn in celebration of Hanukkah was demolished. A few days later a controversial African American professor was invited to our campus as a guest speaker and proceeded to emphasize Jewish involvement in Black oppression. The campus newspaper reported that "Tensions between Black and Jewish students soared in the latter half of . . . [the] . . . speech, as the focus switched to negative Jewish involvement in Black history" (*Daily Collegian*, 1994).

Antisemitism has been documented in writings as early as 300 C.E. and has been called the "longest hatred" (Wistrich, 1991). The term "Semitic" originally referred to a family of languages that included Hebrew and Arabic. In the late nineteenth century, the term "antisemitic" was applied directly to hatred of Jews and not to hatred of all Semitic peoples. Lerner (1992) defines antisemitism as the systematic discrimination against, denigration, or oppression of Jews, Judaism, or the cultural heritage of the Jewish people. In different periods of history antisemitism has taken different forms.

While there is considerable controversy about the extent of antisemitism in the United States, the annual audit of the Anti-Defamation League reported a record 1,879 incidents of antisemitism in 1991, an 11 percent increase over 1990, with for the first time more attacks on people than property (Anti-Defamation League, 1994). Reported incidents of antisemitism on college campuses have also risen sharply in recent years (Sidel, 1994) and have included everything from hate graffiti to a wave of "jokes" about "Jewish American princesses." In a 1992 study on our own campus, 65 percent of 512 undergraduate Jewish students interviewed about their perceptions of campus antisemitism felt that it existed on campus, and the same percentage experienced negative stereotypic remarks from other students (Malaney, 1994).

The Cyclical Dynamics of Antisemitism

Throughout history, overt antisemitic hatred and destruction have regularly subsided to more subtle manifestations and then reemerged with a fury. Those who are aware of this cyclical pattern see the importance of analyzing and confronting antisemitism in all of its forms, no matter how subtle. Those who look at the present without an appreciation of the cyclical nature of this pattern may dismiss antisemitism as a thing of the past, much less important than other forms of oppression in today's world. This course, therefore, emphasizes the understanding of the cyclical historical patterns of antisemitism as fundamental to understanding the complex dynamics of antisemitism today.

For Jews who have family members who lived through or perished in the Holocaust, or for those who know the cycles of antisemitism, incidents of antisemitism on college campuses or in Eastern Europe will be evidence of the here-and-now reality of antisemitism. For those who know little or nothing of the history of antisemitism, graffiti on a campus building, antisemitic remarks by a Russian politician or by Louis Farrakhan or White Power groups, may be overlooked or dismissed as isolated acts, not worth worrying about.

Eastern European Antisemitism

With the fall of Eastern European communist political systems, there has been a mushrooming of antisemitism along with Eastern European nationalism. Along with greater freedom of expression has come the outpouring of age-old latent, anti-Jewish bigotry, reflecting the pattern of antisemitism reemerging in more overt forms during periods of social or economic stress and nationalistic fervor.

Black–Jewish Relations

Many Jews feel alarmed by the expressions of antisemitism by African Americans. Speakers such as Louis Farrakhan and Leonard Jefferies reflect and focus upon many of the negative stereotypes and themes which have haunted Jews throughout history (see Anti-Defamation League, 1993; Austen, 1994; Davis, 1994; Reed, 1986). Because the stereotypes of Jews as wealthy and powerful have grown out of the historical effects of antisemitism, some people of color are unaware of this history and may have difficulty appreciating the harmful effects of perpetuating these antisemitic stereotypes. Black-Jewish tensions are being addressed in balanced ways by authors such as Lerner and West (1992, 1996), Berman(1994), Bulkin, Pratt and Smith (1984), Kaye/Kantrowitz (1992), Kaufman (1988), Strickland (1988), Salzman et al., (1992), Roiphe (1988), Weisbord and Stein (1970), and the new journal *Common Quest.* In fact, one might say there is now a substantial Black-Jewish relations "literature."

Palestinian Rights and Criticism of Israel

The oppression of the Palestinian people by the Israeli government is an important human rights issue that deserves to be expressed and challenged, as it has been by Palestinian, Israeli and American writers (see, for example, Said, 1996, 1993; Yehoshua, 1995, 1981; Grossman, 1993; Doumani, 1992; Fernea & Hocking, 1992; Young, 1992; Falbel et al., 1990; Chomsky, 1983; Memmi, 1975). At the same time, leftist criticisms of Israel and Zionism continue to obscure the boundaries between legitimate criticism of Israeli policy and antisemitism. Implicit in some criticisms is an antisemitic double standard, implying that Jews are a people who have no right to national sovereignty, that Arabs are not perpetrators of antisemitism, and that Israel should be judged by standards of human rights more stringent than those applied to other nations (Lerner, 1992; Friedman, 1989).

Importance of History

Oppression issues are so embedded in the lengthy story of the Jews' fight for survival that the story becomes essential to understanding the faces, features, and factors of antisemitism. We lead up to it by focusing on stereotypic thinking that we as individuals, Jews and non-Jews, carry with us, and that is consistently reinforced by the dominant Christian culture of the West. We then tell the story, bringing to light its central themes, patterns, and concepts. We examine the evolving motives for antisemitism and illustrate how a people's behavior is channeled, influenced, and affected by centuries of oppression. (References we have found most helpful in preparing this history presentation include Castello & Kapon, 1994; Cohn-Sherbok, 1994; Dimont, 1962; Dinnerstein, 1994; Lerner, 1992; Wistrich, 1991; and Boonstra et al., 1989.)

Following the presentation and discussion of the history, we focus on how our individual lives have been touched by the various facets of the history. Given our time constraints, we concentrate on helping participants understand the European and Christian roots and current dynamics of antisemitism in the United States today. We do not examine antisemitism in the Islamic world or other parts of the globe (see Wistrich, 1991; Weinberg, 1986).

Issues of Identity and Self-Definition: What to Expect from Participants

While for Gentiles the course provides a review of issues about the oppressed "other" and their own role in that oppression, for many Jewish students it becomes a significant factor in the renewal of their identities as Jews. Because denial and trivializing of antisemitism by both Gentiles and Jews is a common and important obstacle to overcome, and because the most poignant evidence of antisemitism lies in the personal pain and struggles that individual Jews experience, personal stories help to bring the issues alive. We thus advocate a mixed group approach to this issue.

Jews come in as many different varieties as there are peoples. Self-identified Jews have in common a shared history that dates back 3000 years to the Hebrew tribes of Canaan. This history is cultural, religious, social, and personal and shapes many of the current practices of Jews. Jewishness is not genetic; it is a learned and acquired cultural heritage and identity as well as a shared history reinforced by religious observance and ritual. The ways in which Jews have related to this identity run the gamut from those who don't consider themselves Jewish even though they have Jewish ancestors, to those who practice Jewish customs and rituals every day of their lives. However, whether people of Jewish descent identify themselves as Jewish bears little relation to how they are defined by others, especially those in power. Historically, even when they had converted to Christianity under intense pressure to assimilate, Jews have been designated as the "other" and become targets of oppression.

Jewish students vary in the ways in which they construct their identities as Jews.

Some have strong and clear identities, both religious and cultural; some identify culturally but do not follow religious beliefs and practices; some come from families that have assimilated into Christian culture; some come from mixed parentage. Many of these students come to our courses with questions about what being Jewish means for their identities and lives, and this may seem confusing to non-Jewish participants in the class.

"Gentile" is a term that applies to anyone who is not a Jew. The notion of being a Gentile may be completely new to some students, who are often unaware of their identity as members of that group from the perspective of Jews. It can be painful to come to grips with an aspect of one's social identity that is so closely related to the oppression of others. For Christian Gentiles, feelings of guilt, anger, and confusion sometimes accompany learning about the role of Christianity in Jewish persecution, which seems to contradict everything they were taught about being Christians. And those from mixed Jewish/Christian parentage may experience intense confusion as to how to manage that combination of inherited histories.

Overall Goals

- Understand the historical development and dynamics of antisemitism, including the roots of antisemitic stereotypes.
- Understand how antisemitism is manifested in our personal lives as well as in our society.
- Identify and discuss actions that we can take to interrupt antisemitism.

OVERVIEW OF ANTISEMITISM MODULES
Introductory Module (see chapter 5)

Module 1 (3 hours)
Agenda

1. Introductions, Welcome (30 mins.)
2. Course Description and Goals (10 mins.)
3. Definitions (30 mins.)
4. Stereotypes of Jews (60 mins.)
5. Closing (10 mins.)

Module 2 (3 1/2 to 4 hours)
Agenda

1. History of Antisemitism
   Ancient and Greco-Roman Period
   Rise of Christianity and Middle
   Beginning of Modern Era
   20th Century
2. Historical Themes
3. Closing

Module 3 (3 Hours)
Agenda

1. Check-in (20 mins.)
2. Speakouts of Jews and Gentiles (40 mins.)
3. Caucus Groups: Jews and Gentiles (60 mins.)

Module 4 (3 Hours)
Agenda

1. Action Strategies to Combat Antisemitism (45 mins.)
2. Contracts for Change (60 mins.)
   Option A: Increase Personal Awareness

4. Intergroup Discussion (30 mins.)	Option B: Personal Behavior Change
5. Closing (30 mins.)	Option C: Interrupting Antisemitism
	Option D: Spheres of Influence
	3. Closing (30 mins.)

Handout 9.1. Overview of Antisemitism Modules.

Antisemitism Curriculum Design

Module 1

Time Needed: 3 hours
Goals:

- Define the concept of stereotypes.
- Demonstrate the prevalence of Jewish stereotyping.
- Identify conscious and subconscious negative attitudes about the Jewish people.
- Realize the importance of CONTEXT in understanding stereotypes.

Key Concepts: antisemitism, Jews, Gentiles, stereotypes.

Activities:

1. Introductions, Welcome, Warmup Activity (30 minutes).

Introduce yourself and talk briefly about why you are committed to addressing the issue of antisemitism. Use chapter 5 for suggestions on introductions, class description, and participation guidelines. One approach might be to have participants introduce themselves by talking briefly about the histories of their names, either first name or last name or both. For Jewish students, stories will emerge of Hebrew names, being named for Jewish forebears, names changed upon immigration to the United States. For non-Jewish students, there are various ethnic traditions and family histories that provide material for later discussions of ethnicity as a part of Jewish and other self-identities.

It might be helpful for a Jewish leader to identify her or himself as a Jew rather than as Jewish and explain how it is more difficult to say "I'm a Jew" because historically the word Jew itself has been used with a negative connotation. Also, publicly identifying oneself as a Jew can feel intimidating for some Jewish participants. By mentioning and acknowledging that such public identification is a problem for some Jews, facilitators can draw participants' attention to an identity issue, which in itself is one of the consequences of antisemitism.

2. Course Description and Goals (10 minutes).

Post the agenda, goals, and participation guidelines on newsprint or on a chalkboard (see chapter 5). Keep them visible for the duration of the course, so that you or participants can refer to them. Give special attention to the guidelines for discussions since an atmosphere of trust and safety are important. Ask for questions, additions, revisions, and ask for agreement on the guidelines from the whole group by a show of hands.

3. Definitions (30 minutes).

Brainstorm definitions of key terms and help students clarify what it means to be Jewish or Gentile. Respond to any questions participants may have about the definitions.

Definitions

Antisemitism: "Semitic" originally referred to a family of languages that included Hebrew. But it came to be applied directly to hatred of the Jews. Antisemitism is the systematic discrimination against, denigration, or oppression of Jews, Judaism, and the cultural, intellectual, and religious heritage of the Jewish people.

Jew: The term Jew is derived from Judea, one of the ancient kingdoms of the Hebrew people. Since the scattering of the Jewish people, after the destruction of Judea and Israel, the Jews have thought of themselves as a people, a religion, a culture, joined together by a common history. Whether they assimilated or remained separate, Jews in medieval Europe were "the other" on the basis of their non-Christian religious practice and culture; in modern Europe they were "the other" on the basis of racial hierarchies (Aryan, Serb, and Semite).

Gentile: Derived from the Latin word for "pagan," it has been used by Jews to refer to all non-Jews.

Handout 9.2. Definitions of General Concepts: Antisemitism.

4. Stereotypes of Jews (60 minutes).

Begin this activity by explaining the rules of brainstorming: don't discuss or judge anyone's contribution; it is all right to elaborate on someone else's contribution. Then, either in small groups, or the group as a whole, ask participants to brainstorm anything they've ever heard about Jews. The resulting list on newsprint is used for reference during the history presentation. The history provides the context and explanations for most if not all of the stereotypes usually generated during this activity. After listing the stereotypes, divide participants into groups of two or three and ask them to respond to the following questions:

- What do you notice about the stereotypes? (Example: most are negative.)
- What stereotypes appear most frequently? (Examples: cheap, pushy, J.A.P., clannish.)
- What does it mean that we were able to generate this large list so quickly?

After five minutes call the group back together to discuss their observations and to note common themes raised in the small group discussions.

Present the definition and characteristics of stereotypes. These can be displayed as overheads or posted on newsprint where all can see. Read through and discuss the following:

Stereotype: an undifferentiated, simplistic attribution that involves a judgment of habits, traits, abilities, or expectations and is assigned as a characteristic to all members of a group regardless of individual variation and with no attention to the relation between the attributions and the social contexts in which they have arisen.

Make the following points about the characteristics of stereotypes:

- The dominant group projects self-denied attributes (usually negative but sometimes positive) onto another group.
- Stereotypes often have a grain of truth but are taken out of historical context.
- Attributions are depicted as unchanging.
- Attributions are experienced as hurtful by the targeted group.
- The same attributions may be renamed in a positive way by the dominant group when alluding to themselves.

Post the following chart of agent and target attributes to illustrate.

Targets	**Agents**
They Are . . .	We Are . . .
aggressive	ambitious
stingy	frugal
money-hungry	entrepreneurial
exclusive	discriminating
clannish	loyal
different, strange	unique, individual
clever, shrewd	intelligent
unethical, cheats	doing business
stiff-necked, stubborn	independent

Handout 9.3. They Are, We Are.

Discuss how stereotypes function to maintain oppression:

- They provide a rationalization for oppression. They place blame on the victim, implying that because of these attributes they ask for and deserve what they get. (Example: If Jews weren't so pushy and aggressive they wouldn't have been mistreated.)
- Stereotypes dehumanize the oppressed in the eyes of the agent group, making it easier for them to deny or rationalize any pain they might inflict. (Example: "The Jews are the cause of our problems, so don't trust them.")
- Specific stereotypes have risen from complex social/historical situations and are the result of adaptations and survival strategies that were created and reenforced by the oppressive practices of the dominant culture. Therefore, the perpetuation of stereotypes is based on two important omissions: they neglect to take into account the historical context within which culture and behaviors were created, and they apply an already shaky generalization to arrive at conclusions about individuals.

This activity helps participants witness the ease with which stereotypes of Jews, mainly negative, can be elicited from a random group of people and how embedded they are in common cultural learnings. These stereotypes provide the "hooks" on which the various elements of the history of antisemitism can be hung.

5. Closing (10 minutes).

Briefly go around the circle and ask participants to note something they are looking forward to learning more about.

Module 2

Time Needed: 3 1/2 to 4 hours
Goals:

- Appreciate the importance of historical context to the understanding of stereotypes.
- Comprehend how certain patterns of oppression and the responses to those patterns were expressed throughout the different periods of Jewish history.
- Become familiar with certain aspects of the story of the Jewish struggle for survival over a 3,000 year period.
- Recognize the connection between today's manifestations of antisemitism and that 3,000 year story.

Key Concepts: cyclicity, collusion.

1. History of Antisemitism (3 1/2 hours).

Activities:
Module 2 is devoted to a chronological and thematic history of antisemitism which can be presented in several ways, depending on the readiness level of the facilitators and the opportunities for prior readings by the students. Each of these alternative approaches juxtaposes a chronological historical account with the emergent and accumulating themes of antisemitism as illustrated in the chart in Appendix 9A. Selections from the readings are listed at the end of this book.

Option 1: Lecture on Chronological and Emergent Themes
Facilitators will prepare themselves by reading one or more of the histories mentioned earlier and then use the historical summaries and emergent themes presented in boxes within the text as historical overviews, emergent themes, and highlights. It is helpful to illustrate this material with maps from sources such as Dimont (1962), and Cohn-Sherbok (1994) and illustrations from historical drawings and engravings of Jewish life in Boonstra et al. (1989), Mosse (1985), Castello and Kapon (1994), and Gilman (1991), as overhead transparencies. These transparencies help the facilitator organize the historical material while focusing and maintaining student attention and interest.

Option 2: Lecture on Historical Vignettes
Depending on the readings that students complete prior to this presentation, facilitators who feel fairly familiar with the history of antisemitism may prefer to focus on historical vignettes rather than attempting to cover the narrative history. For example, such an approach could emphasize the Diaspora, the series of expulsions from medieval towns and cities, the mass murders during the Crusades, the Inquisition and expulsion from Spain in 1492, and the pogroms and mass murders in Poland and Russia in the eighteenth and nineteenth centuries, leading up to the Holocaust. Such an approach would focus on the emergent themes of antisemitism

while using illustrative vignettes. The facilitator who uses this approach would need to be able to allude to similar historical events without presenting a narrative or chronological account.

Option 3: Jigsaw Group Study and Presentation of Historical Highlights

The historical highlights presented in boxes in this chapter can be divided by the number of participants and given out on individual sheets of paper for the students to review in small group discussions. Adjacent historical highlights would be discussed within small groups, and students would report out the highlights and themes they have discovered in chronological fashion. This option is more interactive and participatory for students who have completed historical readings, while still covering the historical information and focusing attention on the emergent themes. A film such as *The Longest Hatred* provides a dramatic teaching aid.

Option 1: Lecture on Chronological and Emergent Themes

The history is divided into four major historical phases separated by small group discussion.

Overview of History Presentation

The Ancient and Greco-Roman Eras: Jews as "Other."
Ancient or Pagan Antisemitism
Greco-Roman Antisemitism

The Rise of Christianity and The Middle Ages: Jews as anti-Christ, satanic, linked to usury.
Christian Religious Antisemitism
(Processing Break)
Economic and Political Antisemitism
(Processing Break)

Beginning of the Modern Era: Jews as economic exploiters and political scapegoats.
Beginnings of Modern Europe
Age of Enlightenment
(Processing Break)

The Twentieth Century: Political and Racial Antisemitism—Jews as political conspirators and inferior species, Jews as nationalistic human rights violators, exploiters of the oppressed, power holders.
Modern Antisemitism
(Processing Break)

Handout 9.4. Overview of History Presentation.

In preparation for the small group discussions, ask participants during the history presentations to take notes on the following questions, which should be posted on newsprint:

- What are the sources for the stereotypes we have listed?

■ What are emergent themes, patterns of oppression, and Jewish responses?

Explain that B.C.E. means "before the common era" and C.E means "the common era." These designations are not Christian based as are B.C. and A.D., although the pervasive influence of Christianity is still evident in how we measure time, B.C.E and C.E

In preparing for this presentation facilitators may find it useful to organize the history in some of the following ways:

a. Use historical and contemporary maps from sources listed above as overhead transparencies.

b. Post a history timeline around the room.

c. Prepare the blocked sheet date summaries of each lecture for distribution and/or overheads, so that participants can follow the history presentation.

d. Display on newsprint the historical phases covered in the presentation.

e. Prepare illustrative overhead transparencies.

f. Divide among co-facilitators the various alternating presentation segments.

g. Assign appropriate readings in advance of the course (see contents of reader at the back of the book).

Ancient Era: 2000 B.C.E to 400 B.C.E

Key Events:

B.C.E. 2000–1100: Wanderings in Canaan (Abraham). Exodus of Jews from Egypt and wanderings in Sinai. Settle in Canaan.

B.C.E. 1100–800: Independence period.

B.C.E. 800–700: Assyrians conquer Israel. Jews in Israel taken captive and dispersed. End of Israelites.

B.C.E. 600–500: Babylonian conquest. Fall of kingdom of Judah. Temple destroyed. Jews dispersed. Many deported to Babylonia. Jews in Babylonia codify laws and keep culture alive.

B.C.E. 500–400: Persian domination. Some Jews allowed to return to Jerusalem. Temple rebuilt.

Jews oppressed for:	**Oppressed via:**
—being a rival national and religious group	—forced migrations —dispersions (Diaspora)

Handout 9.5. Ancient Era: 3000–400 B.C.E.

Key Points: Ancient Era

■ During this period, the Jews developed their spiritual and national identity. Their country, Canaan (Palestine/Israel), existed between four huge empires, Egypt, Babylonia, Assyria, and Persia, that were often at war. Canaan was strategically important, fell to frequent invasions, and became a vassal state to one empire or another. Only during a period of about three hundred years (1200–900 B.C.E.) was Canaan an independent Jewish kingdom ruled by the kings Saul, David, and Solomon. Solomon's temple in Jerusalem was destroyed by successive Assyrian and Babylonian invasions.

■ After each invasion, most of the population was taken back to the conquering nation in captivity. These were the first of many dispersions of the Jewish people, which would eventually spread Jews throughout the world and lead to the stereotype of the "wandering Jew." The dispersions also placed Jews in the role of the Other, as permanent aliens, foreigners in whatever country they moved to. While in captivity, many Jews, bound together by a common monotheistic religion, maintained their cultural and national identity. Here lie the roots of the "return to Jerusalem" theme that was to accompany Jews throughout their history and is remembered each year in the Passover Seder ritual.

- When Babylonia was conquered by Persia (500 B.C.E.), many Jews were allowed to return to Canaan to restore a Jewish community in Jerusalem and to rebuild their temple. Many of the Jews still living in different parts of the world paid a "temple tax" to support this center of Jewish religion in the Jewish homeland.
- Wherever Jews were, maintaining the Jewish religion depended on literacy in comprehending and codifying Gods law. This may be a root of Jewish literacy and intellectualism.

Greco-Roman Era: 334–63 B.C.E.

Key Points:

B.C.E. 334–322: Greeks defeat Persians. Jews under Grecian influence. Greco-Roman period begins.

B.C.E. 300–200: Hebrew scriptures translated into Greek. Foundations for Christianity are set.

B.C.E. 168–4: Macabbean revolt. Independent Jewish state reestablished.

B.C.E. 63: Palestine conquered by Romans.

Jews oppressed for:
—preserving religious and cultural differences
—not assimilating
—rebelling

Oppressed via:
—enslavement
—non-citizenship
—special taxation
—confiscation of property
—rules against proselytizing and conversion
—murder

Handout 9.6. Greco-Roman Era: 322–100 B.C.E.

Note emergent themes and then continue lecture using the above box.

Key points: Greco-Roman Era

- During this period many Jews became Hellenized and Romanized. As they spread throughout the Greek and Roman empires, sometimes by choice and sometimes as captives, many became involved in trade and commerce, using the Diaspora connections whenever they could. Jewish merchants were among the first to take part in a growing seaborne trade with the East (Arkin, 1975). Because of the shared language and religious heritage during the Diaspora, Jews had entree to a world trade community not generally available to their Gentile competitors. This may have stimulated the roots of the stereotypes of Jews as international conspirators, consumed by business, an exclusive club.
- Periodically, however, Greek and Roman rule became increasingly aggressive in its attempts to convert Jews to the Greco-Roman way of life, leading, at certain

times, to the outlawing of the Jewish religious observances. There were also outright slaughters of portions of the Jewish population. Those Jews who insisted on adhering to their religious beliefs were branded by Greco-Roman writers as "degenerate outcasts, hated by the gods and men" (Wistrich, 1991).

On several occasions Jews revolted against Roman persecution. The Macabbean Revolt (168–164 B.C.E.) led to an independent Jewish state and is commemorated in the celebration of Hanukkah. After the Romans conquered Palestine in 63 B.C.E. the Jews did not have a national homeland until Israel was founded in 1949.

Beginning of Christian religious antisemitism: 100–600 C.E.

C.E.—Jesus born
1–100: Pontius Pilate procurator of Judea. Christ crucified by Romans.
100–200: Jewish rebellions. Jews dispersed throughout empire. Palestine destroyed and rendered off-limits to Jews.
300–400: Emperor Constantine converts to Christianity. Beginning of Holy Roman Empire. New Testament canonized. First laws limiting rights of non-Christians.
400–600: Christianity spread throughout empire. Papacy established. Jews the only non-Christians in a Christian empire.

Jews oppressed for:
—not converting
—"past sins"; deicide

Oppressed via:
—labels: Christ killers, evil ones, devils
—Judas and the Wandering Jew as Jewish archetypes
—loss of citizenship and rights to practice their religion

Handout 9.7. The Rise of Christianity: 100–600 C.E.

Key points: Christian Religious Antisemitism

- Christianity began as a Jewish sect and for a long time converts were sought primarily from among other Jews. Then Christianity separated from Judaism and spread among the Gentiles. Much of early Christian theology sought to discredit traditional Judaism and establish Christianity as the one true religion. Jews who would not convert were seen as rebels against God's purpose. Since some explanation had to be offered for why many Jews would not accept Christ as the son of God sent to earth in human form, Jews were labeled heretics and agents of Satan. Images of Jews having horns and tails were among the many popular beliefs that identified Jews as "Other" and as a people to be feared and hated. Perhaps the longest lasting and most damaging myth can be traced to the Fourth Gospel of John, in which Jews as a group are held responsible for the death of Jesus, thus establishing and codifying the concept of "deicide" in the New Testament and Christian teaching.
- Until very recently many Christians were taught that the Jews killed Christ. What actually did happen remains speculative and many of the "eyewitness" reports in the Gospels were written several decades later by people trying to discredit

Judaism and appease Rome. It is clearly stated by most sources, however, that Jesus was tried, convicted, and sentenced by Roman law and Roman judges, and crucified by Roman soldiers. It may be that some of the leaders of the Jewish community saw Jesus as a threat to both Roman rule and their own power, but they were not representative of the larger portion of Jews at the time who were living under the often harsh domination of Roman law. And even if a few Jews did encourage and support the conviction of Jesus, it is absurd to make all Jews forever responsible.

Despite this absurdity, this myth of deicide was probably the single most widely used excuse for the persecution of Jews over the course of the next 1,600 years in Christian Europe. Other related myths and libels, such as charging Jews with kidnaping Christian babies and using their blood for religious purposes, were repeatedly used in later years as rationales for attacks on Jewish communities and the mass murder of Jewish people. As time went on, Jewish misfortunes and their dispersion from their homeland were explained as punishment for having killed Jesus. They were believed to have been condemned to wander the earth until Christ's 'second coming.'

Processing Break: The History Presentation Thus Far

Option 1: Processing Breaks

Divide the class into discussion groups of three to five for processing breaks during the history of antisemitism presentation. These groups will discuss the questions already presented, concerning 1) sources of stereotypes and 2) emergent themes, patterns of oppression, and Jewish responses. Four breaks for small group processing are scheduled in the outline that follows: after discussion of Christian Religious Antisemitism, after Economic and Political Antisemitism, and before and after Modern Antisemitism.

Option 2

If instructors have focused on specific moments of antisemitism, such as the Diaspora, the Crusades, the Inquisition, expulsion from Spain, and the Polish pogroms of the late nineteenth century, films such as *Genocide* from The World at War series can be used to capture important historical themes that lead to the Holocaust. We recommend that ample processing time be devoted to individual writing and discussion in pairs following this film because students are often overwhelmed by the graphic portrayal. We also recommend that the film *Courage to Care* be shown later the same day or in the following class period to illustrate that many Gentiles and Jews fought back often at tremendous personal risk. Excerpts from *Weapons of the Spirit* can be substituted for *Courage to Care* if one has time for a longer film. These films can also be used to change modalities in the *Option 1* history presentation. A video resource list appears at the end of this volume.

Economic Antisemitism: 500–1500 C.E.

Key Events

500–650: Forced conversions in Spain and France.

500–800: Jews invited to settle in France, Italy, and Germany. Organized mercantile establishments and became Europe's middle class.

900–1100: Jews invited to England with William the Conqueror. Expanded moneylending activities.

1040–1350: Crusades: Thousands of "heathen" Jews killed along the crusader's route to Palestine. Jews burned alive in their temples.
1100–1300: First ritual-murder and Host-desecration libels. First burning of Talmud. Jews banished from England.
1215: Council of Lateran orders Jews to wear a distinctive sign, yellow Jewish badges. (Yellow stood for "racial disgrace.")
1300–1500: Jews expelled from France (1400). Banished from Spain and Portugal. Persecutions increasingly are economically motivated.

Jews oppressed for:
—not converting
—ritual murder and desecration of the Host
—economic oppression
—causing the bubonic plague
—usury

Oppressed via:
—forced conversions
—exclusion
—segregation (Jewish badges)
—extermination

Handout 9.8. Economic Antisemitism: Medieval Period: 500–1350 C.E.

Key points: Economic Antisemitism

- With the fall of Rome and the beginning of the Dark Ages, the Catholic Church emerged as the main organizing force in Europe. For periods of time during the early Middle Ages, Jews were able to live in relative peace and security with no overt persecution directed against them. However, their position as the only non-Christians in a Christian world and their status as permanent aliens with no homeland led them to play a unique economic role of moneylending ("usury"), a role which eventually led to more resentment and prejudice against them.
- When they had first migrated to Europe during the Greco-Roman period, many Jews worked on the land, but as agriculture became more important to the European economy, Jews were forced out of this way of livelihood by burdensome taxes, confiscation, and periodic expulsions. They instead often became merchants, peddlers, moneylenders, and tax collectors. For survival purposes, Jews developed "portable professions" that didn't require ownership of property, given the pattern of expulsion with confiscation of wealth and property, just as their religion was "portable" and could survive anywhere in the world.
- Jewish occupations were needed in the developing economies of the Middle Ages but held in low esteem and, especially in the case of moneylending, perceived as sinful and restricted by the Church. This situation led to stereotypes of Jews as money-lovers, misers, shrewd, and unscrupulous traders.
- Money has been important to Jews as a portable asset, useful to have in case one should suddenly have to leave home. It could also be used to bribe the authorities and to "buy one's way out" of oppressive regimes. For many Jews, money came to represent relative safety and was used as a tool for survival (Krefetz, 1982).
- A three-class system developed in the feudal economy of rulers, serfs, and Jews. Jews represented a pre-capitalist middle class and performed essential commercial and monetary functions. Jews were invited by many rulers throughout Europe to come to their region for the services they could provide and the taxes

they were required to pay for the right to live there. But because of their role as tax collectors and moneylenders, Jews were frequently blamed by serfs and peasants for the problems of the feudal system. The rulers often encouraged this scapegoating, which frequently led to attacks and massacres. The rulers also would expel the Jews in order to confiscate their money and cancel their debts. This pattern of being invited into a region to fill gaps in the economy, being blamed for the problems of the economic system, and finally being expelled or massacred was repeated regularly throughout European history (Wistrich, 1991; Boonstra et al., 1989).

- During the thirteenth century, Jews in northern Europe were increasingly identified as town-dwellers, restricted to certain quarters called "ghettos," marked by distinctive clothing, denied the right to bear arms, forbidden to leave their rulers' jurisdiction, restricted to money lending, and forced to rely on money and bribery for self-protection. Not only were they now seen as Christ-killers; they were also stereotyped as usurers, bribers, and secret killers (Langmuir, 1990).
- The combination of the economic resentment and religious prejudice led to periodic outbursts of anti-Jewish violence. Antisemitism could now be stirred up through either economic or religious bigotry, or a dangerous combination of the two.
- Believed to be in league with the devil and gifted with evil powers, Jews were often blamed for misfortunes such as the bubonic plague and were killed as a "cure." (See anti-Jewish myths and legends, ritual murder, desecration of the Host, and the poisoning of the wells, in Boonstra et al., 1989.)

Processing Break

Follow instructions given on page 182.

Beginnings of Modern Europe—Economic and Political Antisemitism: 1350 to 1750 C.E.

1300–1400: Jews banished from England.
1400: Jews banished from France.
1478: Spanish Inquisition.
1492: Jews banished from Spain and Portugal.
1556: Jews confined to ghettos in Italy, Germany, and Central Europe.
1550–1700: Jews readmitted to England, Holland, and France. Settle in Russia.
1648–1655: 100,000 Jews massacred in Poland.

Jews oppressed for:
—non-conversion
—"past sins"
—economic forces and cycles

Oppressed via:
—restrictive economic roles
—forced conversions
—extermination and massacres
—expulsions
—segregation: ghettos, Pale of Settlement

Handout 9.9. Beginnings of Modern Europe—Economic and Political Antisemitism:1350–1750 C.E.

Key points: Beginnings of Modern Europe—Economic and Political Antisemitism

- The end of the feudal era saw the beginnings of capitalism and the emergence of a European middle class. Jews were restricted in the kinds of occupations they could follow; only Christians were allowed membership in the newly emerging guilds. Moneylending and trading in second-hand clothes were delegated to the Jews. Having outlived their usefulness as pre-capitalists and perceived as standing in the way of the advancement of the new middle class, Jews were vulnerable once again.

- During the next few hundred years major practices were developed by host societies to deal with "the Jewish Problem"—Jews were resisting conversion and assimilation, would not disappear, and were now considered irrelevant to the host society.

  This led to four basic religious and economically motivated solutions:

- *Conversion.* "Recalcitrant" Jews who would not accept Christ as their Savior were often seen as a blight on the moral purity of the host nation and the cause of any misfortunes that occurred. Conversion was forcibly imposed. The choice was to convert, be burned at the stake or be banished. Throughout much of the sixteenth century, antisemitism was directed mainly at those Jews who remained overtly faithful to the Jewish religion. Converts were supposedly no longer Jews. This attitude lasted until 1547 when, in Spain, the *Limpieza de sangre* (purity of the blood) statute decreed a person was judged to be of impure blood if his mother were even one-eighth Jewish. The purity requirement endorsed the Spanish Inquisition's search for "closet" Jews who had formerly converted but maintained their Jewish religious practices in secret. They were known as *Marranos* (swine). Thousands of supposed Marranos were burned at the stake before Ferdinand and Isabella banished all the Spanish Jews in 1492.

- *Expulsion.* Jews were forcibly expelled from cities, towns, and entire countries, their property and wealth confiscated, and the roles they had occupied in the economy taken over by members of the indigenous population. In 1492, 150,000 Jews who refused to convert were driven out of Spain. By the end of the fifteenth century, Jews were excluded from almost all of Western Europe.

- *Segregation.* In most of Europe, where Jews still lived or were allowed to return, they were forced into ghettos (separate walled off parts of cities) or restricted to certain areas of settlement (the Pale in Eastern Europe). This "solution" limited the economic roles Jews could play and limited their potentially "subversive" and "contaminating" contact with the rest of the population.

- *Extermination.* The Crusaders slaughtered tens of thousands of Jews on their way to the Holy Land. The Spanish Inquisition killed thirty thousand people. One hundred thousand Jews were massacred in Poland in the seventeenth century. This strategy set the stage for Hitler's "final solution" of the "Jewish question."

Age of Enlightenment: Economic and Political Antisemitism and the Beginning of Racial Antisemitism

Key events:
1750: Russian "Pale of Settlement" established.
1787: French revolution bestows French citizenship on Jews.
1821: Russian military conscription laws.

1850–1900: Pogroms in Russia. In enlightened Western Europe, many Jews become members of literary, financial, and political elites.
1880: Mass Jewish emigration from Russia and Eastern Europe to the United States, Western Europe and Palestine.
1894: Antisemitism becomes more politicized. Dreyfus Affair in France. Beginnings of Communism and Zionism.
1905: Protocols of Zion forged and circulated in Russia.

Jews oppressed for:
—alleged economic and political power
—"past sins"
—being members of an inferior race

Oppressed via:
In Western Europe:
—racist theories of antisemitism
—political affiliations both left and right
—discrimination and quotas
In Eastern Europe:
—restricted areas of settlement
—restricted rights and economic opportunities
—conscription into the army
—pogroms: assaults and massacres

Handout 9.10. Age of Enlightenment: Beginnings of Racial Antisemitism.

Key points: Age of Enlightenment

- The triumph of Enlightenment principles of equality, fraternity, and the "natural rights" of people, embodied in the French revolution, brought the emancipation of European Jews out of the ghettos and, for the first time, into the full political and economic rights of citizenship. With this new freedom, Jews assimilated into Western society as never before. But despite the fact that official legal and official persecution came to an end, anti-Jewish attitudes and bigotry continued to exist. In a dynamic that continues to this day, the more success that Jews attained, the more vulnerable they were to being made scapegoats for economic and political problems. Time and again, economic hard times in Europe and the United States brought politically orchestrated outbursts of antisemitic propaganda and persecution.

- The Dreyfus case in France in 1894 provides perhaps the most noteworthy example of this pattern. Captain Dreyfus was a French Jewish officer who was wrongly accused of selling military secrets to the Germans. In France in 1889 an Antisemitic League was established with its own influential daily, *La Libre Parole*, which publicized its hatred against the Jews for multiple and often contradictory reasons.

- The rise of science and the decline of the superstitions underlying religious antisemitism also laid the basis for a new, more insidious form of antisemitism, based on the notion that biology in general and race in particular were major determinants of human characteristics and personal behavior. As ideas of racial determinism became more popular, theories developed describing Jews as the archetypal inferior race, with many identifiable negative characteristics. As belief in these theories grew, antisemitism based on religion, economics, and politics was supplemented with a new racism. From the racist point of view, conversion could no longer save Jews from persecution. One's genes and not one's religious or political perspectives were the determining factors. Once a Jew, always a Jew.

- In Eastern Europe, including Russia, where the ideology of the Enlightenment did not take hold, Jews were still restricted to certain areas of settlement, limited in their economic and political rights, and, starting in the 1850s, conscripted into the Czar's army. The first author's father told him many tales of what it was like for a Jew to be forced to serve in the Russian army with its completely different Gentile life-style and hatred of Jews. Also during this period, organized and random assaults on Jewish communities, known as pogroms, became a fact of life for Jews. These were exacerbated in part by widespread libels alleging a Jewish conspiracy for world domination, based on the forgery "Protocols of the Elders of Zion"(see Larrson, 1994; Wistrich, 1991; Mosse, 1985). Homes were pillaged, women raped, and men, women, and children murdered or maimed in politically endorsed mob action. In response to this heightened oppression, hundreds of thousands of Jews began emigrating to the United States, Western Europe, and Palestine.
- It became clear to some Jews in both Western and Eastern Europe that antisemitism would always be present and that they would never be safe living in an alien country. A movement for a Jewish homeland in Palestine began. Zionism was a new name for an old ideology, meaning a return to Zion, the original name for a Jewish stronghold in Jerusalem. This idea of returning to Jerusalem has been part of Jewish thinking ever since the earliest days of the Diaspora (Dimont, 1962).

Processing Break: Follow previous instructions.

Twentieth Century—Cultural, Religious, Economic, Political, and Racial Antisemitism: 1880 to 1994

Europe

1880–1980s: Jews emigrate to USA and Palestine.
1919: Paris Peace Conference. Germany humiliated. 1933–1935: Nazi rise to power.
1935: Nuremberg laws.
1942: Death camps begin operation.
1942–1945: Nazis murder 12 million. Six million Jews exterminated.
1953: In Russia, Jewish doctors imprisoned on false charges of poisoning Stalin.

Mid East

1917: Balfour declaration opens Palestine to limited Jewish immigration.
1939: British White Paper. Immigration to Palestine further restricted.
1941: Grand Mufti of Jerusalem seeks support from Hitler.
1948: U.N. proposes dual Palestinian-Israel state. Arabs reject proposal. Israel declares independence. First Arab-Israeli war.
1952: Nasser of Egypt promotes "Protocols of Zion."
1956, 1967, 1973, 1982: Arab-Israeli wars.
1975: U.N. supports resolution equating Zionism with racism.
1985: Syrian minister of defense publishes "Matzoh of Zion," citing Jews as ritual murderers.

1948–present: Series of publications denying and excusing the Holocaust and claiming Jews paid the price for still not accepting Jesus. Rise in Eastern European expressions of antisemitism.
1993: Israel begins negotiations with PLO on Palestinian self-rule.

United States
1988–1994: Acts of desecration continue. Rise in Black antisemitism. Jews charged with playing key role in slavery. "Protocols of Zion" distributed at UC Berkeley. Propagation of Jewish world conspiracy theories. Also on campuses JAP (Jewish American Princess) slurs: stereotype of young Jewish women as crass, materialistic, and vulgar.

Handout 9.11. Twentieth Century: 1880–1994.

Key points: Twentieth Century

- Germany's defeat in World War I and its humiliation at the Paris Peace Conference sets the stage for the triumph of Hitler and the Nazis in the 1930s. The Nazis blamed defeat in the war and all of Germany's problems on the "inferior" and "diabolical Jews" who were contaminating the pure blood of the Aryan race. Jews had been more assimilated into German society than they had been in any other society, but that didn't save them.
- After the Nazis came to state power in 1933, antisemitism became institutionalized as it had not been in centuries. In 1935 the Nuremberg laws deprived Jews of citizenship, forbade intermarriage and the employment by Jews of German domestics under the age of forty-five. They also increasingly caused the re-ghettoization of Jews and the incarceration of many in special camps, especially after 1939 as Nazi forces conquered countries with larger Jewish populations to the East.
- In 1942, the death camps began operation as Hitler launched his "Final Solution" to the "Jewish Problem": the extermination of all of Europe's Jews. He succeeded in killing nearly six million, approximately one-half of the Jews in the world (see a detailed sequence of phases in the Final Solution in Boonstra et al., 1989, 89–91).
- "The fact is that the Jews, as well as the rest of the world, were at first totally unaware of the existence of the 'final solution,' which was kept in strictest secrecy by the Nazis. When the horrible truth did begin to seep out, the Jews, along with the rest of the world, refused to believe that anyone could be so inhuman" (Dimont, 1962, 381–82).
- During the war and the Holocaust, many Jews fought in the allied armies and in the underground resistance movements (see the Warsaw Rebellion in Dimont, 1962, 383–85). Those who could, escaped from Nazi-controlled areas. Most countries, including the United States, refused entry to these refugees, so many emigrated to Palestine despite the British restriction of immigration into the area (Wyman, 1984).
- After the war, the United Nations, the newly formed "conscience" of the postwar world, proposed that Jews finally be given an independent homeland within the British colony of Palestine, with the other half of Palestine becoming a Palestinian Arab nation. The Arabs did not recognize Jewish rights to any of this

area and declared war on the fledgling Jewish state. Israel fought off this challenge and in 1949, after two thousand years without a homeland, Jews once again had a nation they could call their own.

The opening sections of this chapter summarize some of the contemporary issues facing Jews in this country as well as in other parts of the world. The assimilation of Jews in the United States is the most successful in Jewish history. The United States, in contrast to its legal discrimination against Blacks, never made laws which took away the rights of Jews. Most antisemitism has taken the form of institutional and individual acts, such as quota systems until the 1960s limiting number of Jews who could be admitted to colleges and professional schools. These institutional policies have all but disappeared (see Dinnerstein, 1994 for the complete documentation). Given the long history of antisemitism and its recurrent patterns, it is no surprise that many Jews remain wary of their human rights status in this or any society other than Israel.

Post-History Summary and Processing:

a. After all of the history presentations and small group processing, ask each group to post their lists of patterns and stereotype roots on newsprint on walls.

b. Ask each group to present and explain their lists and respond to any questions from participants.

c. Have participants compare their Stereotype Roots list with the one generated in the first activity and try to connect each with a historical context.

d. Conclude with the following presentation on major cumulative patterns of antisemitism.

2. Historical Themes (20 minutes).

(1) ***Cumulative Factors (see Appendix 9A):*** Jews have been oppressed because of their cultural differences, religious beliefs, economic activities, political affiliations, and supposed racial characteristics. Throughout history, each factor was added cumulatively to those previously established, thus multiplying the possibilities for antisemitism. Today antisemitism can be stimulated through any of these factors, alone or in combination. Jews are still being accused of being Christ-killers, media manipulators, exploiters of the oppressed, secret power brokers, and possessors of non-Aryan (read inferior) genetic and physical characteristics.

(2) ***Cyclicity:*** Antisemitism is characterized by alternating periods of apparent tolerance and assimilation, followed by periods of violent antisemitic attacks. During periods of economic growth and political calm, Jews can assimilate, and overt manifestations of oppression are less obvious. When there is economic and political stress, scapegoating and persecutions become more blatant and violent in a cycle that continues to operate today. As national and world economic and political tensions increase, in Eastern Europe as well as sporadically in America, acts of desecration and overt expressions of antisemitism also increase.

(3) ***Buffer Role:*** In order to survive and avoid exile, Jews filled whatever economic roles were open to them. At times throughout history, those roles have involved serving as agents of rulers or ruling classes. These roles have placed some Jews in a vulnerable "buffer" position between the actual ruling classes and eco-

nomically oppressed groups in society. In this position, Jews were highly visible as they carried out economic transactions between the two classes and as their religious and cultural practices separated them from mainstream society. Rulers were thus able to blame all Jews for any emerging economic problems and encourage the oppressed to vent their frustrations on the Jewish people rather on the rulers themselves. In the Middle Ages and seventeenth and eighteenth centuries, Jews serving as merchants, administrators, moneylenders, and tax collectors were scapegoated by the French royalty and Russian nobility for the economic problems of the peasants and working classes.

How does this dynamic of antisemitism function currently in the United States? When the "visibly" oppressed groups look to see who it is that is oppressing them, they don't see the Fortune 500 companies and the corporate owners. Instead, scapegoating stereotypes about Jews (all Jews are rich, Jews own the media, Jews control Hollywood, Jews control Congress), are used to pit economically oppressed groups against Jews. The reality that groups like Jews can be oppressed even if they are not, per se, economically impoverished, has been understandably hard for many economically disadvantaged groups to fully grasp. Even more to the point, the existence of these antisemitic stereotypes keeps these other oppressed groups from identifying and challenging the real sources of exploitation. Antisemitism involves a convoluted dynamic: the systematic creation of vulnerability, followed by the effort of Jews to overcome that vulnerability by accommodating to oppressive forces, which are, in turn, only too willing to let Jews become the more visible "agent" of and scapegoat for the oppression of others.

(4) ***Target of All Political Affiliations:*** Antisemitic attitudes involve some of the following, often contradictory, beliefs: "Jews are lefties and communists and revolutionaries who foment radical social upheaval; they are anti-bourgeois and anti-capitalist. Jews are capitalistic and imperialistic power brokers who oppress the economically disadvantaged. Jews have an international conspiracy to control the world. Jews are spineless and will never fight for anything they believe in" (Lerner, 1992, 58). During the thirties and the McCarthyism of the fifties, Jews were accused of being the radical element in this society, but in the last twenty-five years Jews have been increasingly attacked by the Left as capitalists and imperialists, especially by Third World anti-Israel advocates (see Lerner, 1992, for examples and counter-argument).

Facilitation Issues:

As a result of this complex and intense history presentation, participants will likely experience an array of strong feelings. For Jews, these are often feelings of rage, grief, and fear, as well as pride and amazement at what the Jewish people have endured and managed to survive. For Gentiles, there are often similar feelings of rage and grief, as well as admiration for the strength and resilience of the Jewish people. In addition, Gentiles often experience guilt, shame, disbelief, and anger at what has been done in the name of Christianity. Both Jewish and Gentile participants often feel overwhelmed by the long history and magnitude of antisemitism and may express frustration and hopelessness about ever countering such a disease. A closing activity that allows for expression of some of these feelings is a useful way to end the session.

3. Closing Circle (10 minutes).

Have the group sit in a circle. Ask each person to jot down three or four of their most pronounced feelings. Then, ask one person at a time to share the words they wrote accompanied by one or two brief sentences of explanation. Encourage people to simply listen to what each member has to say. [If this activity ends the day, let the group know that we will spend a short time the next day continuing to report our responses to the history and then in the next activity examine how this story gets played out in individual lives.]

Module 3

Time Needed: 3 to 3 1/2 hours
Goals:

- Understand how the history of antisemitism is manifested through individual Jewish and Gentile personal experiences.
- Make connections between antisemitic patterns and stereotypes and their consequences in the lives of the participants.
- Discuss what Jews and Gentiles may have in common, related to their experience of antisemitism.
- Cite examples of internalized oppression.

Key Concepts: collusion, internalized oppression, privilege.

Activities:

1. Check-In: (20 minutes).

Ask participants to pair up and discuss key points from the previous session. Discuss any questions or issues they raise using this time to highlight important concepts from the history presentation.

2. Speakouts of Jews and Gentiles: (40 minutes).

Introduce this activity by explaining that, having spent several hours learning about the history of European antisemitism, we want to focus now on the present and on the effects of antisemitism on individual human beings now. We will do this through speakouts. Speakouts involve individuals, both Jews and Gentiles, telling personal stories of their experiences with antisemitism.

Option 1:
Each instructor, one who is a Jew and one who is a Gentile, does a speakout.

Option 2:
During the previous portions of the workshop, participants can be identified who appear comfortable in relating and reflecting on their personal experience as Jews or Gentiles as potential participants in a speakout. They should be able, if they are Jews, to disclose any phases and conflicts they went through in trying to feel more secure about being Jewish, or, if they are Gentiles, to identify conflicts and phases of their own identity with regard to the Jewish people and their own awareness of antisemitism.

Option 3:

Invite speakers who are not workshop participants, who will be able to convey their experiences as Jews or as Gentiles.

In any of the three options, speakers respond to the following questions:

For Jews:

- What was it like growing up a Jew?
- What phases have you gone through in the development of your Jewish identity?
- What has been most difficult about being Jewish?
- What are you most proud of? What has pleased you most about being Jewish?

For Gentiles:

- What did you learn about Jews early in your life?
- When were you first aware of antisemitism?
- Were there any turning points in your awareness of antisemitism?
- How has antisemitism affected you?

Facilitation Issues:
It is important to remember that speakouts can be emotionally draining. Choose speakers with care and be sure support is provided for each individual as she or he speaks. The speakouts are likely to raise issues that can be discussed separately for Jews and Gentiles in the caucus groups which come next.

3. Caucus Groups: Jews and Gentiles (60 minutes).

Ask students to form groups comprised of all Jews or all Gentiles. There should be four to seven students in each group. If there are students who are not sure whether they identify as Jews or Gentiles, ask them to choose a group depending on which part of their identity they want to explore at this point in the class. (Caucus groups are discussed more fully in chapters 6 and 8.) Ask students to take five minutes per person to share feelings and reactions to what they heard in the speakouts.

Next ask students to respond to the speakout questions listed above for Jews or Gentiles, as appropriate. If there are students who are not sure whether they identify as Jews, ask them to respond to any of the questions they would like.

Explain that telling these stories can be difficult. Our purpose is to listen and understand. We may or may not like what we hear, but now is not the time for debate. Therefore, the other students will listen with care and attention. They may ask questions for clarification and make statements to acknowledge what they hear, but they should not begin a discussion. The focus is on listening to each person's story, one by one. Ask each group to select a timekeeper who will let each student know when her or his time is nearly up.

If this workshop is being co-led, ideally by a Jew and Gentile, each can take responsibility for respective caucus groups. If there is only one leader, a participant should be designated as process-monitor for the reporting.

4. Intergroup Discussion (30 minutes).

Post the following sentence stems on the chalk board or on newsprint. Tell students they will have a chance to complete any of them that they would like to while other students listen without responding. Remind students of the participation guidelines and tell them that the purpose of this activity is hear the thoughts and feelings of the people in the other caucus group.

Sentence Stems for the Jewish Caucus:

- Something I never want to hear said about Jews again is . . .
- Something that makes me proud to be a Jew is . . .
- Something I want Gentiles to know about Jews is . . .
- Something I learned about antisemitism is . . .
- Something I value about Gentile allies is . . .

Sentence Stems for the Gentile Caucus:

- Something that makes me proud to be a ____ (insert religion) is . . .
- Something I want Jews to know about me is . . .
- Something I have learned about antisemitism is . . .
- Something I am committed to doing to address antisemitism is . . .

One way to conduct this activity is with participants sitting in a circle together. Students can speak when they want to, making sure that no one speaks twice before everyone has had a chance to speak once. People can also speak in turn going around the circle, one by one. If this option is used, students should be reminded that they can choose not to speak if they wish.

Another way to do this activity is in a fish bowl format in which, in turn, each caucus group sits as an inner circle while the other group sits as an outer circle. The group on the inside shares their responses to the sentence stems while the outside group listens. Then the groups change places so that the group from the outside is now on the inside. These participants individually respond to the sentence stems while the group now on the outside listens. After both groups have responded to the sentence stems, ask everyone to form one circle and move into the closing activity.

5. Closing (30 minutes).

Ask each participant to note one thing they learned that they hope will stay with them in the future.

Module 4

Time Needed: 4 hours
Goals:

- Identify possible action steps to continue learning and addressing antisemitism.
- Close the workshop.

Activities:

1. Action Strategies to Combat Antisemitism (45 minutes).

Ask students to form groups of four or five. Ask the groups to brainstorm and record on newsprint all private and public actions which they can imagine taking to continue their learning and address antisemitism. (Examples include deliberate monitoring of one's own behavior, getting more information through reading, taking more courses, interrupting antisemitic comments or jokes, discussing antisemitism with others.) Refer to action continuum in Appendix 6C and adapt it to antisemitism.

Ask each small group to report one action from their list. Continue going around the groups, asking participants to name actions not already named.

Lead a large group discussion about actions that can be taken, anxieties participants may have about taking action, and support they may need.

2. Contracts for Change (below) (60 minutes).

Tell students that they are to select one of these options for action and follow the worksheet describing the actions they take and the results. After they have filled out the worksheet, ask students to discuss in small groups which options they chose and why. Ask for a report out of some of the actions chosen. They may also form small groups on the basis of the options they select.

Alternatively, facilitators may choose among these options for all participants.

Option A

Increasing Personal Awareness

Identify a project you will undertake which is designed to increase your awareness about Jews and/or antisemitism. Some possibilities include:

(For Gentiles)

- Educating yourself by reading or watching informational videos about antisemitism and Jewish history.
- Attending a Jewish awareness event such as a movie, lecture, or ceremony.
- Visiting a synagogue service.
- Interviewing a Jewish friend about her or his experience about growing up Jewish.

(For Jews)

- Interviewing your family and relatives about how they experienced Jews and Jewishness as they were growing up. The speakout questions can also be used as a guide.

Option B

Personal Behavior Change

This project focuses on changing a personal behavior that you have identified as being based on (for Gentiles) anti-Jewish stereotypes or (for Jews) internalized oppression as defined in chapters 1 and 2. Use this worksheet as a guide.

1. Describe a specific behavior pattern you use that is related to (for Gentiles) a Jewish stereotype or (for Jews) internalized oppression, and which is something you would like to change. This behavior pattern should be something that you notice yourself doing repeatedly in a variety of situations, for example, (for Gentiles) assuming people are or are not Jews because they possess or lack cer-

tain characteristics, or (for Jews) denying, disguising, or hiding your Jewish identity.

2. Think of two or three specific times when your behavior has reflected this pattern.
3. Based on this behavior pattern complete the following sentences:

   Whenever I'm in a situation in which ________________________, I usually experience feelings of ______, _________, ___________, and begin telling myself ____________, ____________, ____________. What I usually do is ______________, ____________, __________.
4. What would you prefer to do? What would a better response look and sound like?
5. If you could change the pattern what might you gain? What opportunities might you lose out on if you could never change that response?
6. How might others respond to your changed pattern? What are the risks?
7. What kinds of support would be helpful to you while you experimented with some alternative responses? Where can you get this support?
8. How might you evaluate your attempt to change the pattern?
9. Try out the change and report and evaluate the results. What would you do again in the same way? What would you change?

Option C

Interrupting Antisemitism

This project focuses on interrupting antisemitism in interpersonal, institutional, or cultural arenas. Use the following as a guide.

1. Describe the specific manifestation of antisemitism you wish to interrupt. Where, when, and how often do you notice it? How have you responded to it in the past?
2. What tells you that this is an example of antisemitism?
3. What action do you want to take to help interrupt this manifestation of antisemitism? Describe in detail.
4. What do you think would be gained by accomplishing your goal?
5. What are some of the possible disadvantages or risks involved?
6. What resistance might you encounter? Are there ways you can decrease that resistance?
7. What resources or materials would you need in order to achieve your goal? How can you get these?
8. Who can help you with your plan?
9. What other personal support will you need? How can you get that support?
10. How can you evaluate your success? How can you tell the difference between slow change and failure?

11. Try out your plan. Report and evaluate the results. What would you do in the same way the next time? What would you do differently?

Option D
Spheres of Influence and Action Plan

This activity asks that students first identify their various spheres of influence, working alone, from most intimate family members or personal relationships outward through friends and family members, neighbors and school or workplace acquaintances to members of their larger communities. (See more detailed accounts of spheres of influence in chapters 6 and 7 and Appendix 7E.) They then share these spheres of influence with each other in groups of two or three. This is followed by personal risk assessments (from high risk to low risk) for interrupting antisemitism with people in one's various spheres of influence. Since risk levels differ, it is important for participants to discuss with each other their own risk estimates and risk-taking thresholds. Finally, still working in groups of two or three, participants come up with one action plan, considering what obstacles they anticipate, what they need to overcome those obstacles, and what supports they can call upon.

3. Closing (30 minutes).

Ask everyone to sit in a circle. Ask each participant to respond in a couple of sentences to the following:

- What new learnings did you get from this experience?
- How will your awareness or behavior change as a result of this experience?
- Close by responding to the questions yourselves.

Appendix 9A

ACCUMULATION OF THEMES IN ANTISEMITISM

Historical Eras	Ancient B.C.E.	Early Christian 0–800	Middle Ages 800–1400s	Early Modern 1500–1750	Age of Nationalism 1750–1900	20th Century 1900s–
Stereotypes	"Other" Obstinate Stiff-necked → Independent	Infidel Christ-killer → Satan	Clannish Moneylenders Exploiters of the poor → Avaricious Source of disease Poisoners of wells	Worldwide Jewish conspiracy Cause of political and economic problems →		Radicals, Bolsheviks → Racially inferior
Forms of Antisemitism	Forced migration Conquest Enslavement	Legal restrictions Loss of some rights of religious practice	Forced conversion Exclusion Segregation Massacres	Expulsion Segregation "Ghettos" Pogroms Massacres	Political and economic restrictions Segregation Scapegoating Pogroms	Restrictions Extermination

10

Ableism Curriculum Design

Laura Rauscher, Mary McClintock

Introduction

Gaining equal access to the benefits and opportunities our society offers has long been a challenge for people with disabilities. Historically, people with disabilities have faced serious and persistent forms of discrimination, segregation, exclusion, and sometimes elimination. People with disabilities have struggled to establish their place in society and secure their basic civil rights. Although the struggle continues, we live in a time when important and far-reaching changes are truly at hand. The passage of the Americans with Disabilities Act of 1990, a watershed for the disability civil rights movement, was the result of the efforts of a cross-disability coalition that took root in the early 1970s. The ADA asserts the equality of people with disabilities and opens the door to the benefits and responsibilities of full participation in society.

What is Ableism?

Ableism is a pervasive system of discrimination and exclusion that oppresses people who have mental, emotional, and physical disabilities. Like racism, sexism, and other forms of oppression, ableism operates on individual, institutional, and societal/cultural levels. Deeply rooted beliefs about health, productivity, beauty, and the value of human life, perpetuated by the public and private media, combine to create an environment that is often hostile to those whose physical, emotional, cognitive, or sensory abilities fall outside the scope of what is currently defined as socially acceptable. This phenomenon has been described by a variety of terms including, handicapism, ableism, disability oppression, disability discrimination, physicalism, and mentalism. No word perfectly describes what the range of disabled people experiences. We use the terms ableism or disability oppression because they reflect the viewpoint that people with disabilities or with physical or mental limitations, are considered to be inadequate in meeting expected social and economic roles.

Disability in its broadest sense identifies a variety of individuals who may or may not use that specific term to describe themselves or their experiences. There is a broad range of disabilities, encompassing a huge diversity of people, including people whose disabilities are:

- Perceptual (such as visual and hearing impairments and learning disabilities).
- Illness-related (such as multiple sclerosis, AIDS).
- Physical (such as cerebral palsy).
- Developmental (such as Down Syndrome).
- Psychiatric (such as bi-polar, chronic depression, manic-depressive syndrome).
- Mobility (such as quadriplegia, paraplegia).
- Environmental (such as asthma, sensitivities to allergens and chemicals in the environment).

The historic treatment of people with disabilities represents a legacy of discrimination, isolation, segregation, and mistreatment. Over time, disabled people have been viewed as menaces to society needing control, as children to be pitied and cared for, and as objects of charity. Many have been imprisoned or committed to hospitals and asylums against their will. Unfortunately, these approaches to dealing with disability are not confined to history but continue today.

People with mental and emotional disabilities continue to be kept in institutions against their will. Fetuses with "defects" are aborted to prevent the birth of people with disabilities. The Human Genome Project—a project to map human genes—and the debate over euthanasia and the right to die raise issues of who decides about the worth of an individual life. People with disabilities face discrimination in employment, housing, and education, despite laws forbidding such discrimination. National and international social and economic policies contribute to the systematic exclusion of people with disabilities from the mainstream of our society. The desire of many people to distance themselves from disability contributes to unnecessary institutionalization, segregation, and isolation of persons with disabilities.

One of the many roots of ableism is the fear of becoming disabled. Disability reminds us of the fragility of life and confronts us with questions about our own mortality. The feelings that disabilities raise for many people have been one of the reasons communities have tended to avoid contact with people with disabilities. And yet, despite efforts to distance from it, disability remains a normal part of human experience. Every racial, ethnic, and religious group includes people with disabilities. One way of thinking about disability is that everyone, if s/he lives long enough, will have some form of disability. In fact, given the overall aging of the United States population, particularly the aging of the "baby boomers," increasing numbers of people will have age-related disabilities. According to recently released data from a population-based survey by the Bureau of the Census, the number of persons with disabilities in the United States is estimated to be forty-nine million. Of these persons, about half, or twenty-four million, are considered to have a "severe" disability (defined by measures such as extent of assistance needed with daily activities and by specific diagnoses)(U.S. Bureau of the Census Report, Americans with Disabilities, 1994).

Combating Ableism: Recent Legislation and the Disability Rights Movement

In recent years, comprehensive approaches to addressing disability and the oppression of people with disabilities have taken the form of legislation to eliminate discrimination and social barriers within our society. Recent legislation, including legislation related to housing, air travel, and transportation, has begun to have an impact. The Americans with Disabilities Act (ADA) of 1990 provides long-sought recognition of the civil rights of people with disabilities. The ADA prohibits discrimination on the basis of disability in employment, public transportation, state and local government services, public accommodations, and telecommunications. Passage of this landmark legislation is recognized as a significant step toward ending the long history of unequal and unjust treatment of people with disabilities in the United States.

The Disability Rights Movement laid the groundwork for passage of the ADA. The Disability Rights/ Independent Living Movement is a cross-disability approach to change which promotes integration, equality, access, self-determination, and all the benefits of full citizenship.

Language and Identity

Using language to talk about disability, the experience of being disabled, and people who have disabilities is sometimes difficult and has gone through many changes over time. Many terms once used to talk about disabled people in the nineteenth and early twentieth centuries have fallen into disfavor (for example, crippled, deformed, deaf and dumb, insane, and idiot). At the same time, terms such as retarded, handicapped, and mentally ill, acceptable only a few years ago, also have been largely replaced by words such as developmental disability and emotional disability. In addition, some people use euphemistic terms, such as "physically or mentally challenged" and "differently abled" to refer to people with disabilities. The increased use of what is called "people first" language—for example, "a person with a disability"—encourages viewing people who have disabilities as people first and disabled second.

Many people with disabilities have embraced the term "disabled," redefining it as a term describing a powerful and proud group of people with strengths and abilities who are "disabled" by unnecessary social, economic, and environmental barriers more than by a physical, psychological, or developmental "condition." Others reject the term "disabled" feeling it represents a negative label that was forced on them by professionals who did not understand their needs or differences. These people feel that they never had disabilities to begin with, but that they have been greatly affected by negative interactions with health and social service systems, such as the mental health system. These different uses of language reflect the different perspectives held by people with disabilities and the evolution of thinking about disabilities. We use the words "people with disabilities" or "disabled people" because these are the terms most commonly used by the disability rights movement.

Over the last twenty years, a significant segment of people with all types of disabilities have reclaimed and redefined the term "disabled" in a positive way. They identify themselves as part of the political movement for disability rights and independent living in the United States and around the world. They reject the notion that being disabled is an inherently negative experience, or in any way descriptive of something broken or abnormal. From this perspective, "disability" is a positive term. Proponents of this perspective take pride in the differences in their bodies and minds and strive to make others aware of their experiences and accomplishments. Many people with disabilities take part in an ongoing struggle against the oppressive social, economic, and environmental forces that limit their ability to achieve their full potential. They see themselves as "disabled" by the social and environmental structures that were created without them in mind and that now prevent them from taking their rightful place in society. Perhaps most important, these individuals recognize the connections and commonalities among the experiences of people with different disabilities and others who experience other forms of oppression. They strive to work in coalition across disabilities as well as with other oppressed groups.

Teaching about Ableism

The fears raised by considering the possibility of oneself or loved ones becoming disabled and the subsequent oppression one would experience have been key to the systematic oppression of people with disabilities. In order to address ableism effectively, we must address these fears. Before attempting to teach about ableism, facilitators must explore their own relationship to the deeply personal issues that disability raises and be willing to share their own learning process with participants.

Many contemporary educational approaches to ableism focus on "Disability Awareness." These programs use disability simulation activities, panels of persons describing their disabilities, or lists of "dos and don'ts" about interacting with disabled people, to describe specific disabilities. All of these activities focus on disability as a form of *difference* at an individual level rather than ableism as a form of *oppression* that operates on individual, institutional, and societal/cultural levels. We believe it is essential to focus on ableism as a form of oppression and provide participants with accurate information to overcome stereotypes and missing information and to help them understand the systemic nature of ableism. Without this attention to the systemic nature of ableism, education about disability issues does not have a social justice perspective and may serve to reinforce existing stereotypes and beliefs. For example, having participants spend time using a wheelchair to understand the experience of having a mobility disability may reinforce participants' fear of becoming disabled and belief that using a wheelchair is "tragic."

Participant Awareness Levels

In planning courses related to ableism, it is important to consider the awareness level of the students. Most courses on ableism in university or college settings include a diverse participant group including those

- with and without disabilities,
- with hidden disabilities (such as chronic health conditions, learning disabilities, or psychiatric/emotional disabilities),

as well as those

- who have close friends and loved ones with disabilities,
- who don't know anyone with disabilities, and
- who are from a range of cultural backgrounds that have varying cultural norms about disabilities.

Participants will also differ in their willingness to share their experiences with disability. For example, those with hidden disabilities may or may not disclose this information during the course. Some participants may not even think of themselves as disabled or may come to an awareness that they are disabled as a result of participation in the class. Some participants may disclose this information privately to the facilitators, but not to other participants. Facilitators must be aware of and sensitive to the range in participant awareness levels in order to facilitate a meaningful experience for all, including students both in the agent group and in the target group.

All participants should have an opportunity to explore their feelings about disability, including fears about their own fragility, loss of control, and death. Able-bodied participants often talk about how these fears cause them to avoid disabled people. They also report being angry at disabled people for reminding them of these realities of life. Opportunities to express these feelings help participants to understand their fears, to avoid projecting them onto others, and to begin to move from fear and anger to understanding and action. Discussion and support from others with similar feelings encourages participants to accept their own fragility as well as to recognize their own and others' resiliency and the strengths they bring to situations in their lives. Accepting one's fragility and one's strengths leads to less fear of interacting with people with disabilities. Providing participants with the opportunity to interact with people with disabilities directly brings them to a new level of accepting themselves and others.

Assumptions

Whatever specific activities we choose for a course on ableism, our teaching is guided by a set of assumptions we have about disability and oppression. These include:

- Disability is not inherently negative.
- Becoming disabled involves major life changes including loss as well as gain, but it is not the end of a meaningful and productive existence.
- People with disabilities experience discrimination, segregation, and isolation as a result of other people's prejudice and institutional ableism, not because of the disability itself.
- Social beliefs, cultural norms, and media images about beauty, intelligence, physical ability, communication, and behavior often negatively influence the way disabled people are treated.
- Societal expectations about economic productivity and self-sufficiency devalue persons who are not able to work, regardless of other contributions they may make to family and community life.
- Without positive messages about who they are, persons with disabilities are vulnerable to internalizing society's negative messages about disability.
- Independence and dependence are relative concepts, subject to personal definition, something every person experiences, and neither is inherently positive or negative.
- Disabled people's right to inclusion in the mainstream of our society is now protected by law, yet they are still not treated as full and equal citizens.

OVERVIEW OF ABLEISM MODULES
Introductory Module (see chapter 5)

Module 1 (2 1/2–3 hours)	**Module 2 (2 3/4–3 hours)**
1. Introductions/Goals/Agenda Review (30 mins.) 2. Recall (30 mins.) 3. Myths & Stereotypes (30 mins.) 4. Journal Period (5 mins.) 5. Lecture on Definitions (30 mins.) 6. History, Part I (40 mins.) 7. Closing (10 mins.)	1. History, Part II (60 mins.) 2. Disability Rights/ Key Legislation (30 mins.) 3. Roles, Part I (60 mins.) 4. Journal Period (5 mins.) 5. Closing (10 mins.)
Module 3 (3 hours)	**Module 4 (3 hours)**
1. Check-In/ Roles, Part II (30 mins.) 2. Panel of People with Disabilities (90 mins.) 3. Discussion after Panel (30 mins.) 4. Journal Period (5 mins.) 5. Closing (10 mins.)	1. Visioning an Accessible/Inclusive Society (90 mins.) 2. Journal Period (5 mins.) 3. Barriers to Action/ Action Continuum (30 mins.) 4. Personal Commitments for Action (30 mins.) 5. Closure and Evaluation (30 mins.)

Handout 10.1. Overview of Ableism Modules.

Overall Goals

- Increase awareness of the existence and manifestations of ableism at all levels.
- Increase understanding of the experience of being disabled in an oppressive society.
- Increase knowledge about strategies for interrupting and eliminating ableism.

Module 1

Time Needed: 2 1/2–3 hours
Goals:

- Increase awareness of early personal influences that shape perceptions of disability and disabled people.
- Increase knowledge of common stereotypes and myths about people with disabilities.
- Increase knowledge of the historical treatment of persons with disabilities and the origins of ableism.

Key Concepts: socialization, connections to oppression, stereotypes, historical perspectives.

1. Introductions, Housekeeping, Guidelines for Participation, Review Goals and Agenda (30 minutes).

- Introduce facilitators.

- Review housekeeping issues (schedule, restroom location, etc.).
- Review class goals, agenda, and guidelines for participation.
- Students share names, experience with this issue, and one thing they hope to gain from the course.

2. Recall Exercise: Early Learnings about Persons with Disabilities (30 minutes).

The purpose of this activity is to help students identify their own beliefs about disability and disabled people by looking at what they have learned.

- Individual time with handout containing 4 or 5 questions:
  10 minutes to privately reflect/write answers
- Pairs discussion of answers: 10 minutes, 5 minutes per person
  Suggested questions for handout include:

1. What are your earliest memories of, or experiences with people with disabilities?
2. What images, impressions, or feelings did you have as a child about people with disabilities?
3. What messages did the people around you (parents, teachers, friends) pass on to you about people with disabilities?
4. How did these messages affect how you thought about yourself?
5. As an adult, what impressions, thoughts, feelings, or beliefs do you have about people with disabilities? How have they changed or stayed the same over time?

Processing:
Large group discussion, with several students sharing what was discussed in pairs. Suggested questions for processing include:

1. What were some early messages and from whom or what did they come?
2. What are some commonalities or themes that you notice in these messages?
3. What forms of disability (physical, mental, emotional) were included in early memories? What forms were not included?
4. What was it like to recall those early experiences, feelings, thoughts?
5. What are one or two lingering notions or impressions from the past that you would like to explore further in the class?

Acknowledge students' experiences, without judgment, and affirm that fear, discomfort, and confusion are not unusual. Remind students that many of the images and themes they have begun to identify will be discussed later in the course.

3. Myths and Stereotypes (30 minutes).

The purpose of this activity is to help students recognize the many myths and stereotypes about people with disabilities.

- Brainstorm session: 10 minutes of students calling out examples of common stereotypes, myths, and/or words they have heard used to describe people with disabilities, even those that might be derogatory or offensive.
- Record on chalkboard or newsprint visible to all students.

- Encourage the brainstorming process by offering your own examples. Assure students that no one will assume that individuals necessarily believe items they volunteer. A sample list might include the following:

Stereotypes/Myths such as:	**Names/Words such as:**
Eternal children	Crippled
Evil	Deformed
Depressed	Insane
Deranged	Drunk/Druggie
Bitter	Deaf/Mute
Dependent	Crazy
Burden	Physically Challenged
God's Children	Mentally Ill
"Supercrip"	Survivor
Courageous	Retarded
Ugly	Differently able
Asexual	Patient
Tragic	Idiot
	Slow
	Dumb

Handout 10.2. Stereotypes and Language: Ableism.

Processing:

Lead a discussion in which you point out the length of the list of names and stereotypes and how easy it was to generate. This reflects how much a part of our consciousness these images and words are.

Suggested processing questions include:

1. What themes can you identify?
2. What words or phrases seem out of date? Examples: crippled, retarded, mongoloid, or insane.
3. What contradictions can we identify? Example: evil menace vs. God's children, or dependent vs. "supercrip" (a slang word used among disabled people to describe disabled people who try to do it all).
4. What links exist between the various myths/stereotypes and the media, family, and cultural messages identified in the previous exercise?

Conclude by reviewing the ways in which individuals come to learn these messages, perhaps by briefly explaining the cycle of socialization (refer back to descriptions of the cycle in chapters 5, 7, and Appendix 5C). Reassure students that we all learn such messages innocently through the process of being socialized by institutions such as education and the media, yet we also have an opportunity to gain new information and adjust our perspective.

Commentary/ Facilitation Issues:

Stereotypes and words often govern the reactions of many able-bodied people to people with disabilities. The word "tragic," for example, is often used to describe a disability acquired as a result of an accident or an illness. This reaction can prevent one from understanding that while the initial loss one experiences may be genuinely difficult, it is not appropriate to assume that one's life will be an ongoing tragedy. For many persons with disabilities, becoming disabled has profoundly changed their lives in positive ways, ways that could not be imagined at the time of an accident, or the initial diagnosis of an illness. For increasing numbers of people, becoming non-disabled, even through miraculous cures, is not what they desire.

4. Journal Period (5 minutes).

This is the first of a series of brief individual reflection times built into the class design. It allows students time to reflect on their learnings and experiences in the class so far. Explain the purpose of journal time and ask students to spend five minutes thinking and writing quietly by themselves. Tell participants that anything they write during this time will not be collected, graded, or shared with anyone else. Rather it is for their own use. Suggest a question for reflection such as one of the following:

- What have you learned so far in the class that challenges what you thought previously about people with disabilities?
- What questions do you have about disability issues based on the class so far?
- What would you like to remember—information, feelings, thoughts—about the activities we have just completed?

5. Lecture on Definitions (30 minutes).

Purpose: to provide definitions and accurate information about disabilities. The Lecture on Definitions should include the material listed in Appendix 10A and 10B and can draw on readings assigned from the course reader (contents listed at end of volume).

6. History of Treatment of Persons with Disabilities, Part I (40 minutes).

Purpose: to increase student knowledge of the historical treatment of persons with disabilities.

Prepare handouts with a chronological description of key events (see timeline in Appendix 10C). Separate students into small groups and give each group a handout covering a specific time period. Small groups spend 20 minutes reviewing the information on the handout and preparing to present a summary of the information to the large group at the beginning of Module 2.

7. Closing (10 minutes).

Ask students to identify something they learned from this Module, and something about which they still have questions.

Module 2

Time needed: 2 3/4 hours plus break
Goals:

- Increase knowledge of effects of ableism at the personal level.
- Increase knowledge of systematic consumer-driven social, political, and cultural approaches to eliminating the oppression of disabled people.

- Increase knowledge of the historical treatment of persons with disabilities and the origins of ableism.

Key Concepts: historical perspectives, institutional oppression, empowerment, civil rights, legislation, consumer movements.

1. History of Treatment of Persons with Disabilities, Part II (60 minutes).

Purpose: to increase student knowledge of the historical treatment of persons with disabilities. In chronological order, small groups present an oral summary of events occurring during their assigned time period as well as beliefs or assumptions that shaped the way people with disabilities were treated during that period (twenty minutes for all presentations).

Processing:
After all groups have presented information from their time periods, ask students the following questions:

- What themes in the treatment of people with disabilities can we identify?
- What are some of the various perspectives held about people with disabilities over time?
- What are some of the origins of stereotypes and myths, about people with disabilities?
- Give examples of historic events that continue to influence the treatment of people with disabilities today.

Allow at least thirty minutes for this discussion to take place. Students can also draw parallels to the experience of other target groups during various time periods. For example, sterilization was used at the end of the nineteenth century as a way to prevent a variety of "undesirable" children from being born, particularly African American and poor children. Record key themes and observations on newsprint and post.

Commentary/Facilitation Issues:
Emphasize that this activity focuses on *ableism* and a history of the *treatment* of people with disabilities, rather than a history of the lives of people with disabilities. Other than a few well-known people such as Helen Keller, Bob Dole, or Franklin Delano Roosevelt, little is known about the contributions of people with disabilities. Point out that some people with disabilities disguise their disabilities in order to gain social acceptance and economic opportunity, for example, people who don't tell anyone about their history of treatment for emotional disabilities. Conclude the activity by discussing the important role an historical perspective about the treatment of persons with disabilities plays in shaping a better future for us all.

2. Overview of Contemporary Disability Rights Movement(s) and Key Legislation (30 minutes).

Purpose: to provide students with information about key legislation related to disability, and the philosophy and key objectives of critical consumer movements for social and political change related to disability, including:

- variations in the definition of disability.
- the problems addressed by the movements.
- the approach to change taken.
- different organizing principles, such as a cross-disability vs. singular disability focus.
- differences in strategies, such as using civil disobedience vs. working for internal systemic change.

Provide students with an overview of key legislation that protects the rights of persons with disabilities (see Appendix 10-D and 10-E). While the Americans with Disabilities Act is the most recent and far-reaching civil rights legislation affecting people with disabilities, other disability-related laws should be presented as well, such as the Rehabilitation Act of 1973 and the Architectural Barriers Act of 1968. Use the chart "Understanding Abilities and Disabilities—Toward Interdependency" (Appendix 10-F) to show how perspectives on disabilities have changed over time and have laid the foundation for the disability rights movements.

This information can be presented as a lecture with questions and answers. Post key legislation and related dates ahead of time on a large piece of newsprint. Posters, pictures, books, and other visual aids to communicate a flavor of the social and cultural aspect of the disability rights movement are a helpful complement to the lecture format. Include assigned readings as well as anecdotal information about key events that led to important changes and legislation to give the information a context. Provide information that makes connections to other liberation movements. For example, Karen Thompson's attempts to get guardianship of her life partner, Sharon Kowalski, after Sharon was disabled in a car accident, was a situation in which disability rights groups, women's rights groups, and lesbian and gay rights groups worked together (Thompson & Andrezejewski, 1988). Internationally, women with disabilities organized to make certain that their concerns were addressed by the Platform for Action developed at the United Nations Fourth World Conference on Women held in Beijing in 1995 (Morgan, 1996). This information will help to place the disability rights movement in a larger social and historic context.

Processing:
Ask students to:

- Identify key themes of the movements.
- Identify differences among the movements.
- Review the legislation attempting to address disability- related concerns raised by these movements and discuss its impact.
- Give examples of how these laws have helped to further the goals of the disability rights movements.

Break

3. Roles, Part I (60 minutes).

Purpose: to provide students with an opportunity to consider the impact of having a disability on a range of everyday activities. We believe that this activity helps participants begin to address the fear of becoming disabled, a fear which is one of the roots of ableism. The roles exercise provides an opportunity for participants to consider the effects of becoming disabled as well as their assumptions about such an experience. By participating in this experiential activity before listening to the panel of people with disabilities, students are better prepared to hear about the panel members' experiences with the understanding that having a disability means more than having limitations.

The following is a script for the facilitator to use in presenting this exercise.

The purpose of this activity is to look at roles we play in the day-to-day aspects of our lives, and our strengths and limitations in those roles. First, we'll spend some time thinking about our everyday lives and writing in our journals. For this exercise, use your journal to write down responses to questions and make note of information to share with another person. Next, we'll spend some time sharing in pairs. Then we'll do more thinking and writing, then share again with the same person. Finally, we'll discuss our answers to the questions in the whole group. As with the other activities in this class, you are not required to share anything in this exercise that you do not wish to share.

First set of questions: Choose a role that you currently have (for example, a student in a particular class, worker, daughter, son, or friend). Make sure you select a role for which you can imagine a recent specific situation where you were in that role—for example, if you select the role of student, you would imagine a particular class session. Now, think about yourself in that role in that specific situation and describe yourself in that situation:

- Whom do you relate to/ talk to?
- What tasks do you perform?
- Where are you?
- How did you get there?
- What are your strengths and limitations in that role?
- What does this role say about you as a person?

Spend five minutes thinking and writing about these questions. Then, post these questions on newsprint or the chalkboard so that students can refer to them easily.

After the five minutes, instruct the students: Now, spend about eight minutes with one other person, sharing what you thought of and wrote. Each of you spend four minutes giving a brief description of the role, how you play that role, and your strengths and limitations in that role.

After the eight minutes are up, instruct the students: Now, time for more thinking and writing. Select a disability from this list of disabilities. (Post a list of specific disabilities, such as spinal cord injury allowing movement of body above the waist, partially or completly blind, deaf, learning disabilities that limit ability to read.) If you have a disability, choose a disability that you do not have. Spend a few minutes writing down your understanding of the characteristics of that disability.

Now, think about the role you described before. Spend five minutes thinking about and writing about how you believe having the disability you just selected might affect your being in that role. Answer the same set of questions you wrote about before in describing the role.

After the five minutes are up, instruct the students: Rejoin the same partner and spend fifteen minutes discussing how having that particular disability would affect you in the role you have chosen. How do you feel when you think about having a disability? Discuss your thoughts about this with your partner.

Gather everyone back together as a whole group for a discussion (about twenty-five to thirty minutes). Use the following questions for processing:

- What situations did you select?
- What were your strengths and limitations?
- Which disability did you choose?
- What were your strengths and limitations now with the disability?
- How did it feel to think about having a disability?
- How could your feelings about having a disability impact your attitudes towards people with disabilities?

Conclude the exercise with comments such as the following: The purpose of this activity is to point out that we all, people with disabilities and people who don't currently have any disabilities, have many roles in our lives. In each of these roles, we have strengths and limitations. Having a disability does not mean only loss or limitations; it means having a different set of strengths and limitations. Acquiring a disability doesn't just mean loss; it means adjusting to a new set of strengths and limitations. We will talk more later in the class about what it would be like to have a disability over a long period of time. The members of the panel presentation we will hear have had their disabilities for different lengths of time and fill many roles in their day-to-day lives. Think about what their strengths and limitations are in the roles that they fill as you listen to their presentations.

4. Journal Period (5 minutes).

See directions in Module 1, activity 4.

5. Closing (10 minutes).

Ask the group to identify any themes that stand out from this module. Record these themes on newsprint and post for future reference. When the group reconvenes, use these themes to summarize class learnings or for comparison of changes as learning progresses.

Module 3

Time needed: 3 hours
Goals:

- Increase student understanding of the impact of various disabilities on one's daily life.
- Increase knowledge of the effects of discrimination in the day-to-day lives of people with disabilities.
- Increase student comfort level in interacting with people with disabilities.

Key Concepts: coping strategies, personal strengths, allies.

1. Check-In and Journal/Roles, Part II (30 minutes).

Begin this session with a brief opportunity for students to comment on their reactions to the first two modules of the class. Then, as a follow-up to the roles activity done in Module 2, introduce Journal/Roles, Part 2. The purpose of the second part of the roles activity is to help students understand that people with disabilities go through different stages of dealing with acquiring a disability and do not necessarily remain in the stage of grieving losses.

Use the following instructions: In Module 2, we spent some time considering a particular role we fill in our lives and the impact of acquiring a disability on that role. In the next activity, we want to spend some time considering what it would be like to have a disability over a period of time and its impact on the day-to-day realities of one's life. Think back to the role you selected, the disability you chose, and the strengths and limitations you would have in that role with that disability. Now, imagine that it is five years later.

- What would it be like to fill that role with that disability after having had the disability for five years?
- What resources would you need to fill that role (human, technological, financial)?
- What would your strengths and limitations be in that role?
- What would the difference be in your ability to fill that role five years after acquiring a disability and immediately after acquiring a disability?

Spend a few minutes thinking/writing about these questions and then spend eight minutes with the same partner you had in Module 2—to share your responses to these questions.

Bring the whole group back together and ask for responses to the questions and any reactions to this section of the exercise. Discuss the difference between acquiring a disability and living with a disability over time. Again, emphasize that one would continue to have both strengths and limitations, not just limitations.

As a conclusion to this activity, ask the students to think about the limitations they listed in their ability to fill the role while having a particular disability, and to consider which of those limitations are a result of the actual disabling condition and which are a result of the institutions that do not accommodate people with the disability they selected. Make a list of limitations they identify as being caused by the institutions and post the list on the wall. Point out to the students that for many of the limitations they identified in the exercise, the source of the limitation isn't in the disability itself but rather in the attitudes and beliefs of those around people with disabilities and in the societal systems which exclude people with disabilities.

2. Panel of People with Disabilities (90 minutes).

Purpose: to help students gain a deeper awareness of the personal impact of oppression, primarily at the individual level, and to some extent at the institutional and cultural levels, on people with disabilities and their families.

Pre-class Preparation of Panelists:

Prior to the class, identify panel members and prepare them for their presentations (Directions for setting up panels appear in chapter 8 and in Blumenfeld, 1993.) We have found panel members through a number of sources, including college and university disability service offices, independent living centers, and organizations that provide services for people with disabilities. Select male and female panel members who represent a range of disabilities, ages, ethnic, cultural, and economic backgrounds. The individuals selected should understand ableism and be able to present their personal experiences in the context of discrimination and oppression.

If you are not able to have a panel of speakers with disabilities, we recommend using a video about the lives of people with disabilities as an alternative activity. We suggest *Positive Images: Portraits of Women With Disabilities* or *Look Who's Laughing* (see the video resource list at the end of this volume).

Prepare panelists by informing them about the likely range of student knowledge and experience and the questions panelists might be asked. Panelists should be assured that they will have complete discretion over the extent of personal information they share. Ask panelists to focus their remarks on personal experiences that illustrate discrimination and oppression rather than a description of their disability. Provide panelists with a set of questions in advance to help focus their remarks. These might include:

- What is your disability and how long have you had this disability?
- As a person with a disability, what was your experience growing up and going to school?
- How was the experience of disability handled by your family and friends?
- As a person with a disability, how would you describe the accessibility and attitudes here at (name of college, university, or other setting)?
- As a person with a disability, what has been your experience trying to find employment?
- How has having a disability affected how you are treated in various social situations?
- What are some examples of ways that people can interact with you that feel most respectful?
- What do you think the role of non-disabled people is in the disability rights/independent living movement?
- How can non-disabled persons be allies to persons with disabilities?

In-Class Preparation:
Preparing the students prior to the panel is as important as preparing the panelists. Ask students to write down questions they wish to ask the panel members before the panelists arrive. Encourage open-ended questions that allow them to learn about the panel members' experiences of discrimination, isolation, segregation, and other effects of oppression.

Ask students how they feel about meeting the panel, including any hopes and fears they may have. Encourage students to ask as many of the questions as possible. Individuals who are uncomfortable asking questions aloud can give written questions to the facilitators to pass along to the panel members.

Panel Presentation/Facilitation Issues:
Begin the activity by welcoming the panel and introducing each member. Review guidelines for the panel presentation. Guidelines may include:

- Hold questions until all presentations are complete.
- Respect panelists' right not to answer a question.

- Remember that panelists speak from their own experience, not for all disabled people.

Invite the panel to begin by having each panelist give a five to seven minute autobiographical sketch of his/her life. This can include brief descriptions of and reflections on their disability, family, friends, work, school, goals, dreams, but with emphasis upon their experiences of discrimination related to disability oppression.

Keep track of time, reminding each panelist when their time is up. When all panelists have finished their introductory remarks, invite questions from students. Read questions from the index cards as needed or ask your own questions to insure that issues of oppression are adequately addressed. Generally, however, panels work best when facilitators take a secondary role and panelists and students interact directly with each other.

Students' initial questions often tend to focus on finding out about a person's disability rather than on their experiences of discrimination. Encourage or interject questions that redirect the discussion toward the effects of oppression on the lives of people with disabilities.

3. Discussion after Panel Presentation (30 minutes).

After the panel is over, thank the panelists and take a short break. After the departure of the panelists and the break, facilitate a discussion encouraging students to share their feelings, thoughts, or reactions to the panelists' comments. Some questions to ask include:

- What information surprised you or contradicted something you believed?
- Were there times during the panel when you felt uncomfortable?
- What was the source of your discomfort?
- Refer to the list of myths and stereotypes from Module 1. Which ones were contradicted or confirmed by the panel?
- What questions were left unanswered?
- What examples of individual or institutional ableism did the panelists describe?

Commentary:
One of the goals of a panel presentation by people with disabilities is to put a human face on issues which, for many people, have seemed unconnected to their day-to-day lives. By hearing from and speaking with a group of people with disabilities, students can more easily make the connection between the information presented in the class about ableism and real people's lives. Instead of an abstract notion such as "people with cerebral palsy," students will now be able to think of Joe or Linda whom they met on the panel and who has cerebral palsy.

4. Journal Period (5 minutes).

See directions in Module 1, activity 4.

5. Closing (10 minutes).

Ask students to identify ways in which the lives of the panelists have been affected by the history, legislation, and disability rights movements discussed in the first two modules.

Module 4

Time needed: 3 hours
Goals:

- Create a vision for an accessible/inclusive society.
- Develop personal and group strategies for change.

Key Concepts: institutional oppression, empowerment, equal access, and inclusion.

1. Visioning an Accessible/Inclusive Society (90 minutes).

Purpose: to assist students to creatively explore a vision for the future.

Divide class into small groups with newsprint and markers. Ask each group to:

a) List current barriers for people with a range of disabilities within the university/ college and the local community. The groups can draw upon the information presented by panelists and the previous three modules.

b) Envision an accessible and inclusive university or community, and record on newsprint the characteristics that would make it accessible and inclusive.

c) List some strategies that need to occur to move from the present-day reality to their vision. It might be helpful to brainstorm a list of different resources that can enable people with different disabilities to gain full access to a range of opportunities. Examples include personal care assistants, computer technology, books on tape, sign language interpreters, ramps, large print, accessible rest rooms, elevators, teletypewriters, TTYs.

If needed, provide the small groups with specific areas of the university and community to think about, such as residence halls, classrooms, restaurants, the library, a grocery store, a pharmacy. For example, what would an accessible and inclusive residence life system include to accommodate people with mobility impairments, visual impairments, and other forms of disabilities? It might be helpful to circulate among the groups to help them think of specific accessibility barriers and needed resources to make a change. Display the final product of each group on the wall for reporting back to the whole class. Small groups should work for thirty minutes.

Processing:
Reconvene the class and ask each group to share their vision and the strategies and the resources necessary to achieve that vision. Instruct all groups to listen for key concepts during each presentation that overlaps with other groups' presentations. Ask the class to reflect on the lecture about the disability rights movement and legislation, and to identify examples of strategies that are already being used to address ableism in the particular institutions they described.

2. Journal Period (5 minutes).

See directions in Module 1, activity 4.

3. Barriers to Action/ Action Continuum (30 minutes).

Purpose: to consider that obstacles prevent individuals from taking action against ableism and to identify the range of possible actions one can take.

Introduce the activity by explaining that both internal and external barriers discourage taking action against ableism:

- internal—our own attitudes and beliefs that keep us inactive.

- external—institutions and attitudes and beliefs of others.

For people with disabilities, internalized oppression can be a barrier to taking action. Internalized oppression occurs when a member of an oppressed group, such as a person with a disability, internalizes and believes society's oppressive attitudes about him or herself. An example of internalized oppression would be a deaf person who believes that it would be asking too much to expect a sign-language interpreter at the town meeting in their town.

Ask students to spend a few minutes thinking of barriers to taking action that they encounter. Then, ask them to double up in pairs to discuss *one* of these barriers to taking action against ableism. Finally, conduct a whole group discussion soliciting examples of barriers to action and suggestions of ways to overcome those barriers. An example of a barrier to action is not knowing about the specific ways that ableism manifests itself in the local community; an example of a way to overcome this barrier would be to visit a local independent living center to interview staff members about local issues of concern.

Choose a situation in which ableism is a problem and have students brainstorm a list of possible actions to address this form of ableism. An example might be lack of sign-language interpretation for classes at a university. Actions might include:

- researching the laws related to accommodation for people with disabilities.
- writing a letter to the editor of the student newspaper protesting the lack of interpreters.
- organizing a rally to educate the community about this problem and other examples of ableism in the community.

These examples illustrate that for any situation, there are many different actions an individual or group can take to address ableism (see Action Continuum in Appendix 6C). To conclude this section, ask students to consider which actions from the brainstormed list they could imagine themselves taking.

4. Personal Commitments for Action (30 minutes).

Purpose: to encourage students to identify actions they can take individually or collaboratively to help eliminate ableism within their sphere of influence (see chapters 6 and 8 for examples of Spheres of Influence activities).

In pairs have students discuss actions they might take in some of the different settings discussed during the class. Then, ask each student to select one concrete action that they will commit to completing within one month's time. Ask students to identify and write down

1. any barriers they anticipate that could keep them from following through on their plan,
2. support they will need to carry out their action plan, and
3. how they will celebrate or reward themselves for taking action.

Processing:
Ask the students to share their feelings and fears about making a commitment to take action. Ask a few volunteers to share their commitments with the class. Acknowledge that interrupting oppression is not always comfortable and can involve some personal risks.

5. Closure and Evaluation (30 minutes).

Reconvene the group and ask each student to share one thing they learned during the course and one thing about which they still want to know more. Offer the group an opportunity to give verbal feedback on the content presented, pace and time allotted for each activity, and methods and styles of presentation. This feedback may also be solicited through a written evaluation sheet handed out and returned before students leave the course. Have students complete the evaluation and then reconvene the group for a final moment. At this time, review any further reading or written assignments required of students. The course may be concluded by reading a brief poem or quotation about empowering people with disabilities or becoming allies along with taking a few minutes to appreciate the work that has been accomplished and students' contributions during the course.

Appendix 10A

DEFINITIONS OF DISABILITY

The Rehabilitation Act of 1973 defines a "handicapped individual" as "any individual who . . . has a physical or mental disability which for any such individual constitutes or results in a substantial handicap to employment."

The World Health Organization distinguishes between *impairments, disabilities,* and *handicaps. Impairments* are physiological abnormalities. *Disabilities* are limitations in functional performance stemming from impairments. *Handicaps* are resulting disadvantages that may take the form of arbitrary barriers constructed, consciously or unconsciously, by society (McNeil, 1993, 1).

The Americans with Disabilities Act of 1990 states that someone is disabled if he or she "a) has a physical or mental impairment that substantially limits one or more major life activities; b) has a record of such an impairment; or c) is regarded as having such an impairment."

The Bureau of the US Census' 1990 and 1991 Surveys define disability as "a limitation in a functional activity or in a socially defined role or task" (McNeil, 1993, 3).

Source: McNeil, J. M. (1993). *Americans with Disabilities, 1991/92: Data from the Survey of Income and Program Participation.* Washington, DC: US Dept. of Commerce, Economics, and Statistics Administration, Bureau of the Census.

Appendix 10B

DEFINITIONS OF DISABILITY LECTURE OUTLINE

In addition to the definitions listed on the handout, the Definitions Lecture should include the following material:

- Context of defining disabilities depends on historical and cultural issues.
- Many definitions in the U.S. have focused on a person's ability to work and earn a living; these were the definitions related to early rehabilitation laws.
- The ADA's broad, three-pronged definition of disability focuses on *functional* ability rather than specific medical diagnosis to extend its legal protections to the full range of persons with disabilities. A person with a disability is defined as someone who experiences a physical or mental condition that limits the ability to perform a major life activity such as walking, breathing, seeing, hearing, thinking, or working. The second prong of the ADA definition goes further in defining people who might be discriminated against on the basis of disability by saying that people who have a *record or history* of a disability are also protected from discrimination under this law. In addition, the third prong protects people who have no disability at all but who are *perceived* to have a disability. The second and third prongs of the ADA definitions were established in recognition that disability discrimination is a phenomenon unto itself and that disability discrimination results from misconceptions and prejudice which are partly or wholly unrelated to the reality of disability itself.
- Major types of disabilities include: perceptual, illness-related, physical, developmental, mental/emotional, chronic/acute, and environmental.

Appendix 10C

HISTORY OF ABLEISM IN EUROPE AND THE UNITED STATES—SELECTED TIMELINE
Compiled by Pat Griffin and Mary McClintock

1200s–1700s Accepted belief that mentally ill people (lunacy and idiocy) were possessed by the devil or evil spirits. As a result, they were routinely whipped, tortured, and burned at the stake. Disease or ill fortune taken as a sign of having fallen from spiritual favor. Between 1400 and 1700 more than 100,000 people executed as witches. Many of them probably had some form of mental illness or other disability.

1598–1601 English Elizabethan Poor Laws. People with disabilities ejected from hospitals and monastery shelters for the poor. People with disabilities forced to beg and given a cap in which to collect alms. This was the origin of the term "handicap" which many people with disabilities find offensive because of its origin. Many people with disabilities provided entertainment and endured humiliation in return for food and shelter.

1692 Salem witchcraft trials begin in U.S.

1700s Beginning of special schools for treatment of children with disabilities. First attempts to educate deaf children.

1749 French Academy of Sciences appoints a commission to determine whether deaf people are capable of reasoning.

1760 Academy for the Deaf and Dumb established in Scotland.

1776 "Stephen Hopkins referred to his cerebral palsy when he signed the Declaration of Independence, saying 'My hand trembles but my heart does not'" (Shapiro, 1993, 39).

1780 "Gouverneur Morris, who helped draft the Constitution and was later a U.S. Senator from New York, wore a 'rough stick' to replace the left leg he lost in a 1780 carriage accident" (Shapiro, 1993, 39).

1787 "At the time that Benjamin Franklin was chosen to represent Pennsylvania in the Constitutional Convention of 1787, he was almost immobilized by gouty arthritis, and Philadelphia's officials arranged to have him carried into sessions in a sedan chair. His physically defective body thus did not impede his ability to function as a statesman; although the impairment that prevented his walking remained, he was not disabled" (Liachowitz, 1988, xi).

1800s Science begins to replace religion as the main authority guiding leaders in the West. Biology and science are used to explain the world. Instead of being seen as having a spiritual deficit, people with disabilities are seen as having a genetic deficit.

People with disabilities placed under the care of medical profession, professional educators and social workers. Almshouses, workhouses, institutions, asylums proliferate in U.S.

1817 First school for the deaf in the U.S.: American Asylum for the Deaf and Dumb, Hartford, CT.

1840s "Human curiosities" joined burgeoning amusement organizations such as P. T. Barnum's American Museum in New York City (Bogdan et al., 1987).

1840s until the 1940s "Freak shows" popular in traveling circuses.

Institutionalization

Early 1800s State mental hospitals were the first formal system of public care for the mentally ill in the United States. Such institutions were created:

> in response to criticism of the inhumanity of "outdoor relief" and the practice of incarcerating the insane in local almshouses and jails. In contrast to the pattern of physical abuse, neglect, and ridicule that characterized these settings, the early mental hospitals were championed as repositories of hope and human care for the mentally ill (Morrissey et al., 1980, 2).

While state mental hospitals were started with lofty goals of being more humane, they rapidly became transformed into something quite different.

> Massive waves of European immigration and the growing belief in the incurability of insanity further accelerated the transformation of state hospitals from small, intimate, therapeutically oriented "asylums" to large, impersonal, custodially oriented "human warehouses" (Morrissey et al., 1980, 2).

1849 Massachusetts Legislature appropriated funds to create the Massachusetts School for Idiotic Children and Youth in Boston.

1857 Thomas Gallaudet appointed head of Columbia Institute for the Deaf, Dumb and Blind, later named Gallaudet College.

1850–1920s Beginning of the Eugenics Movement. Goal to improve the quality of the human gene pool.

People with disabilities were segregated and hidden (institutions, asylums, hospitals, segregated schools, sheltered workshops, attics) or placed on display as entertainment (freak shows, circuses).

1859 Darwin's *Origin of the Species* published. The principle of natural selection applied to humans and society by scientists and politicians in the U.S. and Europe (Social Darwinism).

1880 Congress of Milan: An international meeting of educators voted to banish sign language from deaf education and introduced Oralism (belief in the superiority of speech over signing). In 1867 every American school for the deaf taught sign language. By 1907, none did.

Late 1800s Racial Hygiene Movement favored government controlled policies to control reproduction so that only desirable genes passed on. Believed that action should be taken to eradicate diseases and characteristics that "weakened the human race." Used to justify isolation and extermination of Jews, homosexuals, and disabled people in Nazi Germany. Was influential in determining attitudes towards disabled people in many Western countries.

Segregated schools for the blind, deaf, and mentally retarded proliferate. No work or support for graduates. Most work in sheltered workshops such as broom factories with subsistence wages with room and board deducted.

Testing and classification of the "feebleminded" by the medical profession. Treatment: segregation and sterilization.

1907 Indiana became the first of 29 states to pass compulsory sterilization laws directed at people with genetic illnesses or conditions.

1908 First American film version of *Dr. Jekyll and Mr. Hyde.*

1918 Soldier Rehabilitation (Smith-Sears) Act of 1918—vocational rehabilitation for disabled veterans, only for people with physical disabilities.

1920 Vocational Rehabilitation Act of 1920—similar to above, but for civilians; only for people with physical disabilities.

1920–38 States established workers' compensation programs

1922 Harry Laughlin (part of the eugenics movement) drew up a model sterilization law, which served as an example for numerous state legislatures. "It required the sterilization of the following 'defective' classes: 1) feebleminded; 2) insane (including the psychopathic); 3) criminalistic (including the delinquent and wayward); 4) epileptic; 5) inebriate (including drug habitues); 6) diseased (including the tubercular, the syphilitic, the leprous, and others with chronic, infectious, and legally segregable diseases); 7) blind (including those with seriously impaired vision); 8) deaf (including those with seriously impaired hearing); 9) deformed (including the crippled); and 10) dependent (including orphans, ne'er-do-wells, the homeless, tramps, and paupers)" (Pfeiffer, 1993, 726).

1923 Lon Chaney played Quasimodo, "the frightful, crooked, bugeyed, and in other ways deformed Hunchback of Notre Dame, the classic disabled victim of others' violence" (Bogdan, et al., 1982, 33).

1927 *Buck v. Bell,* 274 US 200 (1927). Supreme Court decision that upheld a Virginia statute that forbad "feebleminded"people from marrying or becoming parents. Feebleminded was defined in the 1880s as "anyone who was not able to attain the minimum educational level (about today's third-grade education)." "Included was anyone with a communication problem (vision, hearing, or speech impairment) that impeded learning, or a mobility problem that prevented the adequate socialization necessary to learn or made them unable to attend school" (Pfeiffer, 1993, 724).

1920–30s German Social Darwinists feared that the degeneration of the race was due to 1) medical care of the "weak" that had begun to destroy the natural struggle for existence and 2) the poor and misfits of the world were multiplying faster than the talented and fit. Countries with compulsory sterilization laws: Denmark (1929), Norway (1934), Sweden (1935), Finland (1935), Estonia (1936); Czechoslovakia, Yugoslavia, Lithuania, Latvia, Hungary, and Turkey (late 1930s).

1920s Institutionalization of people with disabilities is seen as best for them and for society. People with disabilities seen as a "drag on civilization."

1930–40s President Franklin Delano Roosevelt's physical disability hidden from the American public for fear that it would detract from his power and status.

1932 "MGM's film *Freaks* capitalized on the horror film/freak show link in order to promote the fear of deformity" (Bogdan, et al., 1982, 32–33).

"From the first horror films to modern-day renderings, physical and mental disabilities have been shown to connote murder, violence, and danger" (Bogdan, et al., 1982, 33).

1933 German Law for the Prevention of Genetically Diseased Offspring passed.

1933 Nazi Sterilization Program begins. Doctors required to register anyone known to have any "genetic illness" such as "feeblemindedness," schizophrenia, manic-depression, insanity, genetic epilepsy, Huntington's chorea, genetic blindness or deafness, severe alcoholism. 400,000 people sterilized. Protestant and Catholic churches cooperated and helped to register people in their institutions.

Sterilization was never classified as a war crime because so many other Western countries, including the U.S., had similar laws.

1937 Poll in the U.S. indicates that 45% of the population favor euthanasia for "defective infants."

1938 Germany, England, U.S.: A movement among some physicians to recognize the "privilege" of death for the "congenitally mindless and incurably sick who wish to die."

33 states pass sterilization laws.

1939 in Germany: End of Nazi sterilization program. Beginning of Euthanasia Program. 70,000 adults and 5,000 children put to death during the official phase and over 200,000 killed in total.

German Committee for the Scientific Treatment of Severe, Genetically Determined Illnesses created to create a process for killing "deformed and retarded" children. Directed all doctors and midwives to register children born with "congenital deformities, idiocy, Mongolism, microencephaly, hydrocephaly, deformities of any kind, crippling deformities." Doctors registered all such children up to 3 years old. They were paid for each registration. The committee processed all registrations and decided on the basis of the paperwork who would be killed (no consultation with doctors or parents).

Children were killed with morphine injections, gassed with cyanide or chemical warfare agents. They were also slowly administered poisons, starved to death, and exposed to cold so that the deaths would appear "natural."

Committee for the Scientific Treatment of Severe, Genetically Determined Illnesses sets up adult euthanasia program. Developed the technology for mass killings that was later used on the Jews. Hospitals and institutions filled out questionnaires about their patients' schizophrenia, epilepsy, senile maladies, paralysis, imbecility, encephalitis, chronic nervous system diseases.

Justification: Get rid of people who "polluted" the Aryan race.

1942 An article in the professional journal of the American Psychiatric Association calls for killing all "retarded children under the age of five": F. Kennedy, "The Problem of Social Control of the Congenital Defective: Education, Sterilization, Euthanasia." *American Journal of Psychiatry*, 99 (1), 13–16.

1943 Nazi Euthanasia Program expanded to include children of "unwanted" races (non-disabled and disabled).

1943 Congress passed the Borden-LaFollette Act, which expanded vocational rehabilitation programs to include mentally ill and mentally retarded people in vocational rehabilitation programs.

1945 *House of Frankenstein* filmed. Boris Karloff plays a doctor who is killed by a psychopathic, hunchbacked killer (Bogdan, et al., 1982, 33).

1950s Laws still on the books in some states prohibiting persons "diseased, maimed, mutilated, or in any way deformed so as to be an unsightly or disgusting object" from appearing in public.

1954 *Brown v. Board of Education.* Education for all on equal terms. Used to argue for desegregating education for children with disabilities in later years.

1959–1961 HR361—A bill to extend independent living services to people incapable of employment was twice defeated in the U.S. Congress.

Deinstitutionalization

Starting in the mid-1950s, there has been a major reform in public mental health services—a movement towards "community mental health."

Deinstitutionalization is "an effort to dismantle and close state mental hospitals and to supplant them by a network of community-based mental health services. . . . Between 1955 and 1975, for example, the resident population of state mental hospitals was reduced by more than 365,000 persons. . . . 'Deinstitutionalized' people have faced hostility and rejection from communities, have been 'dumped' in rooming houses and inner city hotels, have been 'reinstitutionalized' in nursing homes and chronic care facilities, have suffered and died in remaining state hospitals because of money being shifted to community care" (Morrissey, 1980, 2–3).

1960s Substandard conditions at institutions for the mentally retarded exposed in media. Educators begin questioning the desirability of special classes vs. mainstreamed classes.

1962 Disabled students' program at the University of Illinois. First to facilitate community living for people with severe physical disabilities.

1963 Mental Retardation Facilities and Community Mental Health Centers Construction Act of 1963 passed.

1964 Urban Mass Transportation Act of 1964, as amended (49USC1612) requires that systems accepting federal monies authorized under the Act must make those systems accessible to elderly and handicapped persons.

1968 Virginia law that was upheld in *Buck v. Bell* (1927) was repealed, but sterilizations under it continued until 1972. By the 1960s sterilization was used in fewer and fewer cases, but 26 states still had a sterilization law for persons labeled mentally retarded and in 23 states it was compulsory (Pfeiffer, 1993, 726).

Architectural Barriers Act of 1968 (42USC4151) requires that all buildings built with federal funds must be accessible.

1970s Independent Living movement begins, grass roots effort by disabled people to acquire new rights and entitlements, control over their lives. Begins to reshape relationship of disabled people with physicians and other rehab professionals. Disability Rights Movement locates problem not in the individual but in the environment (attitudes and barriers, lack of services).

Judy Heumann, disabled woman, starts the first political action group for disabled people (Disabled in Action).

1972 First Center for Independent Living, Berkeley, CA. Service agency run by and for people with disabilities. Ed Roberts, a disabled man, instrumental in developing it.

American Sign Language (ASL) accepted as a way to fill the language requirement at NYU.

1973 Rehabilitation Act (Section 504) prohibited discrimination against "otherwise qualified handicapped" individuals in any program or activity receiving federal assistance. Considered the Civil Rights Act of the handicapped. Broadened power of people with disabilities to jointly draw up rehabilitation plans with professionals and addressed architectural and transportation issues.

1973 Rehabilitation Act of 1973 omitted the word vocational from rehabilitation legislation for the first time in the 53 year history of such legislation.

Set of amendments to the Vocational Rehabilitation Act of 1920—three sections—501, 503, 504 mandate nondiscrimination and affirmative action by federal contractors and the federal government.

"Curb cuts in sidewalks, specially designated handicapped parking spaces, accessible public transportation, ramps into public buildings, universities with special services for disabled students, equal employment practices, and many other changes that one can see throughout this society are either partially or wholly a result of section 504" (DeLoach, 1983, 21).

1974 Boston Center for Independent Living opens.

1975 Education for All Handicapped Children Act passes.

1975 Developmental Disabilities Assistance and Bill of Rights Act of 1975 created state developmental disabilities councils for planning and advocacy.

1976 People with disabilities protest at a meeting of Rehabilitation International (mostly non-disabled professionals). A motion that at least 50% of representatives should be people with disabilities was defeated.

1977 Department of Health, Education & Welfare (HEW) issued supporting regulations to implement Sections 501, 503, 504 after unprecedented public demonstrations by people with disabilities.

People with disabilities occupied the HEW office in San Francisco for 25 days: over 120 demonstrators, supported by Butterfly Brigade (a group of gay men), Black Panthers, unions, civil rights groups, McDonald's, Goodwill Industries, priests, rabbis, the mayor of San Francisco (Moscone), and other lawmakers. Joseph Califano,Secretary of HEW, signed the regulations supporting 504 on April 28, 1977.

1978 Rehabilitation, Comprehensive Services and Developmental Disabilities Legislation (P.L.95–602) referred to as Rehabilitation Amendments of 1978.

Title VII of the above is the Comprehensive Services for Independent Living.

Part B, Centers for Independent Living, funded by Congress, enabled every state to begin offering some type of IL services.

P.L.95–602 authorized Independent Living services and advocacy for severely disabled people.

1981 First Congress of Disabled Peoples International: International disability rights organization formed after Rehabilitation International protest in 1976.

1985 All states have workers' compensation programs, although they are not always compulsory.

1986 Voting Accessibility for the Elderly and Handicapped Act (P.L.98–435) requires that all polling places in federal elections be accessible for elderly and handicapped.

1986 Air Carrier Access Act of 1986 (PL99–435) prohibits discrimination "against any otherwise qualified handicapped individual, by reason of such handicap, in the provision of air transportation."

1988 Fair Housing Amendments of 1988 brought protections to disabled people in housing.

1988 Students at Gallaudet College for the Deaf protest when a hearing president is selected by the Board of Trustees.

1980s–1990s Genetic screening and testing to prevent the birth of "genetically defective" children becomes increasingly possible due to technological advances.

Technological advances also result in greater freedom, access, and independence for people with disabilities.

Deinstitutionalization of state-supported institutions for mentally retarded and mentally ill allow them to live and work in the community. While positive in many ways, deinstitutionalization in combination with inadequate funding for services to support people who have been deinstitutionalized, also has meant an increase in homelessness among people who have mental disabilities.

Rise of Deaf Culture and belief among some deaf people that the deafness is not a disability but a different culture that is discriminated against (audism).

1990 Americans with Disabilities Act becomes federal law. Extends protection of the 1973 Rehabilitation Act to private sector. Requires access and prohibits discrimination in public accommodations, state and local government, employment, requires reasonable accommodation, access to transportation and telecommunications. Is specific where 1973 act was vague.

IDEA—Individuals with Disabilities Education Act.

Reauthorization with amendments of the Education for All Handicapped Children Act.

Sources: Information in this Timeline was compiled by P. Griffin and M. McClintock from the following sources: R. Bogdan et al (1982), The Disabled: Media's Monster, *Social Policy,* 13 (2), 32–35; R. Bogdan (1987), The Exhibition of Humans with Differences for Amusement and Profit, *Policy Studies Journal,* 14 (3), 537–50; A. Gartner (1982), Images of the Disabled/Disabling Images, *Social Policy,* 13 (2), 14–15; R.C. Grzesiak & D.A. Hicok (1994), A Brief History of Psychotherapy and Physical Disability, *American Journal of Psychotherapy,* 48 (2), 240–50; L. Kriegel (1982), The Wolf in the Pit in the Zoo, *Social Policy,* 13 (2), 16–23; C.H. Liachowitz (1988), *Disability as a Social Construct: Legislative Roots,* Philadelphia: University of Pennsylvania Press; J. Morris (1991), *Pride against Prejudice: Transforming Attitudes to Disability,* Philadelphia: New Society Publishers; J.P. Morrissey, H. H. Goldman, & L.V. Kierman (Eds.) (1980), *The Enduring Asylum: Cycles of Institutional Reform at Worcester State Hospital,* New York: Grune & Stratton; D. Pfeiffer (1993), Overview of the Disability Movement: History, Legislative Record, and Political Implications, *Policy Studies Journal,* 21 (4), 724–34; J. P. Shapiro (1993), *No Pity: People with Disabilities Forging a New Civil Rights Movement,* New York: Times Books; I.K. Zola (1985), Depictions of Disability—Metaphor, Message and Medium in the Media: A Research and Political Agenda, *Social Science Journal,* 22 (4), 5–17.

Appendix 10D

IMPORTANT TWENTIETH-CENTURY FEDERAL LEGISLATION FOR PEOPLE WITH DISABILITIES

YEAR	LAW OR ACT	IMPACT
1918	Smith-Sears Veterans' Rehabilitation Act	Assistance for World War I veterans with combat injuries.
1920	Smith-Fess Act (Civilian Vocational Rehabilitation Act)	Provided federal vocational assistance to non-veterans.
1935	Social Security Act	Gave permanent status to the vocational rehabilitation program.
1956	Social Security Disability Insurance	Amended the Social Security Act
1964, 1968	Civil Rights Acts	Title VI established that no discrimination is permitted because of race, color or national origin.
1965	Elementary and Secondary Education Act	1966 and 1967 elaborations of this Act included Title VI for educating disabled children.
1968	Handicapped Children's Early Education Assistance Act	Provided assistance for disabled preschoolers.
1968	Architectural Barriers Act	Required businesses, organizations, and government agencies to meet a set of accessibility standards.
1970	The Developmental Disabilities Services and Facilities Construction Act (P.L.1–517)	Introduced the concept of of "developmental disabilities."
1970	Education of the Handicapped Act	Extension of the Elementary and Secondary Education Act.
1972	Supplemental Security Income	Established uniform national benefits for disabled people. 1973 amendments covered "essential persons" such as spouses.
1973	Rehabilitation Act	Prohibited discrimination against disabled people following Title VI of the Civil Rights Acts, Section 504 (Secs. 501–503 also important).
1974	Education Amendments	Extended the Education of the Handicapped Act and required States to provide comprehensive services for disabled students.
1975	Education for All Handicapped Children Act (P.L. 94–142)	Guaranteed free and appropriate education to all children.
1978	Rehabilitation, Comprehensive Services, and Developmental Disabilities Amendment (P.L. 95–602)	Revised the definition of developmental disabilities to emphasize "functionality."

1984	Developmental Disabilities Act Amendment (P.L. 98–527)	Made employment-related activities a priority.
1986	Air Carriers Access Act	Ensured disabled travelers access to air carriers.
1988	Civil Rights Restoration Act	Expanded the limits of the Rehabilitation Act of 1973.
1988	Fair Housing Amendments	Prohibited discrimination against disabled people.
1990	Developmental Disabilities Assistance and Bill of Rights Act	Emphasized empowerment, advocacy, and protection of disabled people.
1990	Education of the Handicapped Act Amendments (P.L. 101–476)	Expanded the definition of disability and emphasized transition planning.
1990	Individuals with Disabilities Education Act	Placed disabled students in in regular classrooms.
1990	Americans with Disabilities Act	Offered civil rights for disabled people: right to access in employment settings, public transportation, public establishments.

Appendix 10E

DISABILITY RIGHTS MOVEMENT LECTURE OUTLINE

Purpose: increase understanding of disability in a political and socio-economic context.

1. Introduction:
Discuss early social/political approaches to disability including key legislation prior to 1970.

2. Shifting Paradigms:
Paradigms have shifted based on the advocacy of people with disabilities, families, and allies to create a society that eliminates inequalities and provides opportunities for full inclusion and maximum self-sufficiency.

- Disability as a medical issue vs disability as a civil rights issue.
- Disabled people as people to be cured or cared for vs educated and empowered to become independent and self-sufficient.

3. Legislation:
Discuss first and second wave of contemporary disability policy and legislation including success and limitations of these efforts.

First Wave:
Key themes—deinstitutionalization, mainstreaming, non-discrimination, access, education, rehabilitation.

- Early Architectural Barriers Laws
- Section 504 of the Federal Rehabilitation Act
- IDEA—formerly called the Education for All Handicapped Children Act
- Similar state level efforts to prohibit discrimination on the basis of disability

Second Wave:
Key themes—non-discrimination, civil rights, equality, inclusion, economic self-sufficiency, self-determination, independence.

- Fair Housing Amendments
- Air Carriers Access Act
- Americans with Disabilities Act
- IDEA Amendments
- Rehabilitation Act Amendments

4. Current Issues/Future Directions:
Discuss current issues and future problems in the context of preserving and expanding civil rights for people with disabilities.

- Genetic discrimination
- Health care/health insurance
- Assisted suicide
- Eliminating entitlements
- Shifting responsibility to states
- Changes in and loss of critical government programs

Appendix 10F

UNDERSTANDING ABILITIES AND DISABILITIES—TOWARD INTERDEPENDENCY

Bob Bureau

	Medical	**Rehabilitation**	**Independent Living**	**Interdependency**
Definition of Dilemma or Problem	That a person has a physical, mental, or emotional impairment.	Given their disability, the person lacks necessary job skills, and needs rehabilitation.	Dependence on medical professionals, family, friends, and the community-at-large to get own needs met.	Historical distance from the heart of society. Viewed as broken, abnormal, and of no essential, genuine value.
Central Issues of Dilemma/Problem	The actual existence of the disability. That it must be eradicated if at all possible.	The person doesn't fit into the society with their disability. They need to adjust/adapt to the situation.	The laws, values, and attitudes of society are set up to rigidly enforce dependency and restrict freedom.	Dualistic society which acts to perpetuate categories of superior/inferior. The intentional oppression of people with disabilities.
Solution to Dilemma/Problem	Research into curing the disability through surgery, drugs, or invasive treatment.	Vocational rehabilitation, sheltered workshops, physical therapy, and adaptive technology.	Mutual support, self-help, removing all barriers. Cross-disability political action, and social change.	Shift control of available resources to people with disabilities. Empowerment and transformation.
Social Role of Person	Medical Patient.	Rehabilitation Client.	Person with a disability and who consumes/uses services.	Respected and valued community member.
Expectations of Person	Absolutely compliant with medical advice, submissive, never question authorities.	Grateful, eager to appear like everyone else again, to be normal. Should complete treatment plan.	Assertive, retains sovereignty over own life, entitled to a full range of options/choices.	Personal freedom, dignity in taking risks, learning, succeeding, creating, and even, at times, failing.
Group which Control Services	Traditional medical schools, licensed doctors who support drugs and surgery.	Funding sources, social service agancies, charities, foundations, and all levels of government.	People with disabilities.	All people with disabilities, and their own genuine chosen community.
Goals and Outcomes	To cure, to do everything possible to get rid of it, or at the least, to numb any existing pain.	Maximum adaptation to the society, to be made as normal as possible, and to get a job.	Independent living in the community, on own terms.	Recognition that our world has tremendous social diversity, which must not be used to justify fearing or dehumanizing anyone.

11

Classism Curriculum Design

Felice Yeskel, Betsy Leondar-Wright

Introduction

The gap between rich and poor in the United States is the greatest it has ever been. According to long-time Republican party advisor Kevin Phillips, "by several measures, the United States in the late twentieth century has led all other major industrial powers in the gap dividing the upper fifth of the population from the lower" (1990). From 1979 to 1995, the share of all United States personal wealth owned by the wealthiest 1 percent of the population increased from 19 percent to 40 percent. The top 1 percent of the population now owns a greater share of the wealth than the bottom 90 percent. Real (after inflation) wages have been falling since the 1970s (Barlett & Steele, 1992). Some of the results of this changing economic picture include more families with dual wage earners, more part-time and over-time employment for working- and middle-class families, significantly less leisure time, and higher overall unemployment. A growing number of people believe that United States society is breaking down and that the economy is in decline. Many of today's social problems are directly linked to this decline, including urban decay, increased homelessness and hunger, increasing numbers of youth not in school or employed, rising drug and alcohol abuse, and an increase in stress-related illnesses. For many Americans, this situation has led to increasing anxiety about the future and a growing disillusionment with government.

The ability of average Americans to analyze and understand the current situation is thwarted by prevailing myths about class and classism and a version of history in which class and classism have been largely invisible (Zinn, 1980). The American Dream of economic prosperity for all, based on the belief that the economic system is fair and open to any person who is willing to work hard to get ahead, is closely linked with democracy and our political system of representative government. This conflation of democracy and capitalism confuses political and economic critique in such a way that challenges to the economic order are immediately perceived as opposing democracy in favor of communism, thus preventing consideration of alternative *economic* policies and structures (Bowles & Gintis, 1987). In fact, democracy in the United States is limited by the extraordinary influence of large corporations over the political process, but this influence isn't understood by most Americans (Bagdikian, 1992; Chomsky, 1989; Greider, 1992). The psychological investment most Americans have in a meritocratic American Dream makes it difficult to challenge and address these issues clearly.

During periods of social and economic crisis, in the absence of a framework for understanding the crisis, people often turn to scapegoats. Thus the underlying factors that create vast inequalities in wealth, and the beneficiaries of these policies, remain largely invisible. Instead, people on welfare are blamed for causing our budget woes; urban young men of color are blamed for crime; immigrants are blamed for taking away jobs; working women and gays and lesbians are held responsible for the breakdown of the nuclear family and the moral decay of society; Jews are labeled as controlling the banks and the media; the Japanese are blamed for stealing American markets. Public policy debates center around welfare reform or getting tougher on crime, while proposals to increase capital gains taxes or to raise the top income tax bracket back to previous levels rarely enter the public debate. The terms of public debate are set in large part by a small number of major media outlets, whose corporate owners and major advertisers have a vested interest in promoting policies favorable for corporate profits. The true beneficiaries of the redistribution of wealth are rarely visible or acknowledged (Lee & Solomon, 1990).

As citizens and voters, our students will find themselves needing to make judgments about proposals for political and economic change which differentially affect various groups in our society. Understanding how social and economic class operates in the United States is important in order for them to be able to participate in these debates in an informed way. This curriculum is designed to introduce students to a framework for understanding classism and considering more equitable alternatives to the current economic structures of society.

Taboos about Class and the Myth of the Classless Society

In the United States, discussions involving issues of class and money are often more taboo than discussing sexuality. Deep-seated prohibitions about disclosing the facts of one's class identity are learned quite early in our lives. Most parents or caregivers do not disclose to us as children how much money they have or earn; if they do tell us, we learn not to discuss these topics with others. Shame at being poorer or richer than others leads to secrecy and silence. This silence powerfully maintains the invisibility of class and supports the dominant myth that this is largely a classless society, or at least one in which class does not matter very much because all are assumed to be able to move up in class if they work hard enough.

The Work Ethic and the Myth of Class Mobility

The American Dream is that people in this country can attain enough income to own their own homes and provide comfortably for their families if they work hard enough. The fact that most Americans can point to at least one example where this is true reinforces the myth of class mobility and assumptions that those who don't move up lack a strong work ethic. While it is true that there is some class fluidity, and that class status may change over the lifetime of many individuals, the reality is that class is much less fluid than most people think. One study shows that one's father's occupation is the best predictor of one's future income level, more important than IQ, level of education, or years in the workforce (de Lone, 1979). Even where mobility does occur, the class-related values, attitudes, and feelings one learned as a child can persist throughout one's life.

Differing Definitions of Class

Participants may not have considered their own class identity prior to this course. When asked to do so, most conclude that, with very few exceptions, we are all more or less middle class. Even if some indicators would link certain participants with the working class or the owning class, most will tend to stress the contradictory indicators that point instead to middle-class affiliation; for example, "Even though my parents had lots of investments, we lived in a small house and mowed our own lawn," or "We were always broke, but because my dad was a preacher, we got lots of respect from the community." Thus we need to define class and classism, as well as discuss criteria for distinguishing different classes, before we can usefully discuss this topic. Economists, sociologists, political scientists, anthropologists, and activists define "class," "social class," and "socio-economic class" differently. For some sociologists "class" is defined by *occupational* status: blue-collar, pink-collar, white-collar, for example. For some economists, "class" is defined by *income and economic* strata, while for other economists, particularly Marxists and neo-Marxists, *ownership, power and control* figure most prominently in defining "class." These varying definitions can be confusing for students who may be considering class for the first time. Our working definition is that class is "a relative social ranking based on income, wealth, status, and/or power" (Yeskel, 1990).

Hidden History

History is usually taught from the perspective of the privileged. Much of what we learn in public school, for example, is told from the perspective of political and military leaders and other famous personages who usually are members of the upper classes. The perceptions and realities of everyday working people are rarely explored. For example, industrialization is typically taught as a positive transformation of society. From the perspective of the average worker at the time, the era brought loss of control over working conditions when factories and assembly lines replaced craft guilds. The economic "progress" of industrial development looks quite different from the perspective of slaves, indentured servants, and impoverished immigrants whose perspectives are usually invisible in our history books (Takaki, 1993; Zinn, 1980). Currently, increased "productivity" to make the United States "more competitive" is widely accepted as a positive goal, despite the fact that "productivity" is often a code word for replacing jobs with machines and thus displacing workers (Noble, 1989). The history of resistance to classism also remains largely invisible. Strikes, boycotts, slowdowns, and labor organizing are all tactics that workers have used to fight classism (Zinn, 1980).

Conflation of Democracy and Capitalism

During the Cold War between the United States and the former Soviet Union, capitalism and communism became polarized. Capitalism was equated with democracy, and communism, by comparison, was equated with undemocratic and totalitarian political systems. Whenever the economic system in the United States has been challenged, the challenge has been framed as an attack on democracy. Raising issues of class inequality is labeled as "anti-democratic," "class warfare," "communist," "red," or "unpatriotic," with the effect of marginalizing or silencing criticism of the economic structure. This conflation of democracy and capitalism confuses political and economic critique so that challenges to the economic order are cast as opposing democracy in favor of communism, thus preventing consideration of alternative economic policies and structures (Bowles & Gintis, 1987). The psychological investment most Americans have in the American Dream makes it difficult to challenge and address these issues clearly.

Economic Mystification

Issues of class may be more unfamiliar than other issues of oppression partly due to secrecy about the personal aspects of class identity and the confusion surrounding the societal aspects. Students who are unfamiliar with even the basics (the difference between gross and net income, GNP, profit, the difference between salary and wages) often feel overwhelmed. Math anxiety and math phobia also contribute to a feeling of disempowerment or distrust of statistical information that documents class issues. Print resources such as Folbre (1995) and Rose (1992) or video resources listed at the rear of this volume can be useful in courses on class.

The Globalization of Poverty

With the rise of multinational business and global markets, class issues in the United States become ever more complex. The same multinational corporations which increased United States prosperity in the 1950s and 1960s by manufacturing here and selling their products around the globe, are now draining the United States and world economies by moving jobs around to wherever wages are lowest or wherever taxes can be avoided. The status of average American workers is ever more closely tied to the economic and working conditions of laborers in "third world" countries, and class politics in the United States often center on international trade issues, such as the debate over the North American Free Trade Agreement (NAFTA). The overall decline in manufacturing jobs which once offered the possibility of attaining a middle-class lifestyle to blue-collar workers has dramatically changed the class picture in the United States, which now has more and more in common with third world countries. While an introductory course on classism cannot address this issue in any depth, and this curriculum design has been deliberately and artificially limited to United States issues, it is important for facilitators to keep informed about these global changes and their effects on the American workforce.

Hopelessness and Helplessness

The intensity of feelings of hopelessness and helplessness that arise when we focus on working against classism can be overwhelming. Interrupting classist slurs or changing classist language seem insignificant in comparison to the immensity and the complexity of the problem. The need to work against classism on a systemic level is overwhelmingly evident, yet what to do is contested. This can lead to an enormous sense of helplessness, based on several factors: the seemingly intractable imbalances in the distribution of wealth, the confusing interplay of interest rates and employment levels, the complexities of economic theory, and the contradictory explanations of experts.

The fact that class inequality is getting worse rather than better, coupled with the failure of the major visible economic alternative, the Soviet Union, can lead to overpowering hopelessness. The linchpin of the hopelessness is the fact that currently there is very little in the way of an organized social movement against classism. However, the recent election of John Sweeney and changes in the AFL-CIO show promise of creating such a movement. In the 1930s and 1960s there were large-scale, visible movements of poor and working-class people; however, during the life-span of most of today's students, corporate greed and individual consumption overshadowed all else. Meanwhile, other social movements have made significant progress during this same time span, starting with African American civil rights, women's liberation, and more recently lesbian, gay, bisexual, and transsexual liberation and disability rights. This apparent lack of change can lead to students' feeling that classism is a fact of life, hopelessly entrenched and unchangeable, or a result of innate human nature or laws of the marketplace.

OVERVIEW OF CLASSISM MODULES

Introductory Module (see chapter 5)

Module 1 (3 hours) Activities	Module 2 (3 1/2 hours) Activities
1. Welcome and Introduction (10 minutes) 2. Common Ground Part 1 (20 minutes) 3. Assumptions, Guidelines, Agenda (20 minutes) 4. First Memories and Class Indicators (40 mins) 5. Class Background Inventory (50 mins) 6. Common Ground, Part II (15 mins) 7. Key Definitions (20 mins)	1. Class/classism Quiz (30 mins) 2. Income Distribution Activity (20 mins) 3. Wealth Distribution Activity (20 mins) 4. Brainstorm Stereotypes (20 mins) 5. First Person Accounts of Diverse Class Experiences (60 mins) 6. Individual, Cultural and Institutional Classism (40 mins) 7. Closing, Homework, Wrap Up, and Feedback to facilitators (20 mins)
Module 3 (3 hours) Activities	**Module 4 (3 1/2 hours)** Activities
1. Cultural Classism (30 mins) 2. Institutional Classism (150 mins) 3. Closing (10 mins)	1. History of Classism and Anti-Classism (45 mins) 2. Allies (30 mins) 3. Classism in Your School (60 mins) 4. Actions against Classism (45 mins) 5. Closing (30 mins)

Handout 11.1. Overview of Classism Modules.

Classism Curriculum Design

Module 1

Time Needed: 3 Hours
Goals:

- Create a safe environment in which participants can discuss difficult issues.
- Reflect on class experience, and name class of origin.
- Understand working definitions and basic concepts about class and classism.

Key Concepts: class indicators, social class, ruling class, owning class, middle class, working class, lower class/poor, classism, class continuum.

Activities:

1. Welcome and Introductions (10 minutes).

Welcome participants to the course, introduce yourselves, and state a bit about your background and experience with the issue of classism. Then ask participants to introduce themselves and state one reason they are taking this course.

2. Common Ground Part I (20 minutes).

In order to help people begin to know one another, ask participants to stand in a circle. Explain that in this activity, you will name a series of categories and those who fit the category will take a step into the center of the circle. Each time they enter the center they should look around and note who else shares common ground. Start with low-risk categories, such as, "Common Ground for everyone who . . .

- got five or less hours of sleep last night.
- would rather be asleep now.
- is an oldest child (youngest, middle, only, twin).
- grew up in a city (rural area, small town, suburbs).
- is first-generation American (a citizen of another country, grew up outside of the U.S.).

Make up other categories as you go and invite participants to suggest categories.

3. Assumptions, Guidelines, Agenda (20 minutes).

Print the goals listed at the beginning of this design on newsprint or overhead transparency and discuss these goals in light of the assumptions discussed in the introduction to this chapter. Review guidelines with the group. These can be brainstormed together or you can post a list from those outlined in chapters 5 and 12. Post the agenda on newsprint and review it in a general way, highlighting major items.

4. First Memories and Class Indicators (40 minutes).

Ask participants to pair up and take turns responding to the following questions:

- What is the first memory you have of someone you thought was richer than you? Why did you think so?
- What is the first memory you have of someone you thought was poorer than you? Why did you think so?

First one person will speak while the other listens; after five minutes ask them to switch roles. Then reconvene the group and ask for volunteers to share the memories they discussed in order to elicit a variety of examples. Note particularly the factors in each instance that indicate different class positions and write these indicators on newsprint. The list should include indicators such as: income, education, housing, occupation, neighborhood, language (accent, vocabulary, grammar), assets or wealth, appearance (dress, condition of teeth, posture), possessions (computers, TV/VCR, portable phones, stereo system, types of cars), leisure (types of activities, hobbies, travel).

5. Class Background Inventory (50 minutes).

Pass out the class background inventory (see Appendix 11A). If you are co-teaching with an agent/target team, try model interviewing each other while participants observe, using the inventory as a guide. Ask each participant to note their own responses to the inventory, then pair up and take turns interviewing each other as the facilitators did. After five minutes, tell them it's time to switch. Next ask each pair to join another pair, creating small groups of four. Ask each person in the group to briefly note a few items from their background, still using the inventory as a guide.

Each participant should then take an index card and, based on the activities so far, write a short description of their class of origin. They will not be asked to share these cards but will periodically review them to add to what they've written. The card will serve as a record of their learning about classism as the course proceeds.

Facilitation Issues:
Facilitators will provide information and model pride about their own class background(s) during this activity. If the facilitators are from different class backgrounds, this activity will help people to feel more at ease in sharing their stories. Encourage participants to jot a few notes rather than extensive responses to the inventory. If participants report confusion or if their class situation changed as they were growing up, suggest that they focus on formative childhood experiences.

6. Common Ground, Part II (15 minutes).

Ask the group to stand in a circle, shoulder to shoulder, with one facilitator in the middle. Reintroduce the activity, this time asking people to step into the circle when the class category fits. "Common Ground for anyone . . . "

" . . . who grew up in rented apartments."

" . . . who has owned a house."

" . . . whose family owns a summer home or other second house."

" . . . who has a credit card their parents pay for."

" . . . who has traveled internationally."

" . . . who is on a scholarship."

" . . . who has worked at a fast food restaurant."

" . . . who has a trust fund or owns stocks and bonds in your name."

" . . . who shared a bedroom as a child."

" . . . who has shopped with Food Stamps."

7. Key Definitions (20 minutes).

Using newsprint or overhead transparencies present the definitions below and give examples. If necessary review definitions of *oppression, prejudice, social power, stereotype, agent, target, and ally* (chapter 5) before presenting and discussing the definitions below.

Class—Relative social rank in terms of income, wealth, status, and/or power.

Classism—The institutional, cultural, and individual set of practices and beliefs that assign differential value to people according to their socio-economic class; and an economic system which creates excessive inequality and causes basic human needs to go unmet.

Class Indicator—a factual or experiential factor that helps determine an individual's class.

Class Continuum—The ranking of individuals or families in a society by income, wealth, status, or power; the range of experiences out of which particular class identities are defined. Lines may be drawn at different points along this continuum, and labeled differently. Class is a relative thing, both subjectively and in terms of resources; our experience varies depending on whether we look up or down the continuum. However, it is clear that everyone at the top end is mostly agent/dominant, while everyone at the bottom end is mostly target/ subordinate. The following visually demonstrates this:

Targets	**Mostly Targets**	**Mostly Agents**	**Agents**
Lower Class/Poor	Working Class	Middle Class	Owning Class Ruling Class

Class Identity—A label for one category of class experience, such as ruling class, owning class, middle class, working class, lower class.

Ruling Class—The stratum of people who hold positions of power in major institutions of the society.

Owning Class/Rich—The stratum of families who own income-producing assets sufficient to make paid employment unecessary.

Middle Class—The stratum of families for whom breadwinners' higher education and/or specialized skills brings higher income and more security than those of working-class people.

Upper-Middle Class—The portion of the middle class with higher incomes due to professional jobs and/or investment income.

Lower-Middle Class—The portion of the middle class with lower and less stable incomes due to lower-skilled or unstable employment.

Working Class—The stratum of families whose income depends on hourly wages for labor.

Lower Class/Poor—The stratum of families with incomes insufficient to meet basic human needs.

Handout 11.2. Definitions of General Concepts: Classism.

Ask students to reflect on these definitions and consider what they might add or change in the description they wrote on their card earlier concerning their own class background. They can add the changes to their card, but should not cross out anything written before, so as to keep a record of their changing understanding of class as the course proceeds.

Facilitation Issues:
People are often reluctant to acknowledge the existence of classism, so it is important to start with participants' lived experience and with indisputable facts such as census data rather than theories and definitions. It is also important to be aware of the political and ideological issues surrounding class and classism, and try to steer clear of ideological treatises. Present theories, definitions, and models as useful concepts and working models rather than as truth. Acknowledge the diversity of thought on this subject and explain your rationale for choices made, rather than argue for a single "correct" framing of the issue.

Module 2

Time Needed: 3 1/2 Hours
Goals:

- Reflect on where participants' personal class experiences fit into the United States class spectrum.
- Increase awareness and understanding of individual, institutional, and cultural manifestations of classism in the United States.
- Develop empathy for people from other class backgrounds.

Key Concepts: income quintiles, stereotypes, class continuum, institutional, and cultural classism.

Activities:

1. Class/Classism Quiz (30 minutes).

Pass out the quiz in Appendix 11B. Ask participants to pair up and work together to determine answers to the quiz, while also noting areas of disagreement and their reasoning. Then review the answers with the whole group (see Appendix 11C) and discuss areas of confusion or surprise.

2. Income Distribution Activity (20 minutes).

This activity was developed by: United For a Fair Economy, 37 Temple Place, 5th Floor, Boston, MA 02111, (617) 423–2148.

Begin the activity by posting a copy of the income distribution chart in Appendix 11D and the following definition:

> *Income Quintiles*—A method of comparing mean incomes of each one-fifth of a country's families. If every family in the United States were lined up in order of income, and then divided into five groups with the same number of families in each group, and the incomes within the groups were averaged, the five resulting numbers could be compared for a measure of income inequality.

To illustrate, draw a line on the board. Ask for a volunteer to come up to the board and divide the line according to their idea of how income is distributed. Ask for several students with differing ideas to come up to the board and mark the distributions. After a few different views have been drawn, review the chart showing average income for United States family income quintiles in 1992, using Appendix 11D.

Next ask for five volunteers to participate in an experiential demonstration that looks at how income growth changed during a fifteen-year period. Ask the volunteers to line up so that each volunteer represents one quintile. The person farthest to the left represents the lowest 20 percent or quintile of the population, the next person the second quintile, the third the middle quintile, the next person the fourth quintile, and the fifth person the top quintile. Ask each to step either forward or backward (each step equals about 10 percent) to represent income growth from 1977 to 1989. (This might seem like the childhood game "mother may I?")

- Between 1977 and 1989, the *lowest quintile* takes *two steps back.* Families in this quintile saw their income decline almost 17 percent. Their average income after taxes in 1990 was $7,000.
- The *second quintile* takes *one step back.* Their income declined by 8 percent, and their average income after taxes in 1990 was $16,000.
- The *third quintile* takes *a small step back.* Their income declined 3 percent, and their average income after taxes in 1990 was $25,000.
- The *fourth quintile* takes *a half step forward.* Their income increased 5 percent, and their after-tax income was $35,000.
- The *top quintile* takes *two big steps forward.* Their income increased over 18 percent, and their after-tax income was $80,000.
- However within the top quintile, there is still quite a disparity: The top 1 percent in the fifth quintile takes another nine big steps forward. Their income increased over 110 percent, and their after-tax average income was $400,000.

Discuss reactions to the activity thus far. Then note that income growth has not always been distributed in this way. Ask the volunteers to return to the starting line to look at the postwar years 1950–1978 for comparison:

- First quintile: thirteen steps forward, for an average income growth of 130 percent.
- Second quintile: ten steps forward, for an average income growth of 100 percent.
- Third quintile: ten steps forward, for an average income growth of 100 percent.
- Fourth quintile: eleven steps forward, for an average income growth of 110 percent.
- Fifth quintile: ten steps forward, for an average income growth of 100 percent.

Ask participants to speculate about why there are differences between these two time periods. Then provide information about how federal tax and spending policies during the period after the Second World War focused on lifting people out of poverty into the middle class to share in the nation's growth, while during the last fifteen years government policy has rewarded asset owners rather than wage earners.

3. Wealth Distribution Activity (20 minutes).

This activity was also developed by United For a Fair Economy, from Wolff (1995).

One way to explain the difference between wealth and income is to think of income as the stream and wealth as the reservoir into which the stream empties. Wealth is what a person owns (assets), minus what they owe (debts). Ask students to brainstorm examples of wealth. For people on the lower end of the continuum, wealth consists of such things as clothing, furniture, or a car. For those in the middle it may be a house or a stake in a pension fund. For people on the upper end of the continuum, wealth consists of stocks, bonds, real estate, businesses, and art work.

To illustrate how wealth is distributed in this country, ask for ten volunteers to stand in front of each of the ten chairs. (Ten chairs without armrests should be set up in preparation for this segment.) Note that in this demonstration *each person* represents one-tenth of the United States *population* and *each chair* represents one-tenth of all the *private wealth* in the United States.

- In 1976, the top 10 percent owned half of all the private wealth and the bottom 90 percent owned half of all the private wealth. So ask the person representing the "top 10 percent" to lay across five of the chairs; and the other nine people to scrunch into the remaining five chairs. Encourage them to make sure all are sitting.
- Now let's look at the present. Less than twenty years later, there has been a dramatic shift in wealth. Now the top 10 percent owns 70 percent of all private wealth (or seven chairs) and the remaining nine must share three chairs. (Urge the top 10 percent person to extend out over the two additional chairs while you evict the occupants and ask them to scrunch onto the remaining three chairs with everyone else.)
- As with income distribution, there is a broad range within the top 10 percent when it comes to distribution of wealth. Let's have the arm of the person who is the "top 10 percent" equal the wealthiest 1 percent of the population. The top 1 percent owns over 40 percent of the wealth, so this arm's share is now equal to four chairs. The top 1 percent now owns more wealth than the bottom 90 percent combined (4 chairs for the top 1 percent and 3 chairs for the bottom 90 percent).

Processing:
Thank the volunteers and ask the viewers to give them a round of applause. Then post a copy of the Wealth Distribution Chart (see Appendix 11E). Ask participants to pair up and discuss their reactions (thoughts, feelings, questions).

- How are you feeling in the bottom 90 percent?
- How are you feeling at the top?
- If you were going to push someone off the chairs to make room who would it be?
- Where is the focus of public-policy discussions—looking up the chairs at the top 10 percent or looking down the chairs at the disadvantaged?
- What information seems to contradict your prior assumptions about class?

After ten minutes bring the group back together, ask for general reactions and respond to questions. In closing, ask participants to revisit their card and consider how they would change their class description based on any of this new information.

4. Brainstorm Stereotypes (20 minutes).

Tape several sheets of newsprint on the wall. On the top of each sheet write one of the following: "Ruling class," "Owning class," "Middle class," "Working class," and "Poor." Break the class into five small groups. Ask each group to gather next to one of the sheets, brainstorm as many images, words, or stereotypes as possible for their particular class group, and then record the stereotypes on the newsprint. Remind them to list everything that comes to mind even if it's negative or they know it's false. Finally ask one person from each group to share the group's list. Common examples are:

> ***Ruling Class:*** cultured, uptight, refined, sophisticated, condescending, greedy.
> ***Owning Class***: effete snobs, incapable of anything physical, greedy, cultured.
> ***Middle Class***: normal, regular, boring, wannabees, stodgy.
> ***Working Class***: tacky, blue collar, bigoted, stupid, bad taste.
> ***Poor People:*** trailer trash, irresponsible, can't delay gratification, lazy, stupid, disorganized, criminals.

After each group has shared its list, ask for any additions or for examples of information they now have that contradicts or challenges any of these stereotypes.

5. First-person Accounts of Diverse Class Experiences (60 minutes).

The purpose of this activity is to help participants develop empathy with people from different classes and clarify their own class experiences. In some locations it may be possible to organize a panel that includes people from diverse classes, or a fishbowl with participants that is representative of class diversity, while in other locations or courses that are more homogeneous you will need to rely on other sources of information. It is often most powerful for participants to meet real people who have different class experiences from theirs, but if this is too difficult to arrange, the other options provide some exposure to a variety of class experiences. Four options are provided below.

Option 1: Panel of People from Diverse Classes

Ideally the panel should include at least one person each raised as owning class and poor, and one or two others in-between, such as working class and upper-middle class. To find an owning-class speaker, contact a local community foundation (call the Funding Exchange in New York City for foundation names) and ask them to suggest one of their donors. To find raised-poor and working-class speakers, contact local anti-poverty groups such as tenant groups, welfare rights groups, service workers unions, or community action agencies, and ask for low-income speakers. Offer to pay for expenses such as transportation and child care and an honorarium if possible. To find middle-class, lower-middle, and upper-middle speakers who are aware of classism may be harder. Try asking professors in economics, sociology, or social work departments, or call unions of professionals or semi-professionals, such as nurses or teachers associations. Give the questions to the panelists ahead of time. (Directions for setting up panels are given in chapter 8 and in Blumenfeld, 1993.)

Questions for panel could include:

- What have you gained from your class background? What advantages did you receive?
- What has been difficult about your class background? What limitations did you experience?
- Provide examples of memories/critical incidents in your awareness of your class.

- What do you want others to know about people of your class?
- How can others be your ally? How have you been an ally for others?
- What strategies do you see for taking action against classism?

Once panelists have spoken and participants have had an opportunity to ask questions, thank the panel members for their participation and allow them to leave. Then hold a discussion among students using the following questions:

- What feelings did you have while you listened to the different panelists?
- How did the speakers challenge stereotypes we listed earlier?
- What similarities and differences of experience did you notice among the panelists?
- In what ways was classism manifested in the different panelists' experiences?

Option 2: Read-around

If no local panelists or participants are available to do live presentations, have participants read aloud excerpts from autobiographies. Choose six to ten short autobiographical excerpts. Try to vary not only the class background of the authors but also their gender, race, religion, sexual orientation, ability/disability, and generational cohort. Good excerpts will have details that bring the author's experience to life and reveal a mix of positive and negative emotions. Distribute excerpts randomly to participants, and have them stand up in turn and slowly read the excerpt aloud. Some possible sources for excerpts include:

- *A Taste of Power: A Black Woman's Story*, by Elaine Brown, Pantheon Books, NY, 1992: page 22 bottom to page 24 top. (Working-class African American girl gets elite education due to mother's efforts.)
- "Journal Notes" by Pesha Gertler, in *Bridges: A Journal for Jewish Feminists and Our Friends*, Volume 3, Number 1, Spring/Summer 1992, P.O. Box 8437, Seattle, WA 98118; pages 64–65, starting with the second full paragraph on page 64, ending either middle of second column on page 64 or middle of first column on page 65. (Girl's Jewish working-class experience described.)
- *We Gave Away a Fortune: Stories of People who have Devoted Themselves and Their Wealth to Peace, Justice, and the Environment*, by Christopher Mogil and Anne Slepian with Peter Woodrow, New Society Publishers, Philadelphia, 1992: page 19 (upper-class white boy has unusual amount of independence as a child) and page 106 (middle-class girl is shocked by seeing extreme poverty and starts working with Catholic Worker soup kitchen).
- *Skin: Talking About Sex, Class, and Literature*, by Dorothy Allison, Firebrand, Ithaca, NY, 1994: bottom of page 17 to top of page 20. (Southern white girl in very poor family experiences sexual abuse and dislocation.)
- "Chicana, Working-class and Proud: The Case of the Lopsided Tortilla," by Terri de la Pena, in *Out of the Class Closet: Lesbians Speak*, edited by Julia Penelope, Crossing Press, Freedom, California, 1994: page 196, starting with "Through a Depression foreclosure sale . . ." through last full paragraph of page 197. (Lower-

middle-class Chicana girl sees contrasts between her life and the lives of both poor people of color and upper-middle-class Anglos living nearby.)

- *Becoming Brothers*, by Howard and Arthur Waskow, The Free Press, NY, 1993, middle of page 17 to middle of page 18. (Boys growing up in a stable Jewish working-class neighborhood in the 1940s learn of the poverty of the prior Depression generation.)
- *Common Ground: Portraits of Blacks Changing the Face of America*, by Bruce Caines, Crown, NY, 1994, page 244, second full paragraph to middle of second column. (Upper-middle-class African American boy, future car-racing star, learns value of hard work on grandfather's ranch.)
- *Worlds of Pain: Life in the Working-Class Family*, by Lillian Breslow Rubin, Basic Books, NY, 1976, quotes from chapter 3, such as page 33 middle to page 34 middle (white girl grows up as "ward of the state" and runaway after alcoholic father leaves) or page 37 bottom to 38 top (white boy's laborer father has no educational aspirations for him).

Some questions for discussion after the read-arounds include:

- What did this person gain from his/her class background? What advantages were received?
- What was difficult about their class background? What limitations did they experience?
- What similarities and differences did you notice among the readings?
- Did any of the readings break a stereotype we listed earlier?
- In what ways was classism manifested in the different stories?

Option 3: Fishbowl Discussion or Panel of Participants

In cases in which participants are diverse in class background and include individuals who have a heightened awareness of classism, you may choose to use a fish bowl discussion or panel of participants from the course. For fishbowls, one group sits in the middle of the circle and its members talk with each other (the "fish"), while the outer circle listens silently (the "bowl"). They can use the same questions listed under "Panel" above, not as a go-round with each speaking in turn, but as a discussion in which participants respond to each other. Some people may not join a fishbowl, or may join it and not speak. Allow the longest time for the group with the lowest class background, regardless of group size. After both groups have had a chance to speak, ask participants to process their reactions by writing in a journal using the questions noted above in Option 1.

Option 4: Slide Show or Video on institutional Classism

One way to help students grasp the pervasiveness and insidiousness of institutionalized classism is through audio-visual materials. One good resource is "We Shall Not Be Moved. " This slide show describes the process of gentrification of a multicultural neighborhood and is distributed by the Institute for Community Economics in Springfield, Massachusetts. If you are unable to get this short and highly effective visual aid, other possibilities are listed in the video resource list at the end of this volume or include the following documentary-style videos that may be available at your local video store or library: *Roger and Me*; *Harlan County, USA*; *America: What Went Wrong*; and *Salt of the Earth*. If none of these are available, excerpts from fictional Hollywood films available on video could be substituted such as: *Norma Rae, Working Girl, Nine To Five, Milagro Beanfield War,* and *Dirty Dancing*. With some extra effort (and two VCRs), a collage of short excerpts could be prepared in advance. These AV resources can be supplemented with selections from the classism section of the Reader (also listed at the end of this volume).

6. Individual, Cultural, and Institutional Classism (40 minutes).

Briefly introduce the concepts of individual, cultural, and institutional classism.

Individual Classism—This term refers to classism on a personal or individual level, either in behavior or attitudes, either conscious and intentional or unconscious and unintentional. Examples include the thought or belief that a certain type of work is beneath you, or the assumption that everyone has the financial resources to go out to an expensive restaurant.

Institutional Classism—This term refers to the ways in which conscious or unconscious classism is manifest in the various institutions of our society. Two examples from colleges—some schools give preference to children of alumni, thus making it harder for first-generation college applicants to get in; some schools reserve the most convenient parking spaces for faculty, even though they usually work more flexible hours than support staff.

Cultural Classism—This term refers to the ways in which classism is manifest through our cultural norms and practices. It can often be found in the ideology behind something, as in the commercial for peanut butter, "choosy mothers choose Jif," implying that if you buy the less expensive store brand you care less about your kids.

Ask the group to brainstorm examples of each type of classism, and be prepared with examples of your own. For example:

- *Individual Classism*—A middle-class person calling secondhand clothes "tacky"; or holding a prejudice that the reason people are poor is because they are lazy or stupid.
- *Cultural Classism*—A newspaper running pictures and a prominent article on a "high-society" wedding, while not listing or highlighting a working-class couple's wedding; TV shows and movies that portray poor and working-class people as stupid buffoons (the Beverly Hillbillies) or as reactionary bigots (Archie Bunker).
- *Institutional Classism*—A hospital keeping a Medicaid patient for fewer days than a privately insured patient with the same condition, because the amount paid to the hospital is less, or schools in poor neighborhoods having fewer resources and larger student-teacher ratios than more affluent neighborhoods, because money for schools is based on local property taxes.

Processing:
Ask participants to form groups of four and come up with additional examples of individual, institutional, and cultural classism. After ten minutes, bring the group back together to share examples and clarify distinctions among the different levels.

8. Wrap Up, Feedback, and Homework (20 minutes).

Review the definition of cultural classism and assign for homework to look in the popular media (magazines, TV, radio, newspapers) and find examples of cultural classism. Ask students to think about the hidden messages or ideology contained in their examples.

Ask participants to pull out the index card on which they described their social class at the end of Module 1, turn to their neighbor and discuss: How would you change your self-description now? How do you feel about what's written there? They can note changes or additions on the card, but should not change what was written there earlier.

Module 3

Time Needed: 3 Hours
Goals:

- Develop emotional empathy with the experiences of people of class backgrounds other than their own.
- Increase awareness and understanding of how a class stratified system works and the power dynamics involved.
- Increase awareness and understanding of individual, institutional, and cultural manifestations of classism in the United States.

Key Concepts: power, privilege, collusion.

Activities:

1. Cultural Classism (30 minutes).

Ask participants to form groups of four or five and share examples of cultural classism they found for the homework assignment. Ask them to consider the following questions: (15 minutes):

- Is this example classist?
- What messages does it give to people of different classes?
- Does it reinforce stereotypes?
- What values does it hold up as better or normative?

Next ask each group to choose two clear examples to share with the whole group, noting the hidden (or not so hidden) messages conveyed. Make a list of these messages as each group reports. Discuss how the media communicates and enforces our culture's ideology about class.

2. Institutional Classism (150 minutes).

Option A: Star Power Simulation

"Star Power" is a simulation game that illustrates the dynamics of power and privilege. The specific rules for playing the game are detailed in the Instructor's

Manual that accompanies the game. Star Power may be ordered for $225 from Simulation Training Systems, P.O. Box 910, Del Mar, CA 92014. The game cannot be played without the Instructor's Manual and simulation materials.

To prepare for this activity, ask participants to put chairs in three equal-sized circles and invite everyone to take a seat in one of the circles. Give each group a symbol for all of its members (star, circle, square). Tell them that Star Power is a game of trading and that the three individuals with the highest score at the end of the game will be declared the winners. Note that winners will receive a prize. (The prize could be anything that is divisible, a cake or other treat.) Go over the "Trading Rules" and "Scoring" detailed in the Star Power Instructor's Manual. Let students know that the facilitators will be taking on specific roles for the duration of the simulation. Perhaps even have a costume to help students differentiate between the facilitator and the role she/he takes in the game. The rules can be confusing, so make sure before starting that the rules are clear. Let students know that you will enforce the rules.

Play the actual game according to the rules for at least one hour. At the end of the time allotted, stop the game. Participants may still be immersed in the game, so ask them to remove their symbols and consciously get out of their roles. Make a display of taking off your costume and getting out of your role as well. Take a short break and then re-group to talk about responses to the game. You might want to do something physical for a few minutes, such as stretch, to help participants mentally remove themselves from the simulation.

Processing:

Students typically have very strong reactions to the Star Power simulation. Ask students to pair up with someone for five minutes and talk about their reactions to the game. Then ask them to come back together and discuss as the whole group. Start with asking about how they felt at different points in the game and how they are feeling now. This will often involve discussing what happened in the game, who did what to whom, and how it felt to those involved. You may need to draw out particular people or groups; for instance, if only Squares are talking, invite the Circles or Triangles to join in. If one member of a group says something, such as "I realized after the first round that the rules were stacked," focus on this issue. Ask the other groups if and at what point they also realized it. Sometimes Squares will be the most clueless about what happened and others will want to tease them. Often members of the Square group will be defensive. Emphasize that one's *role* in the game often determines ones feelings, perceptions, and understanding.

Often the facilitators will observe interactions that participants do not see. Share your perceptions also. Make sure people also process their feelings about the "Director." Sometimes people have the most intense feelings about this role. Processing this can be a challenge if the facilitator is the same as the "Director" in the game, because people may still act out toward the director. If possible, let another person facilitate the processing so that feelings about the "Director" can be aired freely.

When it seems that most issues have been aired and discussed, move the discussion to parallels between the game and the "real world." Help students discuss similarities and differences. Encourage them to look at all levels—personal, institutional, and cultural. Go over the definitions of "power," "privilege," and "collusion," and consider how these were manifested in the game and in the "real world."

Internalized Classism—Acceptance and justification of classism by working class and poor people, such as feelings of inferiority to higher-class people, feelings of superiority to people lower on the class spectrum than oneself, hostility and blame towards other working-class or poor people, and beliefs that classist institutions are fair.

Privilege—One of the many tangible or intangible unearned advantages of higher-class status, such as personal contacts with employers, good childhood health care, inherited money, speaking the same dialect and accent as people with institutional power.

Option B: Institutional Manifestations of Classism (60 minutes)

Post large sheets of newsprint around the room, with the name of a major institution in our society listed at the top of each one. Examples are:

health care	religion	the political system	education
employment/workplaces	military	the judicial system	the tax system

Break the group into the same number of small groups as the institutions posted, with about four to six people in each group. Give each group newsprint and markers, and ask them to write their responses to the following questions:

- Are the policies, procedures, and norms of this institution classist?
- Does it give privileges to some and limit access to others?
- What might it look like without classism?
- How would it be set up to be more equal for all class groups?

After about twenty minutes bring the small groups back together and ask each to summarize their answers to the questions. If there was disagreement within a group, ask spokespeople to summarize the differing positions.

Facilitation Issues:

This section is the transition from individual experience to society-wide systems; if participants fail to make this transition, they will gain little from the remaining focus of the course. At no time is the possibility of going off-track into particular policy debates or tangential issues stronger than during the discussion of institutionalized classism. However, the sheer number of examples presented in the initial presentation, the video, and the exercise, should keep most participants from the misconception that the facilitators are equating classism with advocating a particular solution. Facilitators should point out the recurring themes in the examples and repeatedly restate the definition of institutional classism.

3. Closing (10 minutes).

Ask people to pair up and talk about one thing they learned from this session and one thing they want to learn more about in the next session.

Module 4

Time Needed: 3 1/2 Hours
Goals:

- Identify examples of opposition to classism in United States history.
- Identify ways of taking action against classism in every day life, and make commitments to individual next steps.
- Increase understanding of the roles and importance of allies and cross class alliances.

Key Concepts: allies, cross class alliances, economic justice, labor movement.

Activities:

1. History of Classism and Anti-classism (45 minutes).

Use the sample outline in Appendix 11F but emphasize that this is a very abbreviated version of a much more complex story. Encourage participants to read books and articles from the reading list at the end of this volume. Talk in a lively, dramatic storytelling way, using handouts and visual aids. A useful visual is a simple timeline with decades marked at intervals posted on the wall, to which the presenter can point. Emphasize historical examples of resistance to class inequality.

Processing:
Ask participants to pair up and share their emotional responses, questions, and ideas. Ask them to take turns, and remind them when it's time to switch. Then bring the whole group back together and facilitate a discussion using the following questions:

- What were your reactions to the history presentation?
- What themes or key ideas did you hear?
- What is still confusing or unclear?
- What aspects of this history have you heard before and what, if anything , was new or surprising to you?

Facilitation Issues:
Since most undergraduates don't know much history, the facilitators should expect varied nonhistorical issues to come up. This is a likely point in the course for students to express disagreements with the course material. It is important for facilitators to remain calm and non-defensive, reminding the group of the discussion guidelines if necessary. No matter how heated or interesting the discussion, give a five-minute warning and then draw it to a close after thirty minutes, as the course would be much weaker without the final segments that follow the discussion.

2. Becoming Allies (30 minutes).

Introduce the concept of an ally as someone who speaks up or takes action against oppression not targeted at themselves. Ask participants to think about a time they had an ally and a time they acted as an ally; then pair up, and take turns sharing their examples. In the whole group, ask for examples, especially as they relate to classism. For example, in one course, a student talked about interrupting a store clerk who was disrespectfully treating a customer using food stamps. If necessary, share one or two of your own examples to prime the pump. Ideally, at least one interpersonal example (such as interrupting a "dumb hillbilly" joke) and at least one institutional example (such as not sending kids to private schools but working to make the public schools better) can be shared by students or facilitators.

On a blank piece of newsprint or a chalkboard, write "Qualities of an Ally." Ask participants to draw out characteristics of an ally from the examples in their own pairs and in the whole group, then to think of others. Finally, give participants copies of the handout, "Becoming An Ally," in Appendix 6B.

3. Classism in Your School (60 minutes).

Ask participants to brainstorm examples of classism they have observed at their college. Ask them: "What was a situation in which you wanted to be an ally or needed an ally against classism?" As they speak, write key words on newsprint or chalkboard. Allow clarifying questions and brief reactions, but enforce the rules of brainstorming (no discussions about what happened, whether it was really classist, who was to blame, or what to do about it). If the group is having trouble thinking of examples, prompt them with questions and examples such as these:

(1) How are support staff such as janitors, cafeteria servers, and secretaries treated at this school? Are there any tensions between them and other groups such as students or faculty? For example:

- At one school all the most convenient parking spaces were reserved for faculty, even though they worked fewer and more flexible hours than support staff.
- At another school, some students and faculty crossed picket lines of striking secretaries.
- At many schools, rowdy students create big messes (e.g., torn up lawns, vomit on floors, food fights, vandalized furniture) with disregard for the groundskeepers and janitors who have to clean up after them.

(2) Are there any issues between students whose tuition is paid by scholarships and those whose tuition is paid by their families or between commuting students and those who live on campus? For example:

- Scholarship students at some schools feel uncomfortable because they work in the cafeterias serving food to other students, which publicizes their economic need, places them in a subservient role in relation to their fellow students, and delays their own meals. One student reported being humiliated by students in the food line who made fun of the hat and apron she had to wear.
- At another school, all the comfortable places to sit and chat are located inside the dorms, and the many commuting students have no lounge.

(3) Are there problems with access to educational experiences? For example:

- At some schools, scholarships don't include any money for books, and textbooks cost so much that low-income students have to do required reading in the library, where only one or two copies are on reserve.
- At other schools, plays and concerts are priced too high for some students to attend them, and sports clubs and bands require expensive equipment purchases.

(4) Are there any class biases in who is admitted to the school, hired, promoted, given honors, or admitted to fraternities? For example:

- At one school interviews for fraternities routinely include questions about parents' occupation and type of high school.
- Some schools give preference to children of alumni, thus making it harder for first-generation college applicants to get in.

Ask participants to choose one example from the list that involves face-to-face interactions between people. If participants have trouble coming up with an interactive example of classism from their own school, suggest one of the examples above. Ask for volunteers to play each role in the situation, or assign roles if there are no volunteers. Make sure at least one role is that of an ally against classism. Have the players stand up where the group can see them. Suggest an opening line for one actor, and ask the others to respond in their roles. At key moments, say "Freeze!" and ask the rest of the group to suggest alternative responses. Stop the role-play after a few minutes. Ask those playing anti-classist characters how they felt. "What did you feel worked? What didn't work?" Ask those playing classist characters how it felt to get different reactions to their behavior. If time allows, do another one or two additional role-plays.

4. Actions Against Classism (45 minutes).

Ask participants to pair up with someone in class with whom they feel they made a significant connection. Using the action continuum in chapter 6 as a guide, ask them to discuss ways they could be anti-classist, and then make at least one specific commitment to a particular action against classism. Pass out blank sheets of paper and envelopes. Ask participants to self-address the envelope and to write their future selves a letter reminding them of what they've learned in this course and what commitment(s) they made to an anti-classist action. Tell them you will mail the letters to them in a month.

5. Closing Circle (10 minutes).

Lead a closing activity in which people share what they have learned about classism and one action they plan to take against classism in the future.

Appendix 11A

CLASS BACKGROUND INVENTORY

Please respond to the following questions about social class:

1. When you were growing up, what was your family's source(s) of income? (Investments, public assistance, parent(s) or guardian(s) salaries or wages, from what occupation(s)?)

2. Describe your home(s) and neighborhood(s) growing up. (Own vs. rent, amount of space inside and between houses or apartments, safety, state of repair/etc.)

3. How does the education you are getting now compare with the education of others in your family in this generation, and in the previous two generations?

4. How was your family's leisure time spent when you were growing up? (Travel, camp, hobbies or activities, sources of entertainment?)

5. Circle five values or expectations from the list below that seem to be most valued in your family. Then underline five that seem to be least important.

   getting by/ making a moderate living/ making a very good living/ gaining social status or prominence/ open communication among family members/ going to a place of worship/ keeping up with the neighbors/ being physically fit or athletic/ working out psychological issues through therapy/ helping others/ getting married and having children/ respecting law and order/ defending one's country/ staying out of trouble with the law/ being politically or socially aware/ recognition/ community service/ saving money/ making your money work for you/ enjoying your money/ getting a high school degree/ getting a college degree/ getting an advanced or professional degree/ learning a trade/ helping to advance the cause of one's racial, religious, cultural group/ physical appearance/ being a professional/ being an entrepreneur/ owning a home/ being patriotic/ going to private school/ not being wasteful/ having good etiquette. Other values or expectations not listed above?

5. What do you appreciate or what have you gained from your class background experience?

6. What has been hard for you from your class background?

7. What impact does your class background have on your current attitudes, behaviors, and feelings? (About money, work, relationships with people from the same class/from a different class, your sense of self, expectations about life, your politics, etc.)

Appendix 11B

CLASSISM QUIZ

How much do you know about class in the U.S.?

Life at the Bottom

1) How many people in the U.S. had no health care coverage in 1994?
a) 8 million b) 22 million c) 37 million

2) The best public schools in the U.S. spend over $15,500 per pupil and have class sizes of about 15. What is the average per-pupil spending and class size of the worst schools?
a) About $7,000 & over 40 students per class
b) Under $3,000 & over 60 students per class
c) About $6,000 & over 100 students per class

3) What are the two biggest factors that predict whether an American has an abandoned toxic waste dump affecting his/her local air and water?
a) Proximity to heavy industry; occupation
b) Race; income
c) Rural/urban location; Northern/Southern U.S.

4) In the Netherlands in 1987, over 60% of poor people were lifted out of poverty by government programs. In Britain, the percent was about 45%; Canada, 20%; France, 52%. What percentage of poor people in the U.S. were lifted out of poverty by government programs in 1987?
a) 18% b) Half of 1% c) 7%

5) The majority of people who became homeless in the 1980s were single mothers with children. Why was this true?
a) More teenagers had babies than before.
b) Average rents rose 20% and welfare benefits for single-parent families dropped an average of 23% during the decade.
c) New rules at low-income housing excluded unmarried mothers.

Politics and Wealth

6) Who was the wealthiest person in North America in 1776?

7) The average successful candidate for U.S. Senate in 1992 spent how much of his or her own money on the Senate campaign?
a) $40,000 b) $212,000 c) $660,000

8) The "tax reform" bill of 1986, which was supposed to eliminate tax loopholes, cut the tax bill for Americans with incomes between $10,000 and $20,000 by 6%, or an average of $69 a year. How did it change the tax bill of millionaires?
a) Increase of 3% b) Decrease of 27% c) Decrease of 12%

9) In 1992, the richest 1% of American families paid an average of 7.6% of their income in state and local taxes. The middle 20% paid 10%. What percent of their income did the poorest 20% of American families pay in state and local taxes?
a) 3% b) 18.2% c) 13.8% d) 8.8%

10) The average U.S. household with income under $10,000 got $5,700 in government assistance in 1991. How much did the average household with income over $100,000 get in government benefits and tax breaks?
a) $9,300 b) $5,700 c) $0 d) $3,542

11) In 1976, the wealthiest 1% of Americans owned 19% of the privately-owned wealth and the bottom 90% owned 51%. In 1993, how had these numbers changed? That is, what percent did the wealthiest 1% and the bottom 90% own?
a) 37% and 32% b) 20% and 50% c) 26% and 45%

The Rewards of Work

12) Statistically, the factor that best predicts a U.S. adult's income is her or his:
a) IQ b) Father's occupation c) Level of education d) Number of years in the full-time labor force

13) In constant dollars, taking inflation into account, how did the 1994 pay for entry-level jobs requiring high school diplomas compare (using percentages to express the comparison) with the same jobs in 1979? (In other words, if the 1979 job is represented by 100%, how would you represent the 1994 job?)
a) 109% b) 66% c) 153% d) 74%

14) All of the following greatly decreased for working families in the 1980s and early 1990s except three. Which three increased? (Circle three.)
Leisure time; home ownership; part-time jobs; union membership; second jobs; kids in college; illegal child labor; pension plans; health benefits

15) The percent of all privately owned wealth in the U.S. in 1995 that was acquired not by work or by investment, but by inheritance was
a) 11% b) 34% c) 46% d) 94%

16) In 1974, Chief Executive Officers (CEOs) of U.S. manufacturing corporations were paid an average of 34 times the income of the average worker. In 1990, compensation for the same CEOs was how many times higher than the average worker?
a) 41 times higher b) 120 times higher c) 66 times higher

Appendix 11C

QUIZ ANSWER SHEET WITH BIBLIOGRAPHIC REFERENCES

1) c) An equal number are underinsured, meaning they have no coverage for a preexisting condition or don't have all health care covered. In 1982, 75% of workers at companies employing 100 or more got health insurance for themselves, and 50% got family benefits. By 1989 the numbers were down to 48% and 31%. Source: D. L. Barlett and J. B. Steele (1992), *America: What Went Wrong?* Kansas City, MO: Andrews and McMeel.

2) b) Millions of inner city and rural Southern children attend overcrowded schools without gyms, libraries, playgrounds, audiovisual equipment, or computers, and sometimes without textbooks or windows in classrooms. Source: J. Kozol (1991), *Savage Inequalities,* New York: Crown Publishers.

3) b)Three out of every five African Americans and Hispanic Americans, and half of all Asians, Pacific Islanders, and Native Americans live in communities with uncontrolled toxic waste sites. For families earning less than $6,000 annually, it is estimated that 86% of African American children and 36% of white children have lead poisoning. For families with incomes over $15,000, the lead poisoning rates are 38% for African-American children and 12% for white children. Source: R. Bullard (Ed.) (1993), *Confronting Environmental Racism,* Boston: South End Press.

4) b)Regressive federal taxes (i.e., heavier on lower incomes) push more Americans into poverty than welfare programs pull out. Source: Staff of *Dollars and Sense* magazine (1992), *Real World Macro,* vol. 9, Somerville MA: *Dollars and Sense,* Economic Affairs Bureau, Inc.

5) b) Average rents for low-income single-parent households went from 38% of their incomes in 1975 to 58% in 1987—and federal housing spending dropped by 75% in the 80s. There were actually fewer teenagers having children in the 1980s than the 1950s, 60s and 70s; what changed was the average ability of the fathers to make a wage that could support a family. In 1991, 34% of homeless people were families with children. Source: T. Amott (1993), *Caught in the Crisis, Women and the U.S. Economy Today,* New York: Monthly Review Press; N. Folbre (Center for Popular Economics) (1995), *New Field Guide to the U.S. Economy,* New York: New Press.

6) George Washington.

7) c) In 1995 there were 27 millionaires in the U.S. Senate. Candidate self-financing covered 15% of all campaign expenses in the 1992 Congressional elections, effectively excluding most non-rich candidates from office. Large individual donations (over $200) covered 35%; Political Action Committees (PAC's), mostly from industry, covered 29%. The most democratic source, small individual donations, only covered 19%. Source: Commonwealth Coalition (1995), Boston, MA.

8) b) People with incomes over $1 million got an even bigger tax cut in the 80s: an average of $346,673 in extra spending money each. (Millionaires are people with assets over $1 million, not necessarily incomes over $1 million.) Source: D. L. Barlett and J. B. Steele (1992), *America: What Went Wrong?* Kansas City, MO: Andrews and McMeel.

9) c) Sales and excise taxes fall disproportionately harder on lower-income people because out of necessity they use a higher proportion of their income on local purchases. A book called *The Poor Pay More* documented that lower-income people also pay higher prices

for most items, especially food, than higher-income people who can drive to cheaper stores and buy in bulk. Source: Staff of *Dollars and Sense* magazine (1992), *Real World Macro,* vol. 9, Somerville MA: *Dollars and Sense,* Economic Affairs Bureau, Inc.

10) a) Besides Social Security and Medicare, which go to seniors of all incomes, many very well-off people get large mortgage interest tax deductions for second homes and luxury homes, and some get farm subsidies or various types of investment tax credits. Source: United for a Fair Economy (1995), Boston, MA.

11) a) Over 30% of American families have negative wealth (more debts than assets), and the top half of 1% own 26.9% of all the wealth—the highest concentration in US history since 1929. The biggest factors in this dramatic shift towards more inequality were changes in tax policy to favor the wealthy, soaring home prices driven up by speculative buying and selling, and the decline in decently-paid manual jobs (especially unionized manufacturing jobs). Source: United for a Fair Economy (1995), Boston, MA.

12) b) Regression analysis in R. de Lone (Carnegie Council on Children) (1979), *Small Futures: Children, Inequality, and the Limits of Liberal Reform,* New York: Harcourt Brace Jovanovich.

13) d) Even college-educated workers' average incomes fell 3.1% from 1987–1991. Source: L. R. Mishel & J. Bernstein (Economic Policy Institute) (1993), *The State of Working America,* Armonk, NY: M. E. Sharpe. From 1977–1988, the lowest-income 80% of American families went down in average income, and the highest-income 20% went up. The poorest 10% lost an average of 14.8% of purchasing power, and the richest 1% gained 49.8% of purchasing power. Source: K. Phillips (1990), *The Politics of Rich and Poor,* New York: Harper.

14) Part-time jobs, second jobs, illegal child labor. The number of part-time jobs has in fact soared, partly because of employers avoiding benefits, partly because of the increased numbers of people working two jobs—especially women. By 1989, 3.5 times as many women were working two or more jobs as in 1973. The number of children working illegally tripled from 1983 to 1992. T. Amott (1993), *Caught in the Crisis, Women and the U.S. Economy Today,* New York: Monthly Review Press.

15) c) N. Folbre (Center for Popular Economics) (1995), *New Field Guide to the U.S. Economy,* New York: New Press.

16) b) N. Folbre (Center for Popular Economics) (1995), *New Field Guide to the U.S. Economy,* New York: New Press. Not only did CEO salaries grow so dramatically, reaching an average of $2 million for the 339 largest publicly held corporations in 1988, but there was almost no correlation between size of CEO salary and the success or profit rate of the company. Source: *Business Week* numbers, quoted in K. Phillips (1990), *The Politics of Rich and Poor,* New York: Harper.

Appendix 11D

INCOME DISTRIBUTION CHART

Average Income for United States Family Income Groups, 1992

If you lined up every family in the United States in order of 1992 *income* (not assets), and then divided them up into five groups with an equal number of families in each group, and then averaged each group's income, these are the averages you'd get:

Bottom 20% made an average of	$ 8,130
2nd 20% made	20,090
3rd 20% made	31,970
4th 20% made	47,690

Within the Top 20%:

Lowest 10% made	65,700
Next 5% made	84,700
Next 4% made	132,400
Highest 1% made	676,000

Source: U.S. Bureau of the Census (1992). *Current Population Survey.* Washington, DC: U.S. Bureau of Census.

Appendix 11E

WEALTH DISTRIBUTION CHART

Average Wealth for United States Family Income Groups, 1989

If you lined up every family in the United States in order of 1989 assets (wealth), and then divided them up into five groups with an equal number of families in each group, and then averaged each group's assets, these are the averages you'd get (amounts given in 1989 dollars):

Bottom 20% owned an average of	negative $14,000 (more debts than assets)
2nd 20% owned	$8,000
3rd 20% owned	$45,000
4th 20% owned	$114,000
Within the Top 20%:	
Lowest 10% owned	$243,000
Next 9% owned	$737,000
Next 0.5% owned	$2,984,000
Richest 0.5% owned	$12,482,000

Source: L. R. Mishel & J. Bernstein (Economic Policy Institute) (1993), *The State of Working America,* Armonk, NY: M. E. Sharpe.

Note: According to Edward Wolff's *Top Heavy: The Study of Increasing Inequality of Wealth in America* (New York: The Twentieth Century Fund Press, 1995), you must have a minimum of 2.3 million dollars in wealth to make it into the top 1% of Americans.

Appendix 11F

CLASSISM HISTORY LECTURE OUTLINE

Outline for a Sample Presentation on Class, Classism, and Resistance to Classism in United States History

1) The founding of the United States (Zinn, 1980, chap. 5).

a) Over half of English immigrants came to the colonies as indentured servants, working five to ten years for those who paid their passage. In the harsh conditions of seventeenth century Virginia, two-thirds of indentured servants died before the end of their contracts from deprivation or disease (Amott & Matthaei, 1991, 96–97).

b) The rebellion against Britain was primarily waged and supported by the wealthiest white men in the colonies, who also had to contend with rebellions against their economic and political control by Indians whose land they were invading, by black slaves, and by poor white renters, foot soldiers, and taxpayers (for example, the Whisky Rebellion).

c) Only white male property-owners were given the vote; in some states, only white male property-owners could serve on juries and only large property owners could run for office (Zinn, 1980, 81, 90). Later, in the 1840s, Dorr's Rebellion tried to institute voting rights for white landless men in Rhode Island but was repressed by the state militia (Zinn, 1980, 209–11.)

2) Four main forms of wealth creation put surplus in the hands of a small wealthy elite and a larger number of small owners, while impoverishing millions, who sometimes rebelled:

a) Slavery (Zinn, 1980, chap. 2; Bennett, 1988, chaps. 4–6). Slave rebellions and escapes played a major role in emancipation. The economic oppression of ex-slaves after emancipation left them almost as impoverished as before (Bennett, 1988, chaps. 8, 9).

b) Immigrant labor during industrialization. The massive fortunes of the "robber barons" grew after the Civil War through monopoly control of industries employing thousands at low wages and bad conditions (Zinn, 1980, chap. 11). The labor movement organized working people to improve these conditions, e.g., the 1886 national general strike for the eight-hour day (Zinn, 1980, 263–64) and the 1912 Lawrence Massachusetts women's "bread and roses" strike (Zinn, 1980, 327–29).

c) Land grabs. Land taken from Indians, French, and Mexicans won territory for English settlers (Zinn, 1980, chaps. 7, 8, Amott & Matthaei, 1991, 39–50, 70–73; Takaki, 1993), and military conquest in the Caribbean, Hawaii, the Philippines, and Central America. Poor men sent as soldiers obtained foreign markets for large property owners (Zinn, 1980, chap. 12).

d) Tenant-farming, sharecropping, and farm mortgages. The Anti-Renter Movement in the 1840s to 1860s in New York state (Zinn, 1980, 206–209) tried to lessen the power of the few huge landowners. The Populist Movement of the 1880s and 1890s (sometimes racist, sometimes mixed-race) organized farmers in the South and West against the banks, grain merchants, and railroads that exploited them (Zinn, 1980, 276–289.) In 1894, the Populist and Democratic parties pushed for and won the first peacetime graduated income tax, but the Supreme Court struck it down (Pizzigati, 1992, 42–49.)

3) The Depression and the New Deal (Zinn, 1980, chap. 15).

a) In the 1910s and 1920s, income distribution became more and more unequal, peaking in 1929. In 1913, 44 families had incomes over $50 million a year, and the majority of adult workers earned between $10 and $20 a week. After World War I, Congress, led by multimillionaire Treasury Secretary Andrew Mellon, cut top tax rates from 77% to 25%. A main factor behind the Depression was wild speculation in stocks, creating huge paper fortunes (Pizzigati, 1992, 51–54.)

b) In 1933, one-fourth to one-third of the labor force was unemployed. Massive numbers of evictions left farms and houses empty and the homeless in "Hoovervilles" (shanty-towns).

c) Widespread uprisings by the newly poor included the Bonus Army of unemployed World War I vets marching to Washington in 1932; sit-down strikes; riots; a Sharecroppers Union; and the creation of the Congress of Industrial Organizations.

d) Huey Long, populist Senator from Louisiana, led a popular if flawed campaign against wealth concentration, and in 1932 proposed to the Senate a tax law prohibiting personal income over $1 million/year, fortunes over $100 million, or inheritances over $5 million. He organized Share-the-Wealth clubs that claimed 7 million members in 27,431 clubs in 1935 (Pizzigati, 1992, 37–41.)

e) Although New Deal legislation (Social Security Act, National Labor Relations Board, minimum wage, etc.) gave some benefits to poor and working poor people, it did not change systemic inequalities in the distribution of wealth.

4) Post-World War II boom economy of 1950s and 1960s (Bluestone, 1984).

a) The U.S. came out of World War II the only intact industrial economy in the world. Tremendous economic growth from exports to the rest of the world created a large middle class and stable working class. Skilled and/or unionized working-class people began to own homes and have pensions; the children and grandchildren of poor immigrants and African Americans went to college in large numbers and populated the new sprawling middle-class suburbs (Amott & Matthaei, 1991, 179, 181.)

b) Anti-Communist McCarthyism repressed union organizers and others who spoke up against classism (Zinn, 1980, 422–428). The unmet expectations created by high Black participation in World War II and by economic growth helped spur the Black Civil Rights Movement, which inspired other poor people's movements such as the United Farmworkers, the American Indian Movement, and the National Welfare Rights Organization.

5) De-industrialization and pillage by the rich in the 1970s to the 1990s (Phillips, 1990, esp. chaps. 3, 4).

a) Disappearance of manufacturing jobs and growth in low-paying service jobs threatened the working-class's recent relative prosperity. Real (corrected for inflation) average wages have fallen steadily since 1972, falling 11% by 1986. (Phillips, 1990, p. 18; Amott & Matthaei, 1991, 135–40, 179–91.)

b) Under President Reagan, tax changes gave massive windfalls to the richest Americans, who invested overseas and speculated in real estate; combined with reductions in domestic spending, this created the first widespread homelessness since the Depression. Tax cuts and increased military spending caused exponential growth in the federal deficit, which transferred tax dollars to the wealthy, holders of most government debt. Deregulation led to the savings and loan crisis, which enriched a small number of bankers and investors, and by 1994 had cost taxpayers five times as much as annual welfare spending on Aid to Families with Dependent Children.

c) Changes in family structure created more single-mother families and the shrinking number of working-class jobs paying family wages caused the "feminization of poverty," pushing millions of women and children below the poverty line (Amott, 1991).

12

Multiple Issues Course Overview

Maurianne Adams, Linda Marchesani

The single issue courses described in chapters 6–11 deal with individual forms of oppression taken one form at a time, and are usually presented within a short and intensive time frame. In this chapter we discuss the instructional goals, learning outcomes, and teaching strategies that emerge in a full semester's focus upon multiple social justice topics. In the course description, we interweave and highlight the ways in which a sustained semester's contact with students, focusing on a number of social justice issues, differs qualitatively from the more intensive mode of the two-day weekend course that focuses on a single form of oppression.

Course Context and Content

This multiple issue, social justice course evolved historically from the single issue courses and draws upon the same foundational and pedagogical concepts. Within a fourteen-week semester, the course covers five issues of social oppression (sexism, heterosexism, racism, antisemitism, and ableism) and illuminates commonalities and differences among them. One commonality we explore is the interaction of social and economic class with these five manifestations of oppression.

Most first and second year students live in residence halls, and the course we are describing, geared primarily for second year students, draws upon a thirty-year tradition of small residentially-based discussion classes in the residence halls. This residential base reinforces the informal, collaborative, experiential teaching strategies that characterize our courses and differentiate them from more formal and traditional lecture-based courses that take place in campus classroom buildings. The residential context helps focus student attention upon instances of diversity and oppression most immediately visible in campus life.

This course was designed to meet the diversity requirement of a campus-wide general education curriculum for all university students (in professional schools as well as in arts and sciences). We shaped a course in which specific forms of oppression such as racism and sexism would be interwoven with key concepts taught as curriculum organizers (see chapters 2 and 5 for key concepts).

The curriculum consists of five forms of oppression, each examined in two-week segments over a ten-week period. We use the remaining four weeks to begin and conclude the course, consider parallels and interconnections among the five "isms," and examine the interaction of socio-economic class with other issues, especially with race, gender, and antisemitism.

Sequence of Course Topics	
Week 1:	Course Introductions
Week 2:	Sexism part 1
Week 3:	Sexism part 2
Week 4:	Heterosexism part 1
Week 5:	Heterosexism part 2 (interconnections with Sexism)
Week 6:	Racism part 1
Week 7:	Racism part 2
Week 8:	Parallels and Interconnections (Classism)
Week 9:	Antisemitism part 1
Week 10:	Antisemitism part 2 (parallels with Racism and Classism)
Week 11:	Ableism part 1
Week 12:	Ableism part 2
Week 13:	Parallels and Interconnections, Classism, Student Projects
Week 14:	Closure, Student Projects

Figure 12.1. Sequence of Course Topics.

General Education Curricular Considerations

The general education emphasis upon critical thinking and writing led us to combine traditional aspects of academic work (papers, readings, homework assignments, and final exams) with active, experiential pedagogy. The writing requirement enables us to use student writing as a tool for self-exploration and reflection. The final exam signals to students the intellectual seriousness of the subject matter. The requirement that general education courses be theory-grounded supports our interweaving of social science theory with personal experience.

Learning Goals

The multiple issues course, like the single issue courses, has basic learning goals of awareness, knowledge, and action. In our syllabus, we identify these goals as:

(1) raising awareness,

(2) information-sharing,

(3) conceptual understanding,

(4) recognition of critical incidents that involve classroom to real-life transfer, and

(5) intervention skills or opportunities for taking concrete action.

We believe these learning goals occur sequentially. We use the first three goals of awareness, knowledge, and conceptual understanding to organize our approach to the initial course topics. By mid-semester, as we study racism and antisemitism, we can pay more attention to the latter goal of recognition of critical incidents in everyday life, and begin to develop action plans and appropriate intervention skills. The interplay of learning goals with course topics or "isms" is shown in Figure 12.2 below.

Learning Goals in Relation to Course Topics
(x's indicate relative weight and emphasis)

Topics	Awareness	Information	Concepts	Recognition	Action
Sexism	xxx	xxx	xxx	x	o
Heterosexism	xxx	xxx	xxx	x	x
Racism	xx	xxx	xxx	xx	xx
Antisemitism	x	xxx	xx	xxx	xx
Ableism	x	xxx	xx	xxx	xxx

Figure 12.2. Learning Goals in Relation to Course Topics.

Raising Awareness

This learning goal is met by helping students acknowledge that the "ism" exists, identify their own social identities and experiences with reference to that "ism" (for example, gender or sexual orientation), and explore the institutional and systemic relationships among agent (dominant) and targeted (subordinate) groups represented within each category (for example, men/women; heterosexual/gay, lesbian or bisexual; people of color/whites). The course emphasizes how these differences are regarded in the mainstream culture as well as in the university and classroom.

Agent or mainstream students, in whatever area they may experience dominance, tend to enter the course thinking of "difference" as belonging to the cultural "other." They are relatively oblivious to their own role as culture-bearers and deny or downplay the experiences of students who are socially subordinate or targeted. For example, male students of whatever racial or ethnic heritage, may question what is the "big deal" for women who experience sexual harassment or are victims of acquaintance rape. Students' increased awareness appears less in the form of academic knowledge and more as gradual shifts in student attitudes toward greater receptivity, sensitivity, and openness to "the other."

Students more readily increase awareness, in our experience, when classroom examples are drawn from their immediate campus environment and daily interactions. By focusing discussions on instances of individual prejudice or institutional discrimination that are readily identifiable to undergraduates in their college communities, we connect their personal and local "data" to more abstract historical or sociological information and concepts presented in readings.

Students have numerous opportunities to explore both agent and target aspects of their own multiple identities as their focus shifts from one issue to another throughout the semester. For example, a Latina woman who focuses upon her identity and experiences in relation to her target racial or linguistic status, may be challenged to consider her agent identities if she is also able-bodied, heterosexual, and/or Christian. In this process she may, although often with difficulty, begin to grasp the coexistence and the complexity of her shifting and fluid multiple identities. She may gain empathy with the struggles of students who can't seem to understand "her" issues of racism or sexism, just as she struggles to understand some of "their" issues of ableism or heterosexism or antisemitism.

Information-sharing

Information is drawn from multiple sources, such as autobiographical narratives, historical documents, statistical and demographic data. It comes through various channels, such as assigned readings, lectures, films, peer panels, guest speakers, and students' in-class shared experiences. We use these sources to establish historical and contemporary contexts, to examine sources of misinformation, stereotypes, and prejudices, and to fill in blanks of missing history or social invisibility.

Some of this information is drawn from personal stories or from campus incidents of sexual, racial, or homophobic harassment. Discussions then broaden to include stereotypes in the media; statistical data concerning differential educational, income, and employment opportunities for people of color and for women; historical backgrounds of European antisemitism and racial laws; various exclusionary quotas barring African Americans, Native Americans, Chinese, Japanese, and Jews in this country's history. The cumulative impact of information within the five topics of oppression enables students to grasp and draw parallels among the internal dynamics of oppressive systems with a depth and vividness that is more than the sum of its five parts.

Personal learnings from writing assignments and small group discussions are supplemented by extensive reading in a specially designed course reader with homework questions and follow-up activities (Adams, Brigham, Dalpes, & Marchesani, 1996; contents listed at end of this volume). Students bring questions about the readings back into class for further examination or discussion.

Conceptual Understanding

The theoretical constructs and conceptual organizers that help students to shape and integrate their learning in this course provide intersections or through-lines among the five subject areas. Without blurring the historically situated particulars of racism or antisemitism, sexism or heterosexism, we want students to grasp some of the conceptual parallels and interconnections among them.

There are key concepts we consider essential for students to understand (see chapter 5):

- the process of social role acquisition and learning (conceptualized as a "cycle of socialization"),
- the characteristics of social identity and social group membership, agent and target social status, and systemic privilege and power,
- the levels (conscious and unconscious) and types (personal, institutional, cultural) of oppression in different historical contexts,
- stereotyping,
- historical contexts,
- internalization or collusion, and
- allies.

The semester provides ample opportunity to reiterate these key concepts across the five topics, enriching student understanding of the concepts and allowing them to continue to explore commonalities and differences.

We introduce these key concepts gradually and incrementally, weaving them in and out of our discussions of the various course topics, as shown in Figure 12.3 below.

Key Concepts in Relation to Course Topic Areas

Topic areas:	Cycle	Identity	Agent/Target	Levels & Types	History
Sexism	xxx	xxx	xxx	xx	o
Heterosexism	xx	xx	xxx	xx	x
Racism	o	xx	xx	xxx	xx
Antisemitism	o	xx	xx	xx	xxx
Ableism	o	xx	xx	xx	xxx

Figure 12.3. Key Concepts in Relation to Course Topics.

The conceptual (as distinct from topical) dimension of this course involves a backward and forward recycling of key concepts across the designated subject areas. For example, a consideration of historical context provides multiple instances of the levels and types of antisemitism in nineteenth- and twentieth-century European laws, media, and bureaucracy. At the same time, this historical dimension, although introduced with reference to antisemitism, also suggests new ways to reframe and understand the historical dimension of other forms of oppression. In racism, for example, the historical background of slavery and forced segregation for African Americans, the World War II internment camps for Japanese Americans, the expropriation of Mexican American wealth and property in the early nineteenth century, extermination of entire villages and cultures of Native Americans by colonists and westward settlers, offer startling glimpses into an unacknowledged, often unknown, dimension of our shared American history. These often shock students who want to know more. At midsemester we pause to review the historical and other parallels and interconnections that have surfaced.

Out of the parallels and interconnections that emerge through the conceptual intersections of the course topics, students begin also to explore their agent and target identities and to experience directly the compounding effect of multiple social identities. For example, across issue linkages and interconnections may emerge for students who experience multiple oppressions (an African American lesbian, a hearing impaired Jewish woman, students from mixed racial parentage), for students who experience multiple privileges (a heterosexual white Christian woman, a gay white Christian man, a heterosexual white Jewish man), and for students who focus exclusively on their target status while ignoring or downplaying their areas of privilege (a Jewish woman in relation to race, an African American Christian man in relation to antisemitism). Students begin to understand how their multiple internally interconnected social identities, whether agent, target, or mixed, have internally reinforcing as well as complicating effects. Once students are able to see the interconnections among multiple issues and multiple identities, we can introduce information about the interaction of social and economic class with gender, race, and antisemitism.

Recognition, or Classroom to Real-world Transfer

Recognition as a learning goal names our expectation that students will learn how to look at their social world differently, in a way described by Freire as "critical consciousness" (1970). This goal asks that students be able to recognize the features of individual prejudice and institutional or cultural discrimination in their every day environment. For example, students analyze campus incidents such as homophobic harassment in the residence halls or the baiting of mixed-race couples, exams scheduled on Jewish holidays, or public gatherings that don't take the needs of students with disabilities into consideration. Such recognition also involves students' coming to understand and disentangle the many factors that often muddy or complicate prejudice or discrimination in real-life experience, such as the compounding effects of alcohol on incidents of racial harassment (Hurst, 1988; *Racism 101* video, 1988).

As we try to facilitate the process by which our students gradually recognize course topics in the fabric of everyday life, we have identified three factors or sets of skills. First, students begin to recognize the "figure" of prior classroom insights (examples of stereotypes) in the "ground" of everyday life (peers telling antisemitic or "dumb" jokes based on stereotypes). Second, dominant students often change their prior belief that violence or harassment is "normal," the fault of or exaggerated by the victim, and begin to imagine ways that oppressive situations might be transformed. Third, recognition enables students to transfer learning from the relative simplifications of the classroom to the messy complexities of everyday life.

Our sustained contact with students during the fourteen week semester enables us to structure, facilitate, and follow-up on students' efforts to transfer their insights back and forth between the classroom and their home communities. Examples taken from campus experience are used in lectures or discussions and then examined so that students share each other's vantage points on different racial, ethnic, or gender issues.

Homework or journal assignments, reflective papers and simulations or role plays, help students sharpen their recognition and analytic skills. Students become adept over time in their ability to recognize and record daily instances of oppression in their daily lives.

Intervention and Action

Once students have applied classroom learnings to examples drawn from their own experiences, they may feel ready to develop action strategies and practice intervention skills. They do this, first, by reflecting on their actual behavior in real situations ("What did you actually do? What other options occurred to you at the time?"), and second, by beginning to imagine other possible behavioral responses or proactive interventions ("What do you wish you had done? What alternatives occur to you now, upon reflection? What obstacles or enablers make these alternatives seem either difficult or possible?"). They are then prepared to try out alternative scenarios by projecting re-played and transformed scenarios into the future ("What might you do if . . . ? What obstacles or enablers would block or ease various courses of action?").

Students draw upon the personal relationships they develop with each other during the semester to try out various action strategies and intervention skills, and use each other to practice, affirm, or critique their proposed action plans. As students get to know each other better, they help each other identify their various spheres of influence: immediate or extended family, intimate relationships, friends or peers at work, school, or places of worship; leadership roles in student activities, student government, student newspapers; neighbors in the residence halls, casual interactions on campus, or in classrooms (see Appendix 7E). They also acknowledge that the relatively high or low levels of risk involved in planning action within various spheres of influence may vary inversely with the degree of intimacy or personal attachment.

Principles of Educational Practice

Our primary principle of educational design is the interaction of course topics, learning goals, and conceptual organizers. But we observe other principles of practice as well, such as flexibility, theory-based pedagogy, attention to classroom climate, differentiation of grades and evaluation from personal feedback, and ongoing attention to our own needs as social justice educators.

Flexibility in Adapting Goals and Key Concepts to Learner Needs and Interests

Although our instructors work within an established curriculum that stipulates course content, learning goals, and key concepts, they have considerable flexibility in designing any two week curricular module and making their own judgment calls on the actual design and facilitation of those modules. Some instructors in a given semester may find it necessary to spend more time raising awareness across all five course topics, while others respond to student interest in their sections by emphasizing recognition and action. The degree to which classism (see chapter 11) is woven into discussions of topics such as racism or antisemitism depends both on the sophistication of the students and on the preparation of the instructor (examples given in Figure 12.1, weeks 8, 10 and 13).

Differences in learning style lead to shifts in emphasis toward experiential or lecture-based learning modes. Some instructors may find that their students prefer working with their own and each others' lived experience, while others make more effective use of lectures, readings, or films (see discussion of learning styles in chapters 4 and 15).

Theory-based Pedagogy

The principles of pedagogical practice outlined in chapter 3 pay special attention to social relations within the classroom, the experiential basis for student-centered learning, the self-knowledge and role of the instructor, and the importance of a safe and respectful classroom climate.

These pedagogical foundations emphasize the importance of paying attention to *process*, a term which has several distinctive yet interrelated meanings in our teaching practice. First, by paying attention to classroom process, we mean being constantly alert to what's going on: What are the group dynamics? Who's speaking and who's silent? Who's interrupting whom? What's the feeling in the room just now (excited, tense, fearful, embarrassed)? Second, by paying attention to process we also mean using deliberate, intentional preparatory structures to stage learning activities: questions attached to weekly reading and homework assignments, specific journal assignments, questions to generate personal information in anticipation of writing assignments, newsprint or chalkboard directions to guide simulations or role play. And third, by attention to process (as in the verb, "to process"), we mean providing ample opportunity for students to reflect upon and describe their thoughts, feelings, and reactions to new information or experiential learning activities; to analyse any contradictions, new questions or new perspectives they've noted; to identify themes in their discussions or unresolved questions; and to consider whether there are implications for change in their future attitudes or behaviors (see chapter 13).

For example, as we design various student-centered learning activities, we try to structure these learning activities in such a way that students can engage in a guided learning experience first and then have an opportunity to reflect upon ("process") that experience, noting its personal connections and relating it to topics previously discussed. This sequence may also include a progression from individual reflection, to dialogue in pairs, to smaller or larger group conversations, all the while utilizing intentionally sequenced questions to structure reflection upon what was observed or learned from a film, panel discussion, or simulation. Examples of these progressions appear throughout the single issue courses in this volume (chapters 6–11) and are also discussed as principles of design (chapter 4) and of facilitation (chapter 13).

We especially draw upon theories of social identity and student development to help us anticipate and understand students' responses to and engagement with the subject matter (chapters 2 and 3). The social identity model seems especially helpful for understanding and paying attention to the ways in which anger, denial, or pain may be elicited by the subject matter or by other students' reactions, and may be expressed by our students and felt by ourselves. Social identity development models also help us remember that students may be in different places developmentally within the same social groups as well as across social groups, so that we may acknowledge the challenges presented by the inevitable collision of strongly held world views.

Social cognitive theory provides a framework for understanding college students' tendency to dichotomize complex questions and reduce multiple perspectives to simple either/or choices (see chapter 3). These cognitive developmental lenses help us empathize with the difficulty students often have acknowledging multiple layers of complex reality at the same moment, or in disengaging from their personal experiences in order to reflect on another's experience or their own experience from a broader systemic perspective. Students in agent social groups often see themselves as an individual or "a person" at the same moment in which they group "other" students who are members of targeted groups together in a single, disrespectful category, as "women" or "people of color." In other words, students often resist or deny identification with the agent group, while collapsing all targets into a single undifferentiated social group (all gays or lesbians, all Chicanas or Native Americans).

While acknowledging the role that resistance and denial may play in agents' coming to terms with previously unnoticed forms of oppression, we also may consider the developmental difficulties in taking the perspective of the other.

We have noticed after more than a decade of teaching this course, that within a fourteen week semester students often make developmental shifts from a dichotomous way of understanding to a broader perspective that can accommodate and value multiple points of view (Adams & Zhou-McGovern, 1994).

Creating a Safe Classroom Climate

Our teaching and learning practice includes careful and explicit attention to the means by which we achieve our teaching objectives. This includes paying close attention to classroom climate by early establishing explicit norms and behavioral ground rules for mutual respect, confidentiality, non-confrontation, honesty, careful listening, and speaking for oneself but not for others (see chapter 5).

Throughout the semester, as the emotional nature of this subject matter contributes to "difficult dialogues" (Butler, 1991), we refer back to these guidelines or add to them to maintain a climate of personal safety and mutual respect that "models" the attitudes we are trying to teach (Tatum, 1992; Romney, Tatum, & Jones, 1992; Thompson & Disch, 1992; Cannon, 1990). We consider this principle of practice extremely important because it enables students to acknowledge the initial fears and anxieties they (and we) understandably attach to the strong, contradictory feelings invoked by the subject matter (Weinstein & Obear, 1992) and their equally contradictory fears of hypocrisy or of conflict in peer discussions. We also try to help students recognize the cultural styles in their differing ways of understanding or feeling comfort or anxiety when presented with intergroup conflict.

Three climate issues require special attention in a semester-long course. First, we need to create a climate that does not rank the various oppression issues as more or less serious or important, and to be mindful of students' tendency to focus upon the pain and experience of their own group to the exclusion or diminishment of other groups' pain and experiences. Instructors need to remind students that although they may personally feel that their issue is more important to them, as a class they need to agree that it is neither useful nor productive to allow competition among issues to prevail.

Second, we try to establish a climate that can provide safety for all students in the class, in relation to their target as well as their agent identities. This includes understanding that safety is relative to student perception and involves respect for different cultural styles of expression and communication. We try not to confuse safety with comfort, since discomfort is an important indicator of a student's growing edge (see chapters 5 and 13).

Third, this course shares with any other academic courses the problems of disruptive student behavior (lateness, side-conversations between students, lack of participation). Letting any of these issues ride unattended from one week to another undermines the openness, trust, and sense of basic fairness that are so critical to this kind of learning. Unlike more formal courses dependent on the lecture mode, participants in these courses often pay close attention to their shared group history throughout the semester and unresolved issues will build and heat up. If we disregard African American history when studying racism, and then focus upon the history of antisemitism as the design in this volume suggests (chapter 9), students of color are likely to be angered by our asymmetrical treatment. Similarly, we can be sure that our failure to deal with overt sexist behavior by men of color in the class, for example, will be understood by women to imply a hierarchy of oppressions by which sexism seems less important than racism. How and when to make interventions (openly in class, side comments during breaks or after class, written notes to students) is often a difficult judgment call. Failure to take action invariably carries its own cumulative pricetag.

Differentiate Grades and Evaluation from Feedback

When a course on social diversity and social justice requires that we assign letter grades to our evaluation of student work, we need to differentiate grading or evaluation from the equally important oral or written personal feedback we give to students to challenge their thinking or point up disparities and inconsistencies. Grades and evaluation are based upon assigned student work, such as questions about assigned texts and other readings (Appendix 12A), preparation of homework assignments, and completion of in class activities; written papers that follow a sequence of reflective questions or structured guidelines; and a final essay exam, based on broad conceptual questions prepared in advance that test students' utilization of concepts and knowledge. We may disagree, sometimes even dislike and disavow some of the views expressed by students in these assignments, and we will always ask questions or give feedback (Appendix 12B), but the actual course grades derive measurably from grade points and grade percentages set in advance for each assignment and for various questions inside each assignment (Appendix 12C).

The various written assignments are also designed to be quantified so that the final grades are numerically arrived at from the totality of work completed on time during the semester. This procedure is especially important, we believe, to clearly differentiate our personal feedback on the content or thoughtfulness of student statements from our grading or evaluation of student work. We also want to be able to challenge the more dualistic thinking of some students who reduce complex issues to simpler dichotomies of right/wrong, true/false, good/bad, without lowering their grades for reasons they do not yet understand. Further, some students expect at the beginning of the semester that we will enforce political correctness in a course dealing with social justice. The rigorous, demonstrable differentiation of qualitative or personal teacher-to-student feedback from the quantifable and basically "fair" grading of performance turns around this initial and understandable distrust, and protects the integrity of our open-ended dialogue-and-discussion teaching approach. We have confidence that students who do the assigned coursework will, by the end of the semester, have had to examine and interrogate their prior beliefs and assumptions, increase their knowledge base, grapple with theoretical and conceptual interconnections, recognize course concepts in real-world examples, and, in many but not all cases, consider and try out new forms of behavior and action in their everyday lives.

Instructor Preparation and Community

This general education course is taught by masters and doctoral students who are enrolled in a social justice education graduate program. To qualify for teaching, teaching assistants complete a sequence of graduate courses and facilitate at least two single issue weekend courses like those illustrated in this volume (chapters 5–11). The graduate course and facilitation sequence prepares instructors-to-be in areas of content and pedagogy described in chapters 1–5 and 13–15. First time instructors come to the teaching of this general education course having spent two years studying fundamental questions of social justice education theory and practice in their structured graduate coursework, and three or more semesters' prior co-facilitation in single issue weekend courses. Their initial instructional experience in this course, after completing graduate coursework and facilitation prerequisites, is in a co-teaching role to provide on-the-spot support and alternative perspectives on the weekly design and classroom process and dynamics. After co-teaching once, instructors become solo teachers who may co-teach with or otherwise mentor newer teachers.

We as instructors are deeply committed to this social justice teaching/learning enterprise and engage in continuous reflection, observation, and research. We establish and maintain ourselves as a community of teachers and learners engaged together in bi-weekly instructors' meetings to share information and course designs, assist each other in problem-solving and provide mutual support. These meetings combine newly appointed co-instructors with veteran instructors who have taught for two or three years. We have developed and continue to update an instructor's manual that includes designs created by previous generations of instructors within the course (Adams, Dalpes, & Gallagher, unpublished), along with the regularly updated and published course reader for the multiple as well as the single issue courses (Adams, Brigham, Dalpes, & Marchesani, 1996). In addition, the faculty and more seasoned graduate instructors provide on-going observation and feedback for each other and for novice instructors.

Some of the more taxing issues for instructors teaching a multiple-issue course include the broad knowledge base for five (six with classism) content areas, self-knowledge in relation to multiple target and agent identities, and readiness to draw parallels and interconnections among the course topics. Both faculty and graduate instructors have their own professional and personal needs in that they are continuing students of complex, often volatile topics and must understand the uniqueness of each issue while also remaining alert and open to new parallels and interconnections. We are each members of multiple agent and target groups, sometimes triggered or disturbed by our students' or by each other's interactions. Often we need to adjust to the internal dynamics of moving from agent to target status as we move from one issue to another—for example, a white lesbian would teach from an agent or dominant perspective in relation to race and, perhaps, in relation to anti-semitism or ableism, while teaching from a target or subordinate perspective in relation to sexual orientation and sexism. These shifting identities can also affect classroom dynamics as students look to the instructor for leadership and the modeling of empowerment (when target) and modeling ally behaviors and strategies (when agent). As students feel connected to the instructor in relation to a shared social identity, they may experience a special bond of affinity and trust. These bonds shift as we all change topics and thus change identity statuses in relation to the course topics across the semester, with the potential for changes in the dynamics of student-teacher relationships as well.

In this chapter, we have hoped to create a resource for use by instructors engaged or about to engage with multiple topics of social diversity and social justice courses (see Adams & Marchesani, 1992; Marchesani & Adams, 1992). However, readers may want to adapt the structures or ingredients described in this chapter using elements presented in the single issue courses described earlier, to fit particular institutional contexts or curricular goals. The learning goals and key concepts represented in Figures 12.2 and 12.3 may also be adapted to accommodate other topics or stretched to give more extensive semester-long attention to one topic (sexism or racism), pairs of topics (sexism and racism, sexism and heterosexism), or topics such as race, class, and gender, or ableism in special education.

We cannot stress enough our view that the course we have described, even after all these semesters, remains a "work in progress." It has been and continues to be shaped by the insights, experiences, creativity, and convictions brought to it by changing generations of graduate instructors and the students they teach and learn from. The recent interweaving of classism through the other main topics—sometimes as a sixth "ism" and other times as an interconnection—is but one among many changes that have taken place at the instigation of the instructors. More recently, instructors have begun to experiment with Augusto Boal's Theater of the Oppressed (1995, 1979) as an adaptation of more established simulations and role-plays.

We change, our students change, and the social, cultural, and political climate in which we live, work, teach, and come to better understand social justice issues, also changes. At best, we've presented a map of the terrain as we currently understand it. We encourage readers of this chapter to conduct their own journeys of discovery and to draw freely on ideas stimulated by the single issue chapters, while incorporating them into the context of some of the design and practice ideas suggested here.

Appendix 12A

READING ASSIGNMENTS
Created by Dvora Zipkin

Readings are an important component of this course. They provide additional information and perspectives, aid you in broadening your understanding, and help prepare you for the final exam.

You will be expected to read several articles (40–50 pages every two weeks) related to each form of oppression covered in class and to be prepared both to discuss them in small groups, and to share highlights of your small group discussions with the rest of the class. Your reading group will remain the same throughout the semester and will work as a team, so you are encouraged to also work together outside of class if you want.

Each group of readings highlights some of the concepts of oppression; these are noted along with the reading assignment, and will be introduced in class prior to the reading discussion dates. As you read, keep the Reading Guideline Questions and these concepts in mind. If you take brief notes as you read, you will be better prepared to contribute to the discussions in class.

In addition to being prepared to discuss the readings and related concepts in class, each group will be responsible to contribute at least one example of that form of oppression from current events. This can be in the form of a newspaper or magazine article, TV or radio news story, something that you have personally experienced, or other sources that you identify. Please focus on *current* events.

Group reading discussions should focus on three components:

1) general reactions, based on the Reading Guideline Questions.

2) the conceptual framework(s) related to that form of oppression, and how the readings illustrate them.

3) current events and manifestations of that form of oppression.

Note: The reading discussion group guidelines apply to all the readings except the first section, *Conceptual Frameworks*, and the last section, *Classism*. The Classism readings will be announced later in the semester.

Reading Guideline Questions

What in the readings was particularly interesting, surprised you, or was new information to you?

What are some things that you agree with or identify with? Explain how and why.

What are some things you disagree with? Explain how and why.

In what ways might the information in the reading be useful to you?

How do the readings illustrate the conceptual frameworks?

What questions do you still have about this form of oppression and/ or the conceptual frameworks?

Conceptual Frameworks	*due week 2*	Oppression: Conceptual and Developmental Analysis Common Elements of Oppression Social Identity Development Model Definitions; Cycle of Socialization; Oppression Umbrella Cycle of Oppression/ Breaking the Cycle of Oppression Social Identity Group Affiliations—worksheet—not to be handed in

---

Sexism *due week 4* — ***Readings:***
Squeezed into Gender Envelopes
Backlashes Then and Now
The Language of Sexism
Double Jeopardy: Women of Color in Higher Education
Peer Harassment: Hassles for Women on Campus
A New Vision of Masculinity
He/She?

Conceptual Frameworks: *Cycle of Socialization; Individual Prejudice*

Heterosexism *due week 6* — ***Readings:***
Homophobia: A Weapon of Sexism (in Sexism section)
How Homophobia Hurts Everyone
How This Society Oppresses Lesbians and Gay Men
Gay Male and Lesbian Youth Suicide
Becoming an Ally
Transgender Liberation (in Sexism section)

Conceptual Frameworks: *Institutional Discrimination; Internalized Oppression*

Racism *due week 8* — ***Readings:***
Perspectives on Race
Something About the Subject Makes it Hard to Name
Inequality in America: The Failure of the American System
White Privilege: Unpacking the Invisible Knapsack
Racial and Ethnic Backlash in College Peer Culture

*plus choose any *two* of the following, preferably dealing with racial groups you know least about:
The Demography of Native North America
Chronology of African American History
History: The Hispanics Appear
Asian Americans and the American Economic Order

Conceptual Frameworks: *Concious/Unconcious Oppression; History*

Antisemitism *due week 10* — ***Readings:***
What is Antisemitism?
Origins of the Antisemitic Pathology
Antisemitism
Cycle of Anti-Jewish Oppression; Stereotype/ Origin
Patterns and Themes of Jewish Oppression
The Abandonment of the Jews: America and the Holocaust
Separations
Timeline of Jewish Oppression (will be handed out in class)

Conceptual Frameworks: *Stereotypes and Cultural Bias; History*

Ableism *due week 12* — ***Readings:***
Common Concerns of Disabled Americans: Issues and Options
Disability in Western Culture
Lives Not Worth Living
Disabling Attitudes
The Independent Living Movement
Americans with Disabilities Act Requirements (p. 102)

Conceptual Frameworks: *Genocide; Non-obvious privilege*

Classism *due week 14* — ***Readings:*** Readings to be announced

Appendix 12B

PROMOTING DIVERSITY THROUGH STUDENT WRITING: ISSUES AND TECHNIQUES

Suggestions for how to use written *feedback* to promote diversity and respond to bias in student writing.

1. Ask for concrete examples, clarifications, illustrations, and details.
2. Provide additional information that corrects misinformation or fills in missing information.
3. Ask about *feelings* associated with a situation or, if they have described feeling a certain way, ask more about the situation(s) that prompt those feelings.
4. Inquire about how they act on their beliefs.
5. Provide students with different perspectives—other ways of looking at the same situation—and invite them to try on a different perspective.
6. Provide students with a broader context (historical or global) with which to think about issues.
7. Point out the "loops" in their thinking (changing their views from one statement to the next).
8. Paraphrase your understanding of the intent of their remarks and ask if you are understanding their intentions/arguments correctly.
9. Support indications of new awareness, growth, risk-taking behavior.
10. Provide suggestions for how to take the next step and explore topics further by suggesting books, resources, films, cultural events.
11. Acknowledge the emotional aspects of dealing with these issues.
12. Introduce students to concepts that can help them make sense of their personal experience.
13. Affirm students' willingness to engage with issues.
14. Share examples of your own experience with students.
15. Let them know you've been there too!

Created by L. Marchesani.

Appendix 12C

GRADING INFORMATION

Personal Socialization Paper—(15% of grade)

Code*	Points	Question
G	25	Part 1: Graph, number of examples given
S	20	Part 2: Story—Specific Example from graph
R	40	Part 3: Reflection
O	5	Connection to Outside readings and class discussion
GP	10	General Presentation: clarity, thoroughness, thoughtfulness
Total	100	

Social Conflict Inventory Part I—(10% of grade)

Code	Points	Question
B	20	I. Background information: Location, time, social group membership of all involved, and other relevant information
A	20	II. Actions: Actions, attitudes, beliefs, values of self and others
RS	20	III. Reflections of Self: Thoughts and feelings; social group membership and other factors and their influences on your thoughts, feelings, and behavior
RO	20	Reflections on Others: Thoughts and feelings; social group membership and other factors and their influences on their thoughts, feelings, and behavior thoughts, feelings, and behavior
GP	20	General Presentation: Clarity, thoroughness, thoughtfulness
Total	100	

Social Conflict Inventory Part II—(10% of grade)

Code	Points	Question
CB	10	1. A. Costs and Benefits of what you did and to all involved
R1	15	B. Possible Response #1
R2	15	Possible Response #2
A1	15	C. Action #1—Costs and benefits
A2	15	Action #2—Costs and benefits
I	10	2. Impact of incident
C	10	3. Connection to class concepts
GP	10	General Presentation: Clarity, thoroughness, thoughtfulness
Total	100	

*Codes refer by letter to various parts of guidelines for papers to emphasize specific issues to be addressed in each section of the paper for maximum number of points.

Final Learning Project—(15% of grade) Criteria will be handed out with project outline
Final Exam—(25% of grade) Criteria will be handed out with final exam
Attendance and class participation—(15% of grade)
Homework—reading assignments—(10% of grade)

Prepared by G. Fleck, adapted from P. Brigham.

PART THREE

Issues for Teachers and Trainers

Facilitating Social Justice Education Courses

Pat Griffin

This chapter provides an introduction to some basic issues involved in facilitating social justice education classes. Facilitating, as distinct from lecture-based teaching, requires attention to process issues in the classroom (Schniedewind, 1993; Thompson & Disch, 1992). Social justice education requires a simultaneous awareness of content and process, as well as an ability to both participate in the process and remain outside of it to assess interactions in the group as a whole and among individuals within the group. These characteristics of social justice education provide the basis for identifying facilitation guidelines for teachers. Other facilitation skills are learned through experience, trial and error, and ongoing experimentation. In fact, much of facilitating social justice education requires the teacher to do a lot of thinking on her feet. In this chapter we will address a range of leadership issues to which facilitators must attend and will describe some student reactions and strategy suggestions for facilitators.

Assessing Initial Readiness to Facilitate Social Justice Education

The first task in thinking about facilitating a social justice education course is to assess what personal resources we bring to the task (Hanson & Lubin, 1987; Phillips, 1987; Weinstein & Obear, 1992; Schwarz, 1994). The following questions serve as guides for helping prospective social justice educators to determine facilitator readiness in five areas: a) support, b) passion, c) awareness, d) knowledge, and e) skills (Bailey Jackson, personal communication).

Support. Support refers to the availability of professional and personal support for teaching about social justice issues. Teaching social justice education courses is more rewarding if you have colleagues and friends who can discuss issues, challenge your awareness, provide help, and commiserate when things don't go as planned.

- What is the climate in your school for addressing social justice issues with students? How are social justice issues addressed in other courses?
- What kind of administrative support do you have? Will the administration back you up if there is parental or community concern?
- What kind of personal support do you have from colleagues and friends? Do you know other teachers who are addressing these issues with students?
- Is there someone with whom you can team teach social justice education courses?
- Do you have someone you can talk with who will help you plan and evaluate your lessons?

Passion. Social justice education is challenging work requiring substantial commitment and passion to sustain facilitators when the challenges become temporarily overwhelming. Belief in the importance of social justice education, the possibilty of social change, and a world in which oppression does not exist provide facilitators with visions to work toward.

- How important is it to you to address social justice issues with students?
- Can you articulate a clear rationale to yourself and others for why these issues need to be addressed?
- Are you willing to risk being the center of controversy if there is community or parental objection?
- Have you considered how addressing these issues will affect students' perceptions of you (positively and negatively)?
- How comfortable are you discussing social justice issues?

Awareness. Learning about social justice issues is a lifelong process. Excitement and humility about continuing to learn about one's own social group memberships, one's access to privilege, and ways to empower one's self, not only make for better social justice education but also keep one in touch with the learning process in which students are engaged.

- How much work have you done on your own beliefs and feelings about social justice issues? Are you aware of your own privilege and prejudice?
- Are you aware of how social justice issues are manifested in your school?
- How aware are you of the interrelationships among different forms of social oppression?

Knowledge. The more information facilitators can bring into the classroom, the richer the experience for participants. When social justice educators keep up with research, writing, and current events about different manifestations of social oppression, they are better prepared to integrate this information into the classroom.

- What information do you have about different forms of social oppression?
- How prepared do you feel to provide information about different forms of social oppression to students?

- Do you have access to resources you can use to increase your knowledge (people, books, workshops, courses, videos)?

Skills. Because of the participatory and interactive nature of social justice education, facilitators use an array of different process and leadership skills to help to create a learning environment in which students can engage with the topic and each other productively.

- What leadership skills do you have for leading student discussions?
- How comfortable are you with students expressing a variety of conflicting beliefs during class discussions?
- Can you listen to prejudiced comments in class discussions without becoming emotionally "triggered" or expressing anger?
- Can you plan questions to help students challenge and confront their own stereotypes and fears about different social groups?
- Are you comfortable disclosing some of your own fears and uncertainties as a way to model this behavior for students?

Solo or Co-facilitation

One of the first decisions when planning a social justice education course is whether to teach alone or to work with a co-facilitator. We strongly recommend co-facilitation for a number of reasons. We believe that two teachers, one from the agent group and one from the target group, can work together more effectively than one teacher working alone to identify strategies that maximize student learning in social justice education. Two leadership perspectives enrich all phases of a social justice education course: planning, teaching, and evaluating and co-facilitators can support each other during difficult and challenging class incidents.

We also recommend co-facilitation because we believe that in classes that focus on single issues of oppression in which both agent and target group members are included (women and men in a sexism class, for example), it is more effective for the teaching team to include an agent and target group member (a woman and a man). Some parts of the content and process of the course are more appropriately addressed by a facilitator from the agent group, and others are best dealt with by a facilitator from the target group. This leadership configuration also provides students with role models from both the agent and target groups as they grapple with challenging issues. Leaders from the target group model empowerment and affirmation. Agent leaders model how to be a self-affirming and effective ally. Both teachers can integrate their own experiences into the class discussions to enrich the variety of experiences and perspectives students hear.

As in any co-facilitation experience it is important to discuss leadership compatibility. Co-facilitators must agree on the nature and dynamics of oppression. They need to discuss teaching goals, teaching philosophies, facilitation strengths and challenges, preferred teaching styles, and content strength. Co-facilitators must also discuss their interactions with each other as members of agent and target groups. Co-facilitators need to maintain open communication during the class, provide each other with constructive feedback, and collaboratively redesign classes and activities as the need arises.

Co-facilitation is not a practical option for all teachers. Solo teaching social justice education can also be successful and rewarding when individual teachers can identify ways to create out-of-class support and assistance. Meeting with an outside support group of colleagues who are interested in social justice education or who are solo teaching their own social justice education courses is one way to create support. Providing an in-class perspective different from the solo facilitator's can be accomplished by bringing in outside speakers, choosing a variety of readings, and selecting videos and other activities that present perspectives from different social groups and positions.

Facilitator Responsibilities

Once potential facilitators make decisions about whether or not a solo or team facilitation format will be used, they need to turn their attention to a wide array of responsibilities they will have in planning and teaching social justice education courses (Arnold, Burke, James, Martin, & Thomas, 1991; Bunker, Nochajski, McGillacuddy, & Bennett, 1987; Eitington, 1984; Pfeiffer & Jones, 1975; Sharp, 1993; Silberman, 1990). These responsibilties include a) establishing an effective learning environment, b) choosing appropriate process leadership roles, and c) attending to a variety of leadership tasks.

Establishing an Effective Learning Environment

Attention to four broad areas helps establish an effective learning environment: a) time, b) teaching aids, c) task, and d) climate. These four areas are discussed below.

Time. From the teacher's perspective there never seems to be enough time in a social justice education course. Because institutionally determined course ending times rarely match the natural ebb and flow of learning, especially in a social justice education class, facilitators are constantly monitoring time and making decisions about how to best use the time available. Managing time includes planning activities that are appropriate for the class time, monitoring student participation time to ensure that all students have time to speak in small and large groups, and knowing when to cut short or extend an activity depending on how engaged students are and on the time remaining in the class period.

When planning time to be allotted for an activity, facilitators must include two essential elements: how much time students need to complete an activity and how much time students need to discuss the activity after it is completed. Much of the important learning from an activity comes from this discussion or processing time. In general, most novice facilitators either plan too many activities for a class period or underestimate how long it will take to complete an activity. As a result, there is insufficient time for processing activities. When discussion time is cut short or eliminated, students are left to make sense of activities on their own without the benefits of facilitator guidance or other participant perspectives. We recommend that facilitators allot at least as much time to discuss an activity as it takes to do an activity. For some activities, allotting twice the amount of time for discussion is necessary.

Teaching Aids. Using all available teaching aids enhances student learning by meeting the needs of different learning styles, abilities, and preferences. Using a variety of visual, audio, and computer technology also keeps the class fresh by avoiding routinized presentation patterns. In addition, many professionally produced videos and audiotapes on social justice issues are available and can be used in class or assigned as homework. Some are topically listed at the end of this volume.

Task. Students can participate most fully when they have some sense of control over their learning experience. Knowing the class objectives and agenda ahead of time is one way to provide that control. During the first class meeting, students should be given a class syllabus with evaluation criteria included. Providing clear and specific criteria for student evaluation during the first class is the best way to inform students about the task expectations for the course. We believe it is important to make clear to students from the beginning that they will not be evaluated on the basis of their beliefs and that agreeing with the perspectives presented in class is not a requirement. Instead, students in our courses are evaluated on their ability to describe their beliefs in relationship to class activities, readings, and other assignments. Students are also evaluated on their understanding of reading assignments, ability to analyze content, and complete prepared worksheets that ask specific questions.

Managing individual activities is another task responsibility for facilitators. This task requires that facilitators choose activities apppropriate to specific learning goals for the course. Facilitators must then describe and set up activities with clear directions. They should also prepare materials ahead of time and identify specific discussion questions to maximize learning from the activity. In addition, facilitators also monitor student participation to keep students on task and encourage different students to speak and express a variety of perspectives.

Climate. Climate responsibilities include addressing a) safety, b) comfort, c) tone, d) space, and e) access.

Safety. Establishing a safe environment in which students can discuss ideas, share feelings and experiences, and challenge themselves and each other to reevaluate opinions and beliefs is one of the primary facilitation responsibilities. Identifying a set of interaction guidelines at the beginning of the course is one way to meet this responsibility (see chapters 5 and 12 for more information about participation guidelines). Once identified and agreed upon by students and facilitators, it is the responsibility of the facilitators to monitor how well the guidelines are used and to remind students of them as needed during the course.

Comfort. When the class lasts two or more hours at a time, it is important to attend to a variety of personal comfort issues. Providing students with short breaks is essential. As a guide, we encourage a 10–15 minute break every 60–90 minutes. With day-long classes, meal breaks are important. As part of an introduction to the course, we recommend telling students when breaks will occur and the locations of the closest phones, bathrooms, and snack or drink machines are. Attending to these comfort issues in advance allows students to concentrate more completely on class activities.

Tone. We have found that creating a class atmosphere that is both serious and light works well. This means treating social justice content as the serious issue it is, but incorporating activities that include humor and playfulness as well as activities that can stimulate sadness, anger, or confusion. Planning class activities so that students can experience serious feelings without becoming enmeshed in them is an intentional process of deciding when students need a break, a chance to sit with feelings of discomfort, time to reflect, or a complete change of focus. Light activities refresh students, relieve tension and enable everyone to focus more effectively on the next activities. "Ice breaker" games, singing, or physical activities like group stretches can facilitate transitions between activities. Other activities such as role plays can be simultaneously light and serious as participants create humorous ways to illustrate or address serious issues.

Space. As a manager of space, a social justice education teacher must consider aspects of the physical environment that affect learning. Lighting, room temperature, ventilation, acoustics, room color, distracting noise, chair comfort and placement, access to audiovisual technology, and room cleanliness can all affect how inviting a classroom is and how well students can concentrate. We have found that teaching in classrooms with movable chairs allows students to arrange themselves in a variety of group configurations depending on the class activity. We prefer variations on circles and semi-circles because students can see and hear each other better than they can in a traditional audience style classroom in which all students face the teacher. Circles and semi-circles also encourage students to talk with each other and invite all students to be active participants in the class.

Access. Making sure that the classroom and bathrooms are accessible to students with disabilities is essential. In addition, we believe it is important at the beginning of the course to ask students to identify any particular needs they have that will make class activities more accessible (we ask students to indicate this information either on a written form or in private with the teachers). Teachers must make provisions that enable students with mobility, visual, hearing, learning, or environmental disabilities to participate successfully and fully in all class activities. Facilitators need to identify support services for students with disabilities and arrange to make written, visual, and oral class materials available to all students who need alternative formats.

Choosing Appropriate Process Leadership Roles

Facilitators take on several different process leadership roles that entail simultaneously monitoring individual, group, and intergroup interactions as students engage with the class content and develop as a group. For this reason, a basic understanding of group development and process theory provides facilitators with a way to make sense of group dynamics in the class (Bradford, 1978; Carew, Carew, & Blanchard, 1990; Moosbruker, 1987). We have found the information discussed in the group development and group dynamics literature to offer useful guides in facilitating social justice education classes (Johnson & Johnson, 1987; LaCoursiere, 1980; Walter & Stephan, 1996).

Some of the roles facilitators can play include: a) participant, b) guide, c) teacher, and d) activist. Individual teachers are more comfortable in some of these roles than others. The challenge is to develop the ability to adopt several roles and to know when each is most appropriate during different aspects of a class.

Participant. Social justice education is enriched when the facilitator can comfortably talk with students about her own experiences, feelings, and struggles related to social justice topics. As facilitators, we share with participants a lifelong journey learning about social justice issues. Disclosing some of our own journey with participants can deepen their understanding of these complex issues. This personal disclosure also models for students how to make personal connections themselves. For example, when a white facilitator tells students about his own confusion and fear as a participant in his first racism workshop, he helps white participants who are experiencing similar feelings to acknowledge and work through them. When a lesbian facilitator discusses her experience coming out to her family, she helps heterosexual students understand the fear and isolation many lesbian, gay, and bisexual people feel among their loved ones.

Guide. A social justice education teacher must also develop the ability to pose questions, raise contradictions, encourage and model self-reflection, and summarize group discussions. All of these skills are used to lead students to more sophisticated self-understanding and elaborated awareness of the dynamics of social oppression in their lives. The challenge of providing appropriate guidance is to encourage students to reevaluate "common sense" understandings they have developed through their own socialization without telling students what to believe.

Teacher. When information needs to be presented to students (statistics, research, conceptual models), facilitators need to be able to present it clearly and concisely. This public knowledge is an important part of understanding social injustice and an essential complement to discussions focused on personal experiences, feelings, and beliefs.

Activist. At times it is appropriate to encourage students to act on their beliefs. By providing a range of options and encouraging students to take action, the facilitator assists students in understanding how to transform a concern for social justice into concrete actions toward social change.

Leading Discussions

Leading discussions in social justice education classes is one of the most important and also one of the most difficult responsibilities a facilitator has. Because the activities in a social justice education course are designed to raise contradictions and challenge participants to rethink their understanding of social power relationships, discussions can be intense, and conflicting perspectives are often expressed. Structured activities without the opportunity to collectively reflect on and discuss their reactions to the activities limit the learning that students can achieve. We call this discussion of class activities "processing." Processing is an intentional and systematic guided discussion of a class activity that encourages the expression of divergent perspectives and enables participants to derive cognitive as well as experiential understanding from the activity. Leading these discussions requires teachers to trust the process that students need to go through to deepen their understanding of social justice issues. Effective facilitators guide and monitor discussions, but do not dominate them or become dogmatic (Dillon, 1994).

After each class activity, we lead participants through a processing progression that begins by focusing on their own *individual reactions* to the activity, guides them through a more *abstract analysis* of the oppression issues raised in the activity, and then to a focus on how they can *apply* this new information.

1. Individual Reflection. Immediately after an activity is finished, we ask participants to identify their personal thoughts and feelings about the activity by thinking about their reactions for a few minutes or by writing down their reactions privately. For example, after a panel presentation by a group of people with disabilities in an ableism workshop, we might ask participants to think about or write down their feelings as they heard different panelists talk about the obstacles they encounter in gaining access to public buildings or we might ask, "What feelings did you have as you listened to the panelists' stories?" or "What did the panelists say about their experiences as people with disabilities attending this school that you had never thought about before?"

2. Descriptions of Reactions. We then invite participants to talk about some of the thoughts and feelings stimulated by the activity that they identified during their individual reflection. This phase of processing can be accomplished in pairs, small groups, or with the whole group. The focus of this phase is to listen and understand, not challenge differing reactions. During this discussion, participants often realize that there is a variety of reactions to the same activity.

3. Analysis. After discussing personal reactions, we ask participants to shift their focus to a discussion of how the activity illustrates particular dynamics of oppression. We invite participants to identify questions, contradictions, or insights raised by the activity. We also ask participants to talk about parallels and connections among different forms of oppression that the activity helped them to better understand. For example, following a role-play about sexual harassment, we might ask participants, "How did the actions of men and women in this role play reflect gender socialization?" or "In what ways are the power dynamics in this situation similar to other forms of oppression?" or "How might the experiences of women from different racial groups compare in this situation?"

4. Summary. When drawing a discussion to a close, it is important for facilitators to help students achieve some degree of closure. The goal is not to reach agreement among all participants or to answer all student questions, but to bring participants to a place from which they are ready to make a transition to the next activity or to end the class session. In summarizing a discussion, facilitators and participants identify themes that emerged, unresolved questions asked, divergent perspectives expressed, or other important points made. This time to reflect enables students to step back and summarize learnings to develop a cognitive as well as an experiential understanding of the issues raised in the activity. For example, after concluding the Act Like a Man, Act Like a Woman activity (see chapter 7), the facilitator might say, "This activity shows how we are all socialized into our gender roles and how we learn to accept gender roles as natural rather than learned. Though we had some differences of opinion about the desirability of gender roles, we did agree that the roles are learned rather than innate. The next step is for us to take a look at some of the consequences of gender roles for men and women." During a classism workshop the facilitators might say, "From this discussion it appears that we have several different understandings of how to define social class in this group. Can we name those differences?" or "I can identify a theme in this discussion that focuses on a conflict between what many of us have believed about equal opportunity in the past and what we are beginning to see about the effects of class differences on economic opportunity."

We do not expect students to end a processing discussion feeling that they have completely resolved their discomfort with different ideas and perspectives. Some disorientation is a sign that students are grappling with new awareness and knowledge. We encourage students to notice their discomfort, challenge themselves to stay with it and try on new ideas rather than immediately retreat to the comfort of more familiar perspectives.

5. Application. The intention in this phase of the processing discussion is to help participants begin to identify how they might apply new understandings and information. We might ask participants to reflect briefly on how the information they learned in this activity might affect their future attitudes, beliefs, and actions. To help participants apply what they have learned in an activity during an antisemitism class we might ask, "How might this activity affect your feelings about scheduling group activities on Jewish holidays?" or "What will your response be the next time someone tells a joke that relies for its humor on Jewish stereotypes that you find offensive?" Because our courses include in Module 4 more extensive activities whose purpose is to help participants identify action plans they can carry out, we typically do not spend much time focused on behavioral change after each individual activity.

Discussion Leadership Tasks

During class discussions the leader has a number of possible leadership tasks depending on the needs of the group and the purpose of the discussion. Deciding when each of these tasks is appropriate requires experience and careful attention to the discussion process as it unfolds. The question, "What's the best leadership task for me to fill right now?" can be answered a number of ways.

Some of these roles include a) giving information, b) conceptualizing, c) reflecting, d) using silence, e) monitoring/redistributing, f) questioning, g) challenging, h) observing/reporting, i) accepting the expression of feelings, j) disclosing personal information, and k) addressing conflict.

Giving Information. Sometimes providing factual information in the form of statistics or descriptions of current events is useful. Students may request this information or the facilitator may decide that providing facts is a way to address misconceptions or fill a gap in the information students use to support a particular position. The following examples illustrate the information-giver role.

- A student states that most people are middle class. The facilitator responds, "Though most people tend to think of themselves as middle class, census statistics show that most of the wealth in the United States is controlled by less than 5 percent of the people."
- A student states that gay men are child molesters. The facilitator responds, "Police records show that well over 90 percent of child sexual abuse involves heterosexual men molesting female children."

Conceptualizing. Sometimes feelings overwhelm and cause participants to shut down or a discussion to lose its focus. The introduction of a conceptual model can provide participants with a way to understand their feelings in a broader theoretical context or can focus the discussion so that it can proceed more productively. For example, facilitators can refer to the oppression model, cycle of socialization, identity development theory, or learning edge/comfort zone models discussed in the introductory module to help students understand their experience (see chapter 5).

- Several students are arguing back and forth about whether or not it is reasonable to ask people to avoid wearing perfume in the workplace because someone may have an environmental illness aggravated by scents. The facilitator responds, "I think several of us might be on a learning edge here. Check and see if that is true for you. How can we decide what we each need to do to expand our comfort zone?"
- A white student is ashamed because she could not identify any African American historical figures on a short quiz. The facilitator responds, "How does the cycle of socialization we talked about earlier help us to understand how we have come to know or been kept from knowing about cultures different from our own?"

Reflecting. At times one of the most effective ways to encourage students to reevaluate their positions is to reflect back what they say. This reflection can enable students to understand the impact of their statements and to identify underlying assumptions.

- The facilitator repeats a student's statement, "So, what you are saying is that poor and homeless people have the same opportunity for advancement as people who have more financial resources. They are just too lazy."
- The facilitator repeats a student's statement, "You believe that Jews are not really discriminated against because they are mostly financially secure."

Using Silence. Many teachers and students are uncomfortable with silence in a classroom. After asking a question, teachers need to learn to wait rather than either answering their own question or asking another in order to fill a silence. In the social justice education classroom, silence can have many different meanings. Students often need silence to think about information or perspectives that challenge their understanding of an issue. We often encourage silence by asking students to individually "free write" their reactions to a question or a class activity before beginning group discussions.

Differentiating productive silence from bored or fearful silence is an important facilitator skill. Signs of a fearful or uncomfortable silence include lack of eye contact among students, yawning, physical shifting and movement in seats, or tense expressions on faces. If facilitators believe a silence reflects fear or discomfort, this situation can provide another learning opportunity and deepen the discussion. Asking students to write down their feelings at that moment or turn to a neighbor and share their thoughts provides students with a way to acknowledge and clarify their reactions. Asking students to do a quick "whip" around the circle in which each student in turn says one word that describes their feelings at that moment is another way to understand how students are reacting. Sometimes commenting on silence with the whole group opens the discussion. These strategies can restart discussion and potentially deepen individual understanding.

- In response to a processing question, the group is silent and no one is making eye contact. The facilitator says, "I'm not sure what this silence means. Can anyone say what you are thinking or feeling right now?" or "Let's just sit with this silence and give all of us time to sort out our feelings. When someone feels ready to answer one of the processing questions, please do."
- Following an emotional exchange between a Jew and a Gentile about the prevalence of antisemitism on campus, the participants are all silent for a long period of time. The facilitator says, "Why don't we each take a few minutes to jot down what we are feeling right now. Then we can talk with a partner before we come back to the whole group."

Monitoring/Redistributing. Several cues help facilitators assess how a discussion is progressing. Student engagement is reflected in body posture, the presence of side conversations, the number of students actively participating in the conversation, the attention given to whomever is speaking, and animation in how students are talking with each other. Monitoring the process provides the facilitator with information about what role to take in the discussion. For example, when one student or a small group of students dominate discussions or when some students are always silent, the facilitator can help to make a space for others to participate in a number of ways.

- One student has taken an active role in class discussions, contributing to every conversation. The facilitator says, "Before we hear from you again, Steve, I'd like to see if some of the people who have not spoken up would like to say something."
- The facilitator notices that a quiet participant has been trying to say something, but keeps getting cut off by other more active participants. The facilitator says, "Maria, it looks like you've been trying to get into this discussion. What would you like to say?"

- The facilitator notices that five participants have not said anything during large group discussions. He says, "Let's do a quick pass around the circle. Each person say a short sentence that describes your reaction to this activity. Choose to pass if you wish."
- The facilitator notices that a small group of participants are dominating the discussions. She says, "We have several people here who are comfortable speaking out in the large group and have spoken up a lot. I'm going to ask those who have talked a lot today to count to ten before you speak so that we make it easier for some of the other folks to join our discussion."

Questioning. Asking questions is often an effective way to challenge assumptions, solicit factual information, and redirect discussions. Rather than directly challenging student perspectives, asking questions encourages students to examine their own assumptions and values in a respectful way.

- What kinds of portrayals of Latino/a people do you see in the movies and on television? How do these portrayals affect your perception of what Latino/a people are like?
- What image of people with disabilities do you get when you watch the Jerry Lewis Telethon?

Challenging. Sometimes it is useful to directly challenge what a student is saying if she or he is personally attacking a classmate or if a student says something that is clearly inaccurate and correction is needed.

- A participant is rolling her eyes and looking away when a man tries to challenge her belief in the fairness of affirmative action programs. The facilitator says to the woman, "There needs to be room for all of us to express our beliefs here. We may not all agree, but we need to be able to disagree respectfully. We need to express our disagreement in ways that are consistent with our discussion guidelines."
- A participant states his belief that gay men want to be women. The facilitator says, "People who want to be the other gender are called transsexuals. Transsexuals and other transgender people can be gay, lesbian, heterosexual, or bisexual. Most gay men are as comfortable with their gender identity as heterosexual men are."

Observing/Reporting. Naming what is happening in a group discussion helps students to understand how the dynamics of oppression are operating within the group. This requires the facilitator to be conscious of intergroup and interpersonal dynamics (Gudykunst, 1994; Narayan, 1988; Porter, 1982).

- In a small group discussion of institutional racism, only the two men in the group are talking and they direct all their comments to each other. The facilitator says, "I notice that even though there are more women in this group, the men are talking more and seem to be looking to each other as they talk. Has anyone else noticed this? How can we be sure everyone has a chance to talk and be listened to?"
- In a racism class white students are directing questions to the students of color as if their role in the class is to teach white students about racism. The white facili-

tator says, "I notice that we white folks sometimes tend to ask questions of the black, Asian, Latino/a, and Native American students about racism. Has anyone else noticed this and what do you think of it?"

Accepting the Expression of Feelings. For some teachers and students the expression of feelings in a classroom is an unusual experience and takes some getting used to (Auvine, Densmore, Extrom, Poole, & Shanklin, 1978). Students get angry at each other, themselves, and the facilitators. Sometimes students cry while remembering painful experiences or hearing a classmate tell a painful story. Students feel frustrated by the pervasiveness of social injustice. Other students are angry—they feel deceived because they never understood oppression before. Neither students nor teachers should feel that the expression of intense emotion is required for effective learning. Everyone should be prepared, however, for the expression of honest feelings as they happen at different times in the course.

- A student begins to cry as she recalls how her younger brother who has a developmental disability was teased by classmates at school. The facilitator says, "It seems like that is still a painful memory for you. Thanks for telling us about this experience. I think it really helps us all to feel how deeply name-calling can affect us. Do other people have similar memories?"
- In asking for students to go around the circle and give a one-word description of what they are feeling in reaction to an intense video about the Holocaust, the facilitator says, "Please pass if you want to keep your feelings private right now."

Disclosing Personal Information. When facilitators express feelings in reaction to discussions about social injustice it provides students with models for what is acceptable in class and can help students feel more comfortable expressing their own feelings. Emotional reactions to social justice education are a natural and human response for teachers as well as students. Because of this facilitators can be triggered by statements students make just as students can trigger emotional reactions in each other. When a facilitator is feeling emotionally triggered, it is important to stay in the facilitator role in responding. Having a co-facilitator in these situations is helpful because rarely are both facilitators triggered at the same time, so that the one who is not triggered can think more clearly about what leadership role to take (refer to chapter 5 for more information about triggers).

Facilitators need to choose when to disclose personal reactions or stories and to be clear about the purpose of this disclosure. It is never appropriate for facilitators to work out their own issues during a class. This important work is better attended to at some other time. If facilitators tell too many personal stories or talk about their own experiences too much, participants might begin to discount the course as the facilitator's "personal agenda." All personal disclosure by the facilitators should be for the purpose of helping students achieve a better understanding of the topic, such as telling participants at the beginning of a racism course: "I remember the first racism workshop I went to. I was afraid that I would say something that someone would think meant I was a racist. I was so afraid of making mistakes that I never said a word and never got to ask the questions I needed to." The facilitator in this situation is using a personal disclosure to help students understand that reactions they might be having to beginning the course are not bad or unusual (further discussion in chapters 14 and 15).

Students depend on facilitators to provide a safe and stable class environment. Facilitators need to keep in mind that, though they might disclose personal stories and reactions, they are not participants and need to keep their facilitator's hat firmly in place.

Addressing Conflict. Numerous opportunities for conflict arise in a social justice education class. Conflict can arise at the intrapersonal level as students are confronted with internal conflicts between their unexamined perspectives and information, and experiences they encounter in class that challenge these perspectives (Tatum, 1994). At the interpersonal and intergroup level students encounter conflicting beliefs and experiences among themselves as they interact in class activities. Sometimes students or groups of students are in conflict with facilitators. It is important for students to be able to challenge ideas and behaviors without personally attacking individuals or groups within the class. Our goal is to encourage the expression of conflicting ideas. Conflicts of this nature are an integral part of the learning process necessary to growth and change. Productive conflict means that all partipants have a voice, their right to express differing perspectives is assured, and all participants listen to and challenge each other and the facilitators respectfully.

One of the most important strategies for ensuring productive conflict is to prepare students for it and to help them understand that conflict and dissonant feelings are an expected and helpful part of the learning process. Clearly stated participation guidelines and skillful facilitation of interactions within the group provide students with a process for expressing conflicting ideas, experiences, and feelings. We use such concepts as the "comfort zone," "learning edges," the use of "I statements," and the concept of "triggers" to help students develop a vocabulary and process for recognizing and dealing with conflict (see chapter 5).

Alternative Discussion Formats

We use a variety of discussion formats, including whole class, small groups, triads, and pairs. Whole class discussions are a staple part of all classes. In these discussions facilitators have the most control over discussions and can effectively assume a variety of leadership roles. Two disadvantages of whole class discussions are that some participants are reluctant to speak in front of the whole group, and other students dominate or get locked into face-to-face debate. Therefore, we also use small group discussions (four to six people) to provide a more comfortable discussion environment for participants who do not like talking in whole group discussions and to ensure that all students have the opportunity to speak. We also use triads when we want to provide participants with even more opportunities to talk. In groups of three, students can have an extended conversation that is not possible in the large or small group discussions. Pair discussions are also useful, especially if the topic is potentially more sensitive for students or to help students gather their thoughts before participating in a larger group discussion. Pair discussions are also helpful after conflict or a particularly emotional exchange in the large group to help participants vent their own reactions in a more protected environment. Individual reflection time is used to enable participants to identify and organize their feelings and thoughts before talking in either small or large groups. We encourage students to keep a class journal in which they write their reactions, questions, and thoughts during individual reflection times.

Facilitators can take different roles during small group discussions. They can announce to the groups that they are available if anyone has questions and then allow the groups to work independently unless invited to join them. Facilitators can also "float" among different groups stopping to listen or even participate in the discussions of several groups. We take on both roles at different times during a class, depending on the group task, participant preferences, and our own energy level.

Common Student Reactions to Social Justice Education

Students have a wide range of reactions ranging from excitement about gaining a new perception of social justice issues to anger at having some of their perceptions of social justice issues challenged (Andrzejewski, 1993; Tatum, 1994). In our experience most students enjoy the challenge to their understanding of these complex issues and appreciate the opportunity to engage others in discussions about social justice. It is not realistic, however, to expect students to immediately embrace all, or even most, of the new perspectives they encounter in a social justice education course.

Below I have identified some reactions to having one's world view questioned. I encourage facilitators to review the identity development model presented in chapter 2 and applied in chapters 3, 12, and 15. This conceptual tool is a valuable resource for putting student reactions into a conceptual context and guiding facilitator responses to these reactions. The possible responses to student reactions are discussed in chapters 5–11 in the context of specific single issue courses. I have also summarized some strategies in this chapter at the end of each section describing different student reactions. The student reactions I will describe here are a) resistance, b) anger, c) immobilization, d) disassociation, and e) conversion.

Resistance

When we raise social justice issues in a classroom we unsettle both unconscious and deeply held beliefs about society, self, and social relations. This disequilibrium can create resistance, as familiar ground shifts and students encounter uncertainty, doubt, and self-questioning as they attempt to regain their balance. We see this resistance as an inevitable and potentially valuable part of the educational process.

We make a distinction between psychological notions of resistance within individual psyches and an educational view of resistance as part of the learning process when previously learned ideas and values are exposed to contradiction and challenge. We understand this educational view of resistance as a response to disequilibrium and part of the legitimate questions and challenges students raise as they encounter both intellectual ideas and their own personal experience in light of material presented in class.

Resistance can take many different forms, but is usually expressed as a refusal to explore or attribute credibility to the idea that social oppression is real. Most students in social justice education courses experience some kind of resistance. Having one's world view challenged or being asked to acknowledge unasked for privilege or understanding how one is discriminated against are painful and uncomfortable experiences. Resistance can come from members of both the agent and target groups. Helping students understand their resistance and work through it is a vital part of social justice education.

Students need to be able to express resistance without fear of negative sanctions from the teachers or other students in the class. Unless students feel comfortable about expressing their honest reactions, class discussions are likely to be shallow and forced. Remind students about participation guidelines and rely on the use of questions and contradictions rather than dogmatic or didactic teaching to challenge students' thinking. The following student reactions illustrate different kinds of resistance. This is a list of examples and is not intended to be all-inclusive.

Claim that the status quo is part of a "natural order." For example in a heterosexism class, some heterosexual students might claim that physical anatomy "proves" that homosexual relationships are unnatural and therefore lesbians, gay men, and bisexual people should be discriminated against. In a racism class, some white students might use their belief in the innate intellectual superiority of whites to explain statistics on crime, educational achievement, or welfare.

Invalidation of target group member's experience. When agent group members are confronted with a description of social reality that contradicts their own experience, they sometimes question the credibility of the target group's experience. They may claim that target group members are oversensitive or are exaggerating their experiences. Others may claim that target group members are dwelling too much on past injustice, that the situation has changed and that the issues being raised have already been addressed. Gentile students might claim that the Holocaust happened fifty years ago and that Jews are no longer oppressed, or they might even question whether or not the Holocaust occurred. Students might claim that most people on welfare are taking advantage of the system rather than finding a job and working like everyone else.

Agents' need to have own pain and hurt recognized. When agents do not differentiate between the hurt they experience and the oppression that target group members experience, this lack of distinction can impede learning. For example, in a sexism workshop some men might claim that they, too, are targeted by sexism because of rigid gender roles and the social sanctions applied to men who violate gender stereotypes. We believe that it is important for agents to understand the ways in which their lives are limited or diminished by oppression and for facilitators to provide opportunities for agents to explore how they are hurt by oppression. However, we also believe it is essential for agents to understand the differences between their experience of hurt and the targets' experience of oppression.

Protection of agent group members by target group members. Sometimes in a sexism class, women will join with some of the men claiming either that women do not experience sexism anymore or that men are victims of "reverse sexism." Occasionally women will protest that the men in the course are being criticized unfairly when issues of male privilege are raised.

Agents focus on an identity in which they are members of the targeted group. Some participants have a difficult time thinking about themselves from the perspective of their agent identities. This is often true for students who are very much attuned to and angry about one or more of their targeted identities. They "live" in these targeted identities and find it difficult to shift that part of their identity to the background in order to focus on an agent identity. For example, in a heterosexism class, an African American heterosexual man focuses only on his experience of racial discrimination rather than thinking about the privilege he receives as a heterosexual. Because students bring all of their identities, both agent and target, to every class, it is essential to integrate this complexity into the course and use these multiple identities to help students draw connections across oppressions. A student's experience of oppression as a target group member in one area can provide a bridge of understanding to other issues in which she or he is an agent group member if students are encouraged to see parallels and connections among different forms of oppression.

Invalidation of the teacher. Sometimes students will claim that the teacher is biased, especially if she is a member of the target group in a single issue course. For example, in an antisemitism course, a Jewish facilitator might be criticized by Gentile students as too personally involved to be "objective." On the other hand, facilitators who are members of the agent group are sometimes invalidated by both agent and target group participants because students do not understand how an agent can understand the oppression without personal experience. Students also invalidate teachers by claiming that the class is exaggerating the extent of the oppression or that only a small number of disgruntled target group members are complaining.

Invalidation of the class. Sometimes students attack class assignments and activities rather than focusing directly on perspectives with which they do not agree. Students might also claim that the class is a form of indoctrination in which they are not free to express a range of beliefs or experiences. These students might attribute all attempts to challenge the status quo to "political correctness" and believe that they will be penalized if they do not agree with a particular party line presented in class. This belief allows them to dismiss the entire course and the issues raised in class without critically examining them.

Anecdote raised to the status of generalized fact. A participant, usually a member of the agent group, will sometimes tell a story they heard on the news or from a friend. In this story the agent group is victimized in some way by the target group either directly or as the result of a program or policy intended to prevent discrimination against targets. The participant uses this anecdote to invalidate target group members' experience and even the oppression model. A student might tell a story of an instance where a man of color beat up a white man or how a white person was denied a promotion because of affirmative action.

Domination of class discussion. Occasionally students will resist by arguing every point made in class with which they do not agree. They take more than their share of talking time in class, challenging the legitimacy of information presented or the validity of experiences described and presenting their own perspectives as "truth."

Hostile silence. Sometimes students express their resistance by refusing to participate in small or large group discussions. This silence can be accentuated by such defensive posture as arms folded across the chest, caps pulled down over eyes, or focusing on non-class related reading or other activities.

We try to maintain the perspective that all students are engaged in a learning process and a journey through resistance is not the final destination. The struggles we see in class often result in learnings that emerge later on, sometimes long after the course has ended. Facilitators need to trust the process of the course to persuade students to think about new perspectives and have faith in the potential for change in even the most resistant students.

Several strategies are useful in addressing student resistance. It is imperative that student grades are not dependent on their beliefs (see chapter 12). In addition, facilitators need to make sure they invite all students to discuss their perspectives and that all perspectives are received respectfully, even those that challenge the legitimacy of oppression. Adhering to the participation guidelines established at the beginning of class is essential so that divergent student beliefs can be expressed. In addition, the inclusion of videos, research, statistics, guest speakers, and outside readings provide students with sources of information about oppression other than the teacher and members of the class. The use of journals in which students write their reactions to class discussions and activities can provide a way for them to express their perspectives and feelings. These journals, if written and responded to by the facilitators, can provide a way to encourage private and confidential discussions with resistant students. Inviting students to make appointments for private discussions can also help facilitators better understand student resistance and identify ways to encourage students to consider different perspectives.

Anger

Some students react to what they are learning in a social justice education class with anger. Our goal is to acknowledge anger and provide a constructive way for students to express their feelings. Students who are members of agent groups sometimes are angry that rights they assumed were available to everyone or achievements they have always accepted as earned are described as unearned privileges not equally available to everyone. Target group members experience anger at the injustice they and other members of their social group have experienced. Target members may also experience anger and impatience at some agent classmates' resistance and lack of awareness about oppression issues. Both agents and targets may be angry that their unquestioned belief in basic equality and fairness in the United States is being challenged.

Strategies to address anger include providing students with ample opportunity to express their anger in ways that do not target other participants or the teacher. Journal writing, pair discussions, conferences with teachers, individual written assignments, and time spent in caucus groups are all ways to address anger among students. Teaching as part of a team is an effective way for facilitators to maintain their balance and perspective when dealing with angry students. If the teaching team is mixed, then it is particularly useful for the member of the team who shares the angry student's social group membership to speak with her or him.

Immobilization

Students who feel overwhelmed by new feelings and information in reaction to what they are learning in social justice education courses often feel immobilized. Familiar ways of experiencing the world and social differences in the world are challenged and, in response to this challenge, some students shut down. They feel overloaded and hypersensitive to issues that they may never have been aware of before. These students begin noticing oppression "everywhere" and are overwhelmed by this flood of awareness. These feelings are uncomfortable and shutting down is an attempt to regain a sense of equilibrium. This response can take several different forms.

Withdrawal from participation. Some students might actually physically withdraw from the class or return late from breaks. More typically, these students remain in the class, but do not participate in class discussions.

Sense of powerlessness to change oppressive conditions. Sometimes students, both agent and target members, get stuck in feelings of helplessness. They feel powerless to do anything to change the oppression they now acknowledge exists. To think further about issues raised in the class is painful because they believe they cannot make a real difference. The problems related to oppression feel too pervasive and deeply rooted for them to believe they can effect change.

Fear of being perceived as a bigot. Most students come to a social justice education course with a desire to learn and grow, but they also bring with them a fear of unintentionally saying or doing something in class that will lead others to see them as prejudiced. Because there is so much new information and awareness for some students, they do not fully trust themselves to decide what behavior is appropriate. This fear can stifle discussion and lead to shallow and safe participation as students engage in self-protection rather than self-exploration.

Agent guilt about their agent status. Some students respond to learning about social oppression by feeling guilt and shame about their agent status. They have difficulty taking pride in their agent identities and have difficulty moving beyond feelings of shame and guilt. White students often enter racism courses with an enormous burden of guilt about being white in a world they acknowledge as racist (Tatum, 1994). Unfortunately, some of these students are immobilized by this guilt and even unwilling to move beyond it to taking some responsibility for action against racism.

Fear of conflict and disagreement. Especially when students have a prior relationship with each other outside of the course, they can be reluctant to disagree with each other or to express dissenting perspectives. This can happen in a number of ways. Sometimes students who do not see social oppression as an issue in their lives are afraid to say so when they perceive that the rest of the group does. They may not feel safe enough to disclose their thoughts and feelings. For example, a Latina student might not speak out about her experience of racism on campus if the white students in class do not seem to recognize racism or understand how they benefit from racism on campus.

An effective way to address immobilization is to help students identify the people and groups in their lives with whom they have influence or to remember individual people who have had an influence on their lives. Reviewing the historical treatment of different targeted social groups also enables students to see how oppressive conditions change over time and to find their place in a larger social change context. Identifying specific actions that individuals can take also helps students to feel empowered. Rehearsing new behaviors in small groups or setting up support groups out of class enables students to believe they can make a difference. Providing historical and contemporary models of agents acting as allies against social injustice helps students see how social change can occur. Finally, insure that mixed classes include enough members of both agent and target groups. This encourages and supports individual students and helps them to express divergent perspectives, challenge dominant understandings, and participate fully.

Distancing

When students respond by distancing, they object to social injustice, but they do not understand their own role in perpetuating social oppression. They understand the issues presented and believe it is important for target groups to receive fair treatment, but they distance themselves from the problem.

The need to see only the most extreme bigots as agents of oppression. In a racism course white students will sometimes spend time differentiating themselves from the "real" racists who join white supremacist groups or who actively and intentionally discriminate against people of color. By only focusing on racism in its more extreme or overt forms, these white students avoid examining their own subtle racism.

Willing to focus on the oppression of targets, but not on the privilege of agents. Sometimes agents enter class with the expectation that the course is only about understanding how target group members are oppressed. They believe that discrimination is wrong and see their role in fighting oppression as "helping" target group members. For example, non-disabled students sometimes come to an ableism class feeling pity or empathy for the "plight" of people with disabilities. They are unprepared to have their own attitudes about disability challenged or to explore how their status as temporarily able people provides them with privilege. These participants are often angry and confused to find that an important part of the oppression equation is understanding that they benefit from oppression and that eliminating oppression requires that they acknowledge and give up their self-perceptions as neutral bystanders who can choose to help others or not.

We try to help students avoid distancing themselves from these issues by planning activities that enable them to see the costs of social injustice to them personally. We also spend part of every course focusing on privilege and helping agents understand that they benefit from oppression even if they do not actively promote it. By exploring how they can recognize privilege and decline to take advantage of it or use it in the service of eliminating oppression, agents can take a proactive stand against social injustice.

Conversion

Conversion occurs when students embrace the perspectives presented in class without critical examination. Rather than resisting or feeling angry or immobilized, they become "born again" converts to the struggle against social injustice with little tolerance for anyone with a different perspective. For example, a man may challenge everyone in the class who uses language he thinks is demeaning to women or present himself as superior to other men in the class because of his sensitivity to women's issues, all the while taking far more than his share of "air time" in class discussions and speaking for women in the class as well. Another example is a lesbian who is critical of other lesbians, gay men, and bisexual people in the class who do not come out.

Correcting others. Students who have experienced a conversion often take on the responsibility of monitoring and correcting the language used by other students in the class and generally have little or no tolerance for dissenting views. This reaction can inhibit authentic participation.

It would be disingenuous to pretend that a social justice education course is neutral or objective. Students are correct in perceiving that there is a particular perspective represented in this course. It is essential, however, that there is room in the course for all perspectives to be heard and challenged respectfully. When facilitators or students squelch the expression of views or experiences that are counter to the underlying beliefs guiding the course, we are vulnerable to charges of promoting political correctness. Students who appoint themselves "PC monitors" in a social justice education course can be intolerant of other students who use the "wrong" language or do not reflect the "correct" understanding of oppression. This intolerance contributes to an unsafe class environment in which students cannot explore and challenge their own thinking freely. It is important to assure students that we all have prejudices and that this course is an opportunity to examine them and choose beliefs based on new information and understanding, rather than allowing our prejudices to guide our thinking without conscious reflection.

Romanticizing target groups. Occasionally agent group members who have had conversion experiences in class or who enter the class as converts develop an idealized, unrealistic, and ultimately dehumanizing image of target group members. They defer to target group members in class and are reluctant to disagree with them. They sometimes identify more with target group members and their culture and express discomfort with their agent identity. They also distance themselves from other agents in an attempt to gain favor with target group members. They can become angry or confused when target group members express a need or preference for some class time in separate agent and target groups.

Reversing power dynamics. Target group members sometimes use their status as "victims" to intimidate agent group members in class. In this "tyranny of the targets" they play on agent guilt and confusion and misinterpret the course as an opportunity to tell agents how they should act, what they should believe, or to vent anger at them. These target group members set themselves up as experts who are the final arbiters of acceptable and unacceptable attitudes and behaviors from the agents.

Demonizing agent groups. Target group members sometimes direct their anger about oppression at all members of the agent group. They are critical of everything that agents in the class say or do, and can refuse to participate in small groups with classmates who are members of agent groups. An agent group member might express a lack of identification with or hostility to their own group and a preference for spending time with target group members. Often this preference grows out of a sense of shame about agents' role in perpetuating oppression and a desire to dis-associate themselves from this connection.

Strategies to address conversion reactions include reminding students that stereotyping groups of people based on their group memberships is counterproductive, no matter who is doing the stereotyping. Talking in the beginning of the class about how adhering to a strict set of rules about language can stifle discussion is a proactive way to discourage students from getting into "PC contests." Modeling ways that students can express their perspective without correcting classmates or presenting their perspective as the only acceptable one is also useful. Activities that help students see each others as human beings rather than merely as members of social groups with unequal power can also discourage students from objectifying each other on the basis of social group membership. If caucus groups based on social group membership are used, it is helpful to prepare students for this early on and to prepare them to rejoin the whole group afterwards.

The goal of facilitating social justice education is to create an environment in which participants are invited to discuss and raise questions about common understandings and choose new beliefs and actions based on a critical examination of their own values. Consideration of the facilitation issues discussed in this chapter can assist social justice education teachers in planning and conducting classes in which all students, agents and targets, have a productive learning experience.

14

Knowing Ourselves As Instructors

Lee Anne Bell, Sharon Washington,
Gerald Weinstein, Barbara Love

While much has been written about how to engage students in social justice courses, little attention has been paid to the teachers in these classrooms. Yet few teachers would claim that raising issues of oppression and social justice in the classroom is a neutral activity. Content as cognitively complex and socially and emotionally charged as social justice, is inevitably challenging at both personal and intellectual levels. In the social justice classroom, we struggle alongside our students with our own social identities, biases, fears, and prejudices. We too need to be willing to examine and deal honestly with our values, assumptions, and emotional reactions to oppression issues. The self-knowledge and self-awareness that we believe are desirable qualities in any teacher become crucial in social justice education.

For most faculty, our professional training has not prepared us to address emotionally and socially charged issues in the classroom. Social justice education is not simply new content but often a radical change in process as well. "Among educators there has to be an acknowledgement that any effort to transform institutions so that they reflect a multicultural standpoint must take into consideration the fears teachers have when asked to shift their paradigms" (hooks, 1994, 36).

Weinstein and O'Bear (1992) asked a group of twenty-five university faculty colleagues from different disciplines to respond anonymously to the question, "What makes you nervous about raising issues of racism in your classroom?" These faculty expressed several concerns that are relevant to our topic. Here, we examine these and other concerns identified in our discussions for this chapter. Sometimes we use a common voice in which "we" refers to the four authors. Other times we use a single voice, identified as Sharon, Jerry, Lee, or Barbara. These quotes come from our taped discussions or from the article by Weinstein and O'Bear.

Below, we describe each concern with examples to illustrate how we grapple with it in our own teaching. Although we treat each issue separately, they do in fact overlap and interact constantly. Further, the strategies we discuss are not intended as standardized responses applicable to any teaching situation. Raising oppression issues in the classroom can be exciting and rewarding, but never entirely comfortable or predictable, especially when group interaction is such a central part of the process.

Awareness of Our Own Social Identities

In most traditional classrooms, our particular social and cultural identities as teachers usually remain in the background, but in the social justice classroom where social identity is central to the content, the significance of who we are often takes center stage. In the study by Weinstein and O'Bear (1992), faculty expressed heightened awareness about their social identities that required them to be more conscious of their attitudes and assumptions, and often raised feelings of guilt, shame, or embarrassment at behaviors and attitudes of members of their own social group(s). Whether we are members of the privileged or targeted group with respect to particular issues inevitably influences how we react to material under discussion as well as how our students are likely to perceive us.

> Jerry: Even though I come into the classroom as a professional teacher, I do not leave my social identities at the door. I am a blend of such identities, for example, white, male, Jewish, heterosexual, beyond middle age, working-class background, now middle class. Especially when I am conducting antisemitism courses, I am constantly reminded of my conflicts about being at the same time a member of a group that is targeted by antisemitism and a member of the dominant white, male group in this society, with all of the inequities and privileges associated with each status.

As teachers we can offer our experience with both dominant and targeted identities as a way to join with students, expand the boundaries in the room for discussing these subjects, and model being open to exploring our own relative positions of power and privilege in relation to different oppression issues.

> Barbara: African American students often express difficulty in seeing themselves in the role of dominant or agent of oppression. They are so closely identified with the role of target or victim of oppression that they fail to see how they benefit from agent aspects of their identity. I grew up with a keen awareness of myself as a black person, but with no understanding at all of the ways I benefit from my status as a Christian. I gathered lots of information about disability oppression, but gained a much deeper understanding of systematic exclusion of people with disabilities when I suffered an injury that left me temporarily disabled.

The historical and experiential complexity of social identity further complicates awareness. The various meanings of group membership for people from different geographic regions, historical periods, and family experiences, yet who are members of the same social group, are important to note. As teachers we need to be careful about the categories we use and conscious of how individual members of a social group experience oppression in diverse ways.

> Barbara: Being Black means different things to different African heritage people. A light-skinned middle- or upper-class African heritage person growing up in the Northeast in the 1990s will describe the experience of being Black very differently from a dark-skinned working-class person raised in the South in the 1950s. Neither experience is any more or less authentically Black. While different, both experiences interact with a system of racism that extends through time, geographic region, and particular individual/family locations.

Exploration of our own social identities and relationships with other members of the groups to which we belong can help us as teachers to remember these complexities. Though as individuals we experience the oppression directed toward our group, no one individual can ever embody the totality of group subjugation. This is one of the central limitations of identity politics. We are constantly balancing the broad strokes of group oppression with the finer shadings of individual experience. This balancing extends to assumptions we make about our students. If we can be conscious of our own identity explorations we may be more likely to remember that that they too may be coming from a range of different places.

> Sharon: What may be in the forefront for a student of color at a particular moment may not be race, but sexual orientation, physical ability, or age. Just because a student is in a wheelchair does not mean disability is the issue that is currently primary. At that point in life, a student may be more engaged with issues of gender, race, or sexual orientation.

As faculty, we find it helpful to reflect on the experiences that have shaped our various identities and note the particular issues with which we feel most comfortable as well as those we tend to avoid, distort, or fear. This knowledge can be helpful preparation for engaging with social justice issues in the classroom, and enable us to respond thoughtfully to students even when we ourselves feel exposed.

> Lee: As a white woman, racism is an ongoing learning process for me. I keep realizing new areas where I'm unaware, learning and hopefully growing, but it is never closed and finished content. If I acknowledge my own ongoing learning I can be more open to what students raise for me to look at. Being aware of my own struggles to be honest with myself and open to new information hopefully also helps me to be more empathetic and supportive of their struggles.

As teachers, we can also try to be thoughtful about our own different levels of awareness on particular issues and realize that our own consciousness is likely to shift and change through our ongoing learning about the various forms and manifestations of oppression in our society.

Confronting Our Own Biases

A second issue noted by faculty in the Weinstein and O'Bear study had to do with fear of being labeled racist, sexist, and so on, or discovering previously unrecognized prejudices within ourselves. This included having to question our own assumptions, being corrected or challenged publicly (especially by members of the targeted group), and encountering our own fears and romanticized notions about members of targeted groups.

No one who has taken on the task of teaching about oppression wants to be thought of as homophobic, racist, sexist, classist, antisemitic, or ableist. Yet we know that recognizing and rooting out deeply socialized, and often unconscious, prejudices and practices is difficult. Faculty understandably feel a sense of vulnerability that what is out of our awareness will emerge to confront us as we engage these issues in our classrooms.

> Lee: I grew up in the Midwest and didn't meet a Jewish person, or at least was not aware I had, until I went to college. I thought that meant I couldn't be antisemitic. Slowly I came to realize all the assumptions and stereotypes I breathe in just living in this culture. I still have unexpected moments of new learning when I suddenly become aware of something I have missed or overlooked that is tied to antisemitism. And I think, "Oh no, how could I

> not have seen this?" I can berate myself for not noticing, or try to avoid the discomfort of this awareness, or I can try to be grateful that at least now I can do something about it.

One example of an activity that went awry because of unexamined assumptions is illustrative. Lee had planned an activity to elicit a discussion of male and female gender socialization, using a fishbowl format in which men and women could listen to each other without interruption.

> I was so intent on gender issues in my planning that I didn't anticipate the discomfort a gay man might feel in the rather raucous male-bonding discussion that took place among the men in the fish bowl emphasizing sports and heterosexual dating. I had not anticipated the way a gay man might have a very different relationship to his experiences of maleness. I noticed the student's discomfort and began to guess my mistake, which he confirmed when we talked about it later.

This lesson serves as a helpful reminder in planning courses to continually ask, "Who are the students I am imagining as I do this planning?" and "Who might I be leaving out?"

Barbara notes how encountering previously unrecognized prejudice enables her to be more effective and empathetic with her students:

> An important part of my own learning has been to recognize the ways I have internalized oppression and how it permeates my consciousness without my awareness. For example, learning to confront the homophobia at the heart of my own religious tradition has been vital to being able to support students who are seeking to learn about heterosexism and homophobia while remaining loyal to their own religious beliefs.

This self-examination is a lifelong process. We all have areas of limited vision, particularly where we are members of the dominant group. If we can model openness to ongoing learning, our students will benefit and we can be less judgmental and more self-accepting when we make mistakes or uncover new areas of ignorance or lack of awareness, and not retreat from this difficult but important work.

Responding to Biased Comments in the Classroom

Faculty anxiety about how to respond to biased comments in the classroom is understandable. Those interviewed by Weinstein and O'Bear expressed fears about dealing with biased comments from dominant members in the presence of targeted members, especially when such remarks were made by members of a dominant social group to which they themselves belonged.

Language plays such an important role in perpetuating oppression that miscommunication and misunderstanding can easily arise. Targeted group members usually have a long history of developing sensitivity to negative cues that signal oppressive attitudes. They have been subjected to, suffered from, discussed and thought about such cues throughout the course of their lives and so are highly tuned to note them. Dominant group members on the other hand are often oblivious to the effects of their language on targeted group members and in fact are often shocked to realize this effect. Thus the potential for breakdown in communication, hurt feelings, defensiveness, and recriminations is high. As educators we want to insure that our language does not inhibit discussion or contribute to any student feeling excluded. Setting ground rules and establishing a commonly agreed upon procedure for addressing offensive statements when they arise are ways to address this problem through classroom process (see chapters 5 and 13).

As teachers, we ourselves are not immune to these triggers either and need to recognize beforehand those to which we are most vulnerable.

> Jerry: As a Jew, particularly when I am teaching about antisemitism, I am vulnerable to all the dominant signals concerning my group. Some version of all the stereotyped statements and attitudes that have pursued me my entire life are bound to be expressed. I always experience those expressions and attitudes with some degree of pain, for they restimulate past fears. When I hear those expressions I may get angry and want to retaliate, but I know that acting directly on my feelings would be inappropriate and counterproductive to the goals of the session and my role as teacher and facilitator. By anticipating typical responses that I have experienced before I can prepare myself to use these triggers intentionally and constructively during the class.

Greater self-knowledge about how we typically react in situations of tension can give us more options for responding in thoughtful ways when conflicts arise. For example, we can examine our motives for avoiding conflict, or proving ourselves as unprejudiced, or wanting people to like us. When we pay attention to our internal dialogue in these situations, we can make more conscious choices in the moment:

> Sharon: I make sure that I know myself in relation to the material and the particular issues that give me the most discomfort or anxiety. If I feel like a well of emotion, I remind myself this class is for the students. Once I had someone co-teaching a particular session and this person just lost it and raged at the class. I went away thinking, "Wow, she just threw up all over the class!"

There are several ways to prepare beforehand to deal with our own triggers as they arise. Having a support system, a person or group with whom we can discuss these issues, share feelings, and get support is very important. For example, Sharon regularly meets with a friend and colleague, another African American woman, to debrief and talk about her classes. She has also at times used a journal to note her feelings and reactions as the class progresses. This process is often a helpful reminder at points in a course where resistance is particularly high or she is feeling down on herself, and allows her to recognize that these are predictable parts of the process rather than flaws in the class or her own teaching. These realizations can be very reassuring.

An appreciation for the process people go through in developing awareness about oppression can also help us acquire patience and understanding when dealing with our own feelings as teachers.

> Lee: I can feel very impatient sometimes. But when I shift my frame of reference to one of trying to understand the process by which people can be engaged in unlearning oppressive attitudes, it kind of unhooks me. Then it becomes a challenge to figure out, "Okay, how is this person thinking about these issues now and what is going to be the way to help them to try out a different perspective?"

Attention to process in the moment occurs on two levels. One level relates to our awareness about how students may be thinking about or experiencing what is going on in the classroom: "Why does that student say or think that, and what is getting triggered for him or her?" On a parallel track, we note and try to understand our own reactions to what is occuring: "Why am I so annoyed at this person; What does it trigger for me?"

It is often easy to hold romanticized notions that those who are themselves victimized by bigotry will be more sensitive and vigilant when groups other than their own are targeted. Unfortunately experiencing oppression does not automatically render one an expert or liberate one from bias toward another group. We can easily be triggered when such expectations are shattered.

> Jerry: I have been exposed to Jewish racism and sexism, African American antisemitism and sexism, and white, Gentile women who are racist and antisemitic. I always harbor the wish that all targeted group members would be allies in interrupting bias in all of its forms. However, wishing doesn't make it so. When I am confronted with bias toward my group from other targeted people, I have to overcome my fear of alienating those whom I thought were "on my side" and challenge their beliefs in the same way I would anyone else. However, in the process I try to provide continuous evidence that I am also sensitive to their target group issues.

The challenge is to maintain an openness to both our own internal process and to what may be going on for our students, so that we can respond to biased comments clearly and directly, but also with compassion and understanding for what it means to discover and change oppressive beliefs and behaviors in ourselves (see chapter 5 for further discussion of triggers).

Doubts and Ambivalence About One's Own Competency

Weinstein and O'Bear found that faculty often worry about having to expose their own struggles with the issues, reveal uncertainty, or make mistakes. As college faculty members we are assumed to have expertise in what we teach. To the degree that we expect ourselves to appear certain about what we know, we may find it difficult to encounter hot spots or knowledge gaps exposed by our interactions with students.

> Jerry: This is especially true when targeted group members other than my own describe perspectives to which I am not yet sensitive. Unless I can admit to students that I am still in the process of learning and that there are areas about which I still need to be educated, I may give the impression that there are simple solutions to which I have access. This places great pressure on me to have "the answer." One way of diminishing the pressure is to disclose my own uncertainties to students. It also models that unlearning prejudice is a lifelong process in which there are rarely simple answers.

The issues students raise that challenge our awareness and sensitivity can create a valuable space for opening up the learning process. As we confront misinformation or ignorance and the blindspots of privilege, we create the possibility for modeling honesty and openness to what can be learned by listening to others who are different from us, especially those who have been targets of dominant stereotypes and assumptions.

In our discussions for this chapter, Lee recalled a course in which classism was a central focus. Since most of the class were teachers or human service professionals, she had assumed a predominantly middle-class perspective and focused the class accordingly, only to discover a simmering anger at the cost of textbooks and the amount of time outside of class needed to complete the homework felt by students who were working two jobs and struggling to make ends meet. Once Lee realized her mistake, she told the class the false assumptions she had made and initiated a discussion about how the problems students were experiencing could be addressed in ways that would be supportive and promote learning. The discussion provided an opportunity for the whole class to engage in an exploration of classism and the unexamined assumptions that reinforce class privilege. The discussion also gave Lee useful new ideas about how to select texts for courses, develop a library of books to loan to students, and think about new ways to construct assignments and build a supportive classroom community.

> Sharon: You can't come into the class saying, in effect, "I know everything there is to know about this and let me tell you." When you make a mistake you have to be willing to say , "Well, that was a mistake" or "I've learned something about this now and I'll do it differently next time." I don't know how comfortable most teachers are with doing this, but there is a way to say, "It didn't occur to me" or "I didn't notice, I'm sorry."

Teaching in ways that invite challenge and model ongoing learning demonstrates a different definition of competence than the traditional one of mastery and expertise. Competence becomes instead skill in creating an atmosphere where difficult dialogues can occur (Goodman, 1995), developing processes that enable people (including the teacher) to expose and look critically at their own assumptions and biases, and building a community that encourages risk-taking and action to challenge oppressive conditions within and beyond the classroom.

Need for Learner Approval

Most faculty hope that our students will like and respect us, and leave our classes feeling positive about their experience. Those interviewed by Weinstein and O'Bear named such fears as making students frustrated, frightened, or angry, leaving them feeling shaken and confused and not being able to fix it.

> Lee: I think I'm good at creating community in the classroom and making people feel welcome and supported. Where I have to push myself is to introduce and not smooth over conflict, to challenge students, and risk their not liking me. I do it, but I realize I'm much more comfortable with the community-building part. It makes me feel good, I want students to like me. But there are times when that can get in the way of productive learning.

In the social justice classroom we intentionally create tension to disrupt complacent and unexamined attitudes about social life. These very conditions can cause students to dislike or feel hostile toward us at various points in the course. Confronting oppression invariably involves a range of feelings from anxiety, confusion, anger, and sadness, to exhilaration and joy. We need to remind ourselves that as much as we crave approval from our students, a sense of well-being and long-term learning are not necessarily synonymous. A better indication of our effectiveness might be whether students leave with more questions than they came in with, wanting to know more and questioning core assumptions in their own socialization.

> Jerry: When students left feeling frustrated, upset, and confused I used to regard it as evidence of my failure as a teacher. It was not until we ran a racism workshop for a community college in which the entire faculty and administration were involved that my concept of what constituted successful teaching began to change. On finishing the weekend-long session the participants were not smiling. On the way home my co-leader and I felt that the workshop had been a failure. Over the next three to five years, however, we kept getting reports of systematic changes in that institution that promoted greater racial equity and awareness and that were directly attributed to the workshop.

Dealing With Emotional Intensity and Fear of Losing Control

Faculty worry about not knowing how to respond to angry comments, having discussions blow up, dealing with anger directed at them, and being overwhelmed by their own strong emotions engendered by the discussion (Weinstein & O'Bear, 1992). Johnella Butler describes this process well:

> All the conflicting emotions, the sometimes painful movement from the familiar to the unfamiliar, are experienced by the teacher as well. We have been shaped by the same damaging, misinformed view of the world as our students. Often, as we try to resolve their conflicts, we are simultaneously working through our own (1989, 160).

Many faculty have been taught that emotions have no place in academia. Traditional modes of teaching distance us from the core issues and conflicts that are central to social justice education and can often result in simply skimming the surface. Ultimately, it is questionable whether intellectual and abstract reflection alone effectively change oppressive attitudes and behaviors.

Dealing with tension, anger, and conflict in the classroom is difficult. However, avoiding the feelings that are stimulated by oppression ignores how deeply it is embedded in our psyches and reinforces norms of silence and discounting that ultimately support oppression (Aguilar & Washington, 1990). Often the most significant learning results from the disequilibrium that open confrontation with feelings and contradictory information can generate (Keil, 1984; Zaharna, 1989).

In preparing ourselves to deal with difficult emotions it can be helpful to examine how our own history with the expression of emotion may affect the way we respond to emotion in the classroom.

> Barbara: I have had to examine how anger and other intense emotions were handled in my household to get a better understanding of my current response to emotions in the classroom. Quite apart from my professional training to be carefully neutral and suppress any display of emotion, I was raised in a household where feelings were denied until they erupted. My response has been to deny feelings any place in discussions, and especially to disallow loud voices. Learning to listen to loud voices and to encourage others to be receptive to them has been important for my ability to facilitate authentic discussion. Reminding learners that loud voices sometimes indicate that a person cares a lot about an issue can provide a context that allows "heated" discussion to take place.

If we learn to accept emotional expression as a valid and valuable part of the learning process, we can turn our focus to finding effective ways to enable its expression in the service of learning.

> Sharon: I actually don't really try to control emotions, but I do try to manage outlets for expressing emotions through dyads or journals for example. If people are upset, I say "Be upset! Be angry, whatever, and we'll just notice it." And I just sort of acknowledge that it's part of the process.

We also acknowledge that there may be times when we feel overwhelmed and uncertain about what to do. When emotions are running high and we are uncertain about how to proceed, we have found it helpful to create time-out to reflect and decide on next steps.

> Jerry: There have been a number of times during my anti-bias teaching when I have felt totally helpless in dealing with certain interactions. A participant may say something that stimulates great tension and anxiety, and a dense silence overtakes the group. I may feel upset and paralyzed as all eyes turn to me to see what I will do, expecting me to take care of the situation. I cannot think of any helpful intervention. I am too upset to think clearly. It is a fearsome moment, one I anticipate with dread.

Over the years Jerry has accumulated a few emergency procedures that help him survive these moments:

- Give participants a brief time out.
- Ask people to record their own immediate responses in their notebooks.
- Invite each participant to share their responses with one other person.

The purpose of these strategies is to change the focus momentarily from public to private, so that participants and instructor can reflect upon and articulate to themselves what they are feeling. It then becomes more possible to return to the discussion with greater thoughtfulness and honesty.

In many cases when a supportive climate has been previously established, losing control or facing strong emotions can be a constructive event, one from which both professor and students learn. In fact, students often make fundamental shifts in their perspectives after they have experienced someone "losing" control, letting go enough to share deeper feelings, fears, and experiences.

> Barbara: I teach social justice education from a position of hope and belief that our efforts can make a difference in the elimination of oppression. I was co-teaching an antisemitism course with a Jewish colleague who said that she did not think antisemitism would ever be entirely eliminated and that other Holocausts were and are possible. Before I could catch them, tears coursed down my face as I felt the enormity of the task before me and the challenge to my own optimism. Several students later told me that this was a powerful learning moment for them.

Personal Disclosure and Using Our Experience As Example

We as instructors are also in many ways texts for our students. Our social group identities, behavior in the classroom, and openness about our own process of learning can all be important and challenging aspects of course content. Who we are affects student perceptions of the issues we raise. In some respects we are both the messenger and the message.

Asking students to engage experientially with oppression material requires that we be willing to take the risks we ask of them. Self-disclosure is an important part of this process and one of the most powerful ways of teaching is through modeling the behavior we hope to encourage in others.

> Lee: If we want to create an environment where our students can be vulnerable enough to look at painful issues that challenge our faith in a fair society and ourselves as good human beings, then we have to give ourselves the same permission to be vulnerable and confused. I'm constantly struggling against this image that teachers are supposed to be perfect, in control, totally aware. Which is ridiculous! Nobody can be that. The question is how can I try to be skillful, and at the same time give myself permission to be a fallible human being? If I'm going to ask my students to disclose something, then I should be willing to do that too. I try to disclose ways in which I've made mistakes and where I felt really stupid when I realized what I was saying, to let students know there's not perfection. There's just human beings trying to be humane with each other and not perpetuate this bloody system.

Sharing our own struggles with the issues provides important permission for our students to engage in the difficult process of doing so themselves. This stance can help to avoid expectations of perfection which often block action. Better to take imperfect action and continue to engage with the issues, than to avoid responsibility for action altogether while we search for perfection.

> Sharon: I want students to understand that learning about social justice is part of a lifelong process. I will share with them stories of my own development, both in areas where I was a target of oppression, or stood in the shoes of an agent of oppression with the accompanying privileges.

The amount, context, and nature of personal information that we disclose is a matter of judgment, depending on the nature and size of the group and the amount of time we have together. We try to make clear the relation of our own disclosure to the topic under discussion.

For many teachers, especially those from targeted groups, the risk of self-disclosure needs to be thoughtfully taken. For example, self-disclosure by a gay or lesbian teacher can be a significant boon to learning, especially if the topic is heterosexism. The instructor, however, should be aware of the homophobia and misinformation sure to exist among her students and plan carefully about how and when she will come out.

> Sharon: I know that for myself I'm always conscious about when it is that I'll come out in class, or even if I will. Because I want them to still see me as credible and I believe that as soon as I come out, that piece of knowledge looms in their eyes over everything else. Like all of a sudden their teacher is sexual, and they have to deal with the internal contradictions of respect for teacher along with societal messages that gay men and lesbians are bad, perverse, immoral, etc. So I know that I'm very conscious about when to share that information. I try to wait until after I've gotten their trust so that any trust I lose during that time period can hopefully be re-established before the end of the semester. I have had students deny my being lesbian and think I was only saying it to create a learning opportunity for them!

Our role in disclosing personal experiences differs from that of our students. Students will use their experiences to probe and understand the personal implications of a specific issue. As instructors, we often use personal experience to illustrate a point. Our role is to be inclusive. Understanding the limits of our own experience allows us to consciously develop examples that go beyond our own personal range.

Negotiating Authority Issues

In the social justice classroom, we deliberately challenge the traditional classroom hierarchy in order to build a community of learning in which the teacher participates as a facilitator of process rather than an authority delivering knowledge (Tompkins, 1990). Issues of authority in the classroom are especially complicated for faculty who are members of targeted groups. Much has been written, for example, about the dilemmas faced by faculty of color and female and gay/lesbian faculty who often cope with both institutional and student devaluation of their professional status (Ahlquist, 1991: Arnold, 1993; hooks, 1994; Ladson-Billings, 1996; Aguilar & Washington, 1990; Maher & Tetreault, 1994). Students sometimes perceive them as less authoritative and may discount the legitimacy of what they teach or accuse them of pushing their own agenda.

A professor of color and a white professor teaching about racism, for example, are likely to be perceived quite differently by students of color and white students.

Sharon describes the various issues she often juggles and the common student perceptions she faces as an African American woman teaching about racism.

> The fact that my students are often 99 percent white means that I have to set up an environment where they can talk about their perceptions of reverse discrimination, quotas, affirmative action, etc. I also don't want to come off appearing like it's only my issue, or it's my personal thing, or that I've got a chip on my shoulder. And if I do have students of color in the class, then I'm also concerned about trying to keep them from having to be the authority on all issues of race.

Gender also casts authority issues in particular ways. We are socialized to expect females to defer to male authority, not to be authorities themselves. Women who achieve professional roles often juggle negative social messages about women in power with an internal sense of being imposters in these roles (McIntosh, 1988; Bell, 1990). When we are dealing with emotional issues and feelings in the classroom, female professors can be easily typecast. Students often expect female teachers to be nurturing or to smile; they become angry or challenge our authority when we do not fulfill their expectations (see Culley, 1985).

Institutional Risks and Dangers

One additional concern is the fear related to the institutional risks involved in departing from traditional teaching formats and content. As we engage with social justice issues and change our classrooms accordingly, we often come into conflict with institutional norms of professed objectivity, authority, and professorial distance in ways that can undermine our confidence, lose the support of some of our colleagues, and in some cases jeopardize our positions as faculty.

When we take on the challenge of teaching social justice content and developing a democratic, participatory process in our classrooms, we run very real risks of getting in trouble with our institutions. We are challenging traditional content as well as traditional teaching processes and norms about the teacher-student relationship. We also often encounter problems with grading and evaluation that other instructors rarely deal with.

> Sharon: A student's mother wrote to the Dean and told him that I was a bad teacher and that if her daughter didn't get a B, she was going to take this to the Provost and the President of the university and have them call me on the carpet. And it was really hard holding my own ground. [Did the Dean support you?] The Dean *did* support me but not without questioning me.

Here, we see multiple vulnerabilities. There's the jeopardy of being an African American teacher in a white institution where she cannot necessarily count on the support that white faculty can usually rely on. Then she is introducing subject matter that may not be supported by the institution. Finally she is engaging in a process of teaching that also may not be valued institutionally.

Many of the faculty teaching social justice courses are women, often among them the few people of color on the faculty, and often untenured. Thus the most vulnerable group takes on the most difficult and institutionally risky teaching. Faculty who teach social justice courses also sometimes receive lower ratings on teaching evaluations than those who teach traditional courses, adding yet another layer of institutional danger to an already exposed position. Thus faculty who take on the challenge of teaching social justice, especially if they are members of targeted groups, are often in an extremely vulnerable position institutionally.

Team teaching, particularly with a tenured faculty member, can be a valuable way of building in support for untenured faculty. Other support systems also need to be developed and nurtured so that faculty who teach social justice education can survive and hopefully thrive in these institutions.

Conclusion

We hope that through naming and discussing the fears and concerns faced by faculty who teach about oppression, we can begin a dialogue of support and encouragement that will enable teachers to sustain their commitment to social justice education. More often that not, people who write about multicultural education say very little about their own struggles in the classroom. We want to contribute to a discussion where teachers can expose the problems and difficulties we all face in this work and support each other in being more effective.

We also want to recognize that we are part of a much larger process of change and affirm the importance of the small part each of us individually plays in this process. What we do counts, often in ways that will not come back to us for validation.

> Sharon: I just think it's helpful to know that I am doing the best I can do and not to be too wedded to the here and now. I know ancestors who came before fought for freedom, equality, and justice and made it possible for me to live this life. Even if I don't change the world for me, I have faith that my work can contribute to a better world for the generations yet to come. That's what keeps me doing it, keeps me grounded, being grateful and knowing that my little part counts.

We hope that nurturing this perspective in our students will make it possible for them to become engaged in social justice action and to believe in the importance of the role each of them can play in creating change.

Knowing Our Students

Maurianne Adams, JoAnne Jones,
Beverly Daniel Tatum

This chapter originated in audiotaped conversations among the three authors as we reflected upon our combined years of teaching experience, and set ourselves the following questions: Why do we need to know our students? What do we need to know about them? How do we get to know our students? What theory and knowledge bases help us understand them? What do we want students to know about themselves, about each other, and about us?

These questions are addressed by interweaving narrative descriptions, examples and excerpts from our conversations, and reflections on what "knowing our students" has meant for our practice. Sometimes we use a common voice in which "we" refers generally to the three authors; other times we each use our own voice, identified as Beverly, JoAnne, or Maurianne. We offer examples of how to obtain and apply information about one's students and describe experiences that illustrate succesful strategies or, in some cases, the mistakes we have made when we didn't practice what we preach.

Why Do We Need to Know Our Students?

Some background knowledge about student learning styles (see chapter 4) and prior familiarity with course content is helpful in any teaching situation. However, when the content involves issues of social justice, to which students bring strongly held opinions and beliefs, this knowledge becomes essential. Regardless of age or experience, students do not enter the social justice classroom as blank slates. They bring information and opinions about gender roles, racial stereotypes, "normal" ability, or "appropriate" sexual behavior as part of their socialization from earliest memory. What they have learned, and from whom, affects their attitude about everything presented in the course.

In our dialogue, we identified six specific reasons why we need to know our students. First, we try to match our curricular goals, and the instructional activities that support them, to what we anticipate or learn about our students. Early assessments provide information about students' past experiences and beliefs about social differences. JoAnne recounts an example of beginning a course on issues of oppression with a group of human service professionals. During an opening discussion designed to elicit information about prior experiences with the topic, one participant said emphatically, "I want to tell you this, I don't want any lectures. I'm tired of being lectured to! I want to be able to talk to people here and learn from each other." If JoAnne had started with something didactic, this student would probably have tuned out. By carefully assessing student expectations and remaining flexible, JoAnne was able to alter her design and return to important conceptual material at a time when students were more able to listen responsively.

Second, we want to know enough about our students to be able to anticipate questions or areas of confusion. We need to think about who our students are as we decide how to introduce key terms and concepts. Some students may hesitate to ask us what the words we use mean; they may speak English as a second language or feel embarrassed by their lack of understanding and sensitive to public humiliation. Beverly recounts a training for college staff that focused on racism but inadvertently excluded people through the use of undefined key terms.

> Beverly: Among the staff in attendance was a group of five women from housekeeping who sat together during the workshop. On the last day of the training they came up to us and one of them said she was totally lost. She didn't have a college degree, she said, and the material we had given them to read was difficult. She then said that when someone in the group referred to "nepotism," she didn't even know what the word meant and had been too embarrassed to say this in the group. She had tears in her eyes when she was talking to us. She was embarrassed to admit that so much had gone over her head, but she also didn't want to lose more.

Third, we need to know our students to be able to teach to their current levels of awareness, assumptions, expectations, and information. For example, we sometimes forget how quickly student generational culture changes, and assume that issues such as sexism are readily apparent to most of our female students. Some younger women insist that the women's movement has already solved all issues of gender inequity in the workplace and that sexual harassment is "no big deal."

Knowing or learning about our students does not occur all at once, or just at the beginning of a course. The nature of social justice courses is such that along the way students often discover beliefs, assumptions, and feelings they did not know they held. Students also change as they engage with social justice content, putting old beliefs behind them and embracing new ways of thinking. Our teaching strategies should also change as we, along with our students, make new discoveries about their beliefs and values.

> Beverly: I change things all the time! I think flexibility is a major resource. I'm constantly assessing my educational goals and asking myself whether what we are doing is moving in a useful direction.

> Maurianne: I tend to have backup strategies—depending on where I think the group may go with a particular topic and what the dynamics may be. Although I always give out the "agenda" for a class, students know I am likely to change activities, such as break them into small groups or ask them to write a page on their thoughts or provide a short

impromptu lecture on missing information or conceptual links for clarification. The fact that I revise the agenda during the class tells students that I'm trying to be responsive to who they are and what they seem to need in the moment.

Fourth, we need to know our students to be able to judge whether we are using appropriate and realistic learning goals. Even the fairly basic instructional goals of awareness, knowledge, and action (noted in chapter 4) may be unrealistic, if we find that generating awareness and providing missing information on a topic consumes most of our class time, and we are left with insufficient time or student readiness to think about intervention skills or action strategies until much later in the semester.

Maurianne: Often there's a sharp difference between how I may prioritize my teaching objectives and what I discover is actually possible for my students, given the limitations of time, the number of other courses they are taking, and their actual "learning edge" for a specific social justice issue. In planning our general education "diversity" course, we overestimated the awareness level and readiness of many of our students. We find we can't introduce personal interventions or action until students actually care about these issues and feel personally implicated in them.

Group size also affects one's teaching goals and is important to plan for in advance. Teaching about racism or heterosexism in a class with more than a hundred students might call for more of a lecture format rather than raising awareness through experiential learning.

JoAnne: I might give some experiential taste to provide a frame for the information in a large class of one hundred students located in a lecture hall, but it certainly wouldn't be the "get to know yourself" kind of experience used in a smaller class of twenty or thirty. I think we must be very clear to not raise questions when there is not sufficient time to answer them. If there's only a limited time with a large group of people, I wouldn't want to open people up to self-disclosure.

Still, an introductory activity such as "I am" (described below) can be done with a large group in row seating if students fill out the worksheet individually, turn and pair with the person next to them, or form groups of four with people sitting in front and in back. The benefits of self-reflection and learning about each other in this case can be augmented by the instructor who reads the "I am" worksheets after class and reports back on the overall group demographics in a later class.

Beverly: The "I am" exercise I use asks participants to fill in as many or as few descriptors as they choose. When students have finished writing, I ask for volunteers to read their lists and then ask people to talk about any patterns they notice. Usually somebody will notice that the white people have not mentioned being White but that the people of color have mentioned their ethnicity; the men have not mentioned being male, but the women have mentioned something about being female. I often use this exercise as an introduction to a lecture presentation on the topic of racial identity development.

Fifth, we need to be able to anticipate student reactions to our specific social group identities as instructors, an issue presented at greater length in the preceding chapter, but relevant to our discussion here as well. We have experienced contradictory reactions among students to our various target identities as female, lesbian, or Black. Sometimes, students grant us an expertise on "our" issues that enables them to avoid exposing their own view or struggling with their own experiences. Other times, they discount what we present as overly subjective or self-interested, and write us off as lacking expertise or authority. Either side of this paradox diminishes our effectiveness as teachers in ways that may not hold true for instructors perceived as belonging to dominant groups.

Sixth, we try to know our students well enough to plan for their likely reactions to and interactions with each other in a culturally diverse class setting. We have observed white students who become silenced by their own participation in the larger system of racism. We have seen students of color become frustrated by the slow pace of discussion or by the level of white denial.

> Beverly: One of the things I might be thinking about is, "Well, do we need to break up into small groups? Or, can this continue as a large group discussion?" If there seems to be a lot of animation in the classroom, everybody wants to talk, and, yet we don't have enough time to let everybody talk, does that mean I should put people in pairs, so that everybody can say something to someone, even if they're not participating as a large group? Does it mean that we need to make a change in the order of the content? Those are some of the things I'm prepared to think about on the spot in terms of what's happening in the class: *process* as well as *content*.

What Do We Need to Know about Our Students?

With which social identities are students most or least comfortable? What issues are of greatest concern to them and what is their motivation for being in this class? What is their prior experience with the range of social justice issues and what are their expectations? We have learned that within any group there will be a range of experiences, familiarity with the material, and emotional comfort. We also anticipate that everyone, including the instructor, will bring a certain amount of misinformation and ignorance to any discussion about social diversity. These are assumptions that we make explicit for students at the start of the educational experience.

Social Identity Mixture in the Class and Multiple Social Identities of Individual Students

Prior to the start of a class or during the first class or introductory module, we ask for specific information about social identities to help us assess the racial and ethnic diversity, gender mix, and age ranges of the group. Revealing personal information about one's social identities may be emotionally difficult for many people, so that creating a climate of safety and comfort is important. Beverly tells the story of a man visibly identifiable as Black, who had grown up in a mostly white community and identified culturally with the white community when she divided the class into caucus groups. The people of color caucus group was assigned to a room in one building and the white caucus group in another building, and she found this man in the breezeway between the two buildings.

> He stood there, unsure of which way to go. We stood in the breezeway and talked about it. I didn't say you need to be in that group, but I asked him what it would mean for him to go one way or the other. He said, "I know I'm Black but I still identify with being White." I told him that I knew a lot of folks in his situation, who had grown up in white communities, that I had grown up in a similar situation, and I guessed that there were other people of color in that room with a similar experience. I suggested it might be helpful for him to be in the room with the people of color and talk about his dilemma and what it meant for him. In the end, that's what he chose to do.

Sometimes merely posing a provocative question creates a crisis of meaning for some students that in turn leads to new levels of understanding. The following example illustrates an unexpected response to the introductory "I am" activity (described earlier) and illustrates the strong feelings that can attach to one's social identities, especially when those identities may be in transition, turmoil, or disguise.

> Beverly: At the end of my presentation, a woman came up to me in tears. She had left the room for a period of time during my lecture, because she had been overcome by emotion. At the end she apologized for leaving and said, "It was because when you asked us to do the 'I am' exercise, I didn't know what to put." She had been raised in a Cuban family, but she was not visibly identifiable as Hispanic and had been taught to pass as White. She felt she could not put down White, but was terrified at the idea of writing down that she was Cuban. I had not asked them to write down anything in particular. I had asked them to simply complete the sentence, "I am ______." But this was what she was experiencing. By the end of my presentation, she realized that she had internalized a lot of racism herself. She said she realized the biggest racist was the one inside of her, and that she really wanted to explore and reclaim her identity as Cuban. She said, "I know it doesn't matter, nobody cares, nobody in this room cares if I'm Cuban or not, but I feel like I'm going to be found out." I had never anticipated that this brief exercise would be so powerful for a particular individual in the room.

One aspect of knowing our students is being sensitive to the ways in which social identity can be so internal and ambivalent that what seems obvious to a viewer is far from obvious or simple to the self.

Prior Experience with and Reactions to Social Justice Education

We try to find out whether students have had prior experiences with social justice courses and their reactions to these experiences.

> Beverly: Some students relaxed visibly when I said, "I know you know this material and so I would appreciate it if there's a different way you understand it or a different language you use. Please speak up. I also know there are some people here for whom this is all new." Some know a lot, some know very little, and both will feel anxious unless you acknowledge some way they can move forward together.

In addition to finding out what students already know, we try to learn about their attitudes and beliefs, their expectations for the experience, and their motivation for participating. Gathering some of this information can be a fairly straightforward process. A written assessment of student expectations and concerns about the course can be conducted prior to the start of a class or during the first session. Informally asking students why they are taking the class and what they hope to learn can accomplish this goal as well.

The level of resistance is likely to be quite high if participants are attending a required course or workshop they believe they have been unfairly mandated to attend. Knowing this information in advance allows the instructor to acknowledge the ways people might be feeling and plan activities to help a resistant group move forward in their understanding of the content and their acknowledgment of its importance.

How Do We Find Out the Information We Need to Know Our Students?

Prior Assessments

There are countless formal and informal ways to collect assessment information before the start of a class or during its initial stages. One productive strategy, already noted, is to distribute a questionnaire or needs assessment prior to the start of the learning experience. Participants might be asked to describe themselves in terms of the issues to be covered in the course. For example, if the course is on racism, questions regarding racial identity are appropriate. Questions about expectations, particular learning needs, and previous experiences with similar courses or workshops are useful. Often asking questions about areas of worry or concern will provide insight into the perspectives and issues participants bring.

Sometimes it is possible to have information in advance about the students in one's course (if they are majors in one's department or if the course has a prerequisite with which one is familiar). One can make some assessments on the basis of known demographics of an established student group (entering students in a geographic area, transfer students from certain schools), although mere demographics cannot convey the personal meanings students attach to their age cohort, race, ethnicity, gender, or sexual orientation.

Introductory Activities

We have learned always to confirm prior demographic or attitudinal assessments with information generated face-to-face during the opening segments of classes or workshops. Also, since it is often not possible to obtain critical information in advance, students can be asked to fill out a questionnaire as an opening exercise or the teacher can pose some questions for open discussion. Alternatively, the instructor can engage participants in experiential exercises which bring out information about group membership. For example, during the initial module of a racism course, Beverly has used an exercise called "Common ground" during the beginning phase of a class or workshop.

> Beverly: In this exercise, I ask participants to line up on one side of the room and to remain silent throughout the exercise. Before beginning, I assure them that they always have the right not to participate at any point in the exercise and can simply remain where they are or stand aside. Then I read a series of statements and ask them to step to the other side of the room if the statement is true for them. For example, I might say, "Please step to the other side of the room if you are a woman." Those women who choose to participate cross over to the other side of the room and stand facing the remaining participants. I ask everyone to look and see who is in your group and who is not. Notice what thoughts and feelings you have as you look across the room. After people have had some time to observe who has crossed the room and who has not, those who crossed the room return to the original group. Then I read another statement, for example, "Please cross the room if you are Asian, Asian Indian, or Pacific Islander."
>
> I may read as many as fifteen or twenty group identifications, some of which may be visibly identifiable, some of which may not be. I ask questions such as "Cross the room if you have a visible or hidden disability, or if neither parent attended college, or if you have ever been homeless, or if you have an alcoholic parent, or if you are an immigrant to this country." When no one crosses the room in response to one of the requests, the group can pause to notice. These moments are often very powerful reminders of whose voices are not represented in the class. We did the activity recently at a Catholic college and there was no one Jewish in the room. That was a powerful statement about who's not here, so we

> said, please take note, and then went on to the next question. Or a person of Native American descent may cross the room by herself and it is powerful to see her standing there by herself and then move back again. When you ask for people who grew up poor, white people cross the room with people of color, but often there are still people of color who did not grow up poor standing on the other side.
>
> Afterwards, when we process this exercise, people often talk about their surprise to see that sometimes those who crossed and those who did not did not fit with their expectations. It brings out one's assumptions. For example, when it comes to disabilities, sometimes people cross whose disabilities are not visible. It is a powerful, nonverbal experience. It shows, I'm not just what I look like on the outside. An opening exercise like this one, though not without risks, can quickly and powerfully bring issues for discussion to the surface, allow the group to feel a sense of intimacy, and provide valuable background information to the teacher as well as to the members of the class.

There are many activities that can provide valuable information about students. Some of these activities are public, such as the activity described above; others are more private, such as asking students to write to the instructor.

> Maurianne: At the end of the first class, I give students time to write to me, telling me whatever they want me to know about themselves, such as their background or preparation for the class, their goals for themselves in this class, any worries they may have about the class, or any physical or other disabilities they want me to know about so I can adjust assignments or activities. These are confidential. Then, during the semester, I ask them to write again, telling me how they're doing, what they're struggling with, what questions or problems they have, what aspects of my teaching they find helpful, what they wish I would change. This lets me know what I need to spend more time on and what I should think about changing. I find out about the students on day one and keep learning more throughout the semester.

Another strategy might be to have students call out the identities that are important to them personally and begin conversations in homogeneous caucus groups.

> Beverly: Midway through the course, I ask people to choose an aspect of their identity they would like to talk about, and it is interesting to see that some of the women of color chose the fact of growing up poor, in which they meet with white women who have also grown up poor. Asking class members to name the identities that are important to them allows the group to decide how they are going to caucus without my imposing the important identity on them.

These activities affirm the multiple and interactive nature of social identities; they cue the instructor into the important issues for particular students; they enable students to probe their own experiences and personal meanings more deeply; and, they enable students to get beyond each others' surface appearance or skin.

A variant JoAnne uses as a frame for her graduate courses invites students to meet together in generationally-defined groups (those born between 1940 and 1950, 1950 and 1960, for example) to identify their heroes, favorite music, and memorable public events.

> JoAnne: It was interesting how the historic moment becomes clear and how social forces shape people's understanding of a range of things. We then walk around the room and read newsprinted presentations of what each others' generational groups have talked about and use these as metaphors and identifiers for the rest of the semester. It doesn't

take much of an age range to have a powerful impact. Between twenty and thirty-five you have three generations; between twenty and forty, there are many worlds.

Feedback Mechanisms throughout the Course

The small and large group discussions, the various ways of processing activities, and our responses to student writing assignments can simultaneously serve as teaching, self-reflection, and information generating tools. Processing can mean something as simple as asking, "How are you doing? Does this make sense to you? What was the hardest part of this activity for you? What was the easiest?"

> Beverly: I try to structure in some processing time at the beginning and end of classes. If it's an ongoing class, frequently other people will begin to help with that responsibility. Sometimes I'll check with people privately and sometimes it can be helpful to do that kind of checking publicly: "I noticed that this was really upsetting for you and I wondered how you're doing with it now?"

Similarly, walking around and listening during small group discussions is another useful way for instructors to stay attuned to students' thoughts, concerns, and the level of understanding. We may notice feelings or questions that members of the class can then share. This information can be used as a point of departure for the next segment.

> JoAnne: When people are in small groups and you're circulating the room, you can listen to what's being said about what's just taken place. Sometimes I'll ask the members of group, "Do you mind if I say something about this question that came up?" Sometimes I share it in an anonymous way and say, "As I was circulating, I heard several of you talking about such and such, and this looks like an issue we need to respond to."

We can also notice how the group is coalescing and what issues are central, peripheral, or unmet. What is the learning climate of the group? Who is speaking? Who is silent? What issues are being avoided? Where is the tension? What are the strengths of the group?

We use journals or reflective writing activities as feedback and response mechanisms and to guide future sessions.

> Beverly: I have, in a classroom setting, required writing assignments, reflection papers, or journal writing that will be coming back to me the next time so that I have an ongoing source of information. I have used index cards on which I asked people to write down a burning question or something that has come up for them. And, have them do it anonymously. Often, people will put down a question they would be embarrassed to ask otherwise. Then, I collect the index cards, leaf through them, and read off samples. This allows me to see right away what issues or points of clarification need to be discussed and share some with the group.
>
> A version of this activity occurred one time when it seemed as if my co-facilitator and I had been talking too much and the group was sort of dead. We were trying to think what to do. So, we distributed these index cards and students wrote down their questions, and we read the questions to the group, for the group to answer. We said, "Who thinks they can answer this question?" It got very lively! It was a very useful thing to do both in getting questions from them and also, increasing their own participation.

Maurianne also asks students to bring to class whatever "burning" open-ended questions (questions for which there is no simple or correct answer) they have after completing homework reading assignments. These can be used to start the next class or as questions for small group discussions. Or, as a variation, each person's question can be passed along for one or more written responses, before reading aloud a sampling of questions and responses. This lets everyone know what the key questions are and how various students are thinking about the same issues.

JoAnne invites visual or dramatic symbolic representations of students' experience to draw on different learning styles:

> JoAnne: So far, most of the feedback devices we've been talking about are paper and pencil or talk. I think those are excellent and they work for some people. But, then I think there are other media as well that can get at different ways that people express themselves, such as symbolically representing things that are happening for them. I like to use colors and papers. It also gets people physically into different configurations. They may huddle on the floor. All kinds of changes in structure will bring out different interactions, such as music or silence.

Feedback Strategies at Various Endpoints

We also want to know what students have learned at the end of a given class session or the end of the course. What knowledge and awareness has been gained? What questions or tensions remain? What type of support system is available to students as they apply what they have learned?

Written statements, action plans, and presentations synthesizing a student's learning represent various methods for assessing the impact of the course. We also ask direct questions such as: What have you learned? What has changed in your understanding of these issues? What next steps would you like to take to continue to learn about and address these issues?

Particularly with social justice content, application to real world contexts is an important goal for our teaching. Depending on the duration of a course, students may choose to implement these strategies and report the results back to the class. When time is more limited, a written or verbal description of a proposed action plan helps transfer the learning from classroom to daily life (see Module 4 in chapters 6–11 for examples).

It is important to acknowledge the obstacles inherent in confronting issues of oppression without a community of like-minded people. For some students, there may be limited safety outside the classroom for engaging with social justice issues. A gay student may not yet be able to speak with dorm mates or family. A woman in an abusive family relationship may not be able to act upon gender politics at home. Action plans must be tempered by the real life conditions for students. Issues of safety, risk, comfort, and the legitimization of feelings are important to consider as the learning experience ends. Students need to understand that as their consciousness shifts, they may experience new tensions with friends, family, or colleagues. Discussion about ways to develop an ongoing support network or to maintain whatever supportive relations have been developed within the class are often useful as the semester reaches its close.

What Theory and Knowledge Sources Help Us Understand Our Students?

We and our colleagues have written elsewhere about the ways in which theories about learning styles, social identity and cognitive development inform our overall curriculum, our in-the-moment facilitative judgments, and the ways we devise and respond to various writing assignments (Anderson & Adams, 1992; Adams & Marchesani, 1992; Marchesani & Adams, 1992; Adams & Zhou-McGovern, 1994;

Hardiman & Jackson, 1992; Hardiman, 1994; Romney, Tatum, & Jones, 1992; Tatum, 1992, 1994). The major guiding social identity, cognitive development and learning style theories we use to anticipate and understand student reactions to social justice subject matter are presented in chapters 2, 3, and 4. Here we will say something of how we draw upon and use specific theories to help us better understand our students.

Learning Style Models

Kolb's learning style model (Kolb, 1984) helps us understand students' differing modalities for taking in new information (concrete experience or abstract conceptualization) and for processing or applying new information (reflective observation or active experimentation) (Smith & Kolb, 1986; Anderson & Adams, 1992; Svinicki & Dixon, 1987; chapter 4). Maurianne informally introduces Kolb's learning style and experiential learning theory early in the semester and explains its relevance to the experiential dimensions of the course.

> Maurianne: I ask students to brainstorm (while I chalkboard) their various learning and study behaviors. Some prefer to study alone, take notes, and draw diagrams; others work in study groups, make telephone calls, stop by each others' dorm rooms. Some look for the big picture, others take detailed notes of the facts. I then ask about their most and least preferred teaching styles and again their responses are wide-ranging and sometimes situationally quite specific. In these discussions, examples of all four learning styles keep coming up, so I then have students' personal experiences to illustrate the range of learning styles in the classroom, using Kolb's model.
>
> I then talk about my two learning style objectives for this class. First, I want to make sure that everyone's preferred learning style is matched at least some of the time (so I use Kolb's model as a checklist for my weekly instructional design) and second, I want everyone's learning style repertoire to be stretched by trying out and developing new skills in their less preferred learning styles. This gives me the transition I need to show how Kolb's experiential learning theory rests on the importance of all four learning modalities for a complete process of learning. As a result, the relatively "odd" things we sometimes do in class—unusual when compared to what goes on in other classes at our large research university—make sense and are supported by an established theory of how people learn.

Other learning style models, such as Witkin's bipolar model of field sensitivity and field independence (Witkin & Moore, 1975) have been adapted to describe culturally-based learning style differences (Hale-Benson, 1986; Shade, 1989; Ramírez & Castañeda, 1974; Anderson, 1988) and to differentiate connected and separate learning styles in relation to socialized gender differences (Belenky, Clinchy, Goldenberger, & Tarule, 1986; Lyons, 1983). Learning style models help us to acknowledge and understand the fact that intergroup learning style differences are not deficits for one group and indices of superiority for another. We learn to respect cultural as well as individual learning style differences, and to recognize their existence within-groups as well as between-groups (Anderson & Adams, 1992; Shade, 1989; Tharp, 1989). At the same time, we try to avoid any tendency to restereotype our students through the uncritical, careless, or simplistic application of learning style templates.

As teachers, we also use the various learning style models as self-correcting devices to call attention to learning style limits in our own instructional designs, and to remind us to plan teaching strategies that both match and stretch the variety of learners in our classes.

Social Identity Development Models

Social identity development models (Hardiman & Jackson, 1992; Tatum, 1992; Cross, 1991; Helms, 1990) provide road maps for students as they grapple with who they and others are in relation to racism, sexism, heterosexism, and other forms of oppression (see chapter 2). The social identity models prove especially helpful for understanding the various ways in which the anger, denial, or pain evoked by social justice subject matter may be expressed by students and felt by ourselves (see Cross, 1995; Hardiman & Jackson, 1992; Tatum, 1992).

> Beverly: If you're talking about race, some white students will feel guilty and will wonder whether they are bad people, and what does living in a racist society mean for who they are? Some students of color will feel angry or agitated because of an increased awareness of victimization. They express impatience with slow progress on obvious problems. The clash of their anger and the white students' guilt is predictable. Both groups of students reach a saturation point where they don't want to hear about racism any more. It feels too overwhelming. They pull back, avoid coming to class perhaps, or don't complete the reading assignments.
>
> For me, I need to know, *Is it happening yet?* I have strategies in place to address these issues. I forewarn people that these things are likely to happen. My experience has been that telling people ahead of time is a helpful thing to do. Sometimes, students will tell me, "Oh, that thing you said would happen, is happening now."

It helps to remember that students are likely to have different understandings of racism, sexism, or heterosexism, depending in part on their levels of identity development with relation to specific social justice topics and as their racial, gender, or sexual identities are dominant or targeted. The Jackson-Hardiman racial identity development model (chapter 2) provides a valuable tool for anticipating and understanding these different between-group and within-group perspectives. For example, we note different perspectives among men or women of color on topics in racism and among men and women of color on sexism, which derive from their different life experiences. These perspectives expand and become more multi-faceted as they learn more, for example, in the context of these courses. This expansion is a developmental process. The identity development models help us anticipate and plan for the potential collision in the classroom of contradictory but strongly held world views. As with the learning style models, these identity development models also serve to remind us that we, too, have our own social identity perspectives which both characterize and limit our world views and from which we tend to generalize to what we feel students in our courses ought to do, feel, and think.

Cognitive Development Models

Social cognitive theory (Perry, 1981; Belenky et al., 1986) helps us anticipate the tendency of many students to dichotomize complex questions, reduce multiple perspectives to simple either/or choices, or not see relations between concrete examples of personal experience and broader theoretical principles. Another indicator is students' willingness to listen to one another as sources of knowledge rather than insisting that the teacher be the sole authority. We attempt to moderate the sources of complexity and contradiction by emphasizing one issue, one perspective, or one theoretical construct at a time. We start with the concrete, personal, and experiential before moving to the abstract and conceptual, and process the sources of contradiction and conceptual confusion. For example, rather than starting out with the notion of multiple identities, we gradually and incrementally build multiple perspectives as a semester-long enterprise (Adams & Marchesani, 1992; Adams & Zhou-McGovern, 1994).

For dualistic students, our authority as college teachers can be used to support new and more complex modes of thinking.

> Maurianne: I use my authority to model respect and appreciation for peer perspectives as a valid source of knowledge about social diversity. Gradually, over a semester, authority and leadership are taken over by students in the class. Initially, however, I have found that if I don't use my authority there is a power vacuum that leads to many lost learning opportunities. The more complex thinkers seem readier to pick up different perspectives from a range of sources, including other students.

What Do We Want Students to Know about Themselves and about Each Other?

Multiple Identities

One limitation of social identity models is the tendency to describe social identities as if they existed in equally weighted either/or categories: male/female, Jewish/gentile, people of color/white. These binary categories obscure the complex identities experienced by biracial, bisexual, and multiethnic people, and oversimplify the interactions in all people among multiple social identities. Further, a student is often more conscious of his or her target identities than agent identities.

> Beverly: One of the most important things I want students to know about themselves is that they are both dominant and targeted. Almost everybody can think of themselves in both these ways, although they tend not to. So, in a course on racism, students of color tend to think of themselves as victimized by racism and white students, as unwitting agents of oppression. For students in the dominant group, whatever that area of dominance is, one of the things I want them to become aware of is the power they have to reconceptualize their area of dominance as victimizer into being one of ally, someone who has the power to interrupt racist or sexist or antisemitic acts, for example. Similarly, students who think of themselves primarily as victims need to reconceptualize their target area into one of empowerment, taking pride in that aspect of their identity.
>
> But this leads to multiple identities as well. For instance, there are areas of privilege unacknowledged by students who feel victimized by race. The black male student needs to be aware of his sexism, the Latina woman of her dominance as a Christian perhaps, the heterosexual black woman of the privilege she has because of her sexual orientation.

We have met students for whom membership in targeted groups seems preferable, almost a badge of honor. For such students it is more desirable and socially acceptable to be a "victim" than to be an agent of oppression in order to avoid the guilt, pain, and responsibility of dominant group status. Students who do acknowledge their membership in a dominant group often struggle not to be reduced to a stereotype in other people's eyes. Instructors need to be understanding and help students recognize and name these feelings as part of their learning process.

Students who experience themselves exclusively through their targeted identities may be newly grappling with personal experiences of discrimination and oppression for the first time, and unable to explore other aspects of their identity. They may never before have questioned accepted ways of thinking and find it conceptually difficult to balance the many layers of a complex issue, especially when those layers have deeply personal and sometimes contradictory meanings.

Maurianne: One of my students, a Jamaican American man, was vehemently and openly sexist and homophobic, as well as believing the derogatory stereotypes about Jews to be factually-based and true. As a black man, he didn't see how race and gender could possibly be disentangled. But gradually, by associating gender issues with his mother and grandmother, both of whom he admired, he was able to wonder whether sexism had affected them as women. He also learned a lot from interviews he conducted with black women about their experiences of sexism.

This man's homophobia came from his church minister, a man whom he credited with saving him from the streets. He agreed to try to separate his beliefs (about homosexuality) from his behavior (toward gay, lesbian, or bisexual students), and to change his "unfair" behavior toward gays, lesbians, and bisexuals, especially since he hoped to be hired as a residence assistant. As a residence assistant, he knew that he would have to treat *all* people fairly.

The breakthrough on antisemitism came after a long segment on Jewish history, highlighted by the films *Genocide* and *Courage to Care.* He told the class that he now understood that not all white folks had the same history or life chances. This breakup of a single concept, "all white folks," was powerful for him. By my not pushing too hard, this student begin to disentangle for himself a set of beliefs, which had been based on personal experiences of racism, revered authorities, and efforts to survive.

The Challenge of Inclusivity

The challenge of inclusivity refers to finding ways to make each student feel comfortable as part of a classroom community, without diminishing the reality of the rage, fear, and shame.

Beverly: After we had done the "Common Ground" activity and were processing it, a white mother of biracial children explained that she didn't cross when I asked for people of racially mixed heritage, because the question was about parentage, although she wanted to cross because she had African American children. The next time we used the exercise, we added "If you are a member of a multi-racial family, please cross the room." This would have included her experience.

Making it possible for students to speak up about our unintentional omissions provides opportunities to fill in missing information.

A common example of inclusivity occurs when white students say, "I have no culture" and attempt to find something in their background that will afford them "victim status." Maurianne offers the example of a white, heterosexual man who recently discovered a fraction of Native American ancestry and wanted to focus on exploring this racial heritage rather than his white privilege. While it may be important that he explore a distant Native American ancestry, it is more important that he explore his dominant identities and recognize his corresponding privileges. Only in this way might he be able to understand the hostility felt by other students who struggle with their target identities on a daily basis.

What Do Students Need to Know About Us and Our Own Struggles with Social Justice Issues?

In conversations that led to this chapter, we could not separate our discussion about knowing our students from the need to understand ourselves as teachers and the related question, What do students need to know about us? The amount, context, and nature of personal information that we disclose is a matter of judgment in planning or in the moment. We believe that particularly in the early moments of a course, important modeling takes place. Self-disclosure may seem unusual to many students, especially in an academic climate. We try to make the relation of our own self-disclosure to the topic under discussion clear. We offer our own experience with both dominant and targeted identities as a way to join with students, expand the boundaries for discussing these subjects, and model how such discussions can happen. For example, Beverly usually describes herself sometime during the first session as an able-bodied, African American, heterosexual, Christian female, raised in a middle-class family. She talks about the fact that she is targeted by racism and sexism because she is a black female, but she also acknowledges her struggle to become aware of the daily privileges she receives as a heterosexual, as a Christian, as an able-bodied person with the education she received as the result of her middle-class status. In this way, she establishes connections with students whose primary identification may be with a targeted or dominant group, and encourages her students to consider the range of positions of privilege and marginality they occupy in relation to others.

> Beverly: In a recent workshop I noticed a number of highly verbal black men who talked a lot about racism but interrupted the women all the time. I said we need to look at our ally behavior not only in relation to racism but also to sexism, and I referred to my previous impatience with white people around not understanding white privilege. How can you not notice that? I got less impatient when I became aware of how ignorant or unobservant I was about my heterosexual privilege. Recognizing my own learning process regarding heterosexual privilege helped me be more generous in terms of my understanding of the way white people can struggle around understanding white privilege, or black men can struggle around their sexism.

Maurianne recounts how she talks with her students about her efforts to disentangle her Jewish identity and her white privilege in ways that feel honest and authentic. She does this to help all her students think about their ethnic family histories in relation to race and to help Jewish students balance their conscious experience as targets of antisemitism with their largely unconscious assumptions about white privilege.

> Maurianne: One of my challenges in class is to talk about how I grew up thinking of Jews as a race, partly because of my ancestry in Europe where Jews were stigmatized racially. But I also talk about how I had "passed" as a non-Jew, by ignoring that aspect of my identity and assuming that Jews, like other white ethnic groups, could assimilate if we worked hard and ignored our differences.
>
> This is obviously not a strategy that works for people of color. Acknowledging my personal struggle with these issues, and talking about the similarities and differences among differently racialized ethnic groups in different historical contexts, shows how my own analysis was reshaped over many years to fit my emerging understanding of my experience as a Jew and as a white woman. It's often easier for students to acknowledge their racial privilege, as Whites in this society, if we've already acknowledged where they and their families may have been targeted due to social class, ethnicity, religion, or sexual orientation.

This chapter is about the importance of knowing our students. We identify such needs as knowing how students are processing and making sense of social justice information, and how they are relating to each other and the instructor. We close this chapter with the acknowledgement that social diversity and social justice education involves journeying into life experiences that are often fraught with fear, suspicion, lies, and shame. Questions that may seem innocuous, such as "list your strengths" or "describe your social identities," can pose a crisis to a participant. To know our students means to maintain an attitude of respectful awe at the range, diversity, and elasticity of human experience.

REFERENCES

Adams, M. (Ed.). (1992). *Promoting diversity in college classrooms: Innovative responses for the curriculum, faculty, and institutions.* New Directions for Teaching and Learning, no. 52. San Francisco: Jossey-Bass.

Adams, M., Brigham, P., Dalpes, P., and Marchesani, L. (Eds.). (1996). *Social diversity and social justice: Selected readings,* 2nd edition. Dubuque, IA: Kendall/Hunt Publications.

Adams, M., and Marchesani, L. S. (1992). Curricular innovations: Social diversity as course content. In M. Adams (Ed.), *Promoting diversity in college classrooms: Innovative responses for the curriculum, faculty, and institutions,* New Directions for Teaching and Learning, no. 52 (pp. 85–98). San Francisco: Jossey-Bass.

Adams, M., and Zhou-McGovern, A. (1994). *The sociomoral development of undergraduates in a "social diversity" course: Developmental theory, research, and instructional applications.* Paper presented at the American Educational Research Association Annual Meeting, New Orleans, LA.

Aguilar, T., and Washington, S. (1990). Towards an inclusion of multicultural issues in leisure studies curricula. *Schole: A journal of leisure studies and recreation education,* 5, 41–52.

Ahlquist, R. (1991). Position and imposition: Power relations in a multicultural foundations class. *Journal of Negro Education, 60,* 158–169.

Albrecht, L., and Brewer, R. M. (1990). *Bridges of power: Women's multicultural alliances.* Philadelphia, PA: New Society Press.

American Association of University Women (1993). *Hostile hallways: The AAUW survey on sexual harassment in America's schools.* Annapolis Junction, MD: AAUW.

American Council on Education. (1949). *Intergroup relations in teaching materials: A survey and appraisal.* Washington, DC: American Council on Education.

Amir, Y. (1969). Contact hypothesis in ethnic relations. *Psychological Bulletin,* 71, 319–42.

———. (1976). The role of intergroup contact in change of prejudice and ethnic relations. In P. A. Katy (Ed.), *Towards the elimination of racism* . New York: Pergamon.

Amott, T., and Matthei, J. (1991). *Race, gender and work: A multicultural economic history of women in the United States.* Boston, MA: South End Press.

Anderson, J. (1988). Cognitive styles and multicultural populations. *Journal of teacher education,* 39 (1), 2–9.

Anderson, J., and Adams, M. (1992). Acknowledging the learning styles of diverse student populations: Implications for instructional design. In L. L. B. Border & N. V. N. Chism (Eds.), *Teaching for Diversity,* New Directions for Teaching and Learning, no. 49 (pp. 19–33). San Francisco, CA: Jossey-Bass.

Andrzejewski, J. (1993). Teaching controversial issues in higher education: Pedagogical techniques and analytical framework. In R. Martin (Ed.), *Practicing what we teach: Confronting issues of diversity in teacher education* . Albany, NY: State University of New York Press.

Anti-Defamation League. (1993). *Jew-hatred as history: An analysis of the Nation of Islam's "The secret relationship between Blacks and Jews".* New York: Anti-Defamation League.

———. (1994). *Anti-semitism worldwide, 1994.* Tel Aviv: Project for the Study of Anti-Semitism, Tel Aviv University.

Anzaldúa, G. (1987). *Borderlands/ La frontera: The new mestiza.* San Francisco: Aunt Lute Books.

Aptheker, H. (1993). *Anti-racism in US history: The first 200 years.* Westport, CT: Praeger.

Argyris, C. (1970). *Intervention theory and method: A behavioral science view.* Reading, MA: Addison-Wesley.

———. (1975). Dangers in applying results from experimental social psychology. *American Psychologist,* 30 (4), 469–85.

Arkin, M. (1975). *Aspects of Jewish economic history.* Philadelphia: Jewish Publication Society of America.

Arnold, M. S. (1993). *Breaking the pot: Melting student resistance to pluralism in counseling programs.* Paper presented at The Association for Counselor Education and Supervision, San Antonio, TX.

Arnold, R., Burke, B., James, C., Martin, D., and Thomas, B. (Eds.). (1991). *Educating for a change.* Toronto: Between The Lines.

Austen, R. A. (1994). The uncomfortable relationship: African enslavement in the common history. *Tikkun,* 9 (2), 65–86.

Auvine, B., Densmore, B., Extrom, M., Poole, S., and Shanklin, M. (1978). *A manual for group facilitators.* Madison, WI: The Center for Conflict Resolution.

Bagdikian, B. H. (1992). *The media monopoly,* 4th edition. Boston: Beacon Press.

Bakhtin, M. (1981). *The dialogic imagination.* Austin: University of Texas Press.

Balka, C., and Rose, A. (Eds.) (1989). *Twice Blessed: On Being Lesbian, Gay and Jewish.* Boston: Beacon Press.

Banks, J. A. (1991). *Teaching strategies for ethnic studies,* 5th edition. Boston: Allyn & Bacon.

Banks, J. A., and Banks, C. A. M. (Eds.). (1995). *Handbook of research on multicultural education.* New York: Macmillan.

Barker, P. (1993). *Regeneration.* New York: Plume.

Barlett, D. L., and Steele, J. B. (1992). *America: What went wrong?* Kansas City, MO: Andrews and McMeel.

Bartky, S. L. (1979). On psychological oppression. In S. Bishop and M. Weinzweig (Eds.), *Philosophy and women.* Belmont, CA: Wadsworth.

Batchelder, D., and Warner, E. G. (Eds.). (1977). *Beyond experience: The experiential approach to cross-cultural education.* Brattleboro, VT: The Experiment Press.

Baxter Magolda, M. B. (1992). *Knowing and reasoning in college: Gender-related patterns in students' intellectual development.* San Francisco: Jossey-Bass.

Beam, J. (Ed.). (1986). *In the life: A black gay anthology.* Boston: Alyson.

Beck. E. (Ed.). (1989). *Nice Jewish girls: A lesbian anthology.* Boston: Beacon Press.

Belenky, M. F., Clinchy, M. B., Goldberger, N. R., and Tarule, J. M. (1985). Epistemological development and the politics of talk in family life. *Journal of Education,* 167 (3), 9–26.

———. (1986). *Women's ways of knowing: The development of self, voice, and mind.* New York: Basic Books.

Bell, D. (1992). *Faces at the bottom of the well: The permanence of racism.* New York: Basic Books.

Bell, L. A. (1990). The gifted woman as imposter. *Advanced Development,* 2, 55–64.

Bell, L. A., and Schniedewind, N. (1987). Reflective minds, intentional hearts: Joining humanistic education and critical theory. *Journal of Education,* 169 (2), 55–72.

Bell. L. A., and Weinstein, G. (1982). Anti-oppression education. Unpublished manuscript. Amherst, MA.

Bell, M. (1995). What constitutes experience? Rethinking theoretical assumptions. In R. J. Kraft and J. Kielsmeier (Eds.), *Experiential learning in schools and higher education* (pp. 9–17). Dubuque, IA: Kendall/Hunt Publications.

Benne, K. D. (1964). History of the T-Group in the laboratory setting. In L. P. Bradford, J. R. Gibb, and K. D. Benne (Eds.), *T-Group theory and laboratory method: Innovation in re-education* (pp. 80–136). New York: John Wiley.

Bennett, Jr., L. (1961, 1988). *Before the Mayflower: A history of black America.* New York: Penguin Books.

Berman, P. (Ed.). (1994). *Blacks and Jews: Alliances and arguments.* New York: Delacorte Press.

Bidell, T. R., and Fischer, K. W. (1992). Beyond the stage debate: Action, structure, and variability in Piagetian theory and research. In R. J. Sternberg and C. A. Berg (Eds.), *Intellectual development.* New York: Cambridge University Press.

Bidell, T. R., et al. (1994). Developing conceptions of racism among young white adults in the context of cultural diversity coursework. *Journal of Adult Development,* 1 (3), 185–200.

Block, J. H. (1973). Conceptions of sex role: Some cross-cultural and longitudinal perspectives. *American Psychologist,* 28, 512–26.

Bluestone, B. (1984). *The deindustrialization of America.* New York: Basic Books.

Blumenfeld, W. (Ed.). (1992). *Homophobia: How we all pay the price.* Boston: Beacon Press.

——— (1993). *Speaking out: A manual for gay, lesbian, and bisexual public speakers.* Boston, MA: The Gay, Lesbian, and Bisexual Speakers Bureau (P.O. Box 2232).

Blumenfeld, W., and Raymond, D. (1993). *Looking at gay and lesbian life.* Boston: Beacon Press.

Bly, R. (1990). *Iron John: A book about men.* Reading, MA: Addison-Wesley.

Boal, A. (1979). *Theater of the oppressed* (translated by Charles A. and Maria-Odilia Leal McBride). New York: Urizen Books.

———. (1995). *The rainbow of desire: The Boal method of theatre and therapy* (translated by Adrian Jackson). New York: Routledge.

Bogdan, R. (1987). The exhibition of humans with differences for amusement and profit. *Policy Studies Journal,* 14 (3), 537–50.

Bogdan, R. et al. (1982). The disabled: Media's monster. *Social Policy,* 13 (2), 32–35.

Boonstra, J., Jansen, H., and Kniesmeyer, J. (Eds.). (1989). *Antisemitism, a history portrayed.* Amsterdam: Anne Frank Foundation.

Bornstein, K. (1994). *Gender outlaw: On men, women and the rest of us.* New York: Routledge.

Borton, T. (1970). *Reach, touch, and teach.* New York: McGraw-Hill.

Boud, D., Cohen, R., and Walker, D. (Eds.). (1993). *Using experience for learning.* Bristol, PA: Society for Research into Higher Education and Open University Press.

Bowles, S., and Gintis, H. (1987). *Democracy and capitalism: Property, community, and the contradictions of modern social thought.* New York: Basic Books.

Bowser, B., and Hunt, R., G. (Eds.). (1981). *Impacts of racism on white Americans.* Beverly Hills, CA: Sage.

Bradford, L. (Ed.). (1978). *Group development.* Amsterdam: Pfeffer and Co.

Bradford, L. P., Gibb, J. R., and Benne, K. D. (Eds.). (1964). *T-Group theory and laboratory method: Innovation in re-education.* New York: John Wiley.

Bricker-Jenkins, M., and Hooyman, N. (1986). Feminist pedagogy in education for social change. *Feminist Teacher,* 2 (2), 36–42.

Brookfield, S. (1993). Through the lens of learning: How the visceral experience of learning reframes teaching. In D. Boud, R. Cohen, and D. Walker (Eds.), *Using experience for learning*. Bristol, PA: Society for Research into Higher Education and Open University Press.

Bruffee, K. A. (1993). *Collaborative learning: Higher education, interdependence, and the authority of knowledge.* Baltimore, MD: The Johns Hopkins University Press.

Bulkin, E., Pratt, M. B., and Smith, B. (1984). *Yours in struggle: Three feminist perspectives on antisemitism and racism.* Ithaca, NY: Firebrand Books.

Bunch, C. (1987). Making common cause: Diversity and coalitions. In C. Bunch (Ed.), *Passionate politics: Feminist theory in action* . New York: St. Martin's Press.

Bunch, C., and Powell, B. (1983). Charlotte Bunch and Betty Powell talk about feminism, blacks and education as politics. In C. Bunch and S. Pollack (Eds.), *Learning our way: Essays in feminist education* . Trumansburg, NY: Crossing Press.

Bunker, B., Nochajski, T., McGillicuddy, N., and Bennett, D. (1987). Designing and running training events: Rules of thumb. In W. B. Reddy and C. Henderson (Eds.), *Training theory and practice* . La Jolla, CA: University Associates.

Butler, J. E. (1985). Toward a pedagogy of Everywoman's Studies. In M. Culley and C. Portuges (Eds.), *Gendered subjects: The dynamics of feminist teaching* . Boston: Routledge & Kegan Paul.

———. (1989). Transforming the curriculum: Teaching about women of color. In J. A. Banks and C. A. M. Banks (Eds.), *Multicultural education: Issues and perspectives* (pp. 145–63). Boston: Allyn & Bacon.

———. (1991). The difficult dialogue of curriculum transformation: Ethnic studies and women's studies. In J. E. Butler and J. C. Walter (Eds.), *Transforming the curriculum: Ethnic studies and women's studies* (pp. 1–19). Albany, NY: State University of New York Press.

Cannon, L. W. (1990). Fostering positive race, class and gender dynamics in the classroom. *Women's Studies Quarterly*, 18 (1–2), 126–34.

Carew, D., Carew, E., and Blanchard, K. (1990). *Group development and situational leadership II: The color model.* Escondido, CA: Blanchard Training and Development.

Cass, V. C. (1979). Homosexual identity formation: A theoretical model. *Journal of Homosexuality*, 4, 219–35.

———. (1984). Homosexual identity formation: Testing a theoretical model. *Journal of Sex Research*, 20, 143–67.

Castello, E. R., and Kapon, U. M. (1994). *The Jews and Europe: 2,000 years of history.* New York: Holt.

Chaffee, C. C. (1978). Cross-cultural training for Peace Corps volunteers. In D. S. Hoopes, P. B. Pedersen, and G. W. Renwick (Eds.), *Overview of intercultural education, training, and research, Volume II: Education and training* (pp. 104–26). Washington, DC: SIETAR: Society for Intercultural Education, Training, and Research.

Chickering, W. (1977). *Experience and learning: An introduction to experiential learning.* New Rochelle, NY: Change Magazine Press.

Chickering, A., and Gamson, Z. (1987). Seven principles of good practice. *AAHE Bulletin*, 39, 3–7.

Chodorow, N. (1978). *The reproduction of mothering: Psychoanalysis and the sociology of gender.* Berkeley, CA: University of California Press.

Chomsky, N. (1983). *The fateful triangle: the United States, Israel and the Palestinians.* Boston: South End Press.

———. (1989). *Necessary illusions: Thought control in democratic societies.* Boston: South End Press.

Churchill, W. (1995). *Since predator came: Notes from the struggle for American Indian liberation.* Littleton, CO: Aigis.

Clinchy, B. M. (1993). Ways of knowing and ways of being: Epistemological and moral development in undergraduate women. In A. Garrod (Ed.), *Approaches to moral development: New research and emerging themes*. New York: Teachers College Press.

Coch, L., and French, Jr., J. R. P. (1948). Overcoming resistance to change. *Human Relations*, 1 (4), 512–32.

Cohn-Sherbok, D. (1994). *Atlas of Jewish history.* New York: Routledge.

Cole, J. B. (1991). Black studies in liberal arts education. In J. E. Butler and J. C. Walter (Eds.), *Transforming the curriculum: Ethnic studies and women's studies* (pp. 131–47). Albany, NY: State University of New York Press.

Coleman-Burns, P. (1993). The revolution within: Transforming ourselves. In J. James and R. Farmer (Eds.), *Spirit, Space & survival: African American women in (white) academe.* New York: Routledge.

Collins, P. H. (1990). *Black feminist thought: Knowledge, consciousness and the politics of empowerment.* New York: Routledge.

Comstock, G. D. (1991). *Violence against lesbians and gay men.* New York: Columbia University Press.

Condon, J. C. (1986). The ethnocentric classroom. In J. M. Civikly (Ed.), *Communicating in college classrooms*, New Directions in Teaching and Learning, no. 26. San Francisco: Jossey-Bass.

Cook, L. A. (1954). *Intergroup education.* New York: McGraw-Hill.

Cose, E. (1993). *The rage of a privileged class.* New York: Harper Perennial.

Costello, C., and Stone, A. J. (Eds.). (1994). *The American woman: 1994–95.* New York: W.W. Norton and Co./ The Women's Research and Education Institute.

Criticos, C. (1993). Experiential learning and social transformation for a post-apartheid learning future. In D. Boud, R. Cohen, and D. Walker (Eds.), *Using experience for learning*. Bristol, PA: The Society for Research into Higher Education and Open University Press.

Cross, W. E., Jr. (1971). The Negro-to-Black conversion experience: Toward a psychology of black liberation. *Black World*, 20 (9), 13–27.

———. (1978). Models of psychological nigrescence: A literature review. *Journal of Black Psychology*, 5 (1), 13–31.

———. (1991). *Shades of black: Diversity in African-American identity.* Philadelphia: Temple University Press.

———. (1995). In search of blackness and afrocentricity: The psychology of black identity change. In H. W. Harris, H. C. Blue, and E. E. H. Griffith (Eds.), *Racial and ethnic identity: Psychological development and creative expression* (pp. 53–72). New York: Routledge.

Cross, T., Klein, F., Smith, B., and Smith, B. (1982). Face-to-face, day-to-day—racism CR. In G. T. Hull, P. B. Scott, and B. Smith (Eds.), *All the women are white, all the blacks are men, but some of us are brave.* New York: The Feminist Press.

Crumpacker, L., and Vander Haegen, E. M. (1987). Pedagogy and prejudice: Strategies for confronting homophobia in the classroom. *Women's Studies Quarterly,* 15 (3&4), 65–79.

Culley, M. (1985). Anger and authority in the introductory women's studies classroom. In M. Culley and C. Portuges (Eds.), *Gendered subjects: The dynamics of feminist teaching* (pp. 209–17). Boston: Routledge & Kegan Paul.

Culley, M., and Portuges, C. (Eds.). (1985). *Gendered subjects: The dynamics of feminist teaching.* Boston: Routledge & Kegan Paul.

Cyrus, V. (1993). *Experiencing race, class and gender in the United States.* Mountain View, CA: Mayfield Publishing Co.

Daily Collegian, University of Massachusetts. (1994, December 7). Black, Jewish students react to Martin's speech. *CIV* (56), 1.

Damarin, S. (1994). Equity, caring and beyond: Can feminist ethics inform educational technology? *Educational Technology,* 34 (2), 34–39.

Davis, D. B. (1994, December 22). The slave trade and the Jews. *The New York Review of Books,* 12, 15–16.

De Danaan, L. (1990). Center to margin: Dynamics in a global classroom. *Women's Studies Quarterly,* 18 (1&2), 135–44.

de Lone, R. (Carnegie Council on Children) (1979). *Small futures: Children, inequality and the limits of liberal reform.* New York: Harcourt Brace Jovanovich.

DeLoach, C. P., Wilkins, R. D., and Walker, G. W. (1983). *Independent living: Philosophy, process, and services.* Baltimore, MD: University Park Press.

Delpit, L. (1988). The silenced dialogue: Power and pedagogy in educating other people's children. *Harvard Educational Review,* 58 (3), 280–98.

Dill, B. T., and Zinn, M. B. (1990). *Race and gender: Re-visioning social relations.* Research paper #11, Center for Research on Women, Memphis, TN: Memphis State University.

Dillon, J. (1994). *Using discussions in classrooms.* Philadelphia: Open University Press.

Dimont, M. (1992). *Jews, God and history.* New York: Penguin.

Dinnerstein, D. (1976). *The mermaid and the minotaur: Sexual arrangements and human malaise.* New York: Harper & Row.

Dinnerstein, L. (1994). *Antisemitism in America.* New York: Oxford University Press.

Downing, N. E., and Roush, K. L. (1985). From passive acceptance to active commitment: A model of feminist identity development for women. *The Counseling Psychologist,* 13 (4), 695–709.

Downs, J. F. (1978). Intercultural training for government employees and military personnel for overseas assignments. In D. S. Hoopes, P. B. Pedersen, and G. W. Renwick (Eds.), *Overview of intercultural education, training and research, Volume II: Education and training* . Washington, DC: SIETAR: Society for Intercultural Education, Training, and Research.

Doumami, B. (1992). Rediscovery of Ottoman Palestine: Writing Palestine into history. *Journal of Palestine Studies,* 21 (2), 5–28.

Dunn, K. (1993). Feminist teaching: Who are your students? *Women's Studies Quarterly,* 21 (3&4), 39–45.

Echols, A. (1989). *Daring to be bad: Radical feminism in America.* Minneapolis, MN: University of Minnesota Press.

Eitington, J. (1984). *The winning trainer.* Houston: Gulf Publications.

Ellsworth, E. (1989). Why doesn't this feel empowering? Working through the repressive myths of critical pedagogy. *Harvard Educational Review* 59 (3), 297–324. (Reprinted in L. Stone (Ed.) (1994), *The educational feminism reader,* pp. 300–27. New York: Routledge.)

Epstein, S. (1987). Gay politics, ethnic identity: The limits of social constructionism. *Socialist Review*, 17 (3–4), 9–54.
Erikson, E. H. (1964). *Insight and responsibility*. New York: Norton.
———. (1968). Identity, psychosocial. In D. L. Sills (Ed.), *International encyclopedia of the social sciences*, volume 7 (pp. 65–66). New York: Macmillan.
Evans, S. (1979). *Personal politics: The roots of women's liberation in the civil rights movement and the new left*. New York: Knopf/Random House.
Faderman, L. (1991). *Odd girls and twilight lovers: A history of lesbian life in the twentieth century*. New York: Columbia University Press.
Fahy, U. (1995). *How to make the world a better place for gays and lesbians*. New York: Times Warner.
Falbel, R., Klepfisz, I., and Nevel, D. (1990). *The Jewish women's call for peace: A handbook for Jewish women on the Israeli-Palestinian conflict*. Ithaca, N.Y.: Firebrand Books.
Fanon, F. (1967). *Black skin, white masks*. New York: Grove Press.
———. (1968). *The wretched of the earth*. New York: Grove Press.
Feagin, J. R., and Sikes, M. P. (1994). *Living with racism: The black middle-class experience*. Boston: Beacon Press.
Feinberg, L. (1996). *Transgender warriors: Making history from Joan of Arc to Ru Paul*. New York: Farrar, Strauss and Giroux.
Ferguson, A. (1982). Feminist teaching: A practice developed in undergraduate courses. *Radical Teacher*, 20, 26–29.
Fernea, E. W., and Hocking, M. E. (Eds.). (1992). *The struggle for peace: Israelis and Palestinians*. Austin: University of Texas Press.
Finn, P., and McNeil, T. (1987). *The response of the criminal justice system to bias crimes: An exploratory study*. ABT Associates, Inc., 55 Wheeler St., Cambridge, MA 02138–1168.
Firestone, S. (1970). *The dialectic of sex: The case for feminist revolution*. New York: Morrow.
Fisher, B. (1981). What is feminist pedagogy? *Radical Teacher*, 18, 24–29.
———. (1987). The heart has its reasons: Feeling, thinking, and community-building in feminist education. *Women's Studies Quarterly*, 15, 47–58.
Folbre, N., and Center for Popular Economics. (1995). *New field guide to the U.S. Economy*. New York: New Press.
Foucault, M. (1980). *The history of sexuality*. New York: Vintage Books.
Frankenberg, R. (1990). White women, racism, and anti-racism: A women's studies course exploring racism and privilege. *Women's Studies Quarterly* (1&2), 145–153.
———. (1993). *White women, race matters: The social construction of whiteness*. Minneapolis: University of Minnesota Press.
Fraser, S. (Ed.). (1995). *The bell curve wars: Race, intelligence, and the future of America*. New York: Basic Books.
Freedman, E. B. (1994). Small-group pedagogy: Consciousness raising in conservative times. In L. Garber (Ed.), *Tilting the tower* (pp. 35–50). New York: Routledge.
Freire, P. (1970). *Pedagogy of the oppressed*. New York: Seabury.
———. (1972). *Cultural action for freedom*. Middlesex, England: Penguin Books.
———. (1973). *Education for critical consciousness*. New York: Seabury.
———. (1994/1970). *Pedagogy of the oppressed*. (revised edition). New York: Continuum.
Friedman, T. L. (1989). *From Beirut to Jerusalem*. New York: Doubleday.
Frye, M. (1983). *The politics of reality: Essays in feminist theory*. Freedom, CA: The Crossing Press.
Gallos, J. V. (1989). Developmental diversity and the OB classroom: Implications for teaching and learning. *Organizational Behavior Teaching Review*, 13 (4), 33–47.
Geller, T. (Ed.). (1990). *Bisexuality: A reader and sourcebook*. Ojai, CA: Times Change Press.
Gilligan, C. (1982). *In a different voice: Psychological theory and women's development*. Cambridge, MA: Harvard University Press.
Gilman, S. (1991). *The Jew's body*. New York: Routledge.
Gitlin, T. (1987). *The sixties: Years of hope, days of rage*. New York: Bantam.
Goldenberg, I. I. (1978). *Oppression and social intervention: Essays on the human condition and the problems of change*. Chicago, IL: Nelson-Hall.

Golembiewski, R. T., and Blumberg, A. (1977). *Sensitivity training and the laboratory approach: Readings about concepts and applications.* Itasca, IL: F.E. Peacock Publishers.

Gonsiorek, J. C. (1995). Gay male identities: Concepts and issues. In A. R. D'Augelli and C. J. Patterson (Eds.), *Lesbian, gay, and bisexual identities over the lifespan: Psychological perspectives.* New York: Oxford University Press.

Goodman, D. (1995). Difficult dialogues: Enhancing discussions about diversity. *College Teaching,* 43 (2), 47–52.

Goodman, G. (1983). *No turning back: Lesbian and gay liberation for the 80's.* Philadelphia, PA: New Society Press.

Grant, C. A. (Ed.). (1992). *Research and multicultural education.* London: Falmer.

Green, M. F. (1989). *Minorities on campus: A handbook for enhancing diversity.* Washington, DC: American Council on Education.

Gregory, S., and Sanjek, R. (1994). *Race.* New Brunswick, NJ: Rutgers University Press.

Greider, W. B. (1992). *Who will tell the people: The betrayal of American democracy.* New York: Simon and Schuster.

Griffin, C., and Mulligan, J. (Eds.). (1992). *Empowerment through experiential learning: Explorations of good practice.* London: Kogan Page.

Grossman, D. (1993). *Sleeping on a wire: Conversations with Palestinians in Israel.* New York: Farrar, Straus and Giroux.

Gudykunst, W. (1994). *Bridging differences: Effective intergroup communications.* Thousand Oaks, CA: Sage.

Hacker, A. (1992). *Two nations: Black and white, separate, hostile, unequal.* New York: Ballantine.

Hale-Benson, J. E. (1986). *Black children: Their roots, culture, and learning styles,* revised edition. Baltimore: The Johns Hopkins University Press.

Hanson, P., and Lubin, B. (1987). Assessment of trainer skills by self, peers, and supervisors. In W. B. Reddy and C. Henderson (Eds.), *Training theory and practice* . La Jolla, CA: University Associates.

Hardiman, R. (1979). White identity development theory. University of Massachusetts, Amherst. Unpublished manuscript.

———. (1982). White identity development: A process oriented model for describing the racial consciousness of white Americans. Dissertation Abstracts International, A 43/01, p. 104 (University Microfilms No. AAC 8210330).

———. (1994). White racial identity development in the United States. In E. P. Salett and D. R. Koslow (Eds.), *Race, ethnicity, and self: Identity in multicultural perspective* . Washington, DC: National MultiCultural Institute.

Hardiman, R., and Jackson, B. W. (1980). Perspectives on race. Unpublished manuscript.

———. (1992). Racial identity development: Understanding racial dynamics in college classrooms and on campus. In M. Adams (Ed.), *Promoting diversity in college classrooms: Innovative responses for the curriculum, faculty, and institutions* New Directions for Teaching and Learning, no. 52, 21–37). San Francisco, CA: Jossey-Bass.

Harding, S. (1991). *Whose science, whose knowledge?* Ithaca, NY: Cornell University Press.

Harris, M. (1988). *Women and teaching.* New York: Paulist Press.

Harrison, R., and Hopkins, R. L. (1967). The design of cross-cultural training: An alternative to the university model. *Journal of Applied Behavioral Science,* 3 (4), 431–60.

Harro, R. L. (1986). *Teaching about heterosexism: A psychological education design project.* Dissertation Abstract International, A 47/03, p. 774 (University Microfilm No. AAC 8612044).

Hart, M. U. (1991). Liberation through consciousness raising. In Mezirow J. et al. (Ed.), *Fostering critical reflection in adulthood: A guide to transformative and emancipatory learning* . San Francisco: Jossey-Bass.

Hartsock, N. (1983). *Money, sex and power: Toward a feminist historical materialism.* New York: Longman.

Hatfield, S. R. (Ed.). (1995). *The seven principles in action: Improving undergraduate education.* Bolton, MA: Anker.

Hayles, R. (1978). Inter-ethnic and race relations education and training. In D. S. Hoopes, P. B.

Pedersen, and G. W. Renwick (Eds.), *Overview of intercultural education, training and research, Volume II: Education and training* . Washington, DC: SIETAR: Society for Intercultural Education, Training and Research.

Helms, J. E. (1990). *Black and white identity: Theory, research and practice.* Westport, CT: Greenwood Press.

Herrnstein, R., and Murray, C. (1994). *The bell curve: Intelligence and class structure in America.* New York: Free Press.

Hochschild, A. (1989). *The second shift: Working parents and the revolution at home.* New York: Viking Press.

Hoffman, N. J. (1985). Breaking silences: Life in the feminist classroom. In M. Culley and C. Portuges (Eds.), *Gendered subjects: The dynamics of feminist teaching* (147–54). Boston: Routledge & Kegan Paul.

hooks, b. (1984). *Feminist theory: From margin to center.* Boston: South End Press.

———. (1989). *Talking back: Thinking feminist, thinking black.* Boston: South End Press.

———. (1994). *Teaching to transgress: Education as the practice of freedom.* New York: Routledge.

Howe, F. (1984a). Mississippi's Freedom Schools: The politics of education. In F. Howe (Ed.), *Myths of coeducation: Selected essays, 1964–1983* (pp. 1–17). Bloomington, IN: Indiana University Press.

———. (1984b). Women and the power to change. In F. Howe (Ed.), *Myths of coeducation: Selected essays, 1964–1983* (pp. 139–74). Bloomington, IN: Indiana University Press.

Hull, G. T., Scott, P. B., and Smith, B. (Eds.). (1982). *All the women are white, all the blacks are men, but some of us are brave.* New York: The Feminist Press.

Human Rights Watch/Asia. (1996). *Death by default: A policy of fatal neglect in China's state orphanages.* New York: Human Rights Watch.

Hunt, Jr., J. S. (1995). Dewey's philosophical method and its influence on his philosophy of education. In K. Warren, M. Sakofs, and J. S. Hunt Jr. (Eds.), *The theory of experiential education* . Dubuque, IA: Kendall/Hunt Publishing Co.

Hurst, F. A. (1988). *Report on University of Massachusetts Investigation* . Springfield, MA: Massachusetts Commission Against Discrimination.

Hutchins, L. and Kaahumanu, L. (Eds.) (1991). *Bi any other name: Bisexual people speak out.* Boston: Alyson.

Icard, L. (1986). Black gay men and conflicting social identities: Sexual orientation vs. racial identity. In J. Gripton and M. Valentich (Eds.), *Social work practice in sexual problems* (pp. 83–93). New York: Haworth.

Jackson, B. W. (1976a). *The function of a black identity development theory in achieving relevance in education for black students.* Dissertation Abstracts International, A 37/09, 5667 (University Microfilms No. AAC 7706381).

Jackson, B. W. (1976b). Black identity development. In L. Golubschick and B. Persky (Eds.), *Urban social and educational issues.* Dubuque, IA: Kendall/Hunt.

Jacoby, R., and Glauberman, N. (1995). *The bell curve debate: History, documents, opinions.* New York: Times Books.

James, J., and Farmer, R. (Eds.). (1993). *Spirit, space and survival: African American women in (white) academe.* New York: Routledge.

Johnson, D., and Johnson, F. (1987). *Joining together: Group theory and group skills.* Englewood Cliffs, NJ: Prentice-Hall.

Joplin, L. (1995). On defining experiential education. In K. Warren, M. Sakofs, and J. S. Hunt Jr. (Eds.), *The theory of experiential education* . Dubuque, IA: Kendall/Hunt Publishing Co.

Katz, J. (1976). *Gay American history.* New York: Arm.

———. (1995). *The invention of heterosexuality.* New York: Dutton.

Katz, J. H. (1978). *White awareness: Handbook for anti-racism training.* Norman, OK: University of Oklahoma Press.

Kaufman, J. (1988). *Broken alliance.* New York: Charles Scribner's Sons.

Kaye/Kantrowitz, M. (1992). *The issue is power: Essays on women, Jews, violence and resistance.* San Francisco, CA: Aunt Lute Books.

Keen, S. (1991). *Fire in the belly: On being a man.* New York: Bantam Books.

Kegan, R. (1982). *The evolving self.* Cambridge, MA: Harvard University Press.

Keil, F. C. (1984). Mechanisms of cognitive development and the structure of knowledge. In R. J. Sternberg (Ed.), *Mechanisms of cognitive development.* New York: W.H. Freeman.

Kesselman, A., McNair, L., and Schniedewind, N. (Eds.). (1995). *Women: Images and realities—a multicultural reader.* Mountain View, CA: Mayfield Publishing Co.

Kim, J. (1981). Processes of Asian American identity development: A study of Japanese American women's perceptions of their struggles to achieve positive identities as Americans of Asian ancestry. Dissertation Abstracts International, A 42/04, p. 1551 (University Microfilms No. AAC 8118010).

Kimmel, M., and Messner, M. (Eds.). (1989). *Men's lives.* New York: Macmillan.

King, P. M., and Kitchener, K. S. (1994). *Developing reflective judgment: Understanding and promoting intellectual growth and critical thinking in adolescents and adults.* San Francisco: Jossey-Bass.

Kitchener, K. (1982). Human development and the college campus: Sequences and tasks. In G. Hanson (Ed.), *Measuring student development,* New Directions for Student Services, no. 20. San Francisco: Jossey-Bass.

Kivel, P. (1992). *Men's work: How to stop the violence that tears our lives apart.* Center City, MN: Hazelden Books.

———. (1996). *Uprooting racism: How white people can work for racial justice.* Philadelphia: New Society Publishers.

Klein, F., Sepekoff, B., and Wolf, T. J. (1985). Sexual orientation: A multi-variable dynamic process. *Journal of Homosexuality,* 11 (1/2), 35–49.

Klein, R. D. (1987). The dynamics of the women's studies classroom: A review essay of the teaching practice of women's studies in higher education. *Women's Studies International Forum,* 10 (2), 187–206.

Knefelkamp, L. (1974). Developmental instruction: Fostering intellectual and personal growth of college students. *Dissertation Abstracts International,* 36 (127A), (University Microfilms No. 75–21, 059).

Kochman, T. (1981). *Black and white styles in conflict.* Chicago: Chicago University Press.

Kohlberg, L., and Higgins, A. (1989). School democracy and social interaction. In W. M. Kurtines and J. L. Gewirtz (Eds.), *Moral development through social interaction* . New York: Wiley & Sons.

Kolb, D. A. (1984). *Experiential learning: Experience as the source of learning and development.* Englewood Cliffs, NJ: Prentice-Hall.

Kovel, J. (1970). *White racism: A psychohistory.* New York: Pantheon Books.

Krefetz, G. (1982). *Jews and money.* New Haven, CT: Ticknor & Fields.

Kreisberg, S. (1992). *Transforming power: Domination, empowerment, and education.* New York: State University of New York Press.

Kurfiss, J. G. (1988). *Critical thinking: Theory, research, practice, and possibilities;* ASHE-ERIC Higher Education Report No. 2. Washington, DC: The George Washington University, School of Education and Human Development.

Lacoursiere, R. (1980). *The life cycle of groups: Group developmental stage theory.* New York: Human Service Press.

Ladson-Billings, G. (1996). Silence as weapons: Challenges of a black professor teaching white students. *Theory into Practice, 35,* (2), 79–85.

———. (1995). Toward a theory of culturally relevant pedagogy. *American Educational Research Journal,* 32 (3), 465–91.

Langmuir, G. I. (1990). *Toward a definition of antisemitism.* Berkeley, CA: University of California Press.

Larsson, G. (1994). *Fact or fraud? The protocols of the Elders of Zion.* Jerusalem: AMI-Jerusalem Center for Biblical Studies and Research.

Lather, P. (1991). *Getting smart: Feminist research and pedagogy within the postmodern.* New York: Routledge.

Lee, M. A., and Solomon, N. (1990). *Unreliable sources: A guide to detecting bias in the news media.* New York: Carol Publishing Group.

Leong, R. (Ed.). (1996). *Asian American sexualities: Dimensions of the gay and lesbian experience.* New York: Routledge.

Lerner, G. (1986). *Women and history.* New York: Oxford University Press.

Lerner, M. (1992). *The socialism of fools: Anti-semitism on the left.* Oakland, CA: Tikkun Books.

Lerner, M., and West, C. (1992). A conversation between Cornel West and Michael Lerner. In J. Salzman (Ed.), *Bridges and boundaries: African Americans and American Jews*. New York: George Braziller.

———. (1996). *Jews and Blacks: A dialogue on race, religion, and culture in America.* New York: Plume.

Lewin, K. (1948). *Resolving social conflicts.* New York: Harper and Row.

Lewis, M. (1993). *Without a word: Teaching beyond women's silence.* New York: Routledge.

Liachowitz, C. H. (1988). *Disability as a social construct: Legislative roots.* Philadelphia: University of Pennsylvania Press.

Lipksky, S. (1977). Internalized oppression. *Black Re-Emergence,* 2, 5–10.

Lippitt, R. (1949). *Training in community relations.* New York: Harper & Brothers.

Lorde, A. (1983). There is no hierarchy of oppressions. *Interracial Books for Children Bulletin,* 14 (3–4), 9.

———. (1984). *Sister Outsider.* New York: Crossing Press.

Lusted, D. (1986). Why pedagogy?. *Screen,* 27 (5), 2–14.

Lyons, N. P. (1983). Two perspectives on self, relationships, and morality. *Harvard Education Review,* 55, 124–146.

MacKinnon, C. (1989). *Toward a feminist theory of the state.* Cambridge, MA: Harvard University Press.

Maher, F. A. (1985). Pedagogies for the gender-balanced classroom. *Journal of Thought,* 20 (3), 48–64.

Maher, F. A., and Tetreault, M. K. T. (1994). *The feminist classroom.* New York: Basic Books.

Malaney, G. D. (1994). Antisemitism on campus. *Antisemitism Journal,* 31 (4), 252–62.

Marabel, M. (1984). *Race, reform, and rebellion: The second reconstruction in Black America, 1945–1982.* Jackson: University of Mississippi Press.

Marchesani, L., and Adams, M. (1992). Dynamics of diversity in the teaching-learning process: A faculty development model for analysis and action. In M. Adams (Ed.), *Promoting diversity in college classrooms: Innovative responses for the curriculum, faculty and institutions,* New Directions for Teaching and Learning, no. 52 (pp. 9–21). San Francisco: Jossey-Bass.

Marcus, E. (1993). *Is it a choice: Answers to 300 of the most frequently asked questions about gays and lesbians.* San Francisco: Harper San Francisco.

———. (1992). *Making history: The struggle for gay and lesbian equal rights.* New York: Harper Perennial.

Marrow, A. J. (1969). *The practical theorist: The life and work of Kurt Lewin.* New York: Basic Books.

McCarthy, C., and Crichlow, W. (Eds.). (1993). *Race, identity and representation in education.* New York: Routledge.

McIntosh, P. (1988). *White privilege and male privilege: A personal account of coming to see correspondences through work in women's studies,* Working paper #189. Wellesley, MA: Wellesley College Center for Research on Women.

———. (1992). White privilege and male privilege: A personal account of coming to see correspondences through work in women's studies. In M. L. Andersen and P. H. Collins (Eds.), *Race, class, and gender: An anthology*. Belmont, CA: Wadsworth Publishing Co.

McLemore, S. D. (1993). *Racial and ethnic relations in America,* 4th Edition. Boston: Allyn & Bacon.

McNeil, J. (1988). *Taking a chance on God: Liberating theology for gays, lesbians and their lovers, families, and friends.* Boston: Beacon Press.

McNeil, J. M. (1993). *Americans with disabilities, 1991/92: Data from the survey of income and program participation.* Washington, DC: US Dept. of Commerce, Economics and Statistics Administration, Bureau of the Census.

McWhorter, G. A. (1969). Deck the ivy racist halls: The case of black studies. In A. L. Robinson, C. C. Foster, and D. H. Ogilvie (Eds.), *Black studies in the university: A symposium* . New Haven, CT: Yale University Press.

Memmi, A. (1965). *The colonizer and the colonized.* Boston: Beacon Press.

———. (1975). *Jews and Arabs.* Chicago: O'Hara Inc.

Mentkowski, M., Moeser, M., and Strait, M. J. (1983). A longitudinal study of student change in cognitive development, learning styles, and generic abilities in an outcome-centered liberal arts curriculum (ERIC No. ED 239 562). Paper presented at the American Educational Research Association, Montreal, Quebec.

Meyers, C., and Jones, T. B. (1993). *Promoting active learning: Strategies for the college classroom.* San Francisco: Jossey-Bass.

Mill, C. R. (1974). Working with hostile groups. *Social Change: Ideas and Applications,* 4 (1), 1–5.

Miller, J. B. (1976). *Toward a new psychology of women.* Boston: Beacon Press.

Mishel, L., and Bernstein, J. (1995). *The state of working America, 1994–1995.* Armonk, NY: M.E. Sharpe.

Mogil, C., and Slepian, A. (1992). *We gave away a fortune: Stories of people who have devoted themselves and their wealth to peace, justice and a healthy environment.* Philadelphia, PA: New Society Publishers.

Mohanty, C. T., Russo, A., and Torres, L. (1991). *Third world women and the politics of feminism.* Bloomington: Indiana University Press.

Moosbruker, J. (1987). Using a stage theory model to understand and manage transitions in group dynamics. In W. B. Reddy and C. Henderson (Eds.), *Training theory and practice.* La Jolla, CA: University Associates.

Moraga, C., and Anzaldúa, G. (Eds.). (1981/1983). *This bridge called my back: Writings by radical women of color.* New York: Kitchen Table: Women of Color Press.

Morgan, R. (1996). Dispatch from Beijing. *Ms.,* 6 (4), 12–21.

Morris, J. (1991). *Pride against prejudice: Transforming attitudes to disability.* Philadelphia: New Society Publishers.

Morrissey, J. P., Goldman, H. H., and Klerman, L. V. (Eds.). (1980). *The enduring asylum: Cycles of institutional reform at Worcester State Hospital.* New York: Grune & Stratton.

Morrow, R. A., and Torres, C. A. (1995). *Social theory and education: A critique of theories of social and cultural reproduction.* New York: State University of New York Press.

Mosse, G. L. (1985). *Toward the final solution: A history of European racism.* Madison: University of Wisconsin Press.

Mumford, L. S. (1985). "Why do we have to read all this old stuff?" Conflict in the feminist theory classroom. *Journal of Thought,* 20 (3), 88–96.

Narayan, U. (1988). Working together across differences. *Hypatia,* 2 (3), 31–46.

Nieto, S. (1996). *Affirming diversity: The sociopolitical context of multicultural education,* 2nd edition. White Plains, NY: Longman.

Noble, D. (1989). Hightech skills. In S. London (Ed.), *The reeducation of the American working class.* New York: Greenwood Press.

Noronha, J. (1992). International and multicultural education: Unrelated adversaries or successful partners? In M. Adams (Ed.), *Promoting diversity in college classrooms: Innovative responses for curriculum, faculty, and institutions.* New Directions for Teaching and Learning, no. 52 (pp. 53–61). San Francisco: Jossey-Bass.

Oboler, S. (1995). *Ethnic labels, latino lives.* Minneapolis: University of Minnesota Press.

Omi, M., and Winant, H. (1986). *Racial formation in the United States from the 1960's to the 1980's.* New York: Routledge.

Omolade, B. (1987). A black feminist pedagogy. *Women's Studies Quarterly,* 15 (3&4), 32–39.

Oser, F. K., Andreas, D., and Patry, J.-L. (Eds.). (1992). *Effective and responsible teaching: The new synthesis.* San Francisco: Jossey-Bass.

Pascarella, E. T., and Terenzini, P. T. (1991). *How college affects students: Findings and insights from twenty years of research.* San Francisco: Jossey-Bass.

Perry, W. G. (1970). *Forms of intellectual and ethical development in the college years.* New York: Holt, Rinehart & Winston.

———. (1981). Cognitive and ethical growth: The making of meaning. In A. Chickering (Ed.), *The modern American college.* San Francisco: Jossey-Bass.

Pfeiffer, D. (1993). Overview of the disability movement: History, legislative record, and political implications. *Policy Studies Journal,* 21 (4), 724–34.

Pfeiffer, J., and Jones, J. (Eds.). (1972–81). *The annual handbook for group facilitators.* La Jolla, CA: University Associates.

———. (1982–present). *The annual handbook for facilitators, trainers, and consultants.* La Jolla, CA: University Associates.

———. (1975). *The 1975 annual handbook for group facilitators.* La Jolla, CA: University Associates.

———. (1974). *Handbook of structured experiences for human relations training, volumes 1 & 2, revised edition.* La Jolla, CA: University Associates.

Pharr, S. (1988). *Homophobia: A weapon of sexism.* Inverness, CA: Chardon Press.

Pheterson, G. (1990). Alliances between women: Overcoming internalized oppression and internalized domination. In L. Albrecht and R. Brewer (Eds.), *Bridges of power: Women's multicultural alliances*. Philadelphia: New Society Publishers.

Phillips, C. (1987). The trainer as person: On the importance of developing your best intervention. In W. B. Reddy and C. Henderson (Eds.), *Training theory and practice*. La Jolla, CA: University Associates.

Phillips, K. (1990). *The politics of rich and poor: Wealth and the American electorate in the Reagan aftermath.* New York: Harper.

Piven, F. F., and Cloward, R. (1982). *The new class war: Reagan's attack on the welfare state and its consequences.* New York: Pantheon.

Pizzigati, S. (1992). *The maximum wage: A common-sense prescription for revitalizing America—By taxing the very rich.* New York: Apex Press.

Polokow, V. (1993). *Lives on the edge: Women and their children in the other America.* Chicago: University of Chicago Press.

Porter, L. (1982). Giving and receiving feedback: It will never be easy, but it can be better. In L. Porter and B. Mohr (Eds.), *The NTL reading book for human relations training*. Alexandria, VA: NTL Institute.

Proudman, B. (1995). AEE adopts definition. *The AEE Horizon,* 15, 1, 21.

Ramírez, M., and Casteñada, A. (1974). *Cultural democracy, bicognitive development, and education.* New York: Academic Press.

Ramos, J. (Ed.). (1994). *Campañeras: Latina Lesbians.* New York: Routledge.

Ratti, R. (Ed.). (1993). *A lotus of another color: An unfolding of the South Asian gay and lesbian experience.* Boston: Alyson.

Reagon, B. J. (1983). Coalition politics: Turning the century. In B. Smith (Ed.), *Home girls: A black feminist anthology*. New York: Kitchen Table Press.

Reed, A. L., Jr., (1986). Blacks and Jews in the Democratic coalition. In A. L. Reed, Jr. (Ed.), *The Jesse Jackson phenomenon: The crisis of purpose in Afro-American politics*. New Haven, CT: Yale University Press.

Rich, A. (1979). *On lies, secrets, and silence.* New York: Norton.

Rogoff, B. (1984). Introduction: Thinking and learning in social context. In B. Rogoff and J. Lave (Eds.), *Everyday cognition: Its development in social context.* Cambridge, MA: Harvard University Press.

Rogoff, B., Gauvain, M., and Ellis, S. (1984). Development viewed in its cultural context. In M. Bornstein and M. Lamb (Eds.), *Developmental psychology: An advanced textbook.* Hillsdale, NJ: Lawrence Erlbaum.

Roiphe, A. (1988). *Blacks and Jews, A season for healing: Reflections on the Holocaust*. New York: Summit Books.

Romney, P., Tatum, B., and Jones, J. (1992). Feminist strategies for teaching about oppression: The importance of process. *Women's Studies Quarterly,* 20 (1&2), 95–110.

Roscoe, W. (Ed.). (1988). *Living in spirit: A gay American Indian anthology.* New York: St. Martin's Press.

Rose, S. J. (1992). *Social stratification in the United States: The American profile poster revised and expanded.* New York: New Press.

Rothenberg, P. (1985). Teaching about racism and sexism: A case history. *Journal of Thought,* 20 (3), 122–36.

Rozema, H. J. (1988). Role reversals in male/female communication: A classroom simulation. *Feminist Teacher,* 3 (2), 18–20.

Russell, M. G. (1983). Black-eyed blues connections: From the inside out. In C. Bunch and S. Pollack (Eds.), *Learning our way: Essays in feminist education*. Trumansburg, NY: Crossing Press.

Ruth, S. (1990). *Issues in feminism: An introduction to women's studies.* Mountain View, CA: Mayfield Publishing Co.

Ryan, W. (1971). *Blaming the victim.* New York: Pantheon.

Saddington, J. A. (1992). Learner experience: A rich resource for learning. In J. Mulligan and C. Griffin (Eds.), *Empowerment through experiential learning: Explorations of good practice*. London: Kogan Page.

Sadker, M., and Sadker, D. (1992). Ensuring equitable participation in college classes. In L. L. B. Border & N. V. N. Chism (Eds.), *Teaching for diversity.* New Directions for Teaching and Learning, no. 49. San Francisco: Jossey-Bass.

Said, E. W. (1993). *Culture and imperialism.* New York: Knopf.

———. (1996). *Peace and its discontents: Essays on Palestine in the Middle East Process.* New York: Vintage.

———. (1992). *The Question of Palestine.* New York: Vintage.

Salzman, J., Back, A., and Sorin, G. (Eds.). (1992). *Bridges and boundaries: African Americans and American Jews.* New York: The Jewish Museum.

Sandler, B. R., and Hall, R. M. (1982). *The campus climate revisited: Chilly for women faculty, administrators, and graduate students.* Washington, DC: Project on the Status and Education of Women, Association of American Colleges.

Sarachild, K. (1975). Consciousness-raising: A radical weapon. In Redstockings (Ed.), *Feminist revolution* (pp. 144–50). New York: Random House.

Sargent, A. G. (1974). *Consciousness raising groups: A strategy for sex role liberation.* Dissertation Abstracts International, A 36/01, p. 196 (University Microfilms No. 7506084).

———. (Ed.). (1977/85). *Beyond sex roles,* 2nd edition. New York: West Publishing.

Sayres, S. (1984). *The 60's without apology.* Minneapolis: University of Minnesota Press.

Schapiro, S. A. (1985). Changing men: The rationale, theory, and design of a men's consciousness raising program. Dissertation Abstracts International, An 46/09, p. 2549 (University Microfilms AAC 8517150).

Schneidewind, N. (1993). Teaching feminist process in the 1990's. *Women's Studies Quarterly,* 3 & 4, 17–30.

———. (1985). Cooperatively structured learning: Implications for feminist pedagogy. *Journal of Thought,* 20 (3), 74–87.

———. (1987). Feminist values: Guidelines for teaching methodology in women's studies. In I. Shor (Ed.), *Freire for classroom.* Portsmouth, NH: Boynton/Cook.

Schniedewind, N., and Davidson, E. (1983). *Open minds to equality: A sourcebook of learning activities to promote race, sex, class, and age equity.* Englewood Cliffs, NJ: Prentice-Hall.

Schoem, D. (1993). Teaching about ethnic identity and intergroup relations. In D. Schoem, L. Frankel, X. Zúñiga, and E. A. Lewis (Eds.), *Multicultural teaching in the university.* Westport, CT: Praeger.

Schoem, D., Frankel, L., Zúñiga, X., and Lewis, E. A. (Eds.). (1993). *Multicultural teaching in the university.* Westport, CT: Praeger.

Schor, J. B. (1992). *The overworked American: The unexpected decline of leisure.* New York: Basic Books.

Schwarz, R. M. (1994). *The skilled facilitator: Practical wisdom for developing effective groups.* San Francisco: Jossey-Bass.

Sears, J. (Ed.). (1994). *Bound by diversity.* Columbia, SC: Sebastian Press.

———. (1990). *Growing up gay in the South.* New York: Haworth.

Segrest, M. (1994). *Memoirs of a race traitor.* Boston: South End Press.

Sennett, R., and Cobb, J. (1972). *The hidden injuries of class.* New York: Vintage Books/Random House.

Shade, B. J. R. (Ed.). (1989). *Culture, style and the educative process.* Springfield, IL: Charles C. Thomas.

Shapiro, J. P. (1993). *No pity: People with disabilities forging a new civil rights movement.* New York: Random House.

Sharp, P. (1993). *Sharing your good ideas: A workshop facilitator's handbook.* Portsmouth, NH: Heinemann.

Sherif, M. (1967). *Group conflict and co-operation.* London: Routledge & Kegan Paul.

Sherif, M., Harvey, O. J., White, B. J., Hood, W. R., and Sherif, C. W. (1961). *Intergroup conflict and co-operation: The robbers cave experiment.* Norman: University of Oklahoma Book Exchange.

Sherover-Marcuse, R. (1981). Towards a perspective on unlearning racism: Twelve working assumptions. *Issues in Cooperation and Power,* 7, 14–15.

Shor, I. (Ed.). (1987). *Freire for the classroom: A sourcebook for liberatory teaching.* Portsmouth, NH: Heinemann.

———. (1992). *Empowering Education: Critical thinking for social change.* Chicago: University of Chicago Press.

———. (1993). Education is politics: Paulo Freire's critical pedagogy. In P. McLaren and P. Leonard (Eds.), *Paulo Freire: A critical encounter* (pp. 25–35). New York: Routledge.

Shor, I., and Freire, P. (1987). What is the "dialogical method" of teaching. *Journal of Education,* 169 (3), 11–31.

Sidel, R. (1994). *Battling bias.* New York: Penguin.

Silberman, M. (1990). *Active training: A handbook of techniques, designs, case examples, and tips.* San Francisco: Jossey-Bass.

Silvera, M. (Ed.) (1992). *Piece of my heart: A lesbian of color anthology.* Eastheven, CT: Inland Books.

Sleeter, C. (1993). How white teachers construct race. In C. McCarthy and W. Crichlow (Eds.), *Race, identity, and representation in education* . New York: Routledge.

Sleeter, C. E., and Grant, C. A. (1994). Education that is multicultural and social reconstructionist. In C. E. Sleeter and C. A. Grant, *Making choices for multicultural education: Five approaches to race, class, and gender,* 2nd edition (pp. 243–51). New York: Macmillan.

Smith, B. (Ed.) (1983). *Home girls: A black feminist anthology.* Albany, NY: Kitchen Table Press.

Smith, D. M., and Kolb, D. A. (1986). *User's guide for the learning style inventory: A manual for teachers and trainers.* Boston: McBer.

Smith, W. (1976). *The meaning of conscientizaçáo: The goal of Paulo Freire's pedagogy.* Amherst, MA: Center for International Education.

Smith, W., Alschuler, A., Moreno, C., and Tasiquano, E. (1975). Critical consciousness. *meforum,* 2 (1), 12–18.

Spelman, E. (1985). Combating the marginalization of black women in the classroom. In M. Culley and C. Portuges (Eds.), *Gendered subjects: The dynamics of feminist teaching* . Boston: Routledge & Kegan Paul.

———. (1988). *Inessential woman: Problems of exclusion in feminist thought.* Boston: Beacon Press.

Stannard, D. E. (1992). *American holocaust: The conquest of the new world.* New York: Oxford.

Stein, N., Marshall, N. L., and Tropp, L. R. (1993). *Secrets in public: Sexual harassment in our schools.* Wellesley, MA: Wellesley College Center for Research on Women.

Steinberg, S. (1989). *The ethnic myth: Race, ethnicity, and class in America,* updated edition. Boston: Beacon Press.

Stevens, G. I. (1993). *Videos for understanding diversity: A core selection and evaluative guide.* Chicago: American Library Association.

Stoltenberg, J. (1993). *The end of manhood: A book for men of conscience.* New York: Penguin.

Strickland, W. (1988). We can overcome: Reflections on real and imaginary rifts between Blacks and Jews. *Tikkun,* 3 (4), 49–52.

Suzuki, B. H. (1984). Curriculum transformation for multicultural education. *Education and Urban Society,* 16 (3), 294–322.

Svinicki, M. D., and Dixon, N. M. (1987). The Kolb model modified for classroom activities. *College Teaching*, 35 (4), 141–46.

Takaki, R. (1993). *A different mirror: A history of multicultural America.* Boston: Little, Brown, and Co.

Tatum, B. D. (1992). Talking about race, learning about racism: The application of racial identity development theory in the classroom. *Harvard Educational Review*, 62 (1), 1–24.

———. (1994). Teaching white students about racism: The search for white allies and the restoration of hope. *Teacher's College Record*, 95 (4), 462–76.

Terry, R. (1975). *For whites only.* Grand Rapids, WI: William B. Erdmans.

Tharp, R. G. (1989). Psychocultural variables and constraints: Effects on teaching and learning in schools. *American Psychologist*, 44 (2), 349–59.

Thompson, B., and Disch, E. (1992). Feminist, anti-racist, anti-oppression teaching: Two white women's experience. *Radical Teacher*, 41, 4–10.

Thompson, K., and Andrezejewski, J. (1988). *Why can't Sharon Kowalski come home?* San Francisco: Spinsters/Aunt Lute.

Tompkins, J. (1990). Pedagogy of the distressed. *College English*, 52 (6), 653–60.

Tong, R. (1989). *Feminist thought: A comprehensive introduction.* Boulder, CO: Westview Press.

Trinh, T. M. H. (1989). *Woman, native, other.* Bloomington: Indiana University Press.

Turque, B. (1992, September 14). Gays under fire. *Newsweek*, 120 (11), 34–40.

Unks, G. (Ed.) (1995). *The Gay Teen.* New York: Routledge.

U.S. Bureau of Census. (1992). *Current population survey.* Washington, DC: U.S. Bureau of Census.

———. (1994). *U.S. Bureau of Census Report, Americans with Disabilities*. Washington, DC: U.S. Bureau of Census.

U.S. Dept. of Health and Human Services. (1989). *Report of the Secretary's Task Force on Youth Suicide, Volume 3: Prevention and intervention in youth suicide*. Rockville, MD: US Dept. of Health and Human Services.

Vygotsky, L. (1978). *Mind in society.* Cambridge, MA: Harvard University Press.

Wallerstein, N. (1987). Problem-posing education: Freire's method for transformation. In I. Shor (Ed.), *Freire for the classroom: A sourcebook* (pp. 33–44). Portsmouth, NH: Heinemann.

Walter, S., and Stephan, C. (1996). *Intergroup relations.* Boulder, CO: Westview Press.

Warner, M. (1993). *Fear of a queer planet: Queer politics and social theory.* Minneapolis: University of Minnesota Press.

Washington, M. H. (1985). How racial differences helped us discover our common ground. In M. Culley and C. Portuges (Eds.), *Gendered subjects: The dynamics of feminist teaching.* Boston: Routledge and Kegan Paul.

Weiler, K. (1991). Freire and a feminist pedagogy of difference. *Harvard Educational Review*, 61 (4), 449–74.

Weinberg, M. (1986). Because they were Jews: A history of antisemitism. Westport, CT: Greenwood Press.

Weinstein, G. (1988). Design elements for intergroup awareness. *Journal for Specialists in Group Work, 13*, 96–103.

Weinstein, G., and Obear, K. (1992). Bias issues in the classroom: Encounters with the teaching self. In M. Adams (Ed.), *Promoting diversity in college classrooms: Innovative responses for the curriculum, faculty, and institutions,* New Directions for Teaching and Learning, no. 52. San Francisco: Jossey-Bass.

Weisbord, R. G., and Stein, A. (1970). *Bittersweet Encounter: The Afro-American and the American Jew.* Westport, CT: Negro Universities Press.

Weise, E. (Ed.). (1992). *Closer to home: Bisexuality and feminism.* Seattle: Seal Press.

Wellman, D. T. (1977). *Portraits of white racism.* New York: Cambridge University Press.

West, C. (1993). *Prophetic reflections: Notes on race and power in America.* Monroe, ME: Common Courage Press.

Wigginton, E. (Ed.). (1992). *Refuse to stand silently by: An oral history of grass roots social activism in America, 1921–1964.* New York: Doubleday.

Wijeyesinghe, C. (1992). Towards an understanding of the racial identity of bi-racial people: The experience of racial self-identification of African-American/ Euro-American adults and the factors affecting their choices of racial identity. Dissertation Abstracts International, A 53/11 p. 3808 (University Microfilms AAC 9305915).

Wildman, S. (1996). *Privilege revealed: How invisible preference undermines America.* New York: New York University Press.

Williams, R. M., Jr., (1947). *The reduction of intergroup tensions: A survey of research on problems of ethnic, racial, and religious group relations.* New York: Social Science Research Council.

Wistrich, R. S. (1991). *Antisemitism: The longest hatred.* New York: Schocken Books.

Witkin, H. A., and Moore, C. A. (1975). *Field-dependent and field-independent cognitive styles and their educational implications.* Princeton, NJ: Educational Testing Service.

Wolff, E. (1995). *Top heavy: A study of increasing inequality of wealth in America.* New York: Twentieth Century Fund.

Wolverton, T. (1983). Unlearning complicity, remembering resistance: White women's anti-racism education. In C. Bunch and S. Pollack (Eds.), *Learning our way: Essays in feminist education* (pp. 272–84). Trumansburg, NY: Crossing Press.

Women's Action Coalition. (1993). *WAC Stats: The facts about women.* New York: The New Press.

Woog, D. (1995). *School's out: The impact of gay and lesbian issues on America's schools.* Boston: Alyson.

Wright, R. (1992). *Stolen continents: The "New World" through Indian eyes.* Boston: Houghton/Mifflin.

Wyman, D. S. (1984). *The abandonment of the Jews: America and the Holocaust, 1941–1945.* New York: Pantheon.

Wysmierski, D. K., and Kent, S. J. (Eds.). (1996). *Classism.* Amherst: Social Justice Education Program, University of Massachusetts.

Yehoshua, A. B. (1981). *Between right and right.* Garden City, NY: Doubleday.

Yehoshua, A. B. (1995). Israeli identity in a time of peace. *Tikkun,* 10 (6), 34–40.

Yeskel, F. (1990). Understanding class and classism. Unpublished paper. Amherst, MA.

York, D. E. (1994). *Cross-cultural training programs.* Westport, CT: Bergin & Garvey.

Young, E. (1992). *Keepers of the history: Women and the Israeli-Palestininan conflict.* New York: Teacher's College Press.

Young, I. M. (1994). Gender as seriality: Thinking about women as a social collective. *Signs,* 19 (3), 713–38.

———. (1990). *Justice and the politics of difference.* Princeton, NJ: Princeton University Press.

Zaharna, R. S. (1989). Self-shock: The double-binding challenge of identity. *International Journal of Intercultural Relations,* 13 (4), 501–25.

Zinn, H. (1980). *A people's history of the United States.* New York: Harper and Row (updated and revised edition, 1995).

CONTENTS OF COURSE READER(S)

The readings for most of the single issue courses are available in five *single* reading packets. *Bundled together*, they provide a large single reader for the multiple issues course, edited 1996 by Adams, Brigham, Dalpes, and Marchesani, and available from Kendall/Hunt in Dubuque, Iowa. The *Classism Reader* (edited 1996 by Wysmierski and Kent) is not as yet bundled into the larger reader, but is available from The Textbook Annex, University of Massachusetts, Amherst. All of the readings are listed below. The reader also includes homework questions and follow-up activities for each of the "isms."

Diversity and Oppression: Conceptual Frameworks

Blumenfeld, W. J., and Raymond, D. (1993/1988). Prejudice and discrimination. In W. J. Blumenfeld and D. Raymond (Eds.), *Looking at gay and lesbian life*. Boston: Beacon Press.

Harro, B. (n.d.). Cycle of socialization. Amherst, MA: Diversity Works.

Harro, B., and Scott, J. J. (n.d.). Cycle of oppression. Amherst, MA and La Crosse, WI: Diversity Works and Office of Student Activities, University of Wisconsin.

Jackson, B., and Hardiman, R. (1982). Oppression: Conceptual and developmental analysis. Amherst, MA: New Perspectives.

———. (1982). Social identity development model. Amherst, MA: New Perspectives.

———. (n.d.). Oppression umbrella. Amherst, MA: New Perspectives.

Miller, J. B. (1976). Domination-subordination. In J. B. Miller (Ed.), *Toward a new psychology of women*. Boston: Beacon Press.

Pharr, S. (1988). Common elements of oppression. In S. Pharr (Ed.), *Homophobia: A weapon of sexism*. Inverness, CA: Chardon Press.

Young, I. M. (1990). Five faces of oppression. In *Justice and the politics of difference*. Princeton NJ: Princeton University Press.

Sexism:

Aim, R. (1992, August). He/She? *Swarthmore College Bulletin*, 14–16, 62–63.

Blood, P., Tuttle, A., and Lakey, G. (1983). Understanding and fighting sexism: A call to men. In P. Blood, A. Tuttle, and G. Lakey (Eds.), *Off their backs . . . and on our own two feet* (pp. 1–8). Philadelphia: New Society Publishers.

Blumenfeld, W. J. (1992). Squeezed into gender envelopes. In W. J. Blumenfeld (Ed.), *Homophobia: How we all pay the price*. Boston: Beacon Press.

Bosmajian, H. (1983). The language of sexism. In H. Bosmajian (Ed.), *The language of oppression*. Lanham, MD: University Press of America.

Carter, D., Pearson, C., and Shavlik, D. (1987/88, fall-winter). Double jeopardy: Women of color in higher education. *Educational record*, 68/69 (4/1), 98–103.

Chow, E. N.-L. (1989). The feminist movement: Where are all the Asian American women? In A. W. United (Ed.), *Making Waves*. Boston: Beacon Press.

Davis, A. (1981). Working women, black women and the history of the suffrage movement. In A. Davis (Ed.), *Women, race and class*. New York: Random House.

Faludi, S. (1991). Backlashes then and now. In *Backlash: The undeclared war against women*. New York: Crown Publishers.

Feinberg, L. (1992). Transgender liberation: A movement whose time has come. In L. Feinberg (Ed.), *Transgender liberation: A movement whose time has come*. New York: World View Forum.

Frye, M. (1983). Oppression. In *The politics of reality: Essays in feminist theory*. Trumansburg, NY: The Crossing Press.

Herman, D. F. (1989). The rape culture. In J. Freeman (Ed.), *Women: A feminist perspective.* Mountain View, CA: Mayfield Publishing Co.

Hughes, J. O. G., and Sandler, B. R. (1988). *Peer harassment: Hassles for women on campus.* Washington, DC: Center for Women Policy Studies.

Kilbourne, J. (1989, winter). Beauty . . . and the beast of advertising. *Media and Values,* 49, 8–10.

Langston, D. (1988). Women and work: Two jobs for less than the price of one. In J. W. Cochran, et al. (Ed.), *Changing our power.* Dubuque, IA: Kendall/Hunt Publishing.

McBride, L. G. (1985, fall). The slender imbalance: Women and body image. *Journal of NAW-DAC,* 49 (1), 16–22.

Pharr, S. (1988). Homophobia: A weapon of sexism. In *Homophobia: A weapon of sexism.* Inverness, CA: Chardon Press.

Sabo, D. (1994). Pigskin, patriarchy and pain. In M. Messner and D. Sabo (Eds.), *Sex, violence and power in sports: Rethinking masculinity.* Freedom, CA: Crossing Press.

Segel-Evans, K. (1986). Rape prevention and masculinity. In F. Abbott (Ed.), *New men, new minds.* Freedom, CA: Crossing Press.

Sidel, R. (1990). Toward a more caring society. In R. Sidel (Ed.), *On her own.* New York: Viking Penguin.

Thompson, C. (1985, Spring). A new vision of masculinity. *Changing Men,* 14, 2–4, 44.

———. (1991, Winter/Spring). Can white heterosexual men understand oppression? *Changing Men,* 22, 14–17.

Gay, Lesbian and Bisexual Oppression:

Arruda, T. (1994). Things that divide us. In J. Ramos (Ed.), *Compañeras: Latina lesbians.* New York: Routledge.

Blumenfeld, W. J. (1992). How homophobia hurts everyone. In W. J. Blumenfeld (Ed.), *Homophobia: How we all pay the price.* Boston: Beacon Press.

———. (1993/88). Sexuality and the heritage of western religion. In W. J. Blumenfeld and D. Raymond (Eds.), *Looking at gay and lesbian life.* Boston: Beacon Press.

———. (1994). Homophobia. In W. J. Blumenfeld (Ed.), *Ready reference: Ethics.* Englewood Cliffs, NJ: Salem Press.

Blumenfeld, W. J., and Raymond, D. (1993/88). A brief history of homophobia. In W. J. Blumenfeld and D. Raymond (Eds.), *Looking at lesbian and gay life.* Boston: Beacon Press.

Deacon, F. J. (1990). What does the bible say about homosexuality?, *The welcoming congregation: The workshop series.* Boston: Unitarian Universalist Church.

Fox, A. (1991). Development of a bisexual identity: Understanding the process. In L. Hutchins and L. Kaahumanu (Eds.), *Bi any other name: Bisexual people speak out.* Boston: Alyson Publications.

Gibson, P. (1989). *Gay male and lesbian youth suicide: Report of the Secretary's Task Force on Youth Suicide.* Washington, DC: U.S. Department of Health and Human Services.

Goodman, G., Lakey, G., Laskof, J., and Thorne, E. (1983). How this society oppresses lesbians and gay men. In G. Goodman, G. Lakey, J. Laskoff, and E. Thorne (Eds.), *No turning back: Lesbian and gay liberation for the 80's.* Philadelphia: New Society Publishers.

O'Connor, A. (1995). Who gets called queer in school? Lesbian, gay, and bisexual teenagers, homophobia, and high school. In G. Unks (Ed.), *The gay teen.* New York: Routledge.

Sears, J. T. (1990). Black-gay or gay-black? Choosing identities and identifying choices. In J. T. Sears (Ed.), *Growing up gay in the south.* New York: Haworth Press.

Thompson, C. (1992). On being heterosexual in a homophobic world. In W. J. Blumenfeld (Ed.), *Homophobia: How we all pay the price.* Boston: Beacon Press.

Washington, J., and Evans, N. J. (1991). Becoming an ally. In N. J. Evans and V. A. Wall (Eds.), *Beyond tolerance: Gays, lesbians and bisexuals on campus.* Alexandria, VA: American College Personnel Association.

Williams, W. L. (1992). Benefits for nonhomophobic societies: An anthropological perspective. In W. J. Blumenfeld (Ed.), *Homophobia: How we all pay the price.* Boston: Beacon Press.

Yeskel, F. (1991). You didn't talk about these things: Growing up Jewish, lesbian, and working class. In C. Balka and A. Rose (Eds.), *Twice blessed: On being lesbian or gay and Jewish.* Boston: Beacon Press.

Racism:

Bonacich, E. (1989). Inequality in America: The failure of the American system for people of color. *Sociological Spectrum,* 9, 77–101.

Dalton, J. C. (1991). Racial and ethnic backlash in college peer culture. In J. C. Dalton (Ed.), *Racism on campus: Confronting racial bias through peer interventions.* San Francisco: Jossey-Bass.

Hardiman, R., and Jackson, B. W. (1980). Perspectives on race. Amherst, MA: New Perspectives.

Higginbotham, E. (1986). We were never on a pedestal: Women of color continue to struggle with poverty, racism, and sexism. In R. Lefkowitz and A. Withorn (Eds.), *For crying out loud: Women and poverty in the United States.* New York: Pilgrim Press.

Hornsby, A. (1991). Introduction. In A. Hornsby (Ed.), *Chronology of African-American history: Significant events and people from 1619 to the present.* Detroit, MI: Gale Research Co.

Kim, I. (1986). Asian Americans and the American economic order. In H.-C. Kim (Ed.), *Dictionary of Asian American history.* Westport, CT: Greenwood.

Ladner, J. (1986, Sept./Oct.). Black women face the 21st century: Major issues and problems. *Black Scholar,* 17 (5), 12–18.

Marks, J. (1994, December). Black, white, other. *Natural History,* 103 (12), 32–35.

McIntosh, P. (1990, Winter). White privilege: Unpacking the invisible knapsack. *Independent School,* 49 (2), 31.

Moore, J., and Pachon, H. (1985). History: The hispanics appear. In J. Moore and H. Pachon (Eds.), *Hispanics in the United States.* Englewood Cliffs, NJ: Prentice-Hall.

Moraga, C. (1983). La Güera. In C. Moraga and G. Anzaldúa (Eds.), *This bridge called my back.* Latham, NY: Kitchen Table: Women of Color Press.

Staples, R. (1987, May/June). Black male genocide: A final solution to the race problem in America. *Black Scholar,* 18 (3), 2–11.

Steinberg, S. (1981). Racial and ethnic conflict in the twentieth century. In S. Steinberg (Ed.), *The ethnic myth: Race, ethnicity, and class in America.* New York: Scribner/Simon & Schuster.

Stiffarm, L. A., and Lane Jr., P. (1992). The demography of native North America: A question of American Indian survival. In M. A. Jaimes (Ed.), *State of native America: Genocide, colonization, and resistance.* Boston: South End Press.

Wiener, J. (1989, February 27). Reagan's children: Racial hatred on campus. *The Nation,* 248, 260–64.

Yamato, G. (1988). Something about the subject makes it hard to name. In J. Cochran (Ed.), *Changing our power: An introduction to women's studies.* Dubuque, IA: Kendall/Hunt.

Antisemitism:

Beck, E. T. (1988, September). From "Kike" to "JAP": How misogyny, anti-Semitism, and racism construct the "Jewish American Princess". *Sojourner: The women's forum,* 14 (1), 18–20.

Brown, C. (1991). Dynamics of anti-Semitism. *Tikkun,* 6 (2), 26–28.

Bulkin, E. (1984). Separations. In E. Bulkin, M. B. Pratt, and B. Smith (Eds.), *Yours in struggle: Three feminist perspectives on anti-Semitism and racism.* Ithaca, NY: Firebrand Books.

Curtis, M. (1990, January). Anti-Semitism in the United States. *Midstream,* 36 (1), 20–26.

Fogelman, E. (1994, March-April). Rescuers of Jews during the holocaust: A model for a caring community. *Tikkun,* 9 (2), 61.

Gray, P. (1983, May 16). Fakes that have skewed history. *Time,* 48.

Lerner, M. (1992). Israel: Legitimate criticisms vs. Israel-bashing and anti-Semitism. In M. Lerner (Ed.), *The socialism of fools: Anti-Semitism on the left.* Oakland, CA: Tikkun Books.

———. Origins of the anti-Semitic pathology. In M. Lerner (Ed.), *The socialism of fools: Anti-Semitism on the left.* Oakland, CA: Tikkun Books.

———. (1992). What is Anti-Semitism?, *The socialism of fools: Anti-Semitism on the left.* Oakland, CA: Tikkun Books.

———. (1992). Zionism: Its legitimacy and tragic flaws. In M. Lerner (Ed.), *The socialism of fools: Anti-Semitism on the left.* Oakland, CA: Tikkun Books.

Pogrebin, L. C. (1991). The high holy days: New clothes and bare feet. In L. C. Pogrebin (Ed.), *Deborah, Golda, and me.* New York: Crown Publishers.

———. (1991). My hanukkah. In L. C. Pogrebin (Ed.), *Deborah, Golda, and me.* New York: Crown Publishers.

Rogow, A. (1968). Anti-Semitism. In D. L. Stills (Ed.), *International Encyclopedia of the Social Sciences,* Vol. 1 (pp. 345–49). New York: Crowell Collier and Macmillan.

Roiphe, A. (1988). Blacks and Jews: A lost friendship. In A. Roiphe (Ed.), *A season for healing: Reflections on the Holocaust.* New York: Summit Books.

Sauvage, P. (1983). A most persistent haven: Le Chambon-Sur-Lignon. Los Angeles, CA: Friends of Le Chambon.

Schnur, S. (1987, Fall). Blazes of truth: When is a JAP not a yuppie? *Lilith Magazine,* 17, 10–11.

West, C. (1993). On black-Jewish relations. In *Race matters.* Boston: Beacon Press.

Wyman, D. S. (1984). The abandonment of the Jews: America and the Holocaust. In *The abandonment of the Jews.* New York: Random House.

Ableism:

Ambo, M. (1985). Speaking out. In S. E. Browne, D. Connors, and N. Stern (Eds.), *With the power of each breath: A disabled women's anthology.* Pittsburgh: Cleis Press.

Bogdan, R., Biklen, D., Shapiro, A., and Spelkoman, D. (1982). The disabled: Media's monster. *Social Policy,* 13 (2), 32–35.

de Balcazar, Y. S., Bradford, B., and Fawcett, S. B. (1988). Common concerns of disabled Americans: Issues and options. *Social Policy,* 19 (2), 29.

Deegan, P. E. (1992, January). The independent living movement and people with psychiatric disabilities: Taking back control over our own lives. *Psychosocial Rehabilitation Journal,* 15 (3), 3–19.

———. (1993). Recovering our sense of value after being labeled mentally ill. *Journal of Psychosocial Nursing and Mental Health Services,* 31 (4), 7–11.

Dolnick, E. (1993, September). Deafness as culture. *Atlantic Monthly,* 272 (9), 37–49.

Filipczak, B. (1993, March). Adaptive technology for the disabled. *Training Magazine,* 30 (3), 23.

Finger, A. (1985). Claiming all of our bodies: Reproductive rights and disability. In S. E. Browne, D. Connors, and N. Stern (Eds.), *With the power of each breath: A disabled women's anthology.* Pittsburgh: Cleis Press.

Gillespie, C. (1993). Prejudice against the handicapped. In D. Gioseff (Ed.), *On prejudice: A global perspective.* New York: Doubleday Anchor.

Jarrow, J. (1991, Winter). Disability issues on campus and the road to ADA. *Educational Record,* 72 (1), 26–31.

Johnsen, L. A. (1985). My learning disability and how it affected me. In S. E. Brown, D. Connors, and N. Stern (Eds.), *With the power of each breath: A disabled women's anthology.* Pittsburgh: Cleis Press.

Morris, J. (1991). Disability in western culture. In J. Morris (Ed.), *Pride against prejudice: Transforming attitudes to disability.* Philadelphia, PA: New Society Publishers.

———. (1991). Lives not worth living. In J. Morris (Ed.), *Pride against prejudice: Transforming attitudes to disability.* Philadelphia, PA: New Society Publishers.

Seabon, P. (1992, Fall). The black deaf experience: Striving for excellence and equality in education. *NTID Focus (National Technical Institute for the Deaf),* 1, 12–15.

Solomon, A. (1994, August 28). Defiantly deaf. *New York Times,* 143 (49, 802), 38–45, 62, 65–68..

Thornburgh, R. (1991). The Americans with Disabilities Act and the future for children. *Exceptional Parent*, 21 (2), W8–W12.

Wright, P. (1987, Spring). Disabling attitudes. *Contact Magazine*, 12 (3), 4–9.

Classism:

Allison, D. (1994). A question of class. In D. Allison (Ed.), *Skin: Talking about sex, class and literature* (pp. 13–36). Ithaca, NY: Firebrand.

Castellano, O. (1990, February). Canto, locura y poesia. *Women's Review of Books*, 7 (5).

Ehrenreich, B. (1986). What makes women poor? In R. Lefkowitz and A. Withorn (Eds.), *For crying out loud.* New York: Pilgrim Press.

———. (1992, September/October). Are you middle class? *Utne Reader*, 53, 63–66.

Erkel, R. T. (1994, November/December). The mighty wedge of class. *Utne Reader*, 66, 100–103.

Funicello, T. (1992). The poverty industry. In P. S. Rothenberg (Ed.), *Race, class and gender in the US.* New York: St. Martin's Press.

Jong, E. (1993). Who's got class? *New England Review*, 15 (2), 23–30.

Langston, D. (1988). Class and inequality: Tired of playing monopoly? In J. W. Cochran, D. Langston, and C. Woodward (Eds.), *Changing our power: An introduction to women's studies*. Dubuque, IA: Kendall-Hunt.

Lewis, G., Holland, P., and Kelly, K. (1992). Working-class students speak out. *Radical Teacher*, 42, 10–12.

Loewen, J. W. (1995). The land of opportunity. In J. W. Loewen (Ed.), *Lies my teacher told me: Everything your American history textbook got wrong.* New York: New Press.

Mantsios, G. (1992). Rewards and opportunities: The politics and economics of class in the U.S. In P. Rothenberg (Ed.), *Race, class, and gender in the US.* New York: St. Martin's Press.

Omatsu, G. (1995, Spring). Racism or solidarity? Unions and Asian immigrant workers. *Radical Teacher*, 46, 33–37.

Russell, M. (1995, November/December). Newtspeak is devolving disability rights. *The Disability Rag and ReSource*, 14–18.

Tillmon, J. (1995, July/August). Welfare. *Ms.*, 6 (1), 50–61.

Wilkerson, I. (1992). Middle class blacks try to grip a ladder while lending a hand. In P. S. Rothenberg (Ed.), *Race, class and gender in the US.* New York: St. Martin's Press.

Williams, T. (1995, September/October). Voices from the tunnel. *Utne Reader*, 71, 92–101.

SELECTED VIDEO RESOURCE LIST

The videos listed below are only a few of the large selection of video resources available for diversity and social justice education. These videos have been selected because they are either short enough to fit into a classroom unit or because we select short segments from them for classroom use. We have used and recommend these videos as alternatives for the modules presented in this volume. For further video listings, consult Stevens (1993), the listings of PBS or other video companies listed by Stevens, or contact the Social Justice Education Program at the University of Massachusetts, Amherst, 01003 for our updated annotated listings available at cost. Videos marked with an * in this list are reviewed in Stevens (1993).

General Overview:

A tale of "O": On being different (user's manual included) (1993).[videotape (two versions, 0:27 full and 0:18 training)]: Goodmeasure, Inc., One Memorial Drive, Cambridge, MA 02142.

A class divided: Then and now (video, facilitator's guide, and book set) (1985).[videotape, 0:60]: PBS Video, 1320 Braddock Place, Alexandria, VA 22314-1698; 800-344-3337; Book: Peters, W. (1987). *A class divided: Then and now*, expanded edition. New Haven, CT: Yale University Press.

Breaking through stereotypes (1994).[videotape, 0:15]. Educational Video Center, 55 East 25th Street., Suite 407, New York, NY 10010; 212-725-3534 ext. 103; fax: 212-725-6501 attn. Stephanie.

Distorted image: Stereotypes and caricature in America: Popular graphics (1973).[videotape, 0:28]: ADL, 823 United Nations Plaza, New York, NY 10014; 212-490-2525.

Facing difference: Living together on campus (1990). [videotape, 0:10]: ADL, 823 United Nations Plaza, New York, NY 10014; 212-490-2525.

Names can really hurt us (Teens talk about their experiences of prejudice) (1994).[videotape, 0:26]: ADL, 823 United Nations Plaza, New York, NY 10014; 212-490-2525.

Racism:

Affirmative action and reaction (Discussion with Lani Guinier) (1996).[videotape, 0:27]: Films for the Humanities, PO Box 2053, Princeton, NJ 08543.

All American hiring practices (Racial codes used by employment agencies) (Feb. 11, 1990).[videotape, 0:25]: CBS, 60 Minutes, 800-934-NEWS; 212-975-2875.

Black and white America (Five college students) (1993).[videotape, 0:26]: Films for the Humanities, PO Box 2053, Princeton, NJ 08543.

Chicano! (four part series, 60 minutes each) (1996).[videotape, 0:60 each]: National Latino Communication Center, PO Box 39A60, Los Angeles, CA 90039; 800-722-9982.

Color adjustment (depictions of race in TV from 1948 on) (1991).[videotape, 1:28, two parts: 0:48 & 0:40]: California Newsreel, 149 Ninth St., #420, San Francisco, CA 94103.

Color of fear (1994).[videotape, 1:30]: Stir Fry Productions, 1904 Virginia Street, Berkeley, CA 94709, 510-548-9695.

Domino: Interracial people and the search for identity (1995).[videotape, 0:44]: Films for the Humanities, PO Box 2053, Princeton, NJ 08543.

Ethnic notions: Black people in white minds (1986).[videotape, 0:58]: Resolution, Inc. /California Newsreel, 149 Ninth St./420, San Francisco, CA 94103.

Eyes on the prize I: America's Civil Rights Years 1954–1965 (6 videotapes) (1986*).[videotape, 0:60 each]: PBS Video, 1320 Braddock Place, Alexandria, VA 22314-1698; 800-344-3337.

Eyes on the Prize II: America at the Racial Crossroads 1965–1985 (eight one-hour videotapes)

(1990*).[videotape, 0:60 each]: PBS Video, 1320 Braddock Place, Alexandria, VA 22314-1698; 800-344-3337. Study guide: "*Eyes on the Prize: America at the racial crossroads: 1965–1985: A viewer's guide to the series*" from Blackside, Inc., 486 Shawmut Ave., Boston, MA 02118.

A family gathering (Japanese American family memories of World War II internment) (1988).[videotape, 0:60]: PBS Video, 1320 Braddock Place, Alexandria, VA 22314-1698; 800-344-3337.

Goin' to Chicago (1994).[videotape, 0:11]: California Newsreel, 149 9th St., #420, San Francisco, CA 94103; 415-621-6196.

In the white man's image (Native Americans) (1991).[videotape, 0:60]: PBS Video, 1320 Braddock Place, Alexandria, VA 22314-1698; 800-344-3337.

Race against prime time (TV coverage of African Americans) (1985).[videotape, 0:60]: Resolution Inc./ California Newsreel, 149 Ninth Street, San Francisco, CA 94103.

Racism 101 (1988).[videotape, 0:58]: PBS Video, 1320 Braddock Place, Alexandria, VA 22314-1698; 800-344-3337.

A single shade of protein (multiracial youth talking about their experiences) (1992).[videotape, 0:43]: ABC: Oprah Winfrey Special, 312-591-9444.

Skin Deep (includes study guide) (Excerpts appear separately as Talking about Race, Parts 1 and 2, 12 minutes each (includes instructors manual) (1995).[videotape, 0:53]. Iris Film Library, 22-D Hollywood Avenue, Ho-Ho Kus, NJ 07423; 1-800-343-5540, fax: 201-652-1973.

Teaching indians to be white (Off reservation boarding schools for Native American children) (1993).[videotape, 0:28]: Films for the Humanities, Inc., PO Box 2053, Princeton, NJ 08543.

True colors (Black and White testers reveal racism in everyday life) (1991).[videotape, 0:19]. Northbrook, IL: ABC Prime Time, MTI Film & Video, 420 Academy Drive, Northbrook IL 60062; 888-777-8100.

Sexism:

DreamWorlds (TV and film images, includes discussion guide) (1990).[videotape, 0:60]: Foundation for Media Education, 26 Center Street, Northampton, MA 01060; 413-586-4170.

DreamWorlds 2: Desire, sex, power in music video (1995).[videotape, 0:56]: Foundation for Media Education, 26 Center Street, Northampton, MA 01060; 413-586-4170.

The fairer sex (male and female testers reveal sexism in everyday life) (Oct. 7, 1993).[videotape, 0:20]: ABC: Primetime, Diane Sawyer; ABC News Videos, PO Box 2249, Livonia, MI 48151; 800-913-3434.

Sex with the unreal woman: Men and pornography (Duke University students talk about effects of pornography on stereotypes and relationships) (Jan. 29, 1993).[videotape, 0:17]: ABC 20/20; ABC News Videos, PO Box 2249, Livonia, MI 48151; 800-913-3434.

Men, sex, and rape (1990).[videotape, 0:50]: ABC News: Peter Jennings Special; ABC News Videos, PO Box 2249, Livonia, MI 48151; 800-913-3434.

Playing the game (Date rape perspectives) (Discussion guide) (1993).[videotape, 0:16]: InterMedia, 1300 Dexter Ave. N, Seattle, WA 98109; 800-553-8336.

Rape: An act of hate (myths about rape, why men rape, how women can protect themselves)(Includes discussion guide) (1993).[videotape, 0:30]: Films for the Humanities, PO Box 2053, Princeton, NJ 08543.

Stale roles, tight buns: Images of men in advertising (1988).[videotape, 0:29]: OASIS, 15 Willoughby Street, Boston, MA 02135, 617-782-7769.

Still killing us softly: advertising's image of women (1987*).[videotape, 0:32]: Cambridge Documentary Films, PO Box 385, Cambridge, MA 02139; 617-354-2677; fax: 617-492-7653.

Women: The new poor (1990).[videotape, 0:28]: Women Make Movies, 462 Broadway, Suite 500, New York, NY 10013; 212-925-0606; fax: 212-925-2052.

Heterosexism:

Before Stonewall: The making of a gay and lesbian community (1984*).[videotape, 1:27]: Cinema Guild, 1697 Broadway, Suite 802, New York, NY 10019; 212-246-5522.

Gay Youth (with study guide) (1992).[videotape, 0:40]: Wolfe Video, PO Box 64, New Alameda, CA 95042; 408-268-6782.

A little respect: Gay men, lesbians and bisexuals on campus (1990).[videotape, 0:43]: Rutgers Office of TV & Media, Rutgers: The State University of New Jersey.

Out for a change: Addressing homophobia in women's sports (1995).[videotape, 0:28]: University of California Extension, Center for Media and Independent Learning, 2000 Center St., Fourth Floor, Berkeley, CA 94704; 510-642-0460.

Pink triangles: A study of prejudice against lesbians and gays (1982).[videotape, 0:35]: Cambridge Documentary Films, PO Box 385, Cambridge, MA 02139; 617-354-2677.

A question of equality (1994). [videotape, 3:40]: Wolfe Video, PO Box 64, New Almaden, CA 95042; 800-get-wolfe.

Sacred lies, civil truths (2 part video, 30 minutes each) (1993).[videotape, 0:30 each]: National Gay, Lesbian, Bisexual Task Force, 1734 14th Street, NW, Washington, DC 20009; 202-332-6438; fax: 202-332-0207.

We are family: Parenting and foster parenting in gay communities (1987).[videotape: 0:57]: Filmakers Library, 124 E. 40th St., New York, NY 10016.

Antisemitism:

America and the holocaust: Deceit and indifference (1994).[videotape, 1:30]: PBS Video, 1320 Braddock Place, Alexandria, VA 22314-1698; 800-344-3337.

Backgrounds: A brief history of Israel and the Arab/Palestinian Conflict (1992).[videotape, 0:29]: First Run/ Icarus Films, 153 Waverly Place, New York 10014; 212-727-1711.

The courage to care (1986).[videotape, 0:28]: Zenger Video, 10200 Jefferson Blvd., Room 902, PO Box 802, Culver City, CA 90232.

Genocide 1941-1945 (Part 20 from the World at War series) (1982).[videotape, 0:52]: A & H Home Video, PO Box 2284, South Burlington, VT 05407.

The longest hatred (2 parts, 1 hour each) (1992).[videotape, 0:60 each]: Films for the Humanities and Sciences, PO Box 2053, Princeton, NJ 08543; 609-275-1400.

Not in our town (N.d.).[videotape, 0:27]: KQED Books and Videos, 5959 Triumph Street, Commerce, CA 90047; 800-358-3000; 800-422-9993.

Weapons of the spirit (classroom version with study guide) (1987).[videotape, 0:28]: Zenger Video, 10200 Jefferson Blvd., Room 902, Culver City, CA 90232 or Friends of Le Chambon, 8033 Sunset Blvd., #784, Los Angeles, CA 90046; 213-650-1174.

Ableism:

How difficult can this be? A learning disabilities workshop, The F.A.T. City Workshop (includes teacher's guide) (1989).[videotape, 1:10]: PBS Video, 1320 Braddock Place, Alexandria, VA 22314-1698, 800-344-3337.

Learning disabilities and social skills: Last one picked . . . first one picked on (teacher's guide) (1994).[videotape, 1:08]: PBS Video, 1320 Braddock Place, Alexandria, VA 22314-1698; 800-344-3337.

Look who's laughing (1994).[videotape, 0:60]: Program Development Associates, 800-543-2119.

Positive images: Portraits of women with disabilities (1989).[videotape, 0:58]. New York: Women Make Movies, 462 Broadway, Suite 501, New York, NY 10013; 212-925-0606.

Selling murder: The killing films of the Third Reich (1991).[videotape, 0:60]: Discovery Channel/ Domino Films for Channel 4. 7700 Wisconsin Avenue, Bethesda, MD 20814; 301-986-0444.

A video guide to disabilities awareness (1993).[videotape, 0:25]: Idea Bank Training Videos, 800-621-1131.

When Billy broke his head (disability, civil rights, intelligent life after brain damage) (1994).[videotape, 0:57]: Fanlight Productions, 47 Halifax St., Boston, MA 02130; 800-937-4113; fax: 617-524-8838.

When the brain goes wrong (7 segments) (1992).[videotape, 0:45 each segment]: Fanlight Productions 47 Halifax St., Boston, MA 02130; 800-937-4113; fax: 617-524-8838.

Classism:

America: What went wrong? (Bill Moyers' Listening to America: 2 parts, 60 minutes each) (1992).[videotape, 0:60 each]: PBS Video, 1320 Braddock Place, Alexandria, VA 22314-1698; 800-344-3337; (Book: Barlett, D.L. and Steele, J.B. (1992) *America What Went Wrong?* Kansas City, MO: Andrews & McMeel.)

America's war on poverty: 5 part series, 60 minutes each (1995).[videotape, each 0:60]: PBS Video, 1320 Braddock Place, Alexandria, VA 22314-1698; 800-344-3337.

Down and out in America (1985).[videotape, 0:57]: MPI Home Video, Dept. 1500, 15825 Robroy Drive, Oak Forest, IL 60452; 800-777-2223.

The global assembly line (1986).[videotape, 0:58]: New Day Films, 121 W. 27th, New York, NY 10001; 212-645-8210.

The Great Depression: 7 part series (1993).[videotape, 0:60 each]: PBS Video, 1320 Braddock Place, Alexandria, VA 22314-1698; 800-344-3337.

Social class (Two high school girls) (1991).[videotape, 0:30]: Insight Media, TSI-114, 2162 Broadway, New York, NY 10024.

We shall not be moved (Slide show re: gentrification of a multicultural neighborhood) (1983).[slide show]: Institute for Community Economics, Springfield, MA. 413-746-8660.

ALTERNATIVE FORMATS FOR SEMESTER-LONG CURRICULUM DESIGNS

FORMATS

Two sample semesters are described below. We encourage users to create their own semester designs by making selections from the topics presented here.

<table>
<tr><th rowspan="2">Weekend Courses</th><th colspan="2">Semester-Long Courses</th></tr>
<tr><th>Semester
1 x week (3 hrs.)</th><th>Semester
2 x week (1 1/2 hrs.)</th></tr>
<tr><td>Module 1
Introductory Session

Friday P.M.
1. Introductions (30 mins.)
2. Course description (15 mins.)
3. Class interaction guidelines (20 mins.)
4. Comfort zones, learning edges, triggers (30 mins)
----
5. Identifying social group memberships (20 mins.)
6. Identifying social group status (20 mins.)
7. Describing an oppression model (60–90 mins.)
8. Closing and preparing for Module One (15–30 mins.)

Supplemental Activities:
9. Agent and target role in eliminating oppression (30 mins.)
10. Levels and types of oppression (30 mins.)</td><td>Session One
----
Extra session needed</td><td>Session One

Session Two

Extra session needed</td></tr>
<tr><td>Racism Curriculum Design
Module 1

Saturday A.M.
1. Welcome, warmup activity, and introductions (30 mins.)
2. Review goals, guidelines, agenda, and assumptions (20 mins.)
Note: Activities one and two may be modified or shortened if continuing from the introductory session with same group
3. Definition of key terms (25 mins.)
4. Ethnic identity and pride activity (40 mins.)
----
5. Personal timeline/cycle of socialization (60 mins.)
6. Closing (10 mins.)</td><td>Session Two</td><td>Session Three
----
Session Four</td></tr>
</table>

Weekend Courses	Semester-Long Courses Semester 1 x week (3 hrs.)	 Semester 2 x week (1 1/2 hrs.)
Racism Curriculum Design Module 2 **Saturday P.M.** 1. Warmup Activity (10–30 mins.) 2. Definitions of cultural and institutional racism (15 mins.) 3. Racism at the cultural level and gallery walk (45 mins.) -------------------------------- 4. Institutional racism (90 mins.) Option 1: Video Option 2: Design a nonracist institution Option 3: Timeline 5. Building a web of racism (30 mins.) 6. Closing (15 mins.)	Session Three	Session Five ---------- Session Six
Racism Curriculum Design Module 3 **Sunday A.M.** 1. Check in/agenda review (15 mins.) 2. Review of definitions of key terms (10 mins.) 3. Caucus groups (105–120 mins.) -------------------------------- 4. Dialogue between caucus groups (60–75 mins.) 5. Closing (15 mins.)	Session Four	Session Seven ---------- Session Eight
Racism Curriculum Design Module 4 **Sunday P.M.** 1. Warmup activity and check-in (30 mins.) 2. Characteristics of allies (20 mins.) 3. Costs and benefits of interrupting racism (15 mins.) 4. Action continuum (15 mins.) 5. Spheres of influence (20 mins.) -------------------------------- 6. Contracts for change (20 mins.) 7. Taking it with you (45–60 mins.) 8. Closing and evaluation (30 mins.) (optional or may be modified if continuing to next module with same group)	Session Five	Session Nine ---------- Session Ten

Weekend Courses	Semester-Long Courses Semester 1 x week (3 hrs.)	 Semester 2 x week (1 1/2 hrs.)
Sexism Curriculum Design Module 1		
Saturday A.M. 1. Welcome, introductions,goals, guideline, and agenda (30 mins.) 2. Hopes and fears (20 mins.) 3. Attitudes toward gender (40 mins.) -------------------------------- 4. Act like a man/act like a woman (45–60 mins.) 5. Definitions: Sex and Gender (10 mins.) 6. Closing (15 mins.)	Session Six	Session Eleven ---------- Session Twelve
Sexism Curriculum Design Module 2		
Saturday P.M. 1. Warmup Activity (10 mins.) 2. Cycle of sexism (30 mins.) 3. Definitions: Sexism and related terms (15 mins.) -------------------------------- 4. Media images of women and men in advertising (120–150 mins.) 5. Homework and closing (15 mins.)	Session Seven	Session Thirteen ---------- Session Fourteen
Sexism Curriculum Design Module 3		
Sunday A.M. 1. Current images of men and women in advertising (30–40 mins) 2. Status of women quiz (30 mins.) 3. Institutional sexism (60–90 mins) -------------------------------- 4. Create a sexist institution (60–90 mins.) Option A: Video Option B: Violence against women (see notes at end of Module Three) Option C: Web of sexism (see notes at end of Module Three)	Session Eight	Session Fifteen ---------- Session Sixteen
Sexism Curriculum Design Module 4		
Sunday P.M. 1. Feminisms: Definitions and theoretical and historical overview (45 mins.) -------------------------------- 2. Men as allies (20 mins.) 3. Strategies for change (30 mins.) 4. Spheres of influence (30 mins.) 5. Action planning and challenging sexism (30–40 mins.) 6. Closing/evaluation (30 mins.) Optional if continuing on to next topic)	Session Nine	Session Seventeen ---------- Session Eighteen

Weekend Courses	Semester-Long Courses Semester 1 x week (3 hrs.)	 Semester 2 x week (1 1/2 hrs.)
Heterosexism Curriculum Design Module 1 **Saturday A.M.** 1. Introductions (30 mins.) 2. Agenda, guidelines, goals (10 mins.) 3. Definitions (10 mins.) 4. Early learnings (45 mins.) ---------- 5. Understanding the complexity of gender and sexuality (45 mins.) 6. Closing (15 mins.)	Session Ten	Session Nineteen ---------- Session Twenty
Heterosexism Curriculum Design Module 2 **Saturday P.M.** 1. Opening (25 mins.) 2. Personal stories (90–105 mins.) ---------- 3. Institutional heterosexism and heterosexual privilege (75 mins.) 4. Homework (10 mins.) 5. Closing (15 mins.)	Session Eleven	Session Twenty-one ---------- Session Twenty-two
Heterosexism Curriculum Design Module 3 **Sunday A.M.** 1. Button activity (45 mins.) ---------- 2. LGB History (90 mins.) 3. Setting up caucus groups (10 mins.) 4. Closing	Session Twelve	Session Twenty-three ---------- Session Twenty-four
Heterosexism Curriculum Design Module 4 **Sunday P.M.** 1. Caucus groups (60 mins.) ---------- 2. Vision of a non-heterosexist world (60 mins.) 3. Action strategies (30 mins.) 4. Closing (45 mins.)	Session Thirteen	Session Twenty-five ---------- Session Twenty-six
End of Semester		
Second semester design, following introductory module (session one).		
Antisemitism Curriculum Design Module 1 **Saturday A.M.** 1. Introductions, welcome (30 mins.) 2. Course description and goals (10 mins.) 3. Definitions of key terms (30 mins.) ---------- 4. Stereotypes of Jews (60 mins.) 5. Closing (10 mins.)	Session Two	Session Two ---------- Session Three

<table>
<tr><th rowspan="2">Weekend Courses</th><th colspan="2">Semester-Long Courses</th></tr>
<tr><th>Semester
1 x week (3 hrs.)</th><th>Semester
2 x week (1 1/2 hrs.)</th></tr>
<tr><td>Antisemitism Curriculum Design
Module 2

Saturday P.M.
1. History of Antisemitism
• Ancient and Greco-Roman period (20 mins)
• Rise of Christianity and middle ages (40 mins.)
• Beginning of modern era (40 mins.)
- - - - - - - - - -
• 20th century (40 mins.)
2. Historical themes and antisemitism today (40 mins.)
3. Closing (20 mins.)</td><td>Session Three</td><td>Session Three
- - - - - - - - - -
Session Four</td></tr>
<tr><td>Antisemitism Curriculum Design
Module 3

Sunday A.M.
1. Check-in (20 mins.)
2. Speakouts of Jews and Gentiles (40 mins.)
- - - - - - - - - -
3. Caucus groups: Jews and Gentiles (60 mins.)
4. Intergroup Discussion (30 mins.)
5. Closing (30 mins.)</td><td>Session Four</td><td>Session Five
- - - - - - - - - -
Session Six</td></tr>
<tr><td>Antisemitism Curriculum Design
Module 4

Sunday P.M.
1. Action strategies to combat antisemitism (45 mins.)
- - - - - - - - - -
2. Contracts for change (60 mins.)
Option A: Increase personal awareness
Option B: Personal behavior change
Option C: Interrupting antisemitism
Option D: Spheres of influence
3. Closing (30 mins.)</td><td>Session Five</td><td>Session Seven
- - - - - - - - - -
Session Eight</td></tr>
<tr><td colspan="3">To follow introductory module or subsitute for other ism</td></tr>
<tr><td>Ableism Curriculum Design
Module 1

Saturday A.M.
1. Introductions, goals, agenda review (30 mins.)
2. Recall (30 mins.)
3. Myths and stereotypes (30 mins.)
4. Journal period (5 mins.)
- - - - - - - - - -
5. Definitions (15 mins.)
6. History activity part I (40 mins.)
7. Closing (10 mins.)</td><td>Session Two</td><td>Session Two
- - - - - - - - - -
Session Three</td></tr>
</table>

<table>
<tr><th rowspan="2">Weekend Courses</th><th colspan="2">Semester-Long Courses</th></tr>
<tr><th>Semester
1 x week (3 hrs.)</th><th>Semester
2 x week (1 1/2 hrs.)</th></tr>
<tr><td>Ableism Curriculum Design
Module 2</td><td rowspan="2">Session Three</td><td rowspan="2">Session Four
----
Session Five</td></tr>
<tr><td>Saturday P.M.
1. History activity, Part II (60 mins.)
2. Disability rights/Key legislation (30 mins.)
----
3. Roles exercise Part I (60 mins.)
4. Journal period (5 mins.)
5. Closing (10 mins.)</td></tr>
<tr><td>Ableism Curriculum Design
Module 3</td><td rowspan="2">Session Four</td><td rowspan="2">Session Six
----
Session Seven</td></tr>
<tr><td>Sunday A.M.
1. Check-in/Roles exercise Part II (30 mins.)
2. Panel of people with disabilities (90 mins.)
----
3. Discussion after panel (30 mins.)
4. Journal period (5 mins.)
5. Closing (10 mins.)</td></tr>
<tr><td>Ableism Curriculum Design
Module 4</td><td rowspan="2">Session Five</td><td rowspan="2">Session Eight
----
Session Nine</td></tr>
<tr><td>Sunday P.M.
1. Visioning an accessible/inclusive society (90 mins.)
2. Journal period (5 mins.)
----
3. Barriers to action/action continuum (30 mins.)
4. Personal contracts for action (30 mins.)
5. Closure and evaluation (30 mins.)</td></tr>
<tr><td colspan="3">To follow introductory module or subsitute for other ism</td></tr>
<tr><td>Classism Curriculum Design
Module 1</td><td rowspan="2">Session One</td><td rowspan="2">Session One
----
Session Two</td></tr>
<tr><td>Saturday A.M.
1. Welcome and introductions (10 mins.)
2. Common ground Part I (20 mins.)
3. Assumptions, guidelines, agenda (20 mins.)
4. First memories and class indicators (40 mins.)
----
5. Class background inventory (50 mins.)
6. Common ground Part II (15 mins.)
7. Key definitions (20 mins.)
8. Personal definitions of class (5 mins.)</td></tr>
</table>

Weekend Courses	Semester-Long Courses Semester 1 x week (3 hrs.)	 Semester 2 x week (1 1/2 hrs.)
Classism Curriculum Design Module 2		
1. Class/classism quiz (30 mins.) 2. Income distribution activity (20 mins.) 3. Wealth distribution activity (20 mins.) 4. Brainstorm stereotypes of class (20 mins.)	Session Two	Session Three
5. First person accounts of diverse class experiences (60 mins.) 6. Individual, cultural and institutional levels of classism (40 mins.) 7. Closing and homework (20 mins.)		Session Four
Classism Curriculum Design Module 3		
1. Cultural manifestations of classism (30 mins.) 2. Star power simulation Part I or Institutional classism Part I (75 mins.)	Session Three	Session Five
3. Star power Part II or institutional classism Part II (75 mins.) 4. Closing (10 mins.)		Session Six
Classism Curriculum Design Module 4		
1. History of classism and anticlassism (45 mins.) 2. Allies (30 mins.)	Session Four	Session Seven
3. Classism in your school (60 mins.) 4. Actions against classism (45 mins.) 5. Closing (30 mins.)		Session Eight

CONTRIBUTORS

Maurianne Adams is a Lecturer in the Social Justice Education Program at the University of Massachusetts/Amherst School of Education. She edited *Promoting Diversity in the College Classroom* (1992). Her research interests include multicultural adult development and learning styles, and she is currently writing a book on the pedagogies of social justice education. She recently co-facilitated a faculty seminar on the history of Black/Jewish relationships, co-edited *Relations Between Blacks and Jews: Historical Perspectives* (in press), and consults widely for faculty development programs.

Lee Anne Bell is Associate Professor at SUNY-New Paltz in a master's program for teachers and human service professionals that focuses on social justice. Her previous writing examined consciousness-raising processes for empowering girls in public schools. Her present interests include how to be an effective ally and build coalitions among diverse groups. She has moderated a Black-Jewish faculty dialogue series and is currently engaged with her students in a study of "race talk."

Diane J. Goodman teaches in the Masters of Professional Studies in Humanistic Education at SUNY/New Paltz. She has been teaching, training, and consulting in diversity and human relations since 1983. She has worked with a range of organizations and has taught at several Universities in the areas of Education, Psychology, and Women's Studies. Her interests in gender issues include women's psychology, gender socialization, and diversity among women.

Pat Griffin is an Associate Professor and Program Director in the Social Justice Education Program at the University of Massachusetts Amherst School of Education. Her research and writing interests include lesbian, gay, and bisexual issues in education. She is nationally recognized for her work in the area of homophobia and heterosexism in sports and athletics.

Rita Hardiman is an adjunct faculty member in the Social Justice Education Program, School of Education, University of Massachusetts, Amherst. She is also a partner in New Perspectives, Inc., a firm that specializes in providing training and consultation services related to social diversity and social justice in organizational settings.

Roberta L. (Bobbie) Harro is Associate Professor of Human Services in the School of Human Services at Springfield College in Massachusetts. She is co-founder of Diversity Works, Inc. and has been working in the field of Social Justice Education for sixteen years. She has been a tenth grade English teacher and directed a primary prevention and education program. Her areas of special interest include education for consciousness raising in heterosexism, racism, adult pedagogy and group dynamics. She uses her experience as a lesbian to help others make connections across social justice issues.

Bailey Jackson is founding faculty member of the Social Justice Education Program, School of Education, and currently Dean of the School of Education, University of Massachusetts, Amherst.

JoAnne Silver Jones is Associate Director of the School of Human Services at Springfield College, Massachusetts. She has presented her work throughout the United States, Canada, and Europe. Her research and teaching interests are primarily in the areas of adult pedagogy and multicultural education, with particular focus on heterosexism, antisemitism, and racism. She consults, lectures, and writes about how to engage adults in the process of change that is both personally empowering and institutionally challenging.

Betsy Leondar-Wright is a long-time activist who has worked for economic justice with many organizations, including Women for Economic Justice, the Anti-Displacement Project, the Share the Wealth Project, and the Massachusetts Human Services Coalition. She lives in Arlington, Massachusetts.

Barbara J. Love is Associate Professor of the Social Justice Education Program at the University of Massachusetts/Amherst. She is a member of National Training Laboratories (NTL) and is on the Board of Directors of the National Black Women's Health Project and The Equity Institute. She has worked with organizations in North America, Europe, Africa, the Middle East, and the Caribbean on issues of diversity and inclusion. Her research focuses on personal and organizational transformation and issues of equity.

Linda S. Marchesani is manager of the Training and Development Unit at the University of Massachusetts and an adjunct faculty member in the Social Justice Education Program, University of Massachusetts/Amherst School of Education. Throughout her career, she has worked with faculty, graduate students and university staff to promote diversity and advocate for social justice.

Mary McClintock is a trainer, organizational consultant, and researcher. Her business, Better-Me-Than-You Research Services, provides on-line and library research for college and university faculty, writers, consultants, and business owners. As a temporarily-able-bodied-and-minded person, she works to promote the full inclusion of people with disabilities in all aspects of society.

Donna Mellen is a core faculty member in the Department of Organization and Management at Antioch New England Graduate School. She also has a consulting practice in organization development. She works with her clients to develop productive, collaborative, creative, and socially responsible organizations. Donna, who was raised as a Protestant, first worked to address antisemitism as a high school social studies teacher, integrating aspects of Jewish history and the history of antisemitism into her European history courses.

Laura Rauscher has been active for over fifteen years in advocating for civil rights and equal opportunity for people with disabilities. She has an undergraduate degree in Community Services and is completing a masters degree in Organizational Development. Her professional career has focused on state and national policy and program development in an effort to increase the availability of a wide range of community-based programs and services that support the independence and self-determination of people with all types of disabilities. As a person with a disability, she is committed to working to promote the full inclusion of people with disabilities in all aspects of society.

Steven Schapiro is a member of the core faculty at Goddard College, where he teaches in the areas of education, psychology, and men's studies, co-directs the Institute on Teaching and Learning, and has formerly held administrative posts as Dean for Academic Affairs and Director of Teacher Education. His research and writing interests focus on men's consciousness raising and identity development. He developed and taught one of the first courses in the country on men and masculinity in the early 1980s.

Beverly Daniel Tatum is Professor of Psychology and Education at Mount Holyoke College in South Hadley, Massachusetts. She teaches courses on the psychology of racism, and lectures extensively on the impact of social issues in the classroom. Her research interests include the racial identity development of Black youth in predominantly White communities, and the impact of anti-racist professional development programs on educators' attitudes and classroom practice. Dr. Tatum is also a licensed clinical psychologist.

Sharon J. Washington is an Associate Professor in the Education Department at Springfield College, and the founder TapestryWorks, a company which provides consultation and workshops in diversity, organizational development, and adventure education. She has been on the faculty at Kent State University and the University of Massachusetts/Amherst.

Gerald Weinstein is currently Professor Emeritus at the University of Massachusetts/Amherst. In his college years he participated in a study of desegregation in the South. During his public school teaching he created classroom procedures for dealing with racism. As a university professor, he continued his anti-racism work, and initiated the first campus workshops on antisemitism. A persistent question throughout all his work is how self-knowledge evolves and how it can be facilitated.

Charmaine L. Wijeyesinghe is National Program Consultant for the National Conference of Christians and Jews in New York City. She has worked in the field of social justice education for almost fifteen years and has presented courses and seminars on diversity, multicultural organizational development, multicultural conflict resolution, and racial identity development. She conducts research, writes, and lectures on multiracial identity development.

Felice Yeskel has been an activist for over twenty years in many social change movements: feminism, lesbian and gay liberation, peace, and disarmament. She is co-director of United for a Fair Economy, an organization working to change public policy and create a fairer and more equitable redistribution of resources. She is also an adjunct faculty member of the Social Justice Education Program at the University of Massachusetts/Amherst and of the Union Institute. Felice is co-director of Diversity Works, Inc., an organization of social justice educators.

INDEX